Lorain County Community College Library

HISTORY:

A Key To The Future

In Memory Of

Vernon G. Gillespie

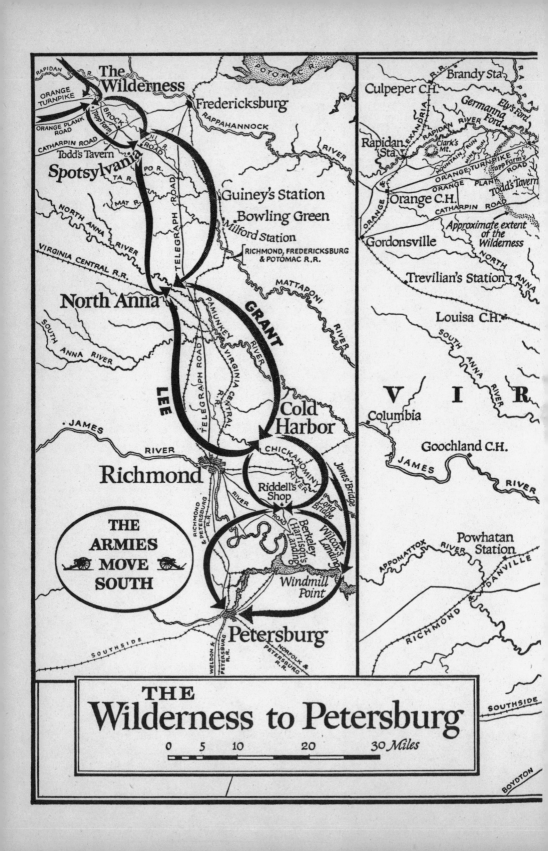

THE
Wilderness to Petersburg

0 5 10 20 30 *Miles*

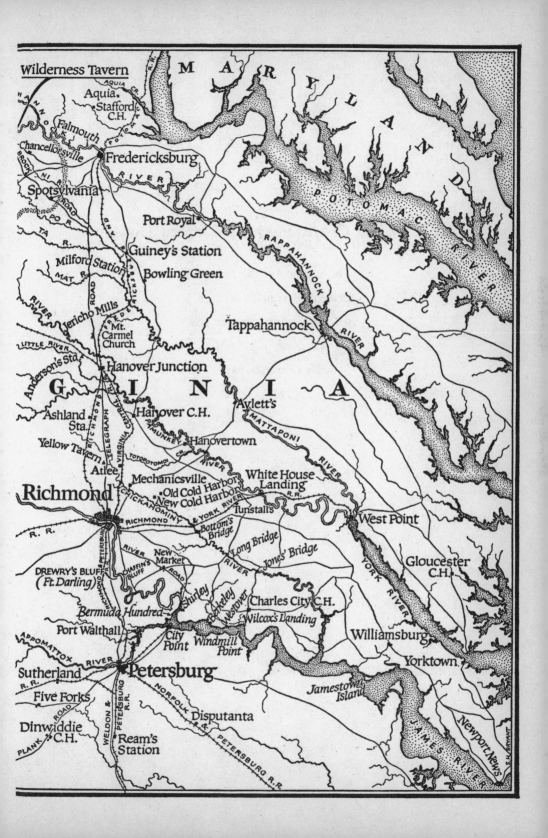

Books on the Confederacy by Clifford Dowdey

BUGLES BLOW NO MORE

EXPERIMENT IN REBELLION

THE LAND THEY FOUGHT FOR

DEATH OF A NATION

LEE'S LAST CAMPAIGN

Lee's Last Campaign

Lee's Last Campaign

The Story of Lee and His Men against Grant — 1864

by Clifford Dowdey

BONANZA BOOKS · NEW YORK

For
John A. S. Cushman
and
Ivan von Auw, Jr.

Contents

Part One: ONE AGAINST THE GODS

I   "The Weight of Empire"   3

II   "There Will Be Nothing Left for Us to Live for"   34

III   "The Army Was Put in Motion Today"   61

IV   "Go Down the Road and Strike the Enemy"   83

V   "If Night Would Only Come . . ."   104

VI   "There Are No Ifs"   137

Part Two: "TO COMMAND IS TO WEAR OUT"

VII   "If It Takes All Summer"   179

VIII   "The Picture Presented Is One of Ultimate Starvation"   217

IX   "Good Health Is Indispensable in War . . ."   249

X   "My Idea Has Been to Beat Lee's Army North of Richmond"   301

XI   "It Will Be a Mere Question of Time"   317

Epilogue: "The Very Best Soldier"   359

Bibliographical Essay with Selected Bibliography   377

Index   401

Maps

The Wilderness, May 5   102-103

The Wilderness, May 6   146-147

The Wilderness to Spotsylvania, Main Contact, May 8   147

Spotsylvania, May 11-12   196

The North Anna, May 23-24   262

Cold Harbor, June 3   295

Grant's Crossing of the James, June 14-16   325

Endpapers: The Wilderness to Petersburg

PART ONE

One Against the Gods

CHAPTER ONE

"The Weight of Empire"

IN THAT SPRING the pageantry was not yet, not quite, gone from the war. Through all privations, general officers in Lee's army managed to turn themselves out well. Though the cadet-gray cloth of their uniforms was usually no more than a thread through the motley of the soldiers' makeshifts, when seen in a group, the generals still suggested the panoply of the chivalric tradition.

On May 2, 1864, the high command of the Army of Northern Virginia formed such a spectacle for the first time since Gettysburg, the year before, and for the last time in their lives. Full-bearded, booted and spurred, with gauntleted hands resting on sword hilts and buttons gleaming on double-breasted coats, the generals stood near their saddled horses like the figures in old lithographs and murals. Even the background, a mountaintop in spring, was almost an idealized setting.

April had been a rainy month, and May came with a sudden flowering of the countryside. Grass and leaves turned freshly green, buds were opening, honeysuckle and dogwood grew in the forests, and purple violets along the roadside. Clark's Mountain was not much of an eminence in itself but, in a generally flat countryside averaging less than 500 feet above the tide, its 1100 feet gave the hill a commanding position. From there Lee and his generals surveyed, across the Rapidan River and beyond the devastated farmland of middle Virginia, the endlessly stretching tented city of the enemy.

Soldiers from the mountain signal station had earlier reported stirrings in the Federal camp. And on that Monday in May, General Lee came for a personal look.

Since November the two armies had camped on opposite sides of the brownish stream, waiting for spring. The Army of the Potomac and the Army of Northern Virginia had fought one another on so many fields that, like two old rivals, each was thoroughly familiar with the potential and the habits of the other. Every soldier in the camps understood as clearly as generals, more clearly than members of their governments, that the invading army waited for spring to attack across the river in the most concentrated blow yet delivered at the Confederate citadel, and that Lee's smaller, physically declining army could only wait for the blow to fall.

Waiting, as General Lee said, "on the time and place of the enemy's choosing" was galling to his nature as a man and antithetical to his principles of warfare. By the fourth year of the war, the resources of the Confederacy had been strained too thin to permit any alternative. Lee's only hope lay in outguessing the opponent and trying to catch the heavily weighted columns at a disadvantage.

From all he revealed, by word or expression, General Lee never appeared more sure of himself than on that second day of May. The General seemed in better health with the turn in the weather and the prospect of action. During the winter he had suffered from "rheumatic pains" and frequently expressed his physical "incapacity." A strongly built and superbly conditioned man, normally possessed of great endurance, his decline had begun the year before. In March of 1863 he had come down with a severe throat infection, his first recorded illness during the war. This was accompanied by what was then diagnosed as a rheumatic attack, but which was probably acute pericarditis. His complexion was florid and he suffered from hypertension which, along with angina pectoris, was to cause his final illness.

Though Lee was unaware of such subsurface undermining as a "heart condition," he had visibly aged at fifty-seven. The classically handsome face of 1861, clean-shaven except for a dark mustache, had become the gray-bearded image of the patriarch. His thinning hair, which had gone from brown to gray, was turning white where it fluffed out over his ears. To the men sharing common cause with him, this patriarchal figure was the "Uncle Robert" or "Mister Robert" — slurred to "Marse" — who rode among them, erect and composed, on the familiar Traveler.

General Lee kept other horses at headquarters during the war, but the seven-year-old Traveler became the favorite of them all.

General Lee called him a "Confederate gray," with black mane and tail. A finely proportioned and strongly built middle-sized horse, his feet and head were small, and he was distinguished by a broad forehead and delicate ears. Though he had a smooth canter and a fast, springy walk, Traveler liked to go at a choppy trot, which was harder on a rider than Lee's horsemanship made it appear. He had been with Lee since before the General assumed command of the army in June, 1862, and was inseparably associated with Lee in the Army of Northern Virginia. The pair of them was like a symbol of indestructibility, a reassuring quality that existed outside the mutations of time and circumstance.

This response to the aura of Lee was not only a product of his spectacular successes. At the time of his emergence in the summer of 1862, Hampden Chamberlayne, a scholarly young Richmond lawyer serving with a howitzer battery, wrote his sister: "When by accident at any time I see Gen. Lee, or whenever I think of him, whether I will or no, there looms up to me some king of men, superior by the head, a gigantic figure on whom rests the world,

> *'With Atlantean shoulders fit to bear*
> *The weight of empire.'* "

The world of the generals who gathered around Lee on that May Monday was placed on those "Atlantean shoulders" in the simplest directness of discipleship. In unquestioning acceptance of Lee as their leader, rather than as commanding general in a chain of command, his subordinates recognized their role as that of followers. The men could be jealous among themselves, and some used all the customary methods for personal advancement, but there was never any of the angling for army command that characterized the politically dominated Army of the Potomac. This was one of the reasons that the officially designated Army of Northern Virginia entered the people's language as "Lee's army" — or, as an old country lady called it that spring, "Mr. Lee's Company."

As a leader, Lee was seen as the personification of a cause, rather than by the living details in which his contemporaries were viewed. Grant was not forever smoking a big black cigar, nor was Jackson forever sucking a lemon while fixing a subordinate with his steely gaze. These habits characterized men by readily perceived idiosyncrasies. By contrast, Lee was observed nearly always in the abstract, by his effect on his fellows, by *their* reaction to the aura of the leader.

The most significant element about this image of Lee is that the legendary aspects were always present. There was no later building of the legend, no collections of sayings or anecdotes; the Lee of the legend emerged full-scale, larger than life, during his command of the army.

Countless efforts have been made to "humanize" the mythical figure, and an abundance of material exists on the intimate details of his habits and character. Much can be recorded about the native sweetness of his disposition, his gentleness, the thoughtfulness of his courtesy, the depth of his emotional attachments, and his devotion to the illimitable members of his family. As a woman-raised child, he was at home in and loved the company of women, was unusually dependent on family life, and probably few professional soldiers were forced to bring such a quality of endurance to the unending monotony of camp life.

Less has been made of his enjoyment of physical luxuries. It was his embracing sense of duty, and not a Spartan nature, which caused him to bear with grace the sparse diet, in which cabbage, corn bread and buttermilk frequently constituted the main meal. Both because he liked to do well by himself and because of his sense of the fitness of things, Lee was particular about his dress and wrote his wife in detail of the new style which must be followed in making his collars. His largely neglected letters to Mrs. Lee are extremely revealing of personal tastes of the man within the aura. As illustration, before the complexities of command absorbed most of his time, he wrote his wife and children graphic details of his surroundings, reflecting a deep appreciation of scenes of nature and unexpected response to the weather. He was very oppressed by rain.

Yet Lee cannot be presented through an accumulation of the minutiae of his days. There was an austere quality in the image, as in the genius of Michelangelo. It was the quality of a powerful force, complete and harmonious.

Too much has been made of Lee's humility. As a devout Episcopalian in a believing age, he walked humbly in the sight of God, but among men he was unselfconsciously aware of what he was.

There was no more false modesty than a need for self-assertion. Leadership was a natural state for Lee. He was a late, the last, product of that heroic age in which Virginia society was distinguished by the development of the superior individual.

To place Lee understandably in relation to his environment, Virginia must be conceived as it was during his impressionable years. One of the largest and most populous of states, Virginia dominated the formative stages of the Republic. Four Virginians — Washington, Jefferson, Madison, Monroe — were Presidents during thirty-two of the first thirty-six years of the nation's life, and this was not a remote statistic to Lee. He was born when Jefferson was President, John Marshall was Chief Justice, and his father, his uncles and his cousins had walked among the giants of the Revolutionary generation which produced the Virginia dynasty.

By 1860, when the last of the great generation had passed from the scene and Virginians were living in an afterglow of the period of power and prestige, Lee's contemporaries had no historic perspective on the passing of an age. They were not aware that the state would never regain its recent glory. The older men in Lee's army had seen the masters of the Virginia dynasty, and the younger men had heard of them in intimate terms as of neighbors and kinsmen and not at all as distant historic figures. To Lee's soldiers, then, he was a continuation of this heroic line, and, as such, the epitome of the best in the civilization they were defending.

For these Southern soldiers were defending a land, with all the unarticulated emotional responses of a personal attachment, and Lee became the personification of their attachments. He never once made a speech about the constitutional rights of their position, nor defined what they were defending. His presence was the definition.

2

This image of Lee truly reflected the man, but the harmonious whole of the man was in turn formed by the image of the heroic generation on which Lee molded himself. The often mentioned composure, the basis of his awesome presence, was the product of a conscious intent, as a work of art is the product of a concept. As multiple elements are arranged in any work of creation, the human conflicts of Lee were resolved within. He had no nervous habits by which he released tension; outwardly, in all circumstances, he revealed a vast capacity for stillness. This is the essence of the statuesque quality in the image of Lee.

The ceaseless inner struggle was reflected in actions which do not seem to express the legendary figure. As a general, he revealed the inner stress by the nature of his orders. Because some of these orders, as revealing actions, do not fit the concept, the tendency has been to explain them away, to place them in a context which permits the image to remain undisturbed. Impulsive actions of Lee in battle which led to failures have been made to appear isolated aberrations, while impulsive actions which led to success have been made to appear the natural result of his self-command.

In his plans, Lee's ability to anticipate the enemy in detail was so consistent that his followers then, and admirers since, tended to regard his foresightedness as a quality of divination. It was, however, the product of intense study. Most painstaking in organizing and analyzing items of information obtained about the enemy, he brought highly developed deductive powers to balancing these indications of the enemy's intentions against a background of known factors.

As the war progressed and high mortality caused a deterioration in command personnel (at a time when losses weakened the army physically), the scope of Lee's counterstrokes became increasingly limited. Inevitably, the more Lee's designed movements were restricted in scope and detail, the more the human element of his surviving generals was exposed to the hazards of extemporized action.

As of May, 1864, a strong factor in Lee's successes was the relationship established between the commanding general and the personnel of the Army of Northern Virginia, from privates to corps commanders. Except for the genius of Stonewall Jackson, the personnel of Lee's army was not necessarily superior to the personnel of other Confederate armies. The difference was in the performance that Lee's leadership could evoke. For, as Lee's men saw him in the patriarchal image, so he led his army more as a patriarch than as the commanding general. In his intuitive understanding of the nature of a patriot army, he recognized that the officers and men were not controlled by an established system.

With his limited source of general officer material, he had to make do with the men he had as they were. In encouraging his generals to exploit their fullest potential, it had been his habit, until the spring of 1864, to give orders designed to promote the men's initiative. Lee's use of these discretionary orders has been cited as a weakness by his critics, but precise orders would have been a denial of the creative participation, the sharing of responsibility, which characterized his army at its best. Stonewall Jackson was the outstanding example of a quick blooming under the discretion given by Lee. (At the Seven Days when Old Jack was forced to operate under precise orders, as a unit in a machine, he fell asleep on the battlefield.) Yet Jackson's response to and achievement under Lee's loose leadership caused Lee to place too much faith in the generals in high command during the period of decline which began in the summer of 1863.

On that Monday, May 2, 1864, when he gathered his ranking generals around him, Lee was caught between his familiar habits of command and a reluctant, incomplete acceptance of the limitations of the generals on whom he depended. These were primarily the three men who commanded his corps.

A corps was a complete military entity in the Army of Northern Virginia and, in Lee's boldest maneuvers of the past, the corps acted separately as semi-independent armies. After Jackson's death, in the campaign which ended at Gettysburg, Lee discovered the flaws in separated corps action without a Jackson.

While he was waiting on Grant's move across the Rapidan, his three corps were of necessity separated by the exigencies of winter assignments. Lee's problem was that in anticipating the enemy, with his limited forces he could only plan countermeasures. Until the coming threat developed, he could not assemble the separated units. Even tentative plans for coordinated action of the three corps must be partly determined by the individual human structures of the men commanding the corps.

These three lieutenant generals were, in order of seniority, forty-three-year-old James Longstreet, forty-seven-year-old Richard Stoddert Ewell, and thirty-nine-year-old A. P. Hill. Each of these three generals had, through a flaw in his human organism, once failed Lee in a crisis. Balanced against the failure were records of stout performance, able administration and devotion. But the inner flaws gave Lee a new unknown factor in his own army as the enemy's vastly expanded invasion program brought a new dimension to the war.

3

James Longstreet was of all Lee's generals the least like what he appeared to be. There was nothing of Cassius's "lean and hungry look" to hint at secret ambitions within the impassive Dutchman. A powerfully built man, deep in the chest, he glowed with the rugged health that suggested his pleasure in outdoor sports. A huge, bushy beard half-covered his stolid features, and clear blue eyes faced the world in aggressive self-assurance. On the surface, he appeared an uncomplicated physical type, and as such he was accepted then and has been historically.

Longstreet has been taken on his own evaluation. Studies have been based in general on acceptance of the substance of his many versions of his war career, though his accounts contains within themselves conspicuous inconsistencies and contradictions. Weighed against known facts, they contain gross inaccuracies and distortions, demonstrable fancies and inventions, and outright lies. There are several reasons for this acceptance of Longstreet as a competent witness for events involving himself.

Had he been a chronic failure and neurotic, like Braxton Bragg, the perversions of self-justification would have been expected; but hearty Longstreet, forthright and securely planted in a world of fighting men, boasted a superior combat record, a high reputation as a corps leader, and the confidence of General Lee. Then, the bitter, prolonged postwar arguments over Gettysburg tended to focus attention on his behavior in that battle, isolating this controversial action from his total record.

Far from being an isolated action of character, Longstreet's conduct at Gettysburg was typical of episodes and events which, viewed in their entirety, formed a pattern of behavior totally at variance with the concept of the stolidly dependable "War Horse." They reveal a Longstreet disturbed by ambitions beyond his limitations and confused, in his absence of self-knowledge, by his compulsion to present to the world the image of his self-evaluation.

The custom has been to pass over the separate incidents, some of which were explained away and others obscured by their historic insignificance. As early as the Battle of Seven Pines (May 31, 1862), there was criticism of Longstreet's lack of cooperation, but the whole battle was bungled and the other generals involved faded from the scene. He was dangerously slow at Second Manassas, but criticisms were forgotten in the glow of final victory. In independent command, his futile siege of Suffolk (May, 1863) was overshadowed by the great victory of Lee and Jackson at Chancellorsville, and his gruesome failure at Knoxville was written off among the Western disasters in the winter of 1863-1864.

In personality difficulties, his earlier clash with A. P. Hill was explained by Hill's emotionality, which led him also to clash with Jackson. Troubles with Hood and Toombs were blamed on these former subordinates. Longstreet's current feuds, in May, 1864, with Lafayette McLaws and Evander Law, were waged through the war office and went largely unnoticed while all attention was focused on the gathering forces of the enemy. Besides, McLaws was a division commander of uninspiring competence and young Law was a bookish brigadier, and neither had strong supporters in the Army of Northern Virginia.

Yet Hill's only two conflicts during the war occurred with Longstreet and Jackson, both of whom had long records of personality clashes. With Longstreet, Hill reacted to a spiteful gesture made by his then superior officer, when Longstreet grew resentful of a newspaper account which glorified Hill during the Seven Days.

With Law and McLaws, the War Department supported both against the persecutions instigated by Longstreet, and the ignored McLaws case was particularly revealing of Longstreet's disturbance. In that, he falsely accused McLaws, as the subordinate, of precisely the same conduct of which Longstreet boasted in himself when he was Lee's subordinate at Gettysburg.

Longstreet's accusal of McLaws read: "You have exhibited a want of confidence in the efforts and plans which the commanding general has thought proper to adopt." In writing about Gettysburg, Longstreet blamed Lee for not changing plans when he, the subordinate, showed his "want of confidence in them." Lee knew, Longstreet wrote, "*I* did not believe in the attack." Since Longstreet showed his opinion of such an attitude by using it in a trumped-up charge against the outraged McLaws, it would seem that he had not regarded himself as a subordinate at Gettysburg. Since that manifestly was his status, Longstreet was clearly a confused person beneath the exterior of bluff self-reliance.

His disturbance did not affect his considerable abilities in fighting and commanding troops at corps level, when he accepted corps command as his post. Beginning in the early winter of 1863, however, the good combat soldier was seized with ambitions for high command. As with many men overtaken by dreams beyond their limitations, he attributed to himself the necessary qualities. Not guileful by nature nor largely shrewd, his maneuvers for high command were clumsy. When he failed in his small independent venture during the winter of the Knoxville campaign, his goaded lunges at McLaws and Law, along with the dismissal of Dr. Jerome Robertson of Hood's old brigade, brought him into the strong disfavor of the President and the war office. Then Longstreet blamed the administration for his troubles.

This personal record was not known in its entirety when Longstreet, having recently rejoined the army, met Lee and his fellow generals on Clark's Mountain. Nor did anyone suspect that he had no liking whatsoever for the role of anybody's "war horse." Nothing in his personal history, as generally known, indicated either his ambitions or suggested his banked resentments of some of his brother officers.

Before the opportunities suddenly presented by the war, Longstreet probably had been the well-adapted extrovert which he appeared. Though born in South Carolina, he came of Dutch stock from New Jersey, moved early to the Lower South, and was not influenced by the strong place-identification of his fellows in the army. In the old army, as typical of all Southerners, his friendships had been formed non-sectionally on a basis of mutual tastes. Much could be learned about the personalities of Lee's officers from the Northerners who had been their friends. A. P. Hill's close friend, for instance, was brilliant, charming McClellan of privileged background; Longstreet's was plain Sam Grant.

As captain in the old army, he transferred from the line to the paymaster department in order to achieve the higher rank and higher pay of major, saying he renounced all dreams of military glory. When he enlisted with the Confederate army, not with the troops of any state, he applied for a secure paymaster post. Having come to Richmond from a New Mexican garrison by way of Texas, he arrived later than most of the officers who came home from army posts, and appeared in the war office precisely when a brigadier was needed for three regiments of Virginia volunteers. By this circumstance, he began as a brigadier when his contemporaries were colonels and at promotion time went to major general when they made brigadier.

When Lee emerged into power and formed the loose hodgepodge of units into two corps of four divisions each, Longstreet was given the First Corps both by seniority and on performance. Jackson's rise to Second Corps command from colonel was more meteoric, and his brilliance caught the imagination of the world as well as the South. Nobody suspected Longstreet's jealousy of Jackson's wider fame. While the army and the public held Old Pete in deep regard as Lee's "War Horse," prudent Longstreet suffered a middle-life resurgence of lust for glory.

It is possible he was influenced by the rise of his friend Grant, a man of his own type, whose similar traits of stubborn tenacity had carried him by 1863 to army command. Also Grant operated in the West where, with competition thinner among gifted leaders, the opportunities to shine were greater. Early in 1863, Longstreet began to maneuver to remove his corps from Lee's army, where he was overshadowed by Stonewall Jackson.

It was when detached from Lee, and trying to effect a transfer of his corps to the poorly commanded Confederate Army of Tennessee, that he failed in the pointless siege of Suffolk, while the army was winning its greatest victory at Chancellorsville. Then Jackson's death in May, 1863, removed his rival from the Army of Northern Virginia, and Longstreet returned to Lee with the undeclared purpose of replacing Jackson as Lee's collaborative right hand. What Longstreet failed to perceive was that Lee and Stonewall had held similar concepts of war, of the strategy for implementing it and of the tactics for executing the strategy. With nothing too audacious for Old Jack, Lee had employed Jackson's mobile striking force for the bolder aspects of his strategy. With Longstreet defense-minded and methodical, Lee had employed his dependables for the orthodox work.

The misunderstanding in the Gettysburg campaign arose when Longstreet, in the thrall of his ambitions, presumed the collaborative partnership with Lee and sought to impose on the commanding general his defense preferences. In seeking the glory, he lost a sense of reality. His mind dominated by a determination to fight a battle under conditions which gave opportunity to his special gifts, the corps commander ceased to react responsibly to the actual conditions on the field. Afterwards Longstreet was never clear about what happened. In some twisted self-justification he opened the Gettysburg issue in a period of bitter feeling between himself and his comrades. The trouble really began when security-minded Longstreet accepted a Federal job in New Orleans from his friend, then President Grant, and of necessity became allied with the Reconstruction occupation government against former Confederates.

Although there is even argument about who started the argument, the first public criticisms of Longstreet came in answer to a letter he allowed to be circulated. Then Longstreet publicly justified his Gettysburg behavior by denigrating Lee, shortly after his death. Already regarded as an apostate, Longstreet brought down on his head the outraged fury of Lee's veterans, a number of whom had apparently been doing some brooding over Gettysburg.

The curious feature of the controversy was that the charges and countercharges ignored what Longstreet actually did to contribute to the Confederate failure in the battle. The arguments centered chiefly on Longstreet's slowness, which was involved in an alleged conflict with Lee over strategy. He undeniably delayed going into action in a sullen spirit observed by many, but this deliberate procrastination was a symptom of his disturbed state and not in itself a decisive factor in the battle.

In the controversy over this red herring, Longstreet justified his slowness on the grounds that he opposed Lee's plans and procrastinated in order to persuade the commanding general to follow his, the subordinate's, superior strategy. In contradictory accounts,

Longstreet wrote some highly dramatic scenes describing arguments with General Lee that seem, at best, improbable.

Considering that the accounts were written after Lee's death, and not one witness of that thoroughly reported battle ever referred to the high-flown dialogue which Longstreet attributed to himself, it is amazing that Longstreet's conflicting versions were ever studied seriously. His after-the-fact rationale of the strategy he claimed to have presented is so at variance with the facts of his erratic behavior that most likely little of his drama with Lee ever happened.

What did happen was glossed over by Longstreet and has been strangely ignored. Four generals and one colonel of his corps, each writing independently of the others and none involved in the controversy, gave a composite account which traced those irrational actions of Longstreet that did seriously affect the outcome of the second day's battle. In a mutinous mood which made him scarcely responsible, he insisted on his subordinates' obeying an old order of Lee's after Longstreet perceived the conditions on the field to be different from the conditions presumed in the order. Except for the refusal of subordinates (particularly Brigadier General Evander Law) to follow his senseless command, Longstreet would have committed two divisions to mass suicide. As it was, he directed one of the most disjointed, ill-managed assaults in the war.

Lee never knew the details of Longstreet's mutinous bungling on the second day and Longstreet never appeared to remember it. Perhaps his memory drew a curtain over the details. Evidently he did recognize that he was not to be Lee's collaborator and replace Jackson, for immediately after the battle Longstreet reverted to the West as the more fertile field for advancement. At Chickamauga, in command of an army wing under Braxton Bragg, he performed at his battlefield best. However, the field victory was negated by Bragg's neurotic ineptitude. Longstreet, instead of finding opportunity, found himself in a disastrous command situation which, he wrote, "called for some such great mind as Lee's." Partly to resolve his difficulties with Bragg, Longstreet was given the independent assignment of the siege of Knoxville. Of this Mrs. Chesnut, the outspoken diarist, recorded: "Away from Lee, what a colossal failure is Longstreet."

It was in trying to avoid this verdict and the consequences that Longstreet became embroiled with subordinates, particularly Major General McLaws and Evander Law, and with maladroit stubbornness tried to impose his will on the President and the War Department. By then the spring campaign was approaching and Lee wanted him back. In a final floundering to retain independent command, Longstreet became suddenly offense-minded and turned to vaporous schemes for taking the war to the enemy.

It was a time when many Confederate leaders, despairing of their fortunes under the existing policies, began to clamor somewhat impractically for counteroffensives. Joining this trend, Longstreet not only abandoned his orthodoxy but also those rudiments of supply and logistics about which, at corps command, he was most meticulous. Before the President decided that Longstreet must return to Lee's army, and while his two divisions were being considered for various of the fanciful strategies then in the air, Longstreet sent the war office a plan which read like the daydream of an amateur Napoleon.

As by then Longstreet enjoyed no friends at court, his suggestions were dismissed with no regard for his feelings. Having grown understandably touchy himself, Longstreet became convinced that, as he phrased it in quotation marks, the "authorities at Richmond" had it in for him. The effect of the administration's rejection of his last desperate effort toward independent command was to turn Longstreet to Lee as his one friend. A thoroughly bewildered Cassius, Old Pete was at last willing to return to his familiar role of Lee's "War Horse."

It is significant that Longstreet's Tennessee campaign was extremely important to him. In the book he wrote thirty years after the war, he devoted more attention to his independent command than to any other aspect of the war. The lack of interest inherent in an abortive secondary campaign, along with the obscuring effects of the Gettysburg controversy, caused this phase of Longstreet's war career to be ignored. If his failure in the West is viewed in the significance which it occupied in Longstreet's mind, his attitude to the war-horse role becomes clearer.

He returned to Lee's army when no other avenues of advancement were open to him, but all evidence indicated that he returned more in a spirit of relief than of reluctance. Whatever of his ambitions may have lingered, he was at last back on familiar ground, where he was welcomed and respected. There was another thing too. A devoted Confederate and a practical man, Longstreet recognized that the South's chance of independence and his family's future resided largely in the ragged forces fielded by Lee.

It is likely that the outwardly stolid Dutchman was in a sounder mental attitude when he took his place among the other generals on Clark's Mountain than he had been since his aspirations began to disturb him in the winter of the year before. Though no one could presume to know his exact state of mind, General Longstreet at least appeared the dependable subordinate of the good days of the army. Certainly General Lee accepted him as such.

4

Richard Stoddert Ewell, successor to the great Stonewall Jackson in command of the Second Corps, was also more complex than he appeared. Outwardly Dick Ewell was the "character" of the army. He capitalized on a "quaint" appearance of almost comically arranged features, emphasized by a dragoon's mustache and bulging eyes, and topped by a bare pate which won him the privately spoken soubriquet of "Old Baldhead." His good days in the old army had come as a captain of dragoons in the rough border service, and he made a point of continuing the role of a fierce, hard-bitten line officer. His voice was high and piping, and in one of his awesome rages, partly histrionics, he seemed like an angry bird.

Before his promotion to corps command, the army was regaled by tales of his eccentric sayings and doings, and such was his love of combat that, when operating as Jackson's division commander, he used to steal away and fight in the lines with the troops. Ewell had been engaged in this foolish pastime during the Second Manassas campaign, in the neighborhood where he had played as a boy, when he took a wound which caused the amputation of his leg from above the knee.

Since both armies used amputees in command, no thought was given to the possible psychological damage an artificial leg would cause a man who prided himself on his wiry agility. Ewell had just been pronounced fit to return to command when Stonewall Jackson died in May, 1863, and he was the logical successor. Even so Lee held misgivings about Ewell's fitness for high command, and at Gettysburg Lee's worst fears were confirmed. Dick Ewell became immobilized at the necessity of making a decision in his first big test, and his paralysis of will was a basic cause of the failure at Gettysburg.

A man honest with himself, Ewell characteristically admitted his mistakes. However, his personal behavior during the fall and winter after Gettysburg so alarmed observers in the Second Corps that they feared for his future performances. At the age of forty-six Old Baldhead had married the propertied Widow Brown, a former childhood playmate whose hand he had long sought, and the young men of his staff traced all their superior's changes to his "doting so foolishly upon his unattractive spouse."

Though many remarks about personalities can be discounted by the bias of the observer, this would not obtain with the most candid recorder, Lieutenant Colonel Alexander Pendleton. His judgments were caused solely by his devotion to the Second Corps and, the youngest chief of staff in the army at twenty-three, "Sandie" Pendleton was an exceptional officer in his own right.

The son of the army's chief of artillery and prewar rector of the church in Lexington, Sandie had graduated from Washington College (later Washington and Lee) at the age of sixteen, the youngest student ever to receive the college's highest academic awards. He was studying for a master's degree at the University of Virginia when he volunteered with his state at the age of twenty. The tall, unassuming, plain-faced young man and Stonewall Jackson had formed an early attachment, and Pendleton rose as Old Jack advanced, becoming chief of staff of the Second Corps when only twenty-two. When Ewell succeeded young Pendleton's hero and friend, he specifically requested that Sandie serve as his chief of staff.

To Old Baldhead, Pendleton gave his fullest loyalty, and devoutly hoped he would carry on the traditions of the Second Corps. Deeply religious, though lacking the strait-laced piety of his father, Sandie was known for a cheerful, optimistic disposition and unfailing enthusiasm. Himself recently married to the daughter of the great house where Jackson had headquartered the winter before his death, the kindly young man would normally have been sympathetic to his forty-seven-year-old superior as a newlywed.

Old Baldhead's marital situation, however, was far from normal for a corps commander. During winter camp, General Ewell had set up an establishment in an abandoned house for his wife and her daughter, and the Widow Brown ran the roost with a heavy hand. Jed Hotchkiss, the Yankee schoolteacher and map maker, and Dr. Hunter McGuire, both of whom dated back to the early days of Jackson's staff, found the presence of the women disturbing to the camp, and McGuire said that Mrs. Ewell's influence was "not very good for the old gent." Moonstruck Ewell showed his own naïveté, and good heart, by cordially inviting Sandie to bring his bride and share the Ewell-Brown ménage.

Sandie was more than disgusted at the Widow Brown's domination of the "superannuated chieftain." In fear for the effectiveness of his beloved Second Corps, he wrote his father, General Pendleton, a sound and fair appraisal of his superior. Ewell possessed "quick military perception and is a splendid executive officer, but lacks decision and is too irresolute." These flaws had existed in Ewell from the beginning, and the young staff officers oversimplified Ewell's changes by attributing them to "petticoat" rule, as Judge Advocate Conner described corps headquarters.

Underneath his fierce façade, Ewell was a gentleman of innate dignity and tenderness, and men privileged to know him intimately soon discovered his capacities for affection and thoughtfulness. Though of a distinguished Virginia family, he had, like Lee, come along when fortunes were low. His father, once a powerfully connected doctor, had mysteriously drifted into obscurity, and Ewell had been educated by his mother and sister, who became schoolteachers. In suffering the lasting effects of genteel poverty, he had long aspired to regain a plantation estate, and his middle-life marriage to a lady of property promoted a natural conservatism in a career soldier who had relinquished the fruits of that career. More than that, the Widow Brown (as Ewell continued to refer to his wife) filled a lonely place, which not even those closest to him had suspected, and she filled it as a dominant, not a passive, personality.

Ewell's relations with the Widow Brown exposed in his personal life what his military relations had indicated in his professional life: he wanted the guiding control of a strong hand. His great performances had come, as division commander, under the iron rule of Old Jack, who allowed no discretion whatsoever. In corps command, he immediately came under the influence of a subordinate, tough-minded Jubal Early, a contemporary and classmate at West Point.

Ewell was too proud to admit this, even had he possessed the self-awareness. Under the dominance of his wife, he was goaded to excel in a command where chance, and not capacity, had placed him. Along with pride, he was a most devoted patriot, a soundly trained soldier and justly confident of his ability to fight troops under controlled conditions. Whether or not he was aware of his limitation in the realm of decisions, it is almost a certainty that Lee recognized it, or, at least, feared it.

When the commanding general studied evidences of the Federal army's intention, from their camp across the Rapidan, he considered no countering move which demanded initiative of Dick Ewell, though the Second Corps was camped along the river, nearest to the enemy.

5

Ambrose Powell Hill, like Ewell, had been promoted by necessity beyond his capacities. Unlike Ewell, sensitive Hill was aware of it and strained against the burden of responsibility to which his nature was unequal.

These limitations in Dick Ewell and Powell Hill should not imply an unique flaw in them nor in the system which promoted them. As with countless Confederate generals of lower rank, they were victims of a circumstance which caused men to be entrusted with assignments for which they were unfitted. Temperament as well as ability was a factor in the fitness of a soldier for corps command. In the history of the Army of Northern Virginia only two generals, Jackson and Longstreet, demonstrated the ability to command a corps with more than adequacy, and only Jackson showed the promise for higher command.

Some of the good men who were lost may have possessed the potential, and some of the late bloomers with Lee in the spring of 1864 may have been at least adequate under the earlier conditions, before the decline of the army's strength and the draining of the shallow pool of general officer material. Yet, in the Army of the Potomac, where less was demanded of a corps commander in a more impersonal, efficient machine, drawing on a far deeper source of material, failures were constant and dependable corps leaders were few. From first to last, none was the equal of Jackson and none superior to Longstreet at his best.

With A. P. Hill, it was not so much that he failed as a corps commander as that he did not excel, and the indefiniteness of his record was the more pointed because of the high expectations held for him. As the greatest division commander in the army's history, unsurpassed in the war as a combat leader, Powell Hill had been the natural choice for lieutenant general when, after Jackson's death, the army was divided into three corps. With Hill, the limitations for the higher rank lay entirely in his temperament.

Curiously, the traits which caused his brilliance as a division commander were the same which caused his inconsistencies in corps command. Had less been expected of him, Hill's performance would not have seemed so vaguely disappointing. As it was, the inconclusiveness of his career in corps command, along with a personality not readily categorized, have caused Powell Hill to come across time with less sharp definition than those of his fellows who could be identified by a single tag, a "war horse" or a "rock," by an eccentricity or a splash of sudden color.

Hill eluded the seekers after the dominant characteristic which fits heroes, dependably one-dimensional, into a handy niche. He has been found "shadowy" and "elusive," an historical enigma. In point of fact, he was one of the most all-too-human men who followed Lee. High-strung and emotional, the nearest to "modern" man of all Lee's generals, "Little Powell" was the only general officer in the army who has been studied as an example of psychosomatic illness.

Though "psychosomatic" is about as vague as Hill's illness was to his contemporaries, his symptoms suggest ulcer or some gastrointestinal disturbance. Hill had inherited a weak constitution from his mother, and contracted yellow fever in Florida, but his attacks of illness in the war coincided with crises in the responsibilities of high command. He turned pale, looked, as they said, "sick as a dog," and his complaint was generalized as "biliousness."

A. P. Hill showed none of this when he commanded his famous Light Division. Then, he directed his six brigades in field action under general orders of superiors who were responsible for the total battle. When his intensity tightened like a spring and his excitement mounted unbearably, he released the strain by going into action. He was a close-up leader, staying with his troops, sword in hand. Something of his released emotionality communicated itself to his men and they fought with a fury that distinguished the Light Division in all its battles.

In attack, the lines kept surging in the face of the heaviest casualties. On defense, once in the late summer heat at Second Manassas, they stood up all day to five successive waves of the enemy's assaults, and they still stayed there when the ammunition was gone and threw rocks and waited, staggering with exhaustion, to close with the bayonet. At Sharpsburg, when Hill drove his men through the dusty heat all day and deployed them, running, into Burnside's flanking movement against Lee's fought-out army, it was only necessary for Lee to say, "And then A. P. Hill came up."

In the lonely sphere of corps command, things were different for Powell Hill. He could find no release in action for his nerves tightening in mounting tension, and the unrelieved emotional stress acted on the susceptible stomach. There also his temperament unfitted him for the demands of a high executive. A fair enough administrator, he was too personal for the exercise of detached authority. He missed the closer companionship of his brigadiers, especially Dorsey Pender. This able, intense North Carolinian, killed at Gettysburg in his twenty-ninth year shortly after his promotion to division command, had been, as a soldier and a man, close to Hill's heart.

Hill was not a group man. His friend Rev. J. William Jones, Third Corps chaplain, said, "His noble traits of heart and mind were best revealed in private friendships." But Hill did not establish intimacies with ease. Very courtly, he had a reserved nature within an outwardly warm manner. He was best remembered across all ranks for his friendly courtesy and easy informality, "genial without familiarity." A courier remembered him as the one general who was unfailingly cheerful even in the tensest action, and a fellow general said, "Of all Confederate officers, he was the most lovable in his disposition."

Yet few men really knew him. What secrets he revealed in his private letters were lost when his family destroyed his papers. His few known letters to old friends, such as the Federals' former commander in chief, McClellan ("Dear Mac"), show him to be unguarded and warm.

His wife, the sister of Confederate raider John Morgan, established a temporary home near camp more often and for longer periods than the wives of most of Lee's generals, though their home life remained separate from army headquarters and Mrs. Hill never intruded her presence, as did Ewell's Widow Brown. Much at home in a general society, Hill was a social favorite in Richmond parlors, where some of Lee's generals, notably Allegheny Johnson and John Hood, had been private jokes.

His well-established family in Virginia's piedmont had been neither planters nor slaveholders. Hill personally was an intense disbeliever in slavery and, like Lee, Stuart, Stonewall Jackson and Ewell, had grown up under the influence of a deeply religious mother. Unlike those Confederates who went unabashedly about their religious devotions under all circumstances, Hill was more typical of the conservative Episcopalians who were what might be called restrained in the outward manifestations of their faith.

Similarly conservative, he affected no oddities of manner or dress. When division commander, during summer fighting, Hill had removed his jacket and attracted considerable attention by leading troops in a fireman's red shirt. Usually, however, he dressed in extreme simplicity and shunned all trappings of military display.

In looks he was striking. Of middle height, he was slight and graceful, and moved well. A bold nose and high brow dominated finely carved features. His cheeks had grown sunken and he wore a high-growing full beard, red-brown, or fox-red. His hair was worn long, parted on the right side. His hazel eyes were deep-set and intense and, by '64, except when he was laughing or animated, a suggestion of melancholy clouded his gaze. One of his Tarheel soldiers thought him "one of the handsomest men I've ever seen."

Much was known about a general by what his soldiers thought of him. While all Lee's other generals were called — like a bourbon — Old Something, Hill's men called him, in affectionate diminutive, "Little Powell." Demanding of them in action, he was casual in camp and indulgent of their needs, and they loved him.

Hill did not concern himself overly with details and he wrote brief, unrevealing reports, as if uninterested in campaigns once they were over. Extremely proud, he never explained, was quick to acknowledge mistakes and generous in assuming responsibilities for failures which involved others. As General Lee considered A. P. Hill's role, in the gathering at the Clark's Mountain reconnaissance post, the problem about his mistakes was their unpredictability. They all resulted from impulsiveness, springing from a nature which did not wish but needed restraint. For quite different reasons from those pertaining to Ewell, Hill could be allowed even less initiative than Old Baldhead.

6

These three men did not constitute an "army command" in the sense of partaking in the decisions made by the high command. The chief of Lee's subordinates, the lieutenant generals shared in the making of strategy no more than the major generals and brigadiers whom they in turn directed. Nor did General Lee's staff bear any relation to a "general staff" in its modern meaning. However, the smallness of Lee's personal staff, those officers who lived at the General's headquarters, has led to the false impression that Lee operated with inadequate staff work.

For all the staffs in his army, as all else, Lee had been forced to find pragmatic methods of getting around the President's bureaucracy without doing violence to Davis's touchiness. Since headquarters staff officers were limited by the tables of organization, Lee introduced the practice of giving relative equality of rank and perquisites to officers of the personal staff and to officers who directed special services. As the commanding general gave all staff officers a flexibility in their areas, this permitted Lee to use non-personal staff officers at headquarters whenever the occasion demanded. In conforming to regulations, Lee seldom retained more than five officers on his personal staff, but with only three personal staff officers, on May 2nd, Lee's available staff numbered sixteen, plus many junior officers as assistants.

His personal staff shifted as Lee relinquished men to field units, and he did not always immediately replace them. Three had transferred in the spring of '64, leaving the General with the three who remained with him constantly from the early days. As majors, later to be promoted to lieutenant colonel, Walter Taylor, Assistant Adjutant General, was something of the executive officer of headquarters; Charles S. Venable, aide-de-camp, was occupied chiefly with inspections; and Charles Marshall, also aide-de-camp, was largely Lee's military secretary. A lawyer and kinsman of Chief Justice Marshall, bespectacled Marshall wrote most of the finished copies of Lee's orders and reports from the commanding general's offhand dictation or rough drafts, as Lee detested paper work.

The officers who comprised the approximation of a general staff directed such bureaus as ordnance, commissary and quartermaster; there were a chief of engineers, a medical director, assistant inspector general, a judge advocate general, and a chief of artillery.

The "chief of artillery" was something of a non-descriptive title for Brigadier General Pendleton, the well-meaning bumbler who had been at West Point with Lee and, turning to the clergy, was serving as rector of the Episcopal Church in Lexington when war came. With military matters in the mists of his youth, the pious Virginia gentleman raised a gun battery manned by college students; this later gained fame with the Second Corps as the Rockbridge (County) Artillery, while Pendleton advanced in administrative work to become chief of artillery reserve. In the army's reorganization into three corps the year before, General Lee, partly in dissatisfaction with the performance of his old friend, abolished the artillery reserve. Yet, unwilling to hurt a cleric of his own faith, and a most devoted patriot, Lee created the nominal post of chief of artillery, which served as an outlet for General Pendleton's fussy preoccupation with details. Though he sometimes interfered with the superbly effective young men who commanded corps artillery, the rector on leave found little ways of being useful (he certainly kept busy) and was a frequent member of the informal staff.

Another officer most likely at the Clark's Mountain gathering was temporary chief engineer, imposingly handsome Major General Martin Smith. This brilliant newcomer to the army was a professional soldier from New York who had built the powerful defenses at Vicksburg. Also frequently in Lee's group were Major Young, judge advocate general, and one-armed Major Peyton, an assistant inspector general who had brought out one of Pickett's shattered brigades at Gettysburg.

The Army of Northern Virginia fielded no mobile telegraph system, and messages from telegraph stations and intra-army messages were carried by the hard-bitten, reckless young men who served as couriers. Important verbal messages from the commanding general were delivered by officers of the personal staff, usually Walter Taylor. This extremely good-looking young man, approaching his twenty-seventh birthday, was from first to last the closest to General Lee.

Born in Norfolk, Taylor attended Virginia Military Institute before family financial reverses caused him to go into business at a relatively early age. With all his attractive good looks and appealing personality, Walter Taylor was an astute businessman, very successful, with a highly organized and literate intelligence. When Lee first set up headquarters as commander of Virginia's forces, Walter Taylor was recommended by a cousin of Lee's, a retired naval captain, whose wife was a relative of Taylor's. So vast are the interweavings of such Virginia families that Taylor had never before seen Lee and the General had never heard of the dark, quiet young man, then attired in the uniform of a Norfolk militia company. Though General Lee had no chief of staff as such, the same quick affinity was established between him and Walter Taylor as between Stonewall Jackson and Sandie Pendleton.

The various interrelations of these men around Lee, by no means extraneous social notes, indicate the kinship, by blood and background, which gave the Army of Northern Virginia the sense of family that made it possible for Lee to lead as something of a clan head. An intense concern was shared about one another's total lives outside the army — their families, homes and neighborhoods.

Lee was constantly forced to separate personal considerations from military necessities throughout the whole army. By the same token, he was gratified when his personal affections for an officer were supported by confidence in his performance. This was fortunately the case with his middle son, Rooney, and his nephew, Fitz, both of whom were division commanders in Stuart's cavalry.

Outside his own family, and since the death of Jackson, Stuart himself was probably the general closest in Lee's affections who also aroused his deepest admiration as a soldier. There was an avuncular quality in Lee's regard for the thirty-one-year-old Jeb Stuart, who had been a cadet at West Point when Lee served a tour as superintendent, and the General placed implicit trust in the commander of his cavalry corps.

No army in the war was as well served by cavalry, in the traditional functions of reconnaissance and screening, as the Army of Northern Virginia by Major General James Ewell Brown Stuart. With the exception of a gaudy side adventure in the Gettysburg campaign, when his exuberant vanity overcame his judgment, Stuart flawlessly served as "the eyes of the infantry" — and the army did not have history's perspective on Gettysburg. It was just one of those operations which seemed doomed from the start.

Like all commanding generals in the war, Lee had to learn the proper use of mounted troops, and the quickness of his mastery of the techniques was undoubtedly sped by Stuart's instinct for his role. The classic distinction between lancers, dragoons and "light cavalry" quickly disappeared in an open country, thinly populated, with fronts the size of European duchies and provinces, and railroads for the first time a military factor in war. "Modern" cavalry, as developed in 1862, in combining all previous functions of mounted troops, and adding new ones, was a precursor of the present air arm, which tactically is a technological development of the cavalry's service as employed by Jeb Stuart.

His dual primary purpose was to obtain information of the enemy's movements and to prevent the enemy from obtaining information about his own infantry. His secondary purpose was to disrupt the enemy's supplies, as by raiding wagon trains and wrecking railroads and supply depots. In its ultimate extension, this disruption of supplies would carry destruction by raids into the enemy's homeland. Though this practice was developed systematically in the Federal forces, traditionalist Lee was opposed to taking war to the civilian population, and Stuart made only one such raid, to Chambersburg, Pennsylvania.

By 1864, the poor condition of Stuart's horses and the superiority of the weapons of the Federal cavalry largely eliminated this secondary function of disrupting military supplies, though the threat influenced the enemy's movements and diverted troops from combat. At the same time, with the declining numbers in Lee's army and the increase in the Army of the Potomac, Stuart's screening operations, which included the guarding of all avenues of approach and the protection of the flanks, forced on his troopers a good deal of fighting as something like mounted infantry. Stuart personally loved combat and had never been happier than during the first two years when, with good mounts, his men fought the enemy's cavalry with relative equality of numbers. But the grimmer days restricted his preferences as they restricted Lee's choices of action.

Nothing, however, affected his irrepressible spirits. He was a stockily built man, powerful in the torso, blessed with an inexhaustible flow of physical vitality and a naturally happy disposition. An iron will to succeed at anything he undertook, along with an instinctive denial of the possibility of the destruction of his known world, gave Stuart a cheerful imperviousness to shifts of fortune. He had endured severe personal losses in staff officers and army intimates. Baron Heros von Borcke, the Prussian volunteer aide, was permanently out with a wound, and another volunteer aide, Farley, the South Carolina Shakespearean scholar and scout extraordinary, was killed. Stuart's dear friend John Pelham, the good-looking young artillerist, and Channing Price, his beloved cousin, were also dead. Blackford had transferred to the engineer corps and Rooney Lee, the General's outsize, Harvard-educated son, was newly occupied with division command. Even Sweeney the banjo player was gone. Yet the outgoing Stuart took life as it came and cavalry headquarters retained a lighthearted atmosphere.

His headquarters were the most informal in the army. His headquarters tent consisted of a tent-fly stretched on rails against a tree, and open at both ends. Underneath was a desk and chair, blankets on the ground, and his two impossibly named setters, Nip and Tuck. John Esten Cooke, prewar professional writer and cousin of Mrs. Stuart, served for a time on Stuart's staff, and he recorded: "The men were perfectly unconstrained in his presence, and treated him more like the chief huntsman of a hunting party than as a major general. . . . [He was] like the king of the rangers."

Preparing for the new campaign, he wrote verses instead of doing paper work, at which his ebullient energy made him fidget, broke off to joke with his staff, and then wrote his wife a letter in which he asked if she knew the words to the new song, "When This Cruel War Is Over." He prepared his uniforms as if for a ball, bedecking himself with gold sash, red-lined cape, and plumed hat. With his huge red beard and great mustachios, Stuart's flamboyant appearance aroused derision among his detractors, but the flash of golden and young-hearted color was a gonfalon to his men and a bright thread to many of the soberest men in the army.

Stuart was not among those gathered on Clark's Mountain. With all his vanity and high spirits, the cavalry chief was all business when he worked. He had his men ranging the bypaths leading from the crossings of the Rapidan, and, the decline in the cavalry demanded his personal attention. Unlike the infantry, Stuart's forces suffered no deterioration in command. A higher proportion of the cavalry came from a class of natural leaders, and in the smaller, more compact force, Stuart, with a sharp eye for command potential, was able to discover men of promise. The decline in the cavalry was entirely physical.

Stuart's paper strength numbered something over eight thousand, 15 per cent below the peak strength of the year before, and his units were widely scattered for forage. Branches of supply and subsistance led from and back to central departments in the bureaucratic system, with the result that the support of armies was in a measure subordinated to the operation of government agencies. While studying Grant's intentions, Lee was writing notes of reports of available forage in various parts of the state, where the worn-out, personally owned mounts could garner a little strength for the coming campaign.

Stuart's total figure included recruits of sixteen-year-old boys and middle-aged farmers whose land had been overrun and who had nothing left to work. The newcomers came straight from their homes, wearing such assortments of clothes as they could provide or their families provide for them. They brought their own horses, saddled and bridled, and the only issue they received was weapons — a single-shot carbine of any of a dozen types, a Colt .44, sometimes a saber, and handfuls of cartridges and caps to put where most convenient.

No especial kindness was shown the recruits by the old-timers. They had to find themselves in the rough banter of case-hardened soldiers, learn both to cook and to stomach the greasy dish of corn meal fried with chunks of fat bacon in a wet pone called "sloosh," and forage for oilcloths from dead Yankees or dead companions. Some wore boots, some shoes. Not even Genghis Khan's hordes looked less like traditional mounted troops devoted to the orthodox work of screening the infantry and gaining information about the enemy.

With no transition from home to the Rapidan, the recruits were simply thrown into the regiments whose numbers were the lowest. Their "camp of instruction" was the soft-banked river, across which they saw moving dark blurs of the enemy in forage caps, magnificently equipped, and firing the new Spencer repeating carbine. There were some thirteen thousand of those enemy troopers, commanded by a big-headed, coarse little man named Sheridan, who had been brought in from the West to show the Easterners what rough war could be like.

All of Stuart's men could ride, though the old farmers might tire and the boys might panic. Having only one shot before they reloaded, the men would make their fire count too, if they stood up to the test. Yet to those most apprehensive about how they might do in combat, something casual and lighthearted emanated from the top. Fitzhugh Lee's frolics might alarm his uncle, the commanding general, and high-shouldered, black-eyed Tom Rosser might follow his sybaritic tastes, but such pleasure-loving sustained a spirit which, in the cavalry, from the beginning was different in quality from the infantry's.

To a stranger, the somewhat gaudy appearance and the lighthearted laughter of the cavalry corps commander might not suggest dependability; but to Lee, Jeb Stuart was one absolutely known quantity. Among the knowns in the potential of his performance was the new limitation imposed on the range of Stuart's probings. Tireless in his vigilance and restless for action, the cavalry leader, like the rest of them, would have to wait on the enemy's move.

7

To Lee, silent on the mountaintop, no definite information from his cavalry or his usual sources guided him in anticipating the thrust the Federal host was obviously prepared to deliver. On Monday, May 2nd, Lee had as a basis for his deductions the premonitory stirrings in the enemy's camp, the known factors of the enemy's general objectives and the immutable terrain. From those elements, he must deduce the time and place of the enemy's thrust, and most particularly the enemy's immediate objective and the probable means of his attempting to achieve it. Would the Federal commander try to reach Richmond by the straightest line or employ a long-range strategy? Would he seek battle with Lee or try to outmaneuver him? Would he push with a heavy concentration or try diversionary tactics?

With a familiar opponent, much would be determined by Lee's knowledge of the man. Grant, the new commander brought in from the West as commander in chief of all the armies, was not only a strange opponent but personally unknown to Lee. More than that: as commander of all the armies, executing the evolved policy of total war with the gathered might of an industrial nation, Grant directed a multi-pronged offensive of which the Army of the Potomac was only the center unit. As the broader offensive threatened points outside of Lee's area of authority, though not outside his area of concern, the General took first things first and pondered over the enemy's imminent movement as it directly affected the Army of Northern Virginia.

Grant's logical choices of approach were through a front restricted to little more than twenty-five miles in width. This followed the course of the Rapidan River from where it branched off the

Rappahannock, ten miles west of Fredericksburg, twenty-five loop-ing miles to the southwest where the river passed to the west of Orange Court House. This small courthouse town, on the Orange & Alexandria Railroad, could be considered an identification point for the western end of the arc of the Rapidan front. The eastern end would come where the Rapidan forked off from the Rappahan-nock. The tented city of the enemy's camp, with a population larger than that of all Virginia cities combined, was spread between the northwest and southwest forks of the Rappahannock, and the Fed-eral army would be forced to cross two rivers if it advanced east of the forks, toward the ravaged small city of Fredericksburg.

Physically, the western end favored the maneuvering of a large army. The farm country, open and rolling, was shy of natural de-fensive positions for a physically weaker army. To the east lay the forbidding belt of woods called the Wilderness. Its narrow roads offered poor passageway for a heavily supplied army, and maneuver would be impossible in the dense thickets.

Lee held his field glasses the longest on the wild country of the Wilderness, where two fords, Germanna and Ely, crossed the river in the heart of freshly flowering jungle. Then he pointed with his wide, strong hand, encased in a leather gauntlet, towards the two fords. Giving no reasons, he said, "Grant will cross by one of those fords."

He made no elaboration of this simple statement, but his general command understood that he meant the Army of the Potomac would throw its full weight at a forced crossing of the river. The gen-erals assumed that Lee meant to defend the crossings. Lee, however, taking no one into his confidence, was considering other plans, the boldest in a career characterized by audacity.

With no further conversation, at least none recorded, the assem-blage of generals and their staffs began to break up. Only a blare of trumpets was lacking to complete the spring pageantry as the handsomely caparisoned officers mounted their horses and turned to leave the mountain. The three corps commanders, Longstreet, Ewell and Hill, would never gather together again. Many of the other generals would never be in any gathering again.

Perhaps because of the solemn overtones of the spectacle of this last meeting of Lee and his generals, men remembered more vividly

Lee's prediction of Grant's move. Because the Army of the Potomac moved within thirty-six hours by the crossings to which Lee had pointed, the aging General became more deeply enmeshed in legend. It was as if a patriarch of the olden times had ascended the mountain and there he experienced a vision; then he came down from the mountain and it was as he had said it would be.

CHAPTER TWO

"There Will Be Nothing Left
for Us to Live for"

ON May 3rd, messages from the Clark's Mountain signal
station advised General Lee of intensified activity in the
enemy's camp, but no troops moved out during the day
and nothing indicated the possible direction of movement. Twenty-
odd miles by winding road from the point where he expected
Grant to enter the Wilderness, Lee waited in his headquarters tent,
pitched with Hill's Third Corps at Orange Court House.

West of the Wilderness and of tidewater, Orange County was
farm rather than plantation country, though Montpelier, the home
of former President James Madison, had been elegantly expanded
by the architect who built the Capitol in Washington. The country,
with its younger men in the armies, some with A. P. Hill's troops,
and its farms hit in a couple of raids, was lean in supplies, but
the people were hospitable at least in spirit, and the soldiers'
temporary community of snugly rude huts had been one of their
more pleasant winter headquarters. The connection of the Orange
& Alexandria Railroad with the Virginia Central, at nearby Gordonsville, made it possible for ladies to visit the soldiers during the
winter. Hill's family quartered with him at a new Victorian mansion called "Mayhurst," where Lee had acted as godfather in the
christening of the Hills' youngest daughter.

As all during the war, Lee lived in a tent, in fear of enemy reprisals on any family whose hospitality he might accept. Though
always accessible and easily approachable, his awesome personal
dignity negated any familiarity or even the desire for it. Neither
orderlies nor sentries were needed to protect the cluster of head-

quarters tents from intrusions; the men's reverential respect for
Lee formed the wall around him.

On this beautiful May day, Tuesday the 3rd, surrounded by
the familiar sounds of camp life, the General made a partial commitment of his army to counter Grant's anticipated move. He
sent an order to Lieutenant General Ewell to break his winter camp
along the Rapidan. There, where the river ran almost due west before taking the southwestward swing beyond Orange Court House,
Ewell was to put the Second Corps immediately in motion toward
the Wilderness. His three divisions were to march eastward along
the old stone Turnpike which, roughly paralleling the river, entered
the Wilderness on Grant's presumed line of march southward. Lee
gave Ewell no detailed instructions and made no mention of general
plans.

Beyond this order to Ewell, Lee did not indicate to anyone the
bold strategy evolving in his mind. It could be observed that Ewell
was to march *toward* the enemy, with no orders to prepare to defend the river crossings, and that was the extent of what Lee revealed to his subordinates.

Hill's troops remained undisturbed in their cheerful quarters, and
Longstreet's incomplete corps, camped ten miles to the south at
Gordonsville, were not alerted. While rudimentary caution would
restrain General Lee from committing Hill and Longstreet on an assumption of the enemy's course of action, more than caution was
involved in Lee's decision against preparing his corps commanders
for moving out. He was restrained by the enormity and complexity
of the offensive projected by the enemy, which threatened too
many points in the area of his responsibility outside the area of his
authority.

General Grant, the newly appointed commander in chief of all
the Federal armies, had the authority to direct the total operation
affecting Richmond and Lee's army, as well as coordinating this
multi-pronged offensive with an overall plan. Lee's authority was
restricted to the Virginia area from the north of Richmond, and his
operations even there were subject to the authority of his commander in chief, President Davis. By this arrangement, field-gen-
eral Lee, in opposing commander-of-the-armies Grant, must work
through an authoritarian superior in order to counter the enemy's

interrelated offensive as it involved his own limited sphere in the total area of operations. As of May 3rd, so limited was Lee by the President's exercise of the authority of commander in chief that he could not assemble his whole army.

Grant's true antagonist was not Lee at all, but Jefferson Davis. As Grant was the first general to design a total plan and execute the details without consulting anyone, Davis was the only Confederate with similar power and similar scope of constituted responsibility. When Lincoln gave Grant the job of carrying a total war of subjugation to the Confederacy, Davis retained the full responsibility of defending the new nation, struggling for survival and its right to survive. By 1864, Davis's policy of a dispersed defense, designed to check the enemy everywhere, provided an ideal arrangement for the success of Grant's use of physical superiority — in numbers, materiel and supporting facilities.

To Lee, the obvious countermaneuver was a concentration against the enemy's main forces, in which the Confederacy would risk largely for the large end of disrupting the enemy's prearranged plans. Since such a risk was antithetical to the President's policy, Lee, though he perceived Grant's total intent more clearly and more in detail than any man in the Confederacy, was forced to attempt to affect the total Federal campaign in the East with his incomplete army in the path of the enemy's chief army. While Grant prepared to deliver his thrust on lines of his choice, Lee prepared to meet him on the lines of Davis's choice.

In this way, Lee, surmising Grant's purposes and recognizing the inadequacy of Davis's system for thwarting them, was committed to fighting the enemy in his front while trying to manipulate the superior at his back. As field commander, he stood in the unique position of waging his lonely fight between the two true antagonists.

2

The key to Lee's problem with Davis was the geographical divisions of departments in an area which militarily comprised one single theater of operations.

In the beginning the Confederacy had been divided along physical boundaries which would have served ideally for the operation of a postal service. In the Virginia-Carolina theater the shape of the departments changed according to the shifts of the war. When Lee first assumed command of the Department of Northern Virginia, his area of authority embraced most of the state. In the summer of 1862, after Lee established a front fifty-odd miles north of Richmond, he continued for a time to direct affairs south of Richmond and related actions in North Carolina. Then, as the enemy abandoned operations immediately south of the James River, Lee's ill-defined authority caused him to give discretionary orders to the generals commanding in the more distant areas.

This did not work well with commanders who subordinated the general plans to the importance attached to some diversionary action in their own areas. Lee wrote Seddon, "the apprehensions of the community exaggerate rumors and create expectations of an immediate attack. The responsibility of the officer charged with the defense tends to produce the same result." After an open conflict with D. H. Hill, Lee wrote Davis that he preferred to be relieved of the responsibility of the distant operations unless provided with the proper authority. As most of the minor affairs concerned those collections of units at scattered points, according to Davis's predilections, the President accepted Lee's ultimatum by relieving him officially of the responsibility.

Gradually, as departments proliferated, a separate department evolved which began at the south bank of the James River. As Richmond was built along the north bank, this water barrier had become the dividing line of Lee's Department of Northern Virginia.

Until 1864, this bureaucratic division worked well enough, while the enemy's chief assaults in Virginia came from north of the Rappahannock and in North Carolina the prime military consideration was the open port of Wilmington. From there the blockade-run supplies were freighted by railroad to Richmond, and the coastal operations were largely peripheral affairs. With the coming of Grant, it became apparent to Lee that the enemy's diversionary actions in coastal North Carolina were to be shifted to a concentration south of the James River in Virginia, to form a joint operation on Richmond with Meade's army striking from the north. Though this secondary Union army would come at the city from south of the James River, the river would serve the Federal forces not as a dividing line but as a connective.

With the Federal naval base at Fort Monroe, on the tip of the Virginia peninsula across Hampton Roads from Norfolk, the forces at Grant's disposal controlled Virginia's inland waterway, and gunboats patrolled the James River to within ten miles of Richmond. The imminent use of these facilities in a joint operation on the capital suddenly made the arbitrary boundary of the James River a division across the area of Lee's responsibility, for of all things he was charged with the protection of Richmond.

The departments remained. Lee was restricted to defending the capital only from the north. The James River, which gradually widened to three miles at the mouth, was only four hundred yards wide at Richmond, but the approaching action to the south of the capital could have been in another country as far as Lee's area of authority extended.

At the Rappahannock, then, Lee was meeting only the enemy's main army in a department which had shrunk considerably since he assumed command. A small force in the Shenandoah Valley, from where another Federal thrust was coming, remained under his authority, but in the eastern section of the Department of Northern Virginia, the enemy (with a Union state government) operated a far larger military establishment than the Confederates. As the days were gone when Lee's army was of a size and strength to pose a threat to the North by its very existence in the field, the General's problem was to defeat the enemy when he lacked the power to maneuver and the authority over his area of military responsibility.

Around Richmond north of the James, Lee had designed a vast system of fortifications which had been completed under his distant direction and urging. From the south side the city was almost wholly exposed. Eight miles to the southeast of Richmond, an ingenious river fort at Drewry's Bluff, on the south bank of the James, held off the United States Navy, but this was lightly manned against ground attack from the land side. This, of course, was known to the enemy. One quick land thrust at Drewry's Bluff could uncover Richmond from the south and lay the capital open to the Federal gunboats. At best, if the fort held, the enemy force on the south side of the river could sever the city's railroad connections with coastal North Carolina and isolate Richmond from the Lower South.

On May 3rd, while waiting for definite information about the Army of the Potomac on his front, Lee devoted himself to the task of persuading the President to change his fixed troop dispositions in anticipation of the enemy's total plans. This he had never succeeded in doing throughout the war. However, never before had Lee prepared to meet an enemy in his front while the capital was in danger of being lost behind him.

To shift troops to Richmond from his own army would be impossible. Davis had already detached six of Lee's thirty-eight brigades and reduced his infantry to a scant forty-five thousand in the Rapidan area. Lee's urgency to reassemble his army before meeting Grant was as great as his need to protect the capital from the south. Pickett's four rebuilt brigades, of Longstreet's corps, and a large brigade from Ewell's corps were scattered in Davis's garrison system. That was standard. Even for the invasion which ended at Gettysburg, Lee could not pry loose from Davis the units to complete his army. However, now, with the heaviest and most closely coordinated blows of the invasion forces about to strike, a full division commanded by one of Lee's brigadiers was occupied in the futile siege of a peripheral position on the North Carolina coast.

In a long-range view of Eastern operations, the inland coastal towns of North Carolina held some military importance. From bases in those towns the Federals threatened the supply railroad from the port of Wilmington and, during the winter lull between major campaigns, retaking the towns constituted a legitimate minor operation. In Confederate hands these inland ports, along with removing the Federal threats, provided a base for shallow-draft boats, including those ingenious monsters called "rams" which the Southerners occasionally sprang on the blockading fleet.

Brigadier General Robert Hoke, while detached from Lee and with sizable aid from one of these rams, the *Albemarle*, had captured Plymouth in a surprise stroke. Upped to major general, he then took on New Bern without support of a ram. That attack failed. Then Davis permitted Hoke to use his new division, including a veteran brigade detached from Ewell's corps, to settle down to a siege while the Federal might massed for major offenses against Richmond and Atlanta.

To complete this pattern of dispersal of inferior manpower, the President held other brigades, the equivalent of two divisions, stationed at various points in the Carolinas *after* the Federals withdrew large forces from the Carolinas for their secondary army with the objective of a back-door attack on Richmond.

When Lee had earlier passed on to Davis the information that this secondary army was composed of troops withdrawn from the Carolinas, he added the conclusion that the removal of these troops showed that the Federals had abandoned "serious intentions" against the Carolina coast. With this conclusion, Lee suggested that, since the coast was temporarily safe, the dispersed Confederate units in that area be concentrated south of Richmond. Believing that the enemy's action was to shift to this new objective, he urged that General Beauregard, commander of the Charleston defenses, be brought on to assume command of the Richmond defense on the south side of the James.

While messages went from Braxton Bragg, the Military Adviser, to the adjutant general toward the end of shifting some of the troops northward from the Carolinas, Davis, instead of bringing Beauregard on, created a new department (the Department of Southern Virginia and North Carolina) and placed Beauregard's name on his charts as its commander. As of May 3rd, Beauregard had set up offices in North Carolina and not one soldier had reached the capital. Lee's six detached brigades remained detached.

Davis had revealed before that his system contained no department of "anticipation." With the imminence of the enemy's massed thrusts obvious to all observers, for Davis the point remained that the enemy had not *yet* moved. After the enemy established his new position, then the commander in chief would rearrange his clerical charts and move units about to meet the situation already created by the enemy.

In working through his superior, Lee never seemed to perceive that this cast of Davis's mind affected all military operations, from grand strategy to small details. Though he accepted the impossibility of convincing the President to concentrate troops in the larger strategy, the General continued to try to persuade Davis to make local concentrations in advance of the enemy's move. On Tuesday the 3rd, Lee once again gathered his patience and marshaled his considerable gift for diplomacy in composing two letters to the commander in chief.

First, to avoid the suggestion of superior knowledge, he repudiated any intelligence on his part in surmising the enemy's intentions (which, as it turned out, he predicted in detail). He based his opinion completely on reports, some of which he enclosed, from spies and scouts and Northern newspapers. Then, when he reached the urgent points of the needs of completing his army and of protecting Richmond from the south side, Lee played on Davis's fear of giving up any ground and appealed to his vanity as the final authority:

If General Beauregard can take care of the flank movement [the secondary army] on Richmond, and I can get all the troops belonging to this army, Pickett, Hoke, and R. D. Johnson [one of the brigades from Ewell's corps], I will endeavor to hold the front. If this can not be done, it may be better for me to be nearer Richmond, which I request the President to decide.

Of all things, Lee knew that the President wanted him to fight on the Rapidan line. Lee had frequently wished to fall back from that line, in order to get maneuvering room, but Davis would relinquish no foot of territory voluntarily for a strategic end. What Lee did not comprehend was that, in Davis's system, his army was an immutable quantity, impervious to time and circumstance, fixed in perpetuity in that barren countryside.

Davis's reliance on the Army of Northern Virginia as a permanent known on the Rapidan missed the point that Lee had previously maintained a resistance through maneuver, and ignored the point that Lee's army was growing weaker as the enemy gathered the mightiest force yet to come at him. Viewing Lee as a fixture, the commander in chief felt free to shuffle units about as if Lee's army was an abstraction, a symbol on the charts, and not a sum of its component parts.

When, earlier in the spring, Davis was seized by a sudden compulsion to mount an offensive in the West, he had considered detaching Longstreet's corps permanently from Lee's army. Then, when Lee secured the return of those veterans, the General had to deny a presidential request for a transfer of veteran division commander Major General Edward Johnson only ten days before Grant moved out. That denial of Lee's was short and blunt, its lack of any sugar-coating revealing the worn patience.

Yet General Lee did not comprehend the basic division between himself and Davis. He never realized that they were talking about quite different things.

3

As commander in chief, Jefferson Davis was praised and blamed for many things which bore little to no relation to his specific role as director of the Confederacy's armed force. No one could question his courage, high principles and unshakable integrity; as President of a hasty collection of fiercely individualistic and largely rural states, sustaining themselves as a republic against invasion from a powerful, mechanized and established nation, he was confronted with problems to tax the resources of any man ever produced on the continent.

If, by chance, the nation he led had won its independence, many of his mistakes would be forgotten and history's rationale would explain how the course of his actions determined the decision. Some of his finest reasonings on constitutional rights would assume an honored place among the arguments on the rights of numerical minorities to govern themselves; Davis would be regarded as a precursor in the application of self-determination as a theory in world government.

As his side lost, his absorption in the abstractions of self-government, have been used as a weakness, and the bitterest irony is that Lincoln's often quoted words — "that government of the people, by the people, and for the people, shall not perish from the earth" — defined the principle for which the South was fighting. At no time did the Confederacy present any danger to the rights of the citizens of the Union to govern themselves.

However, Jefferson Davis's finest constitutionalities bore no more direct relationship to his command of the Confederate armies than did his devotion to his family, or the complex of burdens of his office. Davis chose to neglect the non-military aspects of his office partly in a sincere belief that he could best serve as commander in chief of the armies and partly because that was the center of his interest. His insistence upon retaining supreme military authority during the changing nature of the war, and the worsening Confederate situation, was not, as so often charged, caused by his stiff-necked pride, though that was an element. His retention both of supreme command and of his rigid military policy in commanding derived from a rather pathetic limitation: he knew nothing else to do.

Jefferson Davis was not an adaptable man. Born outside the South's ruling class, he was something of a self-made aristocrat, and his intense awareness of position contributed to a total inflexibility of which his rigidity in command was only a reflection. Beyond that, ambition had developed a derivative intelligence as far as it would go before he was chosen President, and once in that office he relied on the methods which had served him well in his highest former estate, United States Secretary of War. Finally, in his honest conviction that he was the best fitted of all Confederates to control the military destinies, he brought to his self-chosen assignment the bureaucratic methods with which he had operated a peacetime system of garrisons.

In operating this system, the President suffered from the need of the insecure to be infallible and, with his acute sensitivity to criticism and touchiness about his prerogatives, he became impervious to suggestions from generals in the field. Those who presumed to disagree soon found themselves out of favor; sycophants were advanced; among the able generals, only Lee possessed the tact and patience to retain relative control of his own army. Though this unhappy personal record was a failing of the man rather than a result of anything mean in his character, nonetheless it perpetuated a fixed system of operation into 1864 when the changing nature of the war demanded a consideration of changes in the policy.

In the beginning of the war, Davis's system of a dispersed defense appeared sound enough for a political movement of a people whose purpose was to establish their ability to resist aggression. At this time, hope existed for European recognition, which would at least lift the Federal blockade. Southern leaders were strongly influenced in their thinking by the outside intervention which, supporting the colonies' long resistance in the Revolution, was a factor in breaking the British will to hold America in the empire by force of arms. Also, the administration was forced to consider the assertiveness of states, in their separate rights, in the matter of troop dispositions. Even South Carolina, the land of the "fire-eaters" and the Hotspurs, insisted upon sizable quotas of state troops remaining at home. Always local politicians more than supported the practice of manning garrisons on state soil.

Yet a third element, embracing the two practical considerations, was Davis's predilection for departmentalization. This was familiar to him. A departmental structure gave a semblance of coherence to the uncontrollable elements of war, and funneled all control to him.

Davis gave his own rationale to these fixations. He defined the dispersals as a "defensive-offensive" policy, designed to permit of concentrations for counterstrikes against an overextended enemy. This was the theory. In fact, Davis could never bring himself to strip garrisons for any concentration. He simply could not entertain any cause-and-effect principle which, opening the way for the imponderables, removed the situation from his need to control a reassuring paper-structure.

This structure, shrinking in size as areas in the Western Confederacy were overrun, remained propped up into the fourth year of the war for an amalgam of reasons. Chief factors were the stability Lee maintained in Virginia (protecting the Carolinas and Georgia to the south of this buffer), the military mistakes of Lincoln which at least equaled Davis's, and the slowness with which the Union policy of a total war of subjugation evolved.

By May of 1864, when Grant attached himself personally to the Army of the Potomac, the new policy was fully evolved with Grant as its chief implementer. Confederate hope for foreign intervention was long past and with it went any possibility of repeating the long resistance of the Revolution. England then, not wishing to bind a people made permanently dissident by the methods of physical conquest, had fought a traditional war against armies; now the Federal forces, bent on subjugation at any cost, were taking war to civilians and their society on a scale of destructiveness that made it impossible for the people to maintain themselves physically, regardless of their spirit of resistance.

Already, every index revealed the toll of the total war, particularly as reflected in the sub-subsistence level of supplies for Lee's army. At this stage of a war that was to be fought to the finish, the concept of the physically weaker outlasting the physically stronger became a contradiction in nature. To continue the policy of dispersed defenses, on whatever theory, became unrelated to reason.

By then, Jefferson Davis's tenacious grip on his system represented a clinging to the one predictable certainty in the crowding disorder the enemy's forces brought to every facet he had learned about his known world and the order governing it. In this he was like any individual caught in a sequence of personal failures, who can only repeat over and over what worked, or seemed to work, before. By May, 1864, maintaining his system of departments meant to the Confederate President an operation in an orderly macrocosm, in which all contingencies and unpredictables were explained and made rational. The heart of the matter was Davis's belief in his military "genius," as Grant once put it in quotes.

Lincoln, with an ego of sufficient size to accommodate recognized limitations, finally turned the job over to a professional, U.S. Grant. The smaller-caliber ego of Davis needed the delusion that he was the professional without superior. Once, in a moment of anguished anxiety, the Confederate commander in chief admitted to his wife that he considered Lee, and only Lee, his equal in the field. "Oh, if only Lee could take one wing and I the other . . ."

Now, Davis had never led more than a volunteer regiment in the Mexican War. His regular army experience consisted of a brief routine garrison tour as second lieutenant following a mediocre record at West Point. The Confederate President was not unique in equating a love for a profession with talents for it: victims of a similar delusion were scattered in the wake of both armies. But it is given to few men to live this delusion on such a grand scale and enjoy all the trappings of command for such a long period.

In his passion for the military establishment, nothing fascinated him more than charts of organization and the disposition of troops.

As the various failures of the Confederacy gathered — in finance and transportation, in the ability to feed and clothe its people and support its armies — the harassed Mississippian found in those charts a sense of accomplishment. With masses of paper work which belonged properly in the function of clerks, he worked conscientiously into the nights, taxing his one good eye and bringing on acute attacks of neuralgia and dyspepsia. This further strengthened his sense of sacrifice for the cause.

With all the fine aspects and all the pettiness in his character, with all his devoted application to the tasks and mental clarity in phases of it, essentially Jefferson Davis was a victim of ambitions which landed him, a doctrinaire, in a situation which required of all things flexibility. The conscience of no man in the war was clearer, and certainly no "egotism," not in the meaning his detractors gave it, caused his failure to recognize that Lee propped up his system, and not vice versa. The self-limitations of the deluded man were made all too evident in his own writings on the war. With all records available and with years of perspective, he maintained that Lee had always been subject to his orders.

This, of course, was literally true, and nobody knew it better than Lee. What is uncertain is the extent to which Lee recognized that his successes were in proportion to the compromises he wrung from Davis. From the tone of his letters to the President during the spring, Lee was acutely aware of his need to circumvent Davis's policy of fixed dispersals as his own army was affected. However, Lee's appraisal of Davis in the history of their relationship is obscured by his conservative's deference to the constituted authority.

Beyond that, Lee was not one to analyze his fellows, to track down the secret motivations and find the springs of their fixations and compulsions. He took men as he found them and, like Lincoln and Napoleon, judged them on their performance. He could no longer demand high skill, but he insisted upon courage, energy and devotion. He was suspicious of heavy drinkers and would not tolerate personalities whose inner problems caused conflict. As a character, Davis met all of Lee's qualifications, except for his personality difficulties. As these occurred outside the realm of Lee's control, and he believed strife to be inherent in politics anyway, Lee evidently accepted his superior's limitations in performance as he ac-

cepted those of his subordinates. This acceptance is indicated by a
falling off in Lee's letters to Davis. He wrote less frequently, less
warmly, and with a more businesslike brevity.

Before May 3rd, Lee's letters to members of his family revealed
his apprehensions about the coming campaigns across the whole of
the remaining Confederacy, and he risked the President's displeas-
ure by writing him suggestions on the Confederate West. There,
with Atlanta as the objective, an invasion force had gathered under
Sherman to strike simultaneously with the Virginia offensive, and
Davis's reactions to this threat indicated something of a breakdown
in rationality. Infected by the clamors for "offensive" in the atmosphere of growing desperation, the commander in chief began to demand an offensive without disrupting his fixed dispersals to effect
the necessary troop concentration, or even heeding the field general's protests over the inadequate equipment of his existing force.
This general, Joe Johnston, happened to be an enemy both of Davis
and of Braxton Bragg, the President's newly appointed "Military
Adviser."

A gruesome failure as a general in the West and the most hated
soldier in the Confederacy, Bragg performed actually as Davis's
alter ego. In detail work, the neurotic Bragg was efficient and his
services, removed from the field, might have been useful had he
not given Davis sycophantic support in his most irrational orders.
Where these orders concerned Joe Johnston, Bragg's successor with
the betrayed Army of Tennessee, it is possible that Bragg acted
with unconscious malevolence as well as a desire to please his superior.

Bragg had left that chief Western army of the Confederacy in sad
case, with plummeting morale, and Johnston had done a sound job
of rebuilding. However, even by Confederate standards, the army
was too poorly equipped for a major campaign, and Davis's scattering of available manpower gave Johnston something less than one-
to-two in meeting Sherman's tough veterans. Yet Bragg and Davis
insisted that Johnston, a naturally defensive-minded general, open
an offensive against Sherman *before* Confederate forces were concentrated. When Johnston succeeded in the offensive which they demanded, they said, *then* the defensive garrisons would be abandoned
and the troops sent to him.

Lee, in supporting Johnston's reasonable plea for a concentration before attacking, advanced his consistently held conviction of the need for massing their inferior forces at points of their own selection. Prior to 1864, Lee had occasionally written the President little essays on the rudiments of cause-and-effect warfare, in which a counterthrust in force caused the enemy to abandon his diversifying threats in contraction against a heavy blow at his center. Though some of Lee's critics have stressed his preoccupation with Virginia, the range of his concern, in concepts and details, was in fact limitless, and he was the only field general who dared advise the President on a front other than his own. When Davis ignored the advice, there was nothing more Lee could do.

By May 3rd, when General Lee wrote the commander in chief, he directed his persuasive powers toward the primary ends of re-uniting his own army and assembling a force to protect Richmond. To Lee and to Grant, the Army of Northern Virginia and the capital represented a single operation. To Davis, since the secondary threat which Grant was directing toward Richmond would come in a separate department, the operations were two, distinct and separate. Caught between Grant's offensive and Davis's system of fixed dispersals, Lee was, in effect, fighting on two fronts.

In preparing for the meeting with the Army of the Potomac, Lee revealed the effects of the divided pulls at his attention. The awareness of the scattering of troops troubled him perhaps more than meeting Grant before his army was fully gathered. The uncertainty about when, or if, his units would be returned, along with his apprehensions over Richmond's undefended back door, restrained him from acting decisively in executing his plan for rolling back Grant.

General Lee perceived the inevitable end of a policy of passive defense against a stronger opponent, and the purpose behind his evolving plan was not to check Grant. He had resolved upon a strategy designed to inflict upon the main Federal army a field defeat of sufficient decisiveness to wreck the enemy's total offensive at its center. But waiting on the enemy's move on that warm May Tuesday, Lee confronted too many uncertainties to match the audacity of his strategy with bold tactics. With the amorphous nature of the uncertainties affecting his own army, the enemy in his front also contained an unknown element — Grant himself.

4

When U. S. Grant, as commander in chief, attached himself personally to the Army of the Potomac, he was the first general with that politics-plagued army to be free of interference from Lincoln and Washington cabals. General George Gordon Meade, who had commanded the army since just before Gettysburg, remained in nominal command, but obviously Grant was in charge.

This new man was the subject of considerable speculation among the Southern troops. His successful operations, which won him the appointment of commander in chief of all the armies, had been entirely in the West. There, as Lee knew all too well, Grant had been favored by divided and poor Confederate command. Only once, in the Vicksburg campaign — and that against the Confederacy's worst command situation — had he displayed anything like brilliance.

In profiting by the Confederacy's faulty organization, this "Unconditional Surrender" Grant had shown himself to be an uncommonly pugnacious fighter. He drove. Nothing discouraged him and he never stopped trying. In his unspectacular, bulldog fashion, Grant had accomplished what had been expected of brilliant McClellan and of many another general of apparently superior gifts, who had also been presented by the Confederates with favorable conditions.

The problem for Lee was that he knew the McClellans. They were of his own background. General Meade, who commanded the Army of the Potomac against him at Gettysburg, was a personal friend. A literate, old-line Eastern gentleman, Meade fought a traditional war according to a mutually understood code of honor. Like the British in the war over the colonies' secession, Meade was restrained by concern over the future relations of the dissidents and by a personal inability to take total war to people of his own kind.

Grant was of a different background and a harder man. With no prewar political history and no interest either in slavery or Negroes, Grant emerged from a shabby obscurity as a no-holds-barred type of fighter. As the nature of the war changed into a gradually evolved policy of total subjugation, he rose to the top as an instrument of the new policy.

Lincoln assumed the responsibility for the consequences of total war: in the boundlessness of his self-belief and the expediency of his pragmatism, he intended to heal the South's wounds after its society was destroyed. Grant was simply to get the job done. No more concerned about future consequences than about traditional war, he was a professional applying armed might against a people with the single controlling principle of conquest. This was Grant as a commander, a personification of the forces released for the destruction of the world personified by Lee.

As a man, Grant was unknown to Lee. He had a vague recollection of a chance army encounter during the Mexican War, but could not visually place the enemy's new commander. Grant had married a cousin of Longstreet, an intimate since their West Point days. Cadmus Wilcox, one of Lee's division commanders, was another of Grant's friends dating from the Point. This would indicate only, if likes attract likes, that Grant was a physical rather than a mental type.

At West Point, where he had been an indifferent student, Grant impressed his Southern friends with his fine horsemanship. Though taciturn in his manner, he was an amiable man and possessed (as one of Meade's staff officers said) a "rough dignity." He had resigned from the regular army after some personal difficulties and, when the war came, offered his services to a volunteer regiment. He might well have been lost in the shuffle at any stage and he had to survive the jealous maneuvering of superiors as he emerged into prominence, but the unimpressive little man had a knack of being at the right place at the right time.

As soon as he established his headquarters with Meade's army, the new commander in chief showed himself to be all business. He began by banishing from the army the traditional sutlers, those peddlers whose wagons of choice victuals had served no military purpose. Then, as Lee wrote from reports, "All of the officers' wives, sick, etc., have been sent to Washington. No ingress or egress from the lines is now permitted and no papers are allowed to come out. . . . The indications at present are that we shall have a hard struggle."

Lee was certain that Richmond, the three-year citadel, was the goal. He wrote Davis, "All the information that reaches me strengthens the belief that General Grant is preparing to move against Richmond." To get Richmond, he must first dispose of Lee, and there was no evidence to suggest that Grant would try to reach the capital by outmaneuvering him. Almost as if he had heard Grant's directive to Meade, "Lee's army will be your objective," Lee expected Grant would take first things first and try to get at Richmond by overrunning him.

This gave Lee a dual problem. While Grant could take the steps of his objectives in order, first Lee and then Richmond, General Lee could plan no countering move that would expose the city. At that stage of the war, General Lee was influenced in his acceptance of the duality of his assignment by the practical consideration of the capital.

As Paris and London are, and as Washington was not, Richmond was the capital in the full meaning of a nation's heart. However inadequately the supply system operated, Richmond was the supply center for Lee's army, with railroads and roads leading to all points of the compass, and a canal to the west. It was the medical center, which could accommodate twenty thousand sick and wounded, and the center of the interlocking system of private and government manufacture of arms, ammunition, and the materiel of war. Its warehouses and office buildings were used by the government, and the city had expanded with all the activities that gravitate to the hub of operations. The abandonment of Richmond would have caused an irreparable dislocation to the military structure at that time along with an incalculable shock to morale.

Even had Lee preferred to abandon Richmond, his restricted area of authority forced him to operate within Davis's defensive system. Lee's letters indicated that he foresaw the possibility of military necessity forcing the uncovering of Richmond, though his eventuality formed no part of his plans as he plotted to anticipate Grant. His immediate concern was with the tactical plans for protecting his army against the consequences of a wrong guess on Grant's move. Though Lee did not expect Grant to advance far from his bases into the lean countryside around Orange, he could not count on this, and a railroad vital to the army's support ran through that area. The

Virginia Central connected Richmond with the "breadbasket" of the Shenandoah Valley, and Lee would not willingly commit his army to any course that exposed this supply line. As it was, in writing President Davis of his "anxiety" over provisions, he wrote that any "disaster to the railroad would render it impossible for me to keep the army together."

In making his countering move, he must hold Longstreet's two divisions at Gordonsville, the railroad junction ten miles south of Orange, until Grant committed himself. Other units must be held at the river crossings between the Wilderness and Orange Court House, to protect the wagon trains against strikes from the Federal cavalry, built into the most powerful mounted force ever to operate in the East. With these precautionary measures to protect the western end of his line, Lee then confronted the greater risk of losing the Army of the Potomac in its passage of the Wilderness.

5

The Wilderness was not truly a barrens, though certainly the next thing to it. When clearings were hacked out of the primeval forests in the seventeenth century, the soil in the Wilderness area had proven in the main too poor to support farming and the cutover land had gone back to the brush. Any untended forest in eastern Virginia grows thick, briery underbrush and dense screen of vines and creepers, one of the elements that made Indian fighting so difficult for the British gentry at Jamestown. In the Wilderness the rank growths flourished excessively because of the small streams that, branching off from the river, formed boggy ravines to nourish the plants. The Wilderness seemed particularly to encourage stands of wiry saplings. As early as 1732, Colonel William Byrd, an extensive traveler in the Virginia back country, noted that the road "had on either side continual poisoned Fields, with nothing but saplings growing on them."

Colonel Byrd was visiting "the enchanted Castle" built in the wilds by former British colonial governor Spotswood, famed for leading "The Knights of the Golden Horseshoe" to the Shenandoah Valley. Spotswood had founded a town of imported German families in 1710 for the purpose of developing mining in Virginia, but the town, the castle and the mining operation had been reclaimed by the Wilderness, leaving only the name, Germanna, and a corruption of Spotswood's name for the river, Rapid Anne.

Since those days, the primeval forest had also been cut over for its timber. This was used in building the plank road, in the operation of several gold mines which, worked sporadically, yielded small profit on cheap labor, and in Catherine Furnace, which the Wellford family had reopened to help supply the Confederate shortage in iron ore. Some had been sold as timber. Probably no section of the original forest remained. The shadowed density was unbroken except for a few fair-sized holdings, scattered small clearings of subsistence farms, and the stage taverns. By day the entangled thickets around pines, stunted oaks and clusters of saplings were inhabited mostly by moccasins and small animals. At night, when the dark shapes loomed like some weir, the silence was broken only by the call of whippoorwills and the sudden rustled swoop of foraging owls.

Even minus any haunted spirits, the Wilderness, with its narrow roads enclosed by brushy woods, would seem an unlikely stretch for the passage of an army encumbered by sixty-five miles of wagon trains. Yet the Federal army's dependence upon its supporting services guided Lee's reasoning in selecting the Wilderness as Grant's line of march. The Army of the Potomac was supplied and equipped as no armed force ever before on earth. It was followed by herds of live cattle, driven by "cowboys," and had its own telegraph system, with which divisions could set up operations like that of a town. This was an army fitted to operate in a ravaged country, rather than for maneuver, and Grant seemed the type of general likely to use the sheer weight of the Federal force against the thin lines of the weakened Confederate organization.

Lee was not uncertain about Grant's use of the Wilderness passageway as the shortest line between two points. After balancing all factors against Grant's objective, Lee had reached a firm conclusion of the course of action that would seem most logical from the enemy's viewpoint. As Grant's reports reveal, Lee had reasoned as if he had projected himself into his opponent's mind. The uncertain element, the element which contained the enormous risk, was in the manner of Grant's passage through the Wilderness. With all else, Lee's general plan depended upon a slow movement of the total Federal force of 150,000 impeded by wagon trains, supporting services, cattle and horses on the hoof.

A slow movement would spread out the encumbered troops on the narrow, enclosed roads, exposing the columns to attacks on their flank. Three east-west roads, one for each of Lee's corps, led directly across the Federal line of march southward. With the movement of the heavy columns restricted and the dense thickets nullifying the heavier Federal cannon, the Wilderness served as an equalizer for the numbers, and the advantages of the terrain would lie with Lee's assaulting lines. But for this, Grant must move Meade's army precisely as Lee anticipated.

If Grant crossed him and, temporarily risking his supporting services, hurried his 125,000 fighting troops through the Wilderness, everything would be lost for Lee. Grant would cross Lee's front, passing his army, and the enemy would be between Lee's army and Richmond. Of all the maneuvers Lee had made on the hazard of guessing the enemy's intention, he had never planned a movement when a wrong guess involved such finality.

He staked the capital on a gamble that Grant's overconfident attitude would direct an unhurried advance. Lee probably shared the conviction of some of his outspoken officers, and some of Meade's staff officers, that Grant underestimated Lee. The conqueror of the West might well have believed that the Army of Northern Virginia was successful only because it had not met him in battle. Colonel Lyman, of Meade's staff, spoke of the "foolish, cocksure" members of Grant's military family who referred "flippantly" to Lee's army. As Lee reasoned, Grant would rely on his tried bulldozing methods to walk over defensive lines at the river crossings. Finding the river undefended, Grant would assume that Lee had fallen back toward Richmond, and move after him in unhurried confidence through the Wilderness.

Lee was willing to take this gamble in order to seize the initiative. Since his commander in chief would not effect a concentration of forces for the larger end of wrecking the enemy's plan at the center, Lee would try to achieve the larger end with the forty-five thousand infantry he had at hand. To achieve this, with an inferior force, possession of the initiative was imperative. Before he ever heard of Marmont, whose book was published in the South that year, Lee practiced his belief in the French marshal's precept: "The attacking general has, to a large extent, command of the mind of his defensive opponents."

Had General Lee possessed the army of the May before, in the full flowering of its physical power and leadership, he would have moved out as daringly as at Chancellorsville. Where only the simplest maneuvers could be attempted, and he could scarcely trust two of his corps commanders out of his sight, he could be audacious only in the planning.

Though he had started Ewell toward the enemy's line of march, the day of May 3rd passed without Lee informing Hill and Longstreet of the proposed movement of their corps to parallel Ewell into the Wilderness. These relatively cautious tactics for a bold strategy made his projected movement something of a compromise in inception. With all considered, he had little other choice.

The only alternative was to assume the defensive, with a foredoomed end. The weight of numbers would force him slowly backward to the environs of Richmond, where his army would be immobilized. In the field, his army presented a threat to all the enemy's plans in Virginia; once his army was immobilized in works, the decision would be reduced to arithmetic. As the enemy stood at four to one in manpower, with immeasurable advantages in resources, the fight for a decision must be made at the beginning and not at the end of the line.

6

When Lee retired to his tent for the last night's sleep in a peaceful camp, he could not have been sanguine about the approaching test. Many Confederate leaders, along with President Davis, did not regard the enemy's new offensive as introducing a fundamentally different phase of the war. Six Federal generals before Grant had tried an "On to Richmond," and on the surface 1864 need not appear any more decisive than the other years. But Lee, in letters to his family, revealed a preoccupation with the coming campaign that was close to anxiety.

What he privately thought of the Confederacy's chances on the night of May 3rd can only be inferred from those letters to intimates — and from the cautious execution of his most desperate gamble. Not a worrier and never once in his life self-defeated before any struggle of any kind, he did look squarely in the face the practicalities of the South's continuing defense.

As an individual, like Jeb Stuart, it would be difficult for him to conceive the actuality of being personally conquered. By instinct he would fight to win as long as life lasted. As a professional soldier, Lee had been more realistic than Southern civilian leaders since he was forced to the painful decision of either leading an army into his own state or, in defense of his native land, resigning from that army in which he had spent his adult life.

He never entertained those delusions of some Confederate leaders who believed that, if the Southern states failed to win their independence, they could resume their place in the Union with no more ado than if they had lost in a political campaign. With no more respect for rabid secessionists than for abolitionists (both of whom were "factionalists" to him), Lee saw from the beginning that the armed conflict grew from deeper roots than difference of opinion over the Negro's status or even preservation of the Union.

As a product of the great Revolutionary generation, Lee believed the South was defending the rights of man to choose his own government. When "those people," as the Federals became to him, tried to hold together a Union "by bayonets," he said, "Let each man resolve that the rights of self-government, liberty and peace, shall find in him a defender." Lee recognized as few did that, in trying to maintain self-government by arms, the people of the Confederacy were entering a life-and-death struggle. "They may destroy, but I trust will never conquer us," he wrote. "I prefer annihilation to submission."

Unlike those Confederates who continued to think in terms of a disrupted relationship with the Union, and occupied themselves with the constitutionalities involved, Lee understood that only by overcoming force with counterforce would an honorable peace be won. The nation formed by the states who had declared their independence must win a status as unrelated to the states with which they had been associated as the colonies had won from the union of the British empire, with its deeper roots and timeless bonds.

As in the Revolution, the self-determinists could win only by the lapse of will in the stronger power. There was, however, a fundamental difference in the struggles prosecuted by England and the Federal government. The British had been three thousand miles away, with a people little interested in America and some government spokesmen strongly in favor of granting the colonies independence. The Union population had been injected with a crusading spirit by Lincoln's brilliant political war measure, the Emancipation Proclamation. This gave the equivalent of a slogan for the ignorant and the indifferent, while the necessary object of hatred for a crusade — "the chivalry-ridden, slave-holding South" — was provided by the abolitionists and their powers in the Republican Party.

Less than one fourth of Southerners were associated in any way with slavery (scarcely more than ten per cent actually owned slaves) and active emancipationists included Lee, Jeb Stuart and A. P. Hill. The chivalrous attitudes were confined largely to plantation families, but the concept of "chivalry" particularly goaded non-privileged Northerners and was a subject of derision in metropolitan music-hall songs. Under the sanction of the slogan, the anti-Southern Republican Party enjoyed virtually despotic power in its policy of conquering the South by physical destruction.

Yet while there could be no reasonable hope of outlasting the will of this party in power, the Union operated a two-party system, and the non-sectional Democratic Party represented the population which, with no stake in the war, stood to gain nothing by the conquest of the South.

Despite crusades and fomented hatred, as the war entered the fourth year a deep war weariness spread through all classes in all sections of the North. Thoughtful soldiers wrote home that the invasion, far from a crusade, provided opportunities for the personal advancement of connivers and glory-hunters, for plunder and speculation, served as an excuse for hoodlumism and bullying by coarse men suddenly given tyrannical powers. Throughout the East propertied families who were the natural allies of the planter South, in many instances interrelated by marriage, began to think it better to let the Southerners have their freedom than to destroy their civilization. Other segments simply returned to the sentiments of the pre-crusade days and felt, in effect, that the Southern states should go on their way if separation meant enough to them to fight for it. Numerous episodes revealed an antagonism to the Negro. All in all, the Democratic Party, on a peace platform, would have a chance to return to power in the fall elections *if* the Union forces seemed not appreciably closer to winning in 1864 than in the previous three years.

It was the 1864 presidential election which made the new spring campaign the campaign of decision. Lee, and Joe Johnston at Atlanta, needed only to prevent the Federals from achieving decisive victories before fall, *only until fall*, and, as Lincoln privately conceded, the Democrats might well return to power in November.

The Union forces had won battles, taken cities and rivers, seized vast tracts of territory, destroyed personal and public property to such an extent as to impoverish people for generations to come, but the Confederacy still possessed the capacity to field armies and to protect its vital centers of production. Though the Confederacy's West and its great river were gone, that region — except for Nashville (lost early in 1862) — had not contained the major production centers. Atlanta, a railroad center in the Lower South, with Richmond in the Upper South, were the balancing key cities in the more populous and industrially productive Eastern Confederacy.

Between the two, east of the mountains and inland from the coast, the government had developed a string of subsidiary manufacturing plants and depots. On the coast, Wilmington and Charleston sustained the Confederacy's precarious communication with the outside world, and blockade runners delivered cargoes to the ports. With nearly half of its territory lost and the remainder engirdled by the enemy's armies and sea power, the Confederacy held intact those physically vital areas which represented the traditional South. Both in symbol and reality, the unconquered portion could be regarded as the heart of the Confederacy. If no decisive blow was struck within this heartland before the November elections, a peace party could come in and accept the Confederacy's independent status, as Great Britain had accepted that of the Colonies.

To the extent that this eventuality was a possibility, Lee's hope for an honorable peace contained the potential of realization. This potential represented a possibility, not a probability, and the odds against it were high. But Lee had recognized, before a shot was fired, that it would be a war of mathematics, in which the odds would work against the South. He also took a cold look at those odds as his own personal stake was involved.

Because R. E. Lee has been so identified with the abstractions of "honor" and "duty," the element of his personal stake has been ignored. When on resigning from the old army, he said, "I could have taken no other course without dishonor," he referred to the course of self-interest. He was an intensely ambitious man, and the course he renounced — as United States Army commanding general — represented the culmination of his life's strivings.

Though Lee had come of one of the greatest families on the continent, his brilliantly endowed father had squandered a fortune and tarnished the reputation built as Revolutionary cavalry leader, intimate of Washington, U.S. Congressman and governor of Virginia. Lee's impressionable years were spent with his widowed mother, Ann Carter of Shirley, in that peculiarly bitter atmosphere of "genteel poverty." His awareness of their status as poor relations was made the more poignant by the splendor in which his contemporary Carter kinsmen lived. His mother's goad was like that of any widow who instills into her son the need to attain. Only with Robert Lee the nature and the size of the attainment were defined by the high estate from which his immediate family had fallen.

From his entrance to West Point, his course was a steady line of accomplishment. Graduating second in his class, without demerits, he was first assigned to engineering and in that field alone he would have won eminence. In the Mexican War his conspicuous performance on the staff of General Winfield Scott won him the lasting admiration of the commanding general who, at the crisis in 1861, regarded Lee as the top soldier in the country. Recently promoted to full colonel of the 1st Cavalry, Lee was Scott's choice as the officer to assume command of the projected army to be fielded for the invasion of Virginia.

Colonel Lee, saying, "I have not been able to make up my mind to raise my hand against my relatives, my children, my home," relinquished his career at its point of fulfillment in the knowledge that, with his career, went security for his family. Besides his partially crippled wife and three sons, Lee had four unmarried daughters who lived in the great Arlington plantation. (The death of his youngest daughter, in October, 1862, brought Lee his first personal grief during the war.) The Arlington estate was inherited by his wife from her father, George Washington Parke Custis, the grandson of Martha Washington and the adopted son of George Washington. Arlington was particularly meaningful to Lee, since his own family plantation had gone for his father's debts, and he had known the grandeur of his mother's home, the James River manor house of Shirley, only as a visiting cousin. He had foreseen the inevitability of losing his family's home in the first invasion.

Along with this actual loss of the Custis-Lee mansion went the dream, "one of my life's ambitions," as he wrote his wife, of regaining Stratford Hall, where he had been born. Even Martha Washington's home, "The White House," which had come to Lee's middle son Rooney through his Custis grandfather, had been left in ashes by the enemy's armies. With all the magnificence associated with the Lee, Carter and Custis families in Virginia, from the early seventeenth century through leadership in the Revolution, the wife and daughters of General Lee "refugeed" about the state like any other family in the population of the dispossessed that swelled as total war was carried to civilians. His family's safety was another deep concern of Lee's, and he wrote his wife long, and occasionally strong, letters of advice.

As of the night of May 3rd, with the hard-won family security already lost, forever gone, the only security left to fight for was the survival of their personal world. That world of cousins and familiar landmarks ("the graves of my ancestors," as Lee said) represented everything known and cherished. The changed nature of the war revealed that the forces arrayed against them waited only for their defeat by arms to obliterate the society of their beloved land.

Lee wrote his son about the imminent campaign: "If victorious, we have everything to live for. If defeated, there will be nothing left for us to live for."

CHAPTER THREE

"The Army Was Put in Motion Today"

AROUND NINE O'CLOCK in the morning of May 4th, the message came to Lee's headquarters from Clark's Mountain. The Army of the Potomac was crowding toward the two fords, Ely and Germanna, across from the Wilderness. Moving since midnight, the vanguards were then at the pontoon bridges thrown across the two hundred feet of the brown Rapidan. By the time the message reached Lee, the enemy was on the same side of the river with him.

Grant had followed Lee's prediction this far. However, the General's mind was not free of the fearful possibility of the enemy's army hurrying on southward through the Wilderness, though he mentioned this to no one. As far as recorded memories show, he simply issued an order for A. P. Hill to put two of his divisions in motion on the Orange Plank Road, starting toward the Wilderness twenty-five miles away. One division must be held behind for one day as a rear guard for the wagon trains. Hill's two divisions would number less than fifteen thousand infantry to march parallel to Ewell's corps of approximately the same number.

Orders were sent to Longstreet at Gordonsville to prepare to move out with the two divisions with him, about ten thousand infantry. The First Corps would march by the Catharpin Road, south of and parallel to Hill's line of march on the Plank Road. The three fingers projected into Grant's passageway at intervals of two and three quarters and four miles. However, Longstreet was a day's march farther from the intersection than Hill and Ewell. With Hill's rear-guard division to be held for at least a full day, Lee's advance columns would establish contact with barely thirty thousand infantry, and on only two of the three possible openings to the Federal flank.

By being forced to wait on Grant's move before committing himself, Lee was opening his counteroffensive with probing rather than aggressive tactics. In fear of Grant's crossing his front, Lee could not wait for his full force before making contact; but, lacking his full force, he could not make of that contact a full-scale assault. With clarity in his general plan, the details of his tentative execution revealed an absolute self-assurance in his capacities to extemporize and control the situation as it developed.

No act of Lee in the war more clearly illustrated the man's supreme confidence in himself and his soldiers. Staff officer Venable said that Lee's boldness here was based on "his profound confidence in the steady valor of his troops, and in their ability to maintain themselves successfully against very heavy odds." Manifestly, in staking the decision on his soldiers, Lee restricted his moves to actions that placed the burden on the men and not their leaders. As the General said to Hill during that period, "The men know more than the officers."

For their role in the coming campaign the soldiers made such a bedraggled appearance that some Northern newspaper correspondents reported Lee's men to be already finished; without any fight left in them, they were ready to give up for a square meal. Some of the captured men and deserters seen in Union lines were in pitiable condition, and the self-confident members of Grant's staff, never having observed the men in units in action, were inclined to take lightly an army composed of emaciated ragamuffins. Veterans of the Army of the Potomac, who had fought against Lee's men, looked beyond the oddments of patched makeshifts that passed for their "uniforms." As a staff officer of General Meade saw them, "A more sinewy, tawny, formidable-looking set of men could not be . . . they handle their weapons with terrible effect. Their great characteristic is their stoical manliness; they . . . look you straight in the face, with as little animosity as if they had never heard a gun."

To those familiar with the appearance of Lee's army, the soldiers' costumes gave in mass the impression of being uniforms of a sort by the uniformity of their basic garments and the arrangement of their equipment. In this sense they were less variegated than in the early days of their resplendence, when visored caps, gilt-buttoned frock coats and stripe-legged pants made privates look like European courtiers. Most significant of the change from dandies into Confederate soldiers was the absence of those compartmented leather knapsacks that in the first year contained extra clothing, such as white vests, white gloves and dress shirts, for dress parade and parties.

On May 4th, another of the rare May days, the typical Confederate soldier wore a weather-colored slouch hat, its crown dented and the brim, if not too floppy, turned up in front and back. Hair was worn long because that was the style easiest for camp "barbers" to effect on their fellows. The soldier wore a single-breasted jacket — either faded gray of the early days when he furnished his own uniform, or the butternut-colored flimsy of government issue, or a civilian jacket. The buttons in the front bore the seal of his state, not the Confederate seal. The letters CSA were embossed on his belt buckle. He wore a cotton shirt, probably made by his mother or wife, sweetheart or sister. With or without collar attached, he wore no cravat; sometimes a bright pattern of gingham, before it faded, gave him a dash of color about the throat. His pants, rarely matching his jacket, were patched in the seat and frazzled at the cuffless bottoms. His shoes were anything he could find, steal or glean from the dead. They matched those of his fellows in the unpolished discoloration of wear in all weather and in the frayed soles.

Across his body, from his left shoulder to his right hip, he wore a blanket roll in an oilcloth, the latter a capture from the United States government issue. From his right shoulder to his left hip ran a cord attached to a simple canvas haversack. In this he carried a knife, fork and spoon; his comb and razor if he had not stopped shaving; a round mirror in a metal case two inches in diameter; a little needlecase and, at times, a paper package of pins. If still neat about his appearance, he carried a cake of homemade soap and a cloth to serve as a towel. Sometimes a toothbrush went in there, and sometimes in a jacket pocket, where his tobacco was kept.

Any cooked rations that he was issued for a march went into the haversack, if he was not so hungry that he ate it at once. There he cached any oddments of food that he might gather on the march, such as an apple or an ear of corn stolen from a farmer's field, or hardtack gathered from the enemy's dead. In their hunger, men would scrape dried blood off a piece of salvaged hardtack.

Outside the haversack was slung his tin cup, the utensil of all purposes. Pots and pans were carried in the regimental skillet wagon, though some men carried a tin plate that could serve as a saucepan. He might hang his canteen outside the haversack, if the haversack was flat. If it was half full, his canteen swung in the middle of his back from a cord looped over his head. It was a round, tin canteen, holding little more than one pint of water. In the early days, when he got among captured enemy wagons, he filled his canteen with molasses in his hunger for sweets.

Sometimes attached to his belt he wore a leather cartridge case, either CSA or the fancier USA government issue. More frequently he carried his powder-topped cartridges in his pockets. His bayonet, with an eighteen-inch triangular blade coming to a sharp point, was used more for sticking a farmer's stray pig than the enemy, and its open round hilt, which was made to attach to the rifle, was useful as a candle holder when the blade was stuck in the ground. His bright bayonet was next to the tin cup in general usefulness. This total equipment weighed about seven pounds.

By 1864, rifles were available for all soldiers, though even then there were some Southerners so resistant to change that they preferred the prewar smooth-bore muskets which were familiar to them. Confederate issue consisted in part of locally made rifles of all varieties, of which the most practical was the Harper's Ferry 1860 model Springfield, and of imports run in through the blockade, chiefly Enfields. Battlefield gleanings supplemented the regular issue throughout the war. Round shots were gone by 1864, and the rifles fired a leaden slug, a Minié ball (pronounced minnie), which flattened on contact. The calibers ranged from .52 to .69, with .58 perhaps the most common. Superior shots were accurate up to three hundred yards with any of the standard rifles; good shots were accurate up to two hundred yards, and the mediocre shooters around a hundred yards. The sharpshooters were deadly at four hundred yards and up: camp tales claimed fantastic distances. A few of the best sharpshooters had been issued the imported British Whitworth sharpshooter rifle, the best gun in the world. It fired a .58 octagonal bullet, used a telescopic sight, and a crack marksman was accurate with it up to half a mile and even more. A few of these costly rifles (they sold for $1500 gold) had been issued during the spring.

In an inverse way, the apparel and accouterments of Lee's men increased their morale. Their accomplishments despite their privations and hardships tended to promote a conviction of personal superiority in combat over an enemy who could not prevail with all his material advantages and weight of numbers. As with the officers, the men were followers of General Lee, with a sense of discipleship that was given no other commanding general in the war. One of the soldiers said that even the name they gave him, "Marse Robert," derived from the essence of their homeland, "was an act of homage." This explained the reverential quality in their affection, their blind faith in following his orders, and that indefinable blend of belief in his care of them and of their protectiveness of him. With all Lee's aura of "majesty" and of "grandeur," his men's pride in him was personal and self-identifying, as for the head of a family. They always wanted to make him look good and they endured for him to the ultimate limits of endurance.

By May of 1864 many of the best men had passed the limit of their endurance. The morale of some was weakened from behind the lines. Their families' will to resist was broken by the want suffered by children, caused in part by the Confederate government's failure to supply civilian needs. In isolated homes women were menaced by the danger from enemy raiders and marauding bands of deserters from both armies. These wives wrote men in the army of their privations and fears. As the war seemed to go on indefinitely, more and more soldiers answered these appeals and slipped out of the lines at night. After Gettysburg, when all hope went for a decisive Confederate victory, desertions rose into thousands. Though every remedy was tried, the trend was irreversible, and the absence of former companions at morning roll call contributed its own effect on the spirit of the survivors. Beyond all outside influences, beyond the inevitable toll taken by death, wounds, and sickness of the men of strongest morale, in some the flesh had simply failed the spirit. They could not get through the bitter winter of 1863-1864 on their sparse diet with no garments to keep them warm.

In the spring, the government made efforts to fill the decimated ranks with last-ditch conscripts in an act that removed exemptions from farmers and expanded the age limits from seventeen to fifty. Some of the farmers were useful in the undermanned engineering corps, and some of the conscripts tried honestly to serve. Most of them were too fresh from a protected life to adjust to the severity of war at that stage of professionalism in both armies. Some of these poor men fainted at the first bedlam of contact. Others, when retreating with veterans, were seized with panic and ran, never to be seen again. All too many never made much of an effort to adjust; they simply waited for the first chance to slip away from the rude camps of the hard-bitten, derisive veterans. The coming and going of these unwilling, untrained soldiers further undermined the waverers and added grimness to the resolve of the old guard. The hard core of survivors recognized, without articulation, that the struggle was being reduced to them — them and the Old Man.

On May 4th, these survivors were more of a nucleus of "Lee's men" than a cross-sectional representation of the South. Southerners who had not already been molded as "Confederates" by their identification with a group, as Lee's army, could observe more objectively the decline of their fortunes and speculate more realistically on the probabilities of independence. They worked with a dollar that had become worth twenty cents and shopped in markets where a hundred dollars for scarce items were required to buy what one had bought before. Any reasonable person could see that such a cause was nothing to embrace in 1864.

The men with Lee were not reasonable. To them, the war was reduced to the armed enemy across the river and to Uncle Robert. Since nobody could beat him, it must follow that those people "up yonder" would finally give up trying and they could all go home.

2

Though Lee's men were unaware of it, winter had brought a change in the nature of their morale. Soldiers returned from prisons and hospitals observed a lack of the lightheartedness that previously characterized the Army of Northern Virginia even during its grimmest hours. The men still made their jokes out of references to the familiar earthy things of their land, bands still played "Joe Bowers" and "I Lay Ten Dollars Down," and during the winter Rebel pickets (when no officers were about) had played cards with Yankees, using home-grown tobacco as stakes against real coffee. One soldier of the Army of the Potomac became such a favorite that he was smuggled across the Rapidan, provided with a Confederate costume, and taken to a country dance.

There was no single point on which the returning men could say *this* is the difference. The soldiers were resolute, cheerful and confident, but a quality of determination had crept into what had been a casual assumption of ultimate victory. Walter Taylor, Lee's young assistant adjutant general, wrote, "There was no overweening confidence, but a calm, firm and positive determination to be victorious, with God's help." It was an intangible thing, mostly felt by the men who had been removed from the army when the original quality still pervaded the troops.

The year before, on the way to Gettysburg, twenty-three-year-old Sandie Pendleton had been engaged to a girl and in love with the world, and he looked forward to a lovely life in a free Confederate States of America. Though ardently happy in his marriage, Colonel Pendleton viewed the new campaign as continuing an endless ordeal, and his letters changed from ebullience to resolution. The youngest corps chief of staff in the army was not aware of this change in himself nor a similar change in his companions. It was observed by Pendleton's friend and former brother staff officer with Jackson, Henry Kyd Douglas. Major Douglas, captured at Gettysburg, returned from a Federal prison in May, and to him one evidence of change showed in the men's resigned acceptance of the insufficiencies for waging war. In an acute horse shortage, Harry Douglas, assigned to the staff of Major General Edward Johnson, could not even get a mount. As assistant adjutant general of Stonewall Jackson's old division, he was forced to borrow a huge and violent mule, conspicuously white. This horse shortage and the lack of grain for the available animals were indications of the army's physical decline which, accepted by the men without thought, inevitably added a sobering element in their consciousness.

General Lee, having shared the men's ordeals in constant association, was probably unaware of any subtle change in the nature of their morale, as he waited for Hill's soldiers to break camp. He passed the time by writing a letter to his daughter Agnes. His own preparations were quickly completed. As his tents were struck, his body servant packed his personal equipment, extra uniforms and linen, a dress sword, and the metal alloy set of dishes and utensils, looking like pewter, which went into a wooden camp chest. These went into a headquarters wagon, with the sleeping cot and blankets, camp stool and chairs, and the oddments that completed his sparse quarters. Then the General mounted Traveler while he waited for the troops to fall in on the line of march. He was dressed in his neat gray uniform, high black boots and gauntlets, and his brown eyes were shaded by the brim of his light gray, planters' style hat. Seated motionless on the gray horse, the commanding general watched the soldiers hurry through the sad ritual of leaving an old camp.

Though no advance warning to prepare had been given the men, as old soldiers they sniffed approaching action in the air. Already they had disposed of those various little possessions, of no particular value, which they sentimentally acquired for their rude log and mud huts. These articles had been abandoned or bartered, or wistfully hidden against a possible return. If small enough, the objects were stuffed into a pocket. Letters from home were burned, though some men made packets of the letters and placed them in an inside pocket. Some of the soldiers carried small Bibles in pockets and the Episcopalians carried their Book of Common Prayer. Locks of hair and daguerreotypes were pressed into the backs of hunting-case watches. Small round metal lockets, sold to the soldiers of both armies, were also used for articles of remembrance.

The officers sent their personal belongings to the rear. Wagons were allotted only to general officers, brigadier generals and above, who must do paper work and maintain a mess for their staffs. As a gesture to the men, the officers in Hill's corps cut up their tents and passed out pieces among the troops to serve as tent flies. It was unlikely that the soldiers would enjoy much use from such a comfort, but the idea appealed to them.

By the time the men filled their canteens, rolled their blankets and distributed their issue of ammunition about their persons, preparations for their march were being hurried when they went to receive their rations. In the rush the full issue of cornbread had not finished cooking in the few ovens, and many of the men received only half-cooked dough or raw meal. They dropped the rations cheerfully enough into their thin haversacks and took a last look at the winter quarters.

Shortly after noon, the divisions of Wilcox and Heth (pronounced Heath), with men from seven Southern states, formed in columns of four on the plank-bedded road, and the orders to march sang out along the several miles of their ranks extending westward from Orange. When fresh, the men always grew excited at going toward the enemy. With the good-by calls and waving of the women, children and older men who had been their winter neighbors, the unsoldierly-looking soldiers began their march toward the enemy under the warm sun in a festive mood.

3

When they moved out, General Lee rode at the head of the column with A. P. Hill. During the afternoon he was reached by couriers from Jeb Stuart, bringing information of the general movements of Meade's army. The enemy troops were pushing into the obscuring thickets of the Wilderness, with their cavalry ranging well out, and Stuart's riders had gathered no details to indicate whether Grant intended to hurry on through the Wilderness or to move slowly in concentration.

Until that spring, Lee had used his cavalry to gain information more effectively than any commanding general in the war. Now, forced to the unfamiliar role of conserving the waning strength of his cavalry, Stuart had not tried to mount a force to break through the Federal screen. (In February, when Kilpatrick and Dahlgren took their raiding parties toward Richmond, Stuart sent only one token brigade after them.) As a result, the cavalry chief had brought the army commander no information on the size of the enemy.

When the Army of the Potomac came lunging across the Rapidan, unimpeded by a single shot, Stuart's troopers could work close enough in the protective brush of their own land to discover the larger details to send back to the commanding general. The II Corps, commanded by thorny Hancock, had completed its crossing and reached the area of Chancellorsville, on the eastern edge of the Wilderness, around one o'clock. An hour later Major General Gouverneur Warren (who could get along more amiably with Confederate Harry Heth than with his own brother officers) had his V Corps across in the area of the Wilderness Tavern, on the road Ewell was marching. Behind him came Sedgwick's VI Corps.

The "fighting" wagons followed immediately on the troops, and all crossed one of the five pontoon bridges laid by Meade's engineers before the day was over. The light spring-wagons, carrying the officers' personal baggage, crossed with the fighting wagons in immediate support of the infantry. The heavy wagon trains would be twenty-four hours more in crossing the river, with the herd of live cattle. To the soldiers' three days of "full rations" packed in their haversacks, and three days of bread and "small rations" in their knapsacks, the quartermaster department also allotted three days of "beef on the hoof" to each man. This was contained in the army's order of march.

Working out ahead of the infantry and its attendant services in the operation at the river, Gregg's cavalry division ranged along the flowering roads south and east toward the virtually abandoned city of Fredericksburg. To the south and west, Wilson's cavalry division fanned out through the Wilderness as far as Parker's Store on the Orange Plank Road, where Hill's men were marching.

When the general facts of this information were sent westward to calm-faced Lee, riding toward the enemy's concentration, the vital element of numbers was not included. Lee assumed that he would collide with an army equivalent to that which Meade had put in winter headquarters after the inconclusive, post-Gettysburg fighting in Virginia. As late as mid-April, he wrote Davis: "I do not think his army will exceed 75,000." Lee never made a poorer calculation of the might that the enemy could assemble against him.

Before the arrival of Burnside's added IX Corps, the Army of the Potomac reported 127,000 of all arms as "the aggregate present for duty" on the last day of April. Of this "aggregate," something over five thousand were either sick or in prison, and not reported as "equipped for duty." Also in this aggregate were the large numbers of Federal soldiers out of the line on "extra and daily duty." As many as twenty thousand officers and men — a community larger than the adult male population of peacetime Richmond — were detached to subsistence, transportation, medical and similar services, with units to guard the trains. Minus these noncombatant deductions, approximately a hundred thousand fighting men "present and equipped" made the push across the river.

Meade gave contradictory reports of 97,273 and 103,785 as his effective armed strength on the field; his chief of staff, Colonel A. A. Humphreys, struck a balance at 99,438. This would be broken down into roughly seventy-five thousand infantry, more than thirteen thousand cavalry (only two thirds of which crossed the river on the first day), upwards of eight thousand artillerymen for 274 guns, with engineer corps and provost guard.

When Burnside's corps came up with more than twenty thousand infantrymen, Grant could bring onto the field something over a hundred and twenty thousand fighting troops of all arms. Except in Burnside's corps, the units were composed mostly of veterans in an organization founded by that great administrator, McClellan, developed by hard wear and good men, and reorganized for this campaign into a model of American efficiency.

If Lee's army had been fully concentrated, as he wished, he would be outnumbered in combat arms by two to one, not counting the Federal units on detached duty who were available as reserves. The total strength of the Army of Northern Virginia is usually estimated at something between sixty-two and sixty-four thousand. This figure included units on the roster who were detached from Lee when he moved out on Wednesday, May the 4th.

Ewell's thin corps would have been raised to seventeen thousand with the return of his brigades, and Longstreet's corps would have numbered fifteen thousand with Pickett's division. With A. P. Hill at twenty thousand, the infantry would number about fifty-two thousand if all its units were present, though some Confederates claim this figure to be high. Stuart's three light cavalry divisions totaling eight thousand and forty-five hundred artillerymen would complete the strength of all arms as on the roster.

The total force in the Rapidan area, including Longstreet, carried approximately two hundred guns: the count varies from 197 to 203. New Orleans's famed Washington Artillery Battalion was de-

tached south of the James River, where the batteries were waiting for spring grass for the lean horses. The total number of guns,
present and absent, carried on the roster of the Army of Northern
Virginia was 227 — less than Lee wanted.

As Lee marched toward the Wilderness with the twenty-nine
thousand infantry who were to strike the enemy, with fifteen thousand more infantry to come up later in support, he had no notion
that this small force would try to drive an army that approached
one hundred fifty thousand men in its total. Still, it must have taken
some cold nerve to ride into the shadows stretching across the road
with the knowledge of how little he had to attack an enemy's army
even with the strength he believed that army fielded.

4

Before the sun went down, General Lee ordered a halt to Hill's
columns at a roadside village grandiloquently named New Verdiersville. Evidently named for a Verdier family that had once lived in
the area, the scattered cluster of farmhouses was called by the soldiers simply "My Dearsville." The countryside was wooded fairly
heavily there, though still west of the Wilderness. The van of Hill's
corps had marched east on the Plank Road a little more than twelve
miles from Orange Court House, and at Verdiersville the column
was about the same distance from the north-south road over which
the Army of the Potomac was passing through the Wilderness.

At this stage, the corps of Hill and Ewell were, in effect, moving
eastward on parallel tracks which terminated in the main passageway leading south from the fords in the Rapidan River. From this
cross passageway, the Brock Road, Federal cavalry fanned out westward on the Plank Road, toward Hill's infantry. The enemy cavalry
advanced to the western fringe of the Wilderness, no more than
eight miles from where the Third Corps soldiers began building
their campfires along each side of the road.

In the darkening stretches between the Confederate infantry and
the Federal cavalry, General Stuart was personally out patrolling
with some of his troopers. The village of Verdiersville was a sensitive spot with Jeb Stuart. Back in the young days of the war, in '62,

he had experienced a narrow escape there from a dawn capture by an enemy patrol, when he and his staff slept in an unguarded bivouac in the yard of one of the farmhouses. A great horseman, Stuart got off with the loss of his plumed hat and order-book, but Verdiersville was one place the cavalryman would never be easy about. By the time the commanding general's headquarters tent was pitched in a clump of woods, Stuart began sending back his meticulous reports of contacts with the enemy.

No action of any size developed. The blue horsemen were patrolling aggressively, feeling ahead. They moved in complete confidence, firing with the best carbine on the continent: the .54-caliber Spencer repeater. A rim-fire breechloader, which eliminated the cumbersome ramrod used on muzzle-loaders, the handy carbine fired an eight-shot clip and used a brass-base cartridge that did not, like the lead Minié ball, expand on contact. The Confederates had captured some of the repeaters, but none of the resourcefulness of the improvised ordnance manufacture could produce brass for the cartridge cases.

Stuart's reports came in until after eleven o'clock. The reports would seem to indicate that the Army of the Potomac had halted in the sooty shadows of the Wilderness, according to Lee's hopes. How long the halt would endure remained the anxious question. Alone in the candlelit tent, Lee was given no opportunity to plan alternatives in the event that Grant passed his front during the night. The telegraphic communications were still open between Richmond and Guiney Station on the Richmond, Fredericksburg & Potomac Railroad, and during the cool night couriers brought messages to Lee from President Davis.

Now, with Lee on the eve of a crucial battle, the President sent urgent wires to the General informing him that each of the enemy's threats was unfolding precisely as Lee had predicted. Davis made no reference to Lee's advance information on the details of the pattern of the Federals' multiple offensive. With Lee's incomplete army bivouacked ten miles from the enemy's major force and the cavalry already skirmishing, Davis requested Lee to assume responsibility for distant fronts.

In the fertile Shenandoah Valley and around the salt works in the southwest corner of the state, two of the enemy's threats had materialized, and the commander in chief informed the General that he was to direct operations of the small forces scattered through those areas. Brigadier General John Breckinridge, the bourbon-loving former Vice-President of the United States, lacked any military training, and brought mostly an imposing presence and native leadership to his informal command in the Valley. Sensibly he wired Lee for specific instructions. Lee had sent Kentuckian Breckinridge general instructions the day before. On the night of May 4th, the General did not even try to divert his mind into the details of distant forces whose specific circumstances were unknown to him. He sent Breckinridge a four-line wire in which he said, "For the present you will take the general direction of affairs and . . . I trust you will drive the enemy back." He would return to Breckinridge on another day, when the unknowns on his immediate front were more resolved. There was another message of Davis's to be answered right then.

The President wired the grim information that the secondary Federal army, as predicted, was arriving in transports on the south bank of the James River, fifteen miles from Richmond on the opposite shore of the river. Troops numbering more than thirty thousand (more than Lee had immediately with him on that night) were disembarking at the small port of City Point and the old plantation of Bermuda Hundred. This army, a nightmarish materialization of the threat which Lee had vainly tried to persuade Davis to meet in advance, was commanded by Ben Butler, the political general called "Beast" because of his ruthlessness toward civilians. Between Butler and the bridges across the river from Richmond stood only the garrison of the earthen river-fort at Drewry's Bluff. Between Butler and the connecting railroad with Petersburg were only civilian families, already taking flight from their farms and homes at the approach of the "Beast." At the junction city of Petersburg, twenty-two miles south of Richmond, the defense force consisted exactly of Major General George E. Pickett and his staff. Frantic Pickett was waiting both for troops from the Carolinas and for the new department commander, Beauregard, to assume command of the region. As the President had waited for the enemy to appear first, neither Old Bory nor the troops had arrived.

With the enemy at the back gate of Richmond, Jefferson Davis

wired Lee of the changes he was *then* making in his troop dispositions. Lee read of these after-the-fact orders for troops to hurry,
piecemeal, to the threatened point, with an eye to discover the dispositions of his own missing units. Scanning through the details by
which Davis was moving this brigade from here to there, and that
brigade from there to yonder, he found the depressing information
that "the troops called for by you will be up in four days."

By four days it might all be over. Lee began to compose a letter
that was quite different from the two essays in diplomacy he tried
the day before. Writing Davis from the peace of winter camp, however imminent the movement of armies, was not the same as writing from bivouac on the march toward tomorrow's clash. The
day before, the campaign was still in the future. Lee could still hope
for his absent brigades and the gathering of defensive units south
of Richmond. That night he knew in certainty that Davis had done
none of those things urged upon him, and the General lost any impulse toward tactful suggestions.

Writing that "the army was put in motion today" and saying that
the Federal force on the James River "will doubtless now co-operate with Gen. Meade," he stated flatly, "Under these circumstances
I regret that there is to be further delay in concentrating our own
troops." Then he went to the heart of the matter. Referring to the
futile waste of Hoke's division in North Carolina, he wrote:

I fully appreciate the advantages of capturing New Berne, but
they will not compensate us for a disaster in Va. or Georgia. Success in resisting the chief armies of the enemy will enable us more
easily to recover the country now occupied by him, if indeed he
does not voluntarily relinquish it. We are inferior in numbers, and as
I have before stated to your Excellency, the absence of troops belonging to this Army weakens it by more than the mere number of
men.

Unless the force that it will be necessary to leave in North Carolina is able to reduce New Berne, I would recommend that the attempt be postponed, and the troops in N. C. belonging to this army
be at once returned to it, and that Gen. Beauregard with all the
force available for the purpose, be brought without delay to Richmond.

This letter would probably have finished anyone else with the commander in chief. Davis was too busy trying to lock the barn after the horse was gone to heed Lee's unwonted firmness. Lee was too oppressed with the certainty of unavailable manpower, in going against the uncertainties that daylight would bring, to consider his superior's sensitivity. All during the spring he had devoted time and study to the approaching operations, while trying by every known means to build his army, with veterans and supplies, for the coming test. Now all that lay within his control was the direction of the sleeping men around him who, the next day, would offer their lives in faith in his leadership. With the moment at hand, in the realm of uncertainties, Lee apparently worried more about Grant passing his front that night than anyone reported. In the realm of certainties, he knew that he would not have enough of anything, especially not enough veteran units.

5

When Lee wrote Davis that "the absence of troops belonging to this Army weakens it by more than the mere number of men," he expressed a principle that the conscientious President would never understand. What Lincoln knew by instinct was something Davis could not learn in all the application of an unadaptive intelligence: this was the intangible of spirit, of *esprit* or morale. Davis never once in the war made a ringing speech to the hearts of the people, or won loyalty from a dissident by giving him understanding. As Davis felt no response to the intangible qualities that move men, Lee's stress on the need of the "troops belonging to this Army" made no impression on him. In the Gettysburg campaign, when the President palmed off on Lee some second-line strangers as substitutes for detached veterans, the results were very costly. Davis, however, perceived no connection between the cause and the effect.

To Lee, the weakening caused by the absence of his veterans was more than the loss of their skills — their experience in maneuvering themselves in battle, in taking cover, standing up under casualties and producing their tremendous fire power. These were characteristics of most veteran troops. Beyond that, Lee's veterans also had developed those deeper qualities that sustained the spirit on starvation rations against a numerically superior foe who had everything. This was the intangible of a group spirit formed by the individual units accustomed to campaign together as a single force. The units contributed to the whole and the whole to the units.

The group spirit began with a soldier's identification with his company, not likely to be more than sixty or seventy men in 1864. Mostly they would all be neighbors, many kinsmen, and the captain and other officers old friends elected by their fellows. In the ante-bellum militia companies from the cities, men had joined with others of their own social stratum, as in clubs, and their messes continued lifelong associations. As company officers were elected throughout the war, men were often chosen on a basis of personal popularity or leniency in discipline, and line officers in Lee's infantry were frequently poor soldiers. The captain was not the soldiers' big man. This was the colonel, their regimental commander.

Their regiments, of from less than three hundred to more than four hundred men by 1864, were formed of companies from the same county or region, and the regiment was the basic unit of a soldier's pride. The regimental number identified his locale and the battle flag carried the special pride of his home place. In the early days, regiments were such community affairs that parents placed their young sons personally under the care of the colonel, who addressed the private by his first name and was somewhat avuncular as a disciplinarian. Referring to the boy's mother, his reprimand would go something like "Son, what would Miz Lucy say if she knew about your goings-on?"

The basic unit in battle was the brigade, usually four regiments, and in 1864 running from as low as twelve hundred to as high as nearly two thousand. When possible, a brigade was composed of troops from a single state. The men of Jackson's first brigade, which won him his soubriquet at First Manassas, all came from the Shenandoah Valley. Hood's old brigade remained famous as "the Texans," after their depleted ranks were filled out by the 3rd Arkansas; and two tough brigades from Louisiana remained, despite all changes, "the Louisianians."

Rations and the men's supply of ammunition were issued from brigade headquarters, regularly through regimental officers, but in action to any detachment sent back for ammunition. The bullets with the powder attached came ten to a paper package, with a hundred packages in a carton. Ten cartons filled a case — "a thousand to a case," as they said. The cases were carried in the brigade ordnance wagons. The "skillet wagons" were attached to the regiments.

The brigadier was the general with whom the men were familiar, and by 1864 the soldiers were fair judges of their commanders. The brigadiers established their positions in camp. There they showed the extent of their interest in caring for the men's physical needs and moral comforts; they showed, in the nature of their discipline, their own strength of character and turn of mind; and, in the small details of human relationships, they won or lost the respect and liking of the men. The brigades of generals whose personalities did not warm the men, or whose conduct did not win their respect, entered battle with indifferent morale. Occasionally a new brigadier brought his regiments on the field in good condition, and then fought them poorly, and that would be all for him. Usually a brigadier showed in camp those qualities of resolution, judgment and decisiveness that enabled him to handle bodies of men effectively under fire.

The brigadier was the fighting general in the Army of Northern Virginia. He took his men personally onto the field, selected their position and deployed them for action. He must know the weight of fire which they could endure and possess the leadership to hold them to their full capacity for enduring casualties. He must be able to bring them out in order when the going became too rough and shift them on the field of fire without losing direction or too many stragglers. When ordered to attack, he must deliver the thrust with compact regiments aligned on one another, with his attacking line in turn aligned on the next brigade. Of all things he must avoid that drifting of a line or sudden taking of cover that exposed the flanks of other units. In all this action, he must make sure at all times that the men were supplied with ammunition and his superiors with prompt information. Command failure at division or corps level could wreck any movement; but, assuming adequacy in higher command, as the brigades went so went the army.

The division, usually of four brigades, then averaging little more than six thousand, was the largest unit directly commanded by one man, a major general. As Pickett's absent division was the only one then composed of brigades entirely from one state, Virginia, at divisional level the men's identification expanded from place — neighborhood, county or city, state — to a military community. Their pride must extend through each level of identification, though in a division the men were more removed from their commanding officer.

In a major general, good judgment of men was required in the selection of brigadiers, and executive ability in handling those fellow generals and his staff. The staff work of some generals suffered from their self-indulgence in appointing relatives and friends to their official family. As General Lee said, though these made "agreeable companions," they made for poor discipline. Since from staff and field command on up, half the officers were connected by blood or marriage or some close association, the problem was sufficient for General Lee to have formally discouraged the practice of this social incest to which Southerners are particularly addicted.

The major general also needed sound judgment under the pressure of battle, the willingness to act on his own initiative and the ability to make quick decisions. Heavy responsibility was placed on the division commander in battle. He was responsible for the performance of his brigadiers and they were responsible to him. Finally, in times of virtually semi-independent command, he must be able to cooperate with other units in concert of action toward a common objective. In the qualities of military leadership, the step was large from brigadier to major general, and it was essentially in his quality of leadership that the division commander related to his troops.

The final extension of the soldier's identification was with his corps. To most Confederates the corps, of which Hill's, with more than twenty thousand, was then the largest, was the vastest community they had ever known. When a man's loyalty had extended through all stages, his self-identification embraced the corps in the fullness and intensity of his pride. In regiments and brigades, the men carried on derisively good-natured rivalries with units from other localities in their states or with other states, and even divisions within a corps had staged during the winter a full-scale battle with snowballs. The corps was beyond parochial rivalries.

The corps was a small, physically complete army within the command organization of Lee. The corps carried its own artillery, five battalions totaling about seventy-five guns. It carried its own wagon train, and its supporting services operated the services of its component units from the top of the pyramid downward. As military units, the three corps were separate entities that related only at command level through general headquarters. In action, the commanding general could shift a corps' divisions about as he saw fit, without violating the protocol of command, since only the commanding general was responsible for the direction of the battle. Short of such emergency action on the field, the corps commander held complete responsibility for the condition and the performance of his men, from privates to major generals.

The morale and discipline were built in camps and tested in battle. When the troops stood up to the test repeatedly, the shared experiences created the indefinable element of *esprit* that was more than the sum of the parts. Though the corps commander was more removed from the men than any general except Lee, the lieutenant generals gave the corps their individual characters. In some curious communication, a corps commander impressed his characteristics as a soldier on his troops, and personalized the group unit to which the men gave their loyalty.

The biggest jump of all was from division command to corps command. While some men of outstanding promise had been killed, and some of the younger men were then in the process of developing, others had been prevented from developing their full military potential by what falls inclusively under the term of "personality difficulties."

Old army "Shanks" Evans was the classic example. Brigadier General Evans showed every gift of leadership at First Manassas, where his heroic stand determined the nature of the battle and gave the Confederates their chance. He was intuitive in divining the enemy's intent, decisive in making a countering move, meticulous in sending back accurate information, bold and skillful in action, and held his green troops together under casualties that would have been heavy for regulars. But the lean South Carolinian was followed by an orderly who carried on his back a keg of bourbon whiskey, from which the General continuously refreshed himself. This would never do in Lee's army, where Lee, Jackson and Stuart were teetotalers.

By 1864, another factor militated against the full functioning of many officers from colonels to corps commanders. The weight of the odds against which they contended oppressed men with the knowledge that they could afford no mistakes. Enemy generals could and did make the clumsiest blunders. The local action might be affected but the organization was not, and losses would be made up. The awareness that any mistake might be irreparable, and that men lost were gone for good, caused some men to hold back and others to try too hard.

At the very top, the "organization" consisted practically of one man, and Lee knew for a certainty that mistakes would be made among the two hundred men in key positions of command. What he did not know was who would make them this time. When his total army was assembled, the command structure in the infantry would consist of approximately a hundred and fifty regimental commanders. A chain of error could start anywhere from top to bottom or anywhere between. For, in addition to the men who were untested at their new ranks, among the veteran commanders one or more men of proven ability had failed at some crisis in every battle since Fredericksburg, back in December of 1862.

It was Lee's knowledge of his total structure, and familiarity with every detail, that caused him to place his dependence so heavily on veteran outfits. With them assembled, one unit would stand when another broke, try confidently where another had failed, or fill a breach that, widened, might become that chain of disaster. As the *esprit* of each unit was more than the sum of the parts, so the concentration of the units gave the army the spirit that supported Lee's faith in his men.

On that May night of the 4th, in his tent in the woods, General Lee's awareness of the absence of dependable brigades was quickened by the exchanges with Davis. After his messages to the President had been dispatched and the problems of the other fronts cleared from his mind, Lee had suffered a strain caused by the conflict of attention. The aroused awareness of his missing veterans lingered in his mind in the background of the truly calamitous possibilities. If Grant moved on through the Wilderness during the night, with the other Federal army already south of Richmond, it would all be over.

Whatever happened, there was nothing more he could do. He could take the solace of praying for the single heart to do God's will, without the drain of worry about the morrow.

Somewhere around midnight, he turned to his cot for the few hours' sleep before daylight.

CHAPTER FOUR

"Go Down the Road and Strike the Enemy"

BEFORE DAWN came the news that the Army of the Potomac was camped in the Wilderness, and General Lee did not try to hide his relief. During the night he had kept his apprehensions to himself. At breakfast with his staff officers, shortly before five, Uncle Robert showed such a cheerful humor that he talked with unusual candor about his plans. He mentioned his satisfaction at having Meade's army where he had hoped it would be and, in the assurance of finding his risky assumptions confirmed to the last vital detail, seemed unconcerned for the moment over his small numbers. From what the General could read into the information sent by Stuart, it was evident that Grant was not expecting Lee's army on the flank of his march.

It was not before five in the morning that the heavy columns of Lee's old enemy began the push southward over the constricting roads through the Wilderness. For all the bold riding around of Sheridan's cavalry, scant reports of the Confederates had been sent to Grant. As Lee had hoped, the Federal's new commander in chief assumed that, since the river crossing had been uncontested, Lee was falling back to a defensive position. In his assumption, Grant could not know that Lee was ignorant of the size of the force coming at him. At that stage more or less a supervisory commander, Grant seemed bent simply on moving ahead until Lee's army was encountered and then trying to overwhelm it.

With Grant doing precisely what Lee wanted him to, Lee dismissed last night's problems of the surrounding dangers. In the early morning of the 5th, another of the radiant May days, Lee gave A. P. Hill orders to put his two divisions in motion toward the enemy. Then, personally inspecting the folding of the saddle blanket on Traveler and the tightness of the girth, he swung his solid weight up on the gray horse. Though the General never wore sword or side arms, he carried a Colt revolver in the left saddle holster. Adjusting himself in the saddle, he gathered the reins and started the horse forward at a brisk walk.

Moving out, he was joined by A. P. Hill, who wore his short, single-breasted shell jacket and a black hat with a curled brim. Hill wore no insignia of his rank, not even a general's wreath around the three stars on his collar. Jeb Stuart, after riding ahead with a picket line of troopers, joined Lee's group later in the morning. Stuart was turned out in full finery. His gray campaign hat, now weather-stained, still carried a long ostrich feather where the left brim was turned up and pinned to the crown. There were none of the laughing young staff officers who had sung "Ole Joe Hooker, Won't You Come Out of the Wilderness" one year before when Stuart temporarily succeeded to command of Jackson's corps in the battle of Chancellorsville. Approaching the somber screen of the Wilderness, he now was alert, all business, and no singing was heard anywhere.

There is some doubt about the precise beginning of the Wilderness. The winding Plank Road the three generals followed eastward carried them past fewer farms and more woods, of increasing density, but at eight o'clock they had not yet entered the obscuring mazes which the natives considered to be the veritable Wilderness. Around eight o'clock they were joined by Major Campbell Brown, son-in-law and staff officer of General Ewell. At sight of him, General Lee appeared to lose some of the boldness of his confidence. This young man was the son of Ewell's new wife, the lady who had created such a disturbance at Second Corps headquarters, and most likely Brown reminded Lee of the unhappy changes in General Ewell. The very presence of Campbell Brown, instead of Colonel Sandie Pendleton, could have done nothing to reassure Lee, for camp rumors concerned the Widow Brown's finagling to get the chief of staff's job for her son.

Major Brown had ridden across country, from the parallel road, to ask for orders. Until asked for specific orders for the Second Corps, Lee's general orders called for no more than a march to contact with the enemy. From there, with the Wilderness nullifying the use of artillery, a rifle fight would develop as circumstances indicated. For the Second Corps, nothing in the fundamentals required for deployment and position would tax the largely proven generals at brigade and division command, and Lee personally was nearby. The Old Turnpike was sufficiently close to the river to prevent an exposure of Ewell's flank to enveloping movements from the entangled bottomland on his left. On his right, at that stage of the march, the Old Turnpike was close enough to the Orange Plank Road to avoid any appreciable gap between Hill's left flank. Hill's right was protected by Stuart's fanned-out horsemen.

With complete confidence in Ewell, Lee would have felt no need to make the orders more specific. As he began to consider a more definite order to send Ewell, General Lee reverted to that awareness of his scant numbers which had been quickened the night before by Davis's communications. An element of caution restrained the excitement of the early morning impulse to get right at Meade's army. There *were* those dangers gathering on the surrounding fronts and a failure here, in the center, would bring quick and total collapse. As if suddenly looking straight in the face of an action *he could not lose*, and discounting the initiative of the commander of one half of his assaulting force, Lee decided to limit Ewell's action to making contact.

First, he told Major Brown that he wanted Ewell to regulate his march to the pace of Hill's divisions. As the Second Corps had started earlier and their road was straighter, this amounted to no more than an alignment that would be made between any separated troops going into action. Then the General gave the restraining order which reflected his own state of mind. He told Major Brown that he "preferred not to bring on a general engagement before General Longstreet came up."

Of itself, this order was sufficiently direct and uncomplicated. Certainly Lee did not recall that the restriction against a "general engagement" duplicated in part the Gettysburg order which immobilized Ewell. The other part of the Gettysburg order had allowed Ewell the discretion of carrying a position "if practicable." No "if" was attached to the order Lee sent by Major Brown. The only conditional elements were the "preference" of the commanding general and the definition of "general engagement." It was not that either of these unspecific elements should impose any burden on Ewell's limited powers of resolution, provided his contact went according to normal expectations. What Lee failed to consider was the effect that the unexpected might exert on Ewell's powers of resolution when he was forced to determine the stage at which an action became a general engagement and to decide between the commanding general's preference and the immediate necessity.

In trying to limit the scope of the corps commander's responsibility, Lee not only revealed his limited trust in Ewell. He showed, by his disregard of Ewell's potential for collapse in resolution, that the burden of those responsibilities beyond his control was already taking its toll of him.

2

Lieutenant General Richard Stoddert Ewell had started his morning cheerfully enough. At five o'clock the one-legged general was drinking a cup of coffee crouched over a low fire at a crossing of woods' paths in the forest, where he was discovered by a passing artillery officer, Robert Stiles. Young Stiles was a particular favorite of Ewell's, who called him "my child" when they were alone.

This intimacy between a general officer and an artillerist was one of the characteristics of that peculiarly personal army, where equals were accepted across all ranks. In addition to this generality, Stiles belonged to that distinguished group of young men who served in the Richmond Howitzers. The son of a Georgia preacher, Stiles had spent his teens in New Haven where his father answered a "call," was a graduate of Yale and had been studying at Columbia Law School at secession. Though he had visited Richmond only once, he went there to offer his services to the howitzer battalion which contained many of his friends.

The three companies of Richmond Howitzers, which from beginning to end numbered no more than 750 gunners on its four-year roster, boasted the highest proportion of gifted, educated men of any unit on either side. John Esten Cooke, ante-bellum professional writer and later Confederate biographer, began as a private, as did Professor Nichols Crouch, the composer of "Kathleen Mavourneen" — Jeb Stuart's favorite song. William L. Sheppard, the best known of all Confederate artists, came home from art studies in Paris to join the 2nd Company, and the first captain of the

1st Company was George W. Randolph, Jefferson's grandson and later Confederate Secretary of War. Including a book by Stiles himself, the small outfit produced more published works than any unit in the war.

By Stiles's account, General Ewell offered him a cup of coffee. At the time the General was accompanied only by a single courier, who held his own horse, the General's horse and the crutches which Old Baldhead had scorned the year before. Ewell's horse was a flea-bitten gray, named Rifle, and Stiles said the horse was "singularly like" the General, "so far as a horse could be like a man." Ewell's face, decorated with the outlandish mustachios, was naturally pale, but Stiles noticed that the older man seemed unusually pallid, as if he "had been up all night." However, the slightly bulging eyes were bright and his manner alert. When the young artillerist sat down to a cup of coffee, the dew was still on the grass and a low-hanging fog was just lifting. As they chatted — perhaps about absent food, for Ewell was a great cook — Stiles asked the General if he had any objections to telling him his orders.

"No, sir, none at all," Ewell answered briskly. "They are just the orders I like — to go right down the road and strike the enemy wherever I find him."

At his former best, under the iron control of Old Jack, that type of straight-on action was the glory of Dick Ewell. It relieved him of the responsibility of making decisions. But, several hours after his morning coffee with young Stiles, Ewell received the restraining order from the commanding general. He seemed not at all disturbed by the limitations imposed upon his actions nor by any confusion over adapting to Lee's preference. With no pressures being exerted upon him, the loyal subordinate simplified matters for himself by interpreting "preference" to mean "order." He would *not* bring on a general engagement.

A year before, the unregenerate Ewell might have indulged in one of his wrathy spectacles to show his staff the afflictions a good soldier must bear in accommodating the vagaries and vaguenesses of commanding generals. During the Widow Brown's reign, such didos were forbidden. His cursing, which they used to say "could be parsed," became a wasted talent, and as a churchgoer he joined Lee, Stuart, the Pendletons and others in the company of Virginia

Episcopalians. Outwardly at least he accepted his duty with good grace. Riding his flea-bitten horse along the old stone turnpike, General Ewell appeared as self-confident as when he had marched his old division under the rigidly defined assignments of Stonewall Jackson.

The corps commander had every reason for confidence in his troops, and in the organization welded by Old Jack's stern demands. The Second Corps had suffered no losses in general officers in the Gettysburg campaign or since, and the only changes had been made to replace failures.

Ewell's former division was commanded by tobacco-chewing Jubal Early, the best of the later-emerging major generals. Forty-eight years old and a classmate of Ewell's at West Point, Old Jube had cut short a promising army career to turn to law and politics. From the farming country of western Virginia, outside the belt of large slaveholders, Early had fought bitterly against secession. When armed invasion was employed in his own state, Early became an even bitterer enemy of a people who sought to impose their will on him by force.

Though he was close to Ewell, whom he dominated, ambitious Early was one of the most disliked general officers in the army. In his younger years he had been a darkly handsome man with a fine military carriage. During an inconsequential command in the Mexican War he suffered a rheumatic attack which left him stoop-shouldered and bent and, during the war, his lower face was covered by a grizzled beard. Though natively courteous, he had a sardonic turn of mind, was profane in his speech, and made little effort to please. Under slight provocation, Early could become extremely harsh, and he respected no one's feelings in his criticism of others. One of his younger staff officers, who found him "a very pleasant and conservative old gentleman" in the quiet of camp life, wrote his father that when the General "is excited, his manners are so insulting that he is beyond endurance."

Since he was as rough on the enemy as on his own men, and possessed sound military sense, Jubal Early's division boasted a record of high performance. Among his brigadiers, silky-bearded Harry Hays was a proven leader of the famous Louisiana Brigade and John B. Gordon, with his Georgians, was one of the most promising of the younger men in the army. Both came from civilian life. Early's one weakly led brigade at Gettysburg had been the Virginians commanded by "Extra Billy" Smith, the last of the "political" generals in the army and, in 1864, the governor of Virginia. Smith was replaced by John Pegram, a veteran brigadier from the Western armies, where he had commanded a division under Forrest. A West Pointer and professional soldier from Richmond, he was the older brother of Willie Pegram, Hill's greatly loved young cannoneer, and had asked for a transfer presumably to be near home. Only Hoke's old brigade lacked a veteran commander. These stout North Carolinians, then detached from the army in the peripheral operations which gave employment to their former brigadier, were among the dependables whom Davis had advised Lee were four days away. Without them, Early's division moved toward the enemy with three fourths of its strength.

Stonewall Jackson's old division was commanded by Edward Johnson. Called "Allegheny" ostensibly because of an early command in the mountains, the nickname fitted the somewhat rough-hewn quality of his social behavior. A professional soldier of unspectacular competence, the forty-eight-year-old Virginia bachelor, with his undecorative chin beard, was personally something of an eccentric, and in battle wielded a hickory club instead of a sword. Coming to the army in the pre-Gettysburg reorganization, Johnson had proven equal to the task of maintaining control of a division that contained some of the most guilefully dauntless evaders of discipline in the army.

Originally an all-Virginia unit, Johnson's division's losses had been made up by two North Carolina regiments, a Maryland battalion, and a Louisiana brigade. The Louisianians had the only post-Gettysburg brigadier, and Leroy Stafford had won his promotion at Gettysburg by his courageous and superior handling of the brigade during the absence of its regular commander. Stafford's Louisianians were noted for a brigade dog, a feist named Sawbuck, who reportedly recognized every man in the outfit. At one time Sawbuck would follow his friends to battle. After he suffered a leg wound, the dog would hang back out of bullet range, and the men said he acted like an "old soldier."

The other three brigades of Johnson's division were commanded by pre-Gettysburg brigadiers, two of whom, John M. Jones and "Maryland" Steuart, were professional soldiers. The third, James A. Walker, was a Virginia Military Institute graduate whose talents and courage were so high that he had risen despite the grievances that Stonewall Jackson held against him since their days as professor and student.

The third division in Ewell's Corps was commanded by another V.M.I. man, thirty-five-year-old Robert Rodes. A peacetime civil engineer and professor, the magnificent-looking blond had been promoted to major general on the strength of his performance the year before at Chancellorsville. Though Rodes had done nothing to fulfill his promise at Gettysburg, his five-brigade division was improved by replacing two poor brigadiers with good men. Cullen Battle succeeded to Rodes's own former Alabama brigade, and Robert Johnston took over the North Carolina brigade that was then detached from the army, guarding Hanover Junction.

As commanders of the other brigades in his division, Rodes was fortunate in having three of the best younger men in the army. Militarily untrained George Doles was a rock with his Georgians, and West Pointers Junius Daniels and Dodson Ramseur led North Carolina brigades with the blend of cold skill and gallantry that indicated a potential for higher command. At that stage, twenty-seven-year-old Ramseur was, with Gordon, the most promising brigadier with Lee.

In artillery also the Second Corps was well served. When Stapleton Crutchfield's wound prevented his return, Colonel Armistead Long was promoted from Lee's staff to brigadier in command of corps artillery. A thirty-nine-year-old professional soldier from Virginia, Long had received his artillery training in the old army from General Hunt, the Federals' superb chief of artillery and Long's continuing friend. A tall, dark man who sported a sleek "military mustache," Long was very impressive in appearance. Affable in manner and scholarly in his tastes, Brigadier General Long was one of the artillery's best administrators and a soundly knowledgeable battle tactician. The corps carried seventy-three guns in five battalions. As in all of the corps, one battalion was attached to each division, and two formed the corps reserve.

Ewell's troops carried the proud tradition of Jackson's old corps, some survivors dating back to the first days of the Stonewall Brigade (its official name). Old Jack himself had once said proudly of those troops, "They may sometimes fail to take a position, but they have never been driven from one."

3

Some time in midmorning, men and officers were stirred by the sight of dark-clad masses crossing the Turnpike ahead of them. The time is inexact. Federals reported viewing Ewell's columns on the road as early as seven-thirty, while Ewell, who made the only Confederate report on record, stated that he saw the enemy "crossing the pike" at eleven o'clock.

The road from Germanna Ford, traveled by the Union forces, ran along a slight rise, and in the clear morning light the Federal officers could have caught movement miles down the turnpike. Ewell was marching into the sun and approached close to the narrow aperture of the crossroads before movement there became visible to him. As General Ewell halted his column and deployed three brigades before sending his report, his time-date might have been closer to the hour of sending the dispatch than of the encounter. Ewell recorded the time later from memory, and probably he saw the enemy earlier than eleven o'clock. The confusion in time, distances and numbers in many reports on the Wilderness suggest the blurring effect of the entanglements of green brush.

When Ewell saw the enemy force, he knew from familiarity with the country that the Federal troops were moving south on the road from Germanna Ford. That was all he knew. The Second Corps was then in the densest thickets of the Wilderness, with no possibility of a reconnaissance to reveal the enemy's strength or disposition. Even without Lee's restrictive order, Dick Ewell would not have attacked. As it was, he turned the decision completely over to the commanding general.

Halting his columns, he ordered Jones's advance brigade deployed across the road, Battle's brigade to form in support, and advanced another brigade by a side lane to his left, toward the river. Then he sent the information to General Lee, this time by lantern-jawed Sandie Pendleton. Colonel Pendleton soon rode back with a message that, according to Ewell, repeated "substantially the same instructions as before." General Lee *preferred* to avoid bringing on a general engagement. When Ewell received the message, the unseen enemy was firing with the weight of a skirmish line on both sides of the road across Jones's front. Again accepting preference as a specific order, Ewell sent a message to Brigadier General Jones "not to allow themselves to become involved, but to fall back slowly if pressed."

Having found the enemy, Old Baldhead prepared to receive him in sound soldierly fashion. He sent orders to rear brigades, strung out for more than three miles, to hurry forward. He ordered his nearer brigades to deploy on either side of Jones, whose men were then clawing their way through the briers to form a line of battle.

John M. Jones was a professional soldier who had been at West Point (though not in the same class) with Longstreet, Grant, D. H. Hill, and Sherman, and some personal trouble, perhaps similar to "Shanks" Evans's, caused this Virginian to advance more slowly than his contemporaries. He had not made brigadier until before Gettysburg, where he was wounded in the head at Culp's Hill. Soon returning to his brigade in Edward Johnson's division, Jones mastered whatever difficulties plagued him and won the respect of his old army friends on both sides. His soldiers were extremely attached to him. He was a full-faced man, rather sad looking, with a bushy mustache.

Where Jones formed his brigade across the pike, mostly to the right (south side), the green brush of the Wilderness was an almost impenetrable tangle. Not even a small clearing was in sight and the men could scarcely see twenty yards in their front. The firing from the mostly invisible enemy seemed exploratory, lacking volume, and the Federals were shooting high. Under the rattling of bullets through the foliage, the soldiers devoted their attention to hacking out vines in order to form an alignment. The other brigades from Johnson's division followed the country lane which paralleled the pike on the left side. These troops would come up to extend the line from the road northward toward the river. Several hundred yards to Jones's rear, where Battle was forming in support, three other brigades from Rodes's division began to grope their way from the Turnpike into the jungle on the south side to form a reserve line, and extend the right.

This was the relatively routine situation before noon when suddenly — it was very sudden to the troops, since there was no artillery preparation — a full blue division came hurtling through the brushy woods from both sides of the pike.

4

The Federal troops belonged to Griffin's division of Warren's V Corps, and they were no longer feeling out the Confederates. Three large brigades came at Jones's line in full-scale attack.

This opening action of the new campaign demonstrated at once Grant's policy of free-swinging aggression, his opportunism and confidence, and his determination not to surrender the initiative. A boring-in type of attacker, who usually scorned finesse, Grant showed, by his pugnacious reaction to the danger from the Confederate columns, that he believed his army could absorb any punishment Lee could mete out.

At this stage of Grant's supervision, Meade in theory exercised field command of the army under Grant's general orders. It was an awkward arrangement at best and, though each man tried to ease the situation, it was not designed to work in practice. On this opening battle, Meade initiated the orders for meeting the threat of the Confederate approach without first consulting Grant. He immediately reported to Grant and later they joined headquarters in the clearing of one of the few substantial farms in the Wilderness.

Meade's chain of orders, which led to Griffin's attack down the Turnpike, began around seven-thirty, when corps commander Warren informed him that a Confederate column (Ewell) was advancing toward the crossroads used by his V Corps in its southward march. From this point on, the improvised action developed into a battle for the main north-south passageway, the Brock Road.

The Wilderness was laced with narrow roads and country lanes, some no more than a farmer's cowpath. Only three of the relatively major roads concerned the two armies. The Old Turnpike and the Plank Road, running at a slant from southwest to northeast, were simply two ways from Orange to Fredericksburg. Near Fredericksburg the two roads converged, as they did at other points, but approaching the north-south Brock Road the Turnpike and the Plank were separated by a distance of two and three-quarters miles.

Those units of the Federal army which crossed the river at Germanna Ford marched south by the ford road to its terminus on the Turnpike in the area of the discouraged frame building of the old Wilderness Tavern. One-half mile to the east, the Brock Road began its course south from the Turnpike to its intersection with the Plank Road, and on southward to Todd's Tavern.

When Meade learned of the Confederate approach, Warren's V Corps had moved down the Brock Road to the Orange Plank, where his columns turned west. The van was approaching Parker's Store, three miles from the Brock Road. At that point, Hill's corps was advancing on Parker's Store from the other side, some miles to the west.

Hancock's II Corps had crossed at Ely's Ford and moved southward east of the Brock Road. His troops were approaching Todd's Tavern, six miles south of the Brock Road-Plank Road intersection. As of then, Todd's Tavern was the destination of Longstreet, a day's march away.

This progress of march became a dangerous dispersal of troops with Lee's army potentially on the flank of columns compressed on narrow roads. General Meade immediately ordered a contraction of Warren's corps. He pulled the units back from the Plank Road toward the Turnpike, forming battle lines facing west into the jungle. The tail of the column, Griffin's division, became the head, and Meade ordered the division deployed across the Turnpike about one and a half miles to the west of the tavern, facing Ewell. At the same time, Meade halted the southward march of Hancock's corps, and cavalry threw a screen across the Plank Road west of Parker's Store, in the direction of Hill's line of march. South of the Plank Road, Union and Confederate cavalry were skirmishing inconclusively but with sharp fighting on both sides.

These movements were essentially defensive in the vital consideration of holding the Confederates off the Brock Road passageway. But Meade believed that Lee was not planning an assault from the

Old Turnpike. As Lee's retirement from the unprotected river crossing had induced the belief that he was falling back to a defensive position, it was Meade's opinion that the Confederate troops on the Old Turnpike were designed merely to delay the Federal march. Conferring with Grant, Meade explained his intention of attacking down the Turnpike to develop the Confederate strength.

Grant replied that "If any opportunity presents itself for pitching into a part of Lee's Army, do so without giving time for disposition." In complying with this order, Meade had Griffin's division prepared to attack before the other divisions of Warren's corps were properly aligned on his left. Also, the van of Sedgwick's corps, the last to cross the river, had not come up on Griffin's right.

Wright's division of Sedgwick's corps, designed to come up on Griffin's right between the Turnpike and the river, was slowly grappling its way westward on a lane in the same terrain where Johnson's three brigades followed a country road in moving eastward.

Wadsworth's and Crawford's divisions, of Warren's corps, were forming on Griffin's left where, at noon, no Confederates had reached their position. Wadsworth got his division in motion soon after Griffin but, as no contact was established between their flanks, Griffin's division in effect made the initial assault alone.

Griffin was a rough customer whose three veteran brigades, containing some U.S. regulars, numbered more than six thousand men. Under no restraint to avoid bringing on a general engagement, his troops deployed for full-scale attack in the protective woods and then came hurrahing through the brush with everything they had. At the point of collision, the assaulting lines overwhelmed Jones's outside strength of fifteen hundred and enveloped both his flanks.

5

John M. Jones never had a chance to execute Ewell's order to the effect of not allowing "themselves to be involved." His Virginia regiments, several rebuilt with conscripts, took one look at the dark masses bursting through the foliage as far as they could see, and broke. Veterans and unseasoned troops, their flight was to typify the action of outfits of both armies throughout the fighting in the

Wilderness. Something in the eeriness of the surroundings, where the soldiers could not see the extent of the enemy force emerging against them, shook the nerves of the stoutest men.

Poor Jones, after conquering his own weakness, fell dead trying to steady his men, his aide-de-camp dying with him.

By the time Jones's broken regiments reached their own reserve line, the men poured through the troops of Battle's brigade in such a rush as to shake the order of the Alabama soldiers. Cullen Battle, a thirty-nine-year-old, heavy-bearded, peacetime lawyer, had been promoted to brigade command in Rodes's division after Gettysburg for his cool-headed initiative and sure handling of his isolated regiment in a crisis caused by an inept brigadier. With no intention of failing in his first major engagement as brigadier general, Battle held his regiments to their ground. Though in confused order, the troops managed to put some volume in their rifle fire and refused to break.

Major General Robert Rodes, who had won his promotion to division command on this same ground the year before with Stonewall Jackson, was aware of his less than outstanding performance at Gettysburg. The martial-looking blond hurried the deployment of those two of his brigades which had saved his reputation at Gettysburg and sent them crashing to Battle's right. The North Carolina brigade of Junius Daniel, who had won his own place at Gettysburg, and the Georgia brigade of steady-eyed, earnest-looking George Doles groped through the briery vines and saplings toward the support of Cullen Battle's shaky line. Rodes was riding about everywhere on an excited head-tossing black horse whose neck and shoulders were flecked with white froth. Rodes showed his own excitement by catching the ends of his long, tawny mustache between his lips.

He had reason to be excited. His three brigades, one shaken, numbered less than four thousand men against the momentum of Griffin's victorious troops, and Rodes had no more troops at hand. Ramseur's fine brigade was strung out westward on picket duty along the river, and his fifth brigade was detached from the army on orders of President Davis. While the soldiers might be apprehensive about what the green maze concealed, Rodes was reasonably certain that Federals did not send one division alone on an attack of that violence. There was nothing he could do except hold the lines and keep the men shooting. Neither side was firing guns at that time.

This was a field of combat on which Ewell, the old border dragoon, felt most at home. With a quick analysis of the situation, he used a spur on Rifle and personally rode back to the head of the column of Jubal Early's following division. As always, cold-eyed Early's troops were well closed up and, as frequently, the lead brigade, was Gordon's Georgians. Squeaking in his high-pitched voice that "The day depends on you, sir," Old Baldhead sent Gordon into the brush headed for the right flank of Rodes's three brigades.

While this confused action hung in the balance on the right side of the road, fortuitously Edward Johnson's three brigades between the Turnpike and the river came up on the left before Wright's division, of the VI Corps, reached the field. Two guns had by then been tugged into position in a clearing to the left and began to play on the flank of the brigade of Griffin's division north of the pike. When Johnson's hairy, ragged men came yelling through the woods, from the side where the attacking troops expected support, Ayres's brigade fell back across the turnpike, and crowded into Griffin's other two brigades.

With the pressure off Battle, Doles and Daniel (in that order from the pike southward), and with Gordon coming into line on their flank, the Confederates began to push forward over the whole narrow front. Griffin's brigade, still unsupported, fell back slowly.

At that time, Griffin's supports for his left were actually on the field. In the obscuring brush, they had drifted and lost direction. This was the division of Wadsworth, a white-haired old New Yorker who, in the Wilderness, showed more zeal than skill. Coming up on Griffin's left, his troops were so turned around that their left flank was exposed to Daniel and Gordon. These two young men — one a West Pointer in the last days of his life and the other a future governor of Georgia — took instant advantage of the opening. In no time at all, their sharp thrusts drove Wadsworth's exposed brigades backward, uncovering other brigades floundering in the jungle. Soon Wadsworth's whole division retired toward the Brock Road.

Then the confused withdrawal snowballed. Wadsworth had started ahead of Crawford's division on his left. When Crawford's right brigade, McCandless, came fumbling for Wadsworth's left, it became (in the words of Meade's chief of staff) "enveloped by Gordon's brigade." Before McCandless's men could disentangle themselves and fall back, the brigade took heavy casualties in killed, wounded and especially prisoners. The rest of Crawford's division, then isolated from their fellows, could only retire with the retreating line into the thickets.

In terms of a military decision, this phase of the opening clash of the armies ended when the Federals retired with severe losses and Ewell's men began to solidify their position across the Turnpike. Judged from Grant's orders, his troops suffered a distinct reversal. They had taken a severe repulse in trying to drive the Confederates, with the result that their dangerously strung-out army was halted in an exposed position and forced to a confused, reversed movement on narrow roads.

In meeting the enemy, Ewell had done all that could be expected: he had set up the enemy for Lee's stroke.

6

This accomplishment of the seven Confederate brigades who came into battle after Jones's men broke, and turned back the attack of a twenty-five-thousand-man Federal corps, was largely attributable to the Wilderness. The late arrival of Wright's division of Sedgwick's corps on the Confederate left, and the lost direction of the large bodies thrown hastily on the Confederate right, were elements in Lee's calculation of the effect of the Wilderness on heavily laden troops strung out under an overconfident command. Grant's aggressiveness had ordered the assault "without giving time for disposition."

Wright's division did not form in line north of the pike until three o'clock. By then, Johnson's three brigades, having driven Griffin's right, were placed in position and dug in. The woods were burning between the lines — about three hundred yards apart, just beyond accurate rifle range — and wounded Confederates and Federals were struggling to get out of the fought-over ground.

During the afternoon, both sides tried attacks there on the left. Neither could budge the other, but Ewell's corps suffered acutely in loss of command personnel during the exchanges. Leroy Stafford, who won the wreath around his collar stars for his Gettysburg performance, took a mortal wound. John Pegram, who transferred from Forrest to fight near home, went down with a bad wound in his first engagement on his native soil. With poor Jones gone, three of Johnson's four brigadiers were lost in a few hours.

Another loss, felt personally throughout the corps, was the death of Colonel J. Thompson Brown, senior colonel and second in command of the corps artillery. Beginning as a lieutenant in the Richmond Howitzers, Brown, a peacetime lawyer, typified those militarily untrained men who rose on energy, initiative and courage. He had shown his lack of training when he temporarily commanded the Second Corps' guns at Gettysburg but, with his resolution and intelligence, he was highly useful in serving under the professional direction of General Long. Shot dead by a sharpshooter while posting guns, Colonel Brown, with all respect for his accomplishments and example, was chiefly mourned by the men who had campaigned with him for his social graces and genial intellect.

As the battle on the Old Turnpike turned out, Lee's restraining orders had been perfectly adapted to the type of fighting which developed. With less coordination demanded of defensive than assaulting troops, Ewell, with luck on his left and sharp performances on his right, had handled his compact troops with competence. On the Federal side, few attacks ever made by the Army of the Potomac were as poorly coordinated as that movement of Warren's corps and one of Sedgwick's divisions through the smoking brush.

Ewell's fight, however, did not become a part of a total battle. Some time after three in the afternoon, A. P. Hill became heavily engaged on the parallel road to Ewell's right, and a dangerous gap developed between the flanks of the two corps. Long after the threat passed on Ewell's front and Hill became hard pressed on the other side of the open flank, Old Baldhead attended strictly to the action immediately affecting his corps. As Lee had demanded no more initiative of Ewell than of his subordinates, Ewell assumed no initiative for coordinating his corps in an action which, obviously swelling into a general engagement on his right, affected the whole army.

As an obedient subordinate, Ewell had done what he was told to do and with that he called it a day. With the action fading off on his front, he formed his troops, with flanks well protected, along the lines where Jones had first been struck. The men strongly fortified their positions and at dark brought off two guns abandoned by the Federals in the road. When night settled over the ghostly field, with the dead unburied and woods' fires flickering, Ewell sent his report to General Lee and asked if Lee wished him to attack on his front the next day.

As it happened, Colonel Marshall had sent two messages from the commanding general that arrived after Ewell sent his report at eight o'clock. With one message simply verifying the other, Lee introduced the dangerous element of discretion. Passing on the information that the enemy's forces were shifting their weight to the (Confederate) right, he offered Ewell a choice: if Ewell found it practicable to attack the enemy's right in the area of the Wilderness Tavern ridge, and to cut the enemy off from the river, "the General wishes it done." If this could not be done "without too great a sacrifice, you must be prepared to reinforce our right."

This was a different matter from the morning's restraining order. With that, Ewell translated "preference" to "command" and the pattern of the action developed around the sound fundamentals of his stand. This night order demanded a decision.

Perhaps Lee was reassured by Ewell's good performance in the separate action and dared to hope the corps commander would rise to the emergency. Whatever motivated the commanding general's proffer of a choice, Ewell refused to accept the choice of a decision. He did no rationalizing about it, consulted with no one, and never mentioned having received the order in his report. His organism simply rejected the assumption of the initiative required to make a decision. As far as is known, he put the order out of his mind that night.

Neither preparing an attack nor a shift to reinforce the right, the

Widow Brown's new husband devoted his attention to those familiar details he did well. He saw to it that his strongly fortified and well-aligned lines were ready to receive the enemy the next day. By this action, Lieutenant General Ewell divorced his corps from the plans of the army and settled down to continue his separate battle.

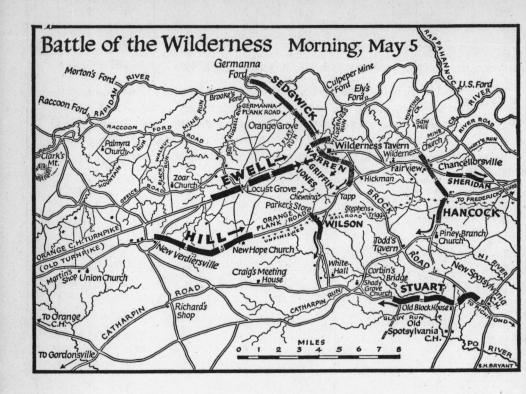

Battle of the Wilderness   Morning, May 5

Battle of the Wilderness · Noon, May 5

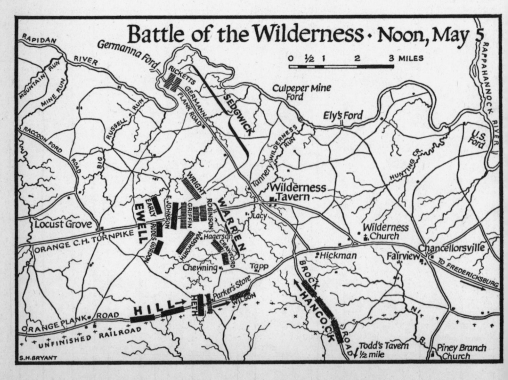

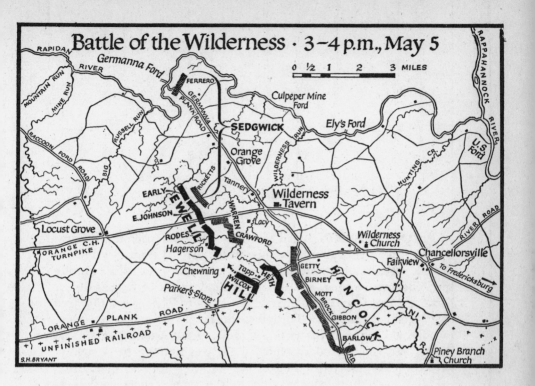

Battle of the Wilderness · 3–4 p.m., May 5

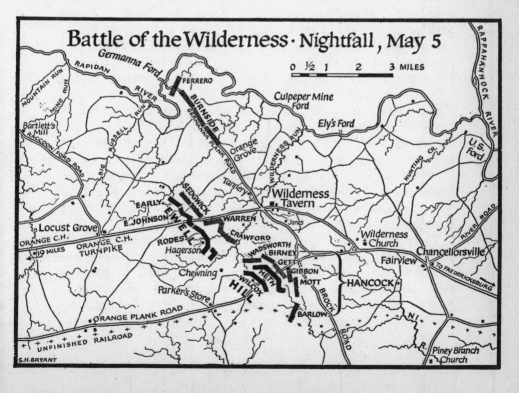

Battle of the Wilderness · Nightfall, May 5

CHAPTER FIVE

"If Night Would Only Come . . ."

AROUND NOON, when Ewell's battle developed on the Turnpike, Hill's advance troops on the parallel Plank Road began
brushing with the enemy's cavalry. Hill's van, then entering
the Wilderness proper, was about three miles west of Ewell's line of
battle. At that stage of the march, the looping Plank Road diverged
away from, south of, the Turnpike, and the jungle created a widening division between the two corps. Though General Lee seemed
unprepared for this contingency, there was nothing to do except
keep the Third Corps marching ahead.

Hill's corps was evidently under the same general orders as
Ewell's, to march to contact. Since Lee was riding with A. P. Hill,
perhaps no definite orders were given. There is a vagueness about
the command situation between Lee and the Third Corps commander during all of May 5th. Lee's battle report was lost, Hill
never got around to writing his, and the recollections of the staff
officers contain no reference to the status.

Some time during the day Powell Hill became sick, though the
exact time is also unknown. Later in the day, one of his division
commanders, Henry Heth, mentioned that Hill was sick in such a
way ("Hill being sick") as to imply that the illness had not come
upon him suddenly. However, when his columns entered the Wilderness, he was riding with his usual grace and a reported exchange
with his chief of couriers would indicate that he appeared well
enough at the time.

The attention of Hill, Jeb Stuart and, at least outwardly, of the
commanding general, was focused on the developments along their
own shrouded road. On the third parallel road, the Catharpin Road
to the south of them, Tom Rosser's cavalry brigade, protecting the
flank of their march, was skirmishing heavily with Federal mounted

troops. At intervals bodies of the blue troopers overflowed from the running fight to pop out of the screen of woods on the flank of the marching columns. One of the smaller groups of enemy horsemen was plainly lost. After startling a brigade of infantry with their sudden appearance, the dozen or so equally surprised riders faded back into the obscuring thickets. A larger unit, on some leader's impulsive bid for glory, came charging out of a side road. General Stuart seemed irritated by these excursions from the direction where his troopers patrolled, and took off southward into the brush, his red-lined cape billowing out behind him.

Shortly after noon, having marched ten miles east from New Verdiersville, the advance skirmishers encountered a determined line of dismounted enemy cavalry at the crossroads called Parker's Store. This one cavalry regiment, later reinforced by a second, expected to be supported from north of the road by Crawford's division of Warren's corps. But those foot soldiers, having been withdrawn eastward, were forming the left of the Federal line then attacking Ewell. Expecting to be supported, however, Colonel Hammond's 5th New York Regiment stood their ground against Hill's line of skirmishers.

Cavalry commanders often magnified the resistance they put up when their troopers fought infantry, and Hammond reported standing off the infantry from six o'clock in the morning—at the time when Hill's men were breaking camp ten miles away. Beyond the exaggeration, the dismounted horsemen with their repeating carbines, shooting at close range from behind trees, did bring the advance line to a halt.

Major General Heth's division was leading the march, with Pettigrew's old brigade deployed in advance. The lamented Johnston Pettigrew, a distinguished North Carolinian before the war and in the army an inspiring leader until his death on the retreat from Gettysburg, was a hard man to follow.

W. W. Kirkland, his successor, was a trained soldier with a good Confederate record, noticeably steady in battle. Yet Kirkland served as an illustration of one of those brigadiers who, for indefinable reasons, did not win the confidence of all his men. Soldiers did not often write in complete frankness about their officers, and their honest opinions were sometimes found through inference. One of

Kirkland's North Carolinians complimented another brigadier who, by inferred contrast to Kirkland, gave the brigade high morale and brought them into position fast "with a feeling of their own confidence."

Kirkland's skirmishers, perhaps expecting no more from the enemy cavalry than another hit-and-run affair, settled down slowly to the business of driving off the troopers. A. P. Hill ordered up a strengthening line to put some weight into the fire. The horsemen, still dismounted, fell back slowly, firing, keeping to the thick cover on both sides of the road.

When the two cavalry regiments began backing up the road, Hill's courier and most constant companion asked the General a favor. Sergeant Tucker's favorite horse had died during the winter, and the courier asked Hill if he might go forward and get himself a horse. About a dozen of the enemy dead were sprawled along the roadside, and stray horses, bearing fine U.S. saddles, were crashing around in the thickets. General Hill appeared cheerful enough when he told Tucker to go ahead. (He promptly lost his courier for the coming campaign, as the sergeant caught a bullet in the thigh and was carried shamefaced to the rear.) Some of the infantry also must have been a little overeager for gleanings from the dead, for the Federal cavalry gathered some prisoners to be sent to the rear for questioning.

With the dismounted cavalry falling back before them in the dense stretches of the Wilderness, the advance skirmishers moved ahead warily. They were only three miles from the Brock Road when the soldiers passed Parker's Store, and the officers supposed the enemy cavalry to be falling back on infantry. Small brush fires began to flicker on both sides of the narrow road, and men peered with squinting eyes over the smoke into the obscuring entanglements. The advance line approached within a quarter of a mile of the vital north-south passageway when the men came under the heavier fire of rifles from mostly invisible infantry skirmishers. Having established contact with the enemy's infantry, the advance line halted and exchanged shots while waiting for orders.

When Heth's skirmishers settled down to something like Indian fighting in the woods, Lee's party halted slightly more than one mile from the Brock Road. A clearing cut into the Wilderness there on their left, the subsistence farm of the Widow Tapp, provided one of the rare sites for gun positions. Lee told Hill to deploy Heth's full division on both sides of the road, to develop the enemy's strength. Guns were to be brought up and posted in the farm clearing.

Kirkland's advance brigade filed off to the left side of the road, in the direction of Ewell's fight then raging unseen to the north. Heth's other brigades began to grapple their way through a heavy stand of saplings on the right of the road. Colonel Poague, with the sixteen guns of the division's artillery battalion, prevailed upon General Heth to abandon his notion of posting a four-gun battery in the road. Leaving only one three-inch rifled piece in the road, Poague ordered the other guns drawn into the clearing.

Before the gunners began bringing up their pieces, Lee, Hill and Stuart (who had then rejoined them) moved off the road into the Widow Tapp's farmyard. Followed by their staffs, the three generals walked their horses past the widow's humble dwelling and dismounted at a rise, where several trees gave some shade. The time is inexact, as the reports vary widely, and a composite would indicate that Lee's group began their wait between two and three o'clock when Ewell's battle was at its peak.

From the clearing at the Widow Tapp's, Lee could distinctly hear the rattle of Ewell's fight on the Turnpike. In the absence of artillery, the firing held a curiously flat sound, making it difficult to determine the extent or progress of the engagement. As no messages had come from Ewell, the commanding general could only assume the Second Corps was holding its own. However, the problem of even greater concern than Ewell's fate was the gap which, contrary to calculations, appeared between the two roads.

The distance between the Turnpike and the Plank Road, from the Tapp clearing north, was two and three-quarters miles, and Ewell's right flank did not extend an appreciable part of that space southward, toward Hill's corps. Because the action developed separately on these two roads, with the dense maze between, the fighting has been largely viewed as two battles. To the anxious Lee they comprised one single and unexpectedly complicated action.

What he designed as a joint movement on the passageway of the Federal forces had turned into the one thing he sought to avoid:

Ewell, fully engaged, was directing an action outside the commanding general's control. To compound this unsettling development, Lee did not know what the enemy was up to in the concealing brush between him and Ewell. At that time the divisions of Wadsworth and Crawford were floundering through the intervening gap toward Ewell's right, but this was unknown at the farm clearing. Though there had been evidence of the withdrawal of those divisions from the Parker's Store area, Lee could not know how far or to where the big divisions had withdrawn.

Having expected to extemporize action, *with the initiative*, Lee's movements became determined by the divided battle. On one wing, Ewell was temporarily out of communication, and the commanding general evidently felt it unwise to turn the Plank Road development-action over to impulsive Powell Hill. Hill's one rash act as a corps commander had occurred among the last major actions before the army went into winter headquarters, and the Bristoe Station disaster could well have been fresh in Lee's mind. Casualties were so heavy that even generally liked Hill came in for public criticism. Though Hill generously assumed all blame, and wrote Lee, "I am convinced I made the attack too hastily," the emotional need for release in action remained a characteristic of the high-strung soldier.

There was also the matter of A. P. Hill's unstable health. He first came down with his mysterious ailment on the opening day at Gettysburg, his first critical action as a corps commander, and since then had noticeably failed in vigor. With all his intensity as a fighter and his appealing social graces, the frail-looking, sensitive Hill could not have been a reassuring presence in that little clearing in the impenetrable, engulfing Wilderness.

By the time the generals dismounted in the farmyard, Lee began to assume tacit control of the Third Corps, and sent orders directly to division commander Heth. This would have been no discourtesy to Hill. He was with Lee at what amounted to general headquarters and, under the tension caused by the separated corps, it was natural for the commanding general to act with some urgency in executing his unrevealed plans.

Evidently General Lee had chosen defensive tactics in his offensive strategy. He was a natural counterattacker to the enemy's lead.

With his veterans on tactical defense, the enemy would lead to their strength.

As it happened, this was one of the occasions when Hill's impetuosity would have served Lee well. Between eleven and two o'clock, only one Federal division, and that minus one brigade, had been available to rush to the intersection of the east-west Plank Road with the north-south Brock Road. When Heth's advance line encountered the Federal skirmishers, Getty's division, of Sedgwick's corps, was hurrying to the intersection with no time to dig in and no supports at hand.

Cool-headed Getty believed that the bold appearance of himself and his staff in the road caused Heth's advance to halt. Getty's staff had really nothing to do with it. From field officers to Lee, no Confederate there suspected that the well-officered Army of the Potomac had exposed itself so vulnerably as to possess only three fourths of one division to send running to a crossroads at which their dispersed army could be cut in half.

For hours the mobile telegraph system of the Federal army sped messages from Meade's chief of staff to officers over half the Wilderness. Hancock, whose van had halted six miles southward at Todd's Tavern, was at two o'clock driving his men northward toward Getty's support. The thin Brock Road was crowded with guns and wagons, littered with the abandoned gear of recruits, and, even under Hancock's lash, the going was slow.

None of this was known to Lee. His cavalry, pressed hard by Sheridan's heavier columns, could do no more than guard Hill's flank and keep the Catharpin Road open for Longstreet. In the absence of specific information about Ewell on the Turnpike or the enemy in his front, as Hill's strung-out divisions came up Lee exercised ordinary discretion in deploying Heth's division before he risked developing what force the brush might conceal.

Yet, with all considerations, Lee seemed to be acting under a self-imposed restraint. Knowing that no mistakes must be made, he approached the clash with a caution which reflected his awareness of the consequence of the engagement and his scant numbers for doing the job. The old reliables of Longstreet's division were on his mind, though the methodical Dutchman could not be expected up before nightfall. Perhaps too much was on his mind, too many uncertainties, including the unpredictableness of A. P. Hill and the absence of a truly inspiring division commander on the field.

For the Third Corps was a makeshift affair and, with a broad spread of competence in its general officers, had developed no outstanding leaders in the two divisions on the Plank Road. On the contrary, Heth illustrated those officers who so continually failed to live up to an early promise that they must be accepted as permanently on that nebulous plateau above mediocrity and below the exceptional.

2

When the Third Corps was formed the year before, after Jackson's death, one division was removed from the First Corps and Hill's six-brigade "Light Division" from the Second Corps; then the four strongest brigades of the Light Division formed a new division under Dorsey Pender, Hill's favorite soldier, and the two weakest brigades were joined by two brigades new to the army to form a new division. This division went to newly promoted Henry Heth, the division commander who would seem to have been the closest to Powell Hill.

Coming of similar Virginia backgrounds, each thirty-nine, they had been companions since childhood, classmates at West Point, and Hill had acted as groomsman at Heth's wedding. Modest and friendly, with the same courtliness and charm of manner which characterized Hill, Harry Heth was generally liked on both sides and was the only officer whom Lee addressed by his first name. Yet as corps commander and subordinate the two lifelong friends established no closeness in their military relationship. Perhaps the men had known each other too well, while being fundamentally too dissimilar.

On his side, Hill was not by nature (as Jackson had been and Longstreet was) a general to rule with an iron hand. Very aware of others, he was generous to his subordinates, as he was indulgent with his men, and quick with praise. Heth, less emotional, more contained, brought conscientiously applied intelligence to his work and was very careful about his personal record. With a performance at division command as inconclusive as Hill's at corps command, Harry Heth had been forced to overcome morale problems in his hodgepodge division.

Archer's veteran Virginia-Alabama brigade, low in numbers, lost its leader when Archer was captured at Gettysburg and operated under a colonel while waiting for his return from prison. However, Archer's health was permanently impaired and he was to die soon after his release.

The frequently orphaned Field-Heth brigade of Virginia veterans, once a pride of the Light Division, had drooped in morale while temporarily under command of Colonel Brockenbrough, fought poorly at Gettysburg and returned to Virginia in sad shape. Since then, the brigade had been taken in hand by a sound though unspectacular professional soldier, Henry Harrison ("Mud") Walker, a Virginian of the 1853 class of West Point. As Walker had been Brockenbrough's lieutenant colonel, the twice passed-over colonel resigned from the army in a huff. Displeased Confederate officers frequently resigned as from a club, though the going of Mud Walker's fellow Virginian on the whole benefited the brigade.

In the original formation of the division, Lee had wanted the return of two of his veteran brigades, then detached by President Davis in peripheral employment. Instead, the commander in chief held the veterans on guard duty and sent Lee two sets of strangers.

One of these, Pettigrew's North Carolinians, had performed well, though losing their brilliant leader. Currently under replacement Kirkland, the soldiers were regarded as sufficiently dependable veterans to form the advance of Hill's corps into the Wilderness.

The other brigade, containing some green troops mixed in with fine Mississippi regiments, had been commanded by the President's inexperienced nephew, Brigadier General Joseph Davis. Under the puny leadership of this peacetime lawyer, the brigade was ragged at Gettysburg despite the inspired performance of those Mississippi units built on the nucleus of ante-bellum militia companies of college students. As Heth was wounded on the first day at Gettysburg, the division's performance was spotty and it returned to Virginia low in spirit and weak in numbers.

The heavy losses were made up by the addition of a fifth brigade, Cooke's North Carolinians, whom Lee had wanted in the original formation of Heth's division. John R. Cooke, Jeb Stuart's brother-in-law and intimate, had grown up in the old army where his father won fame with his dragoons on the Mormon Trail. Young Cooke had eschewed an army career, graduating from Harvard, but as a volunteer he was an able and devoted officer at his rank. In appearance he was distinguished by a hole in his forehead, resulting from a wound taken in battle. John R. Cooke and his father broke off relations when Philip St. George Cooke remained with the Union forces, and the son's men told a story on him at Seven Pines. Hearing that Philip St. George Cooke led a cavalry regiment in his area, John R. Cooke said, "Let's go down and stir up Papa."

Joseph Davis's Mississippians were helped by the continued absence of their brigadier, as senior colonel Stone, though officially only in temporary command, proved an able leader of the no longer green troops.

In rebuilding the morale of this division, Heth revealed his best qualities as a soldier. As they deployed across the Plank Road in feeling out the mostly hidden enemy, his troops were all battle-wise, capable of tremendous fire power and group tenacity. At least adequately led everywhere, the units had by then served together sufficiently to perform in dependable coordination of action. But in command of any development movement against the enemy on the Brock Road was affable Heth, the good soldier who had never enjoyed a really good day as division commander, and who on the road to Gettysburg had blundered into the Federal infantry and precipitated the battle before Lee was ready.

Coming up behind Heth were the four brigades from the old Light Division, now Wilcox's division. The regiments in this division were mostly built on volunteer units from the earliest days, some extending from elegant prewar militia companies. The South Carolinians were particularly distinguished by the social prominence of the private soldiers and in the first year their messes had been marvels of splendor.

By May of 1864, the soldiers of illustrious lineage were indistinguishable from the canebrake and red-hill boys, but their leaders still reflected the background of the units. With not a single of the original brigadiers surviving with the division (most were dead), the present brigade commanders provided an unique illustration of a patriot army: none was a professional soldier and each was a learned man of privilege.

The North Carolina brigade was led by thirty-one-year-old James Lane, a tidewater Virginian of plantation background, educated at V.M.I. and the University of Virginia; a college professor in North Carolina when war came, Lane joined a volunteer regiment commanded by his friend and Jackson's brother-in-law, D. H. Hill. The other North Carolina brigade was led by Alfred Scales, a thirty-seven-year-old lawyer and politician, who had served one term in the United States Congress; he enlisted as a private.

With the Georgia brigade was Edward Thomas, thirty-nine, a scholarly planter who had often refused political office; with experience in the Mexican War, Thomas had been personally authorized by Davis to raise a regiment for the Confederacy. The somewhat bedraggled survivors of the South Carolina dandies were commanded by flamboyant Samuel MacGowan, lawyer and politician, also with Mexican War experience.

Their dates of rank were in the pre-Gettysburg era and, though none was considered for higher command, each was capable where he was and all were devoted and energetic. Their long association gave them an almost casual familiarity with the others' type of performance, and provided that coordination of action which Lee felt to be essential in his outnumbered army. This quality was particularly necessary in a division which had first lost its idolized leader when A. P. Hill was promoted to corps command and then lost Dorsey Pender, their first division commander in the new organization.

Plain-looking, chunky Cadmus Wilcox had come to them as a stranger after Pender was killed at Gettysburg. A forty-year-old bachelor, born in North Carolina of parents from Connecticut, Wilcox was a professional soldier, graduating with Stonewall Jackson, McClellan and Pickett in the great 1846 class at West Point. Powell Hill had matriculated in that class, though he dropped out of the Point for a year due to illness. Hill had not known Wilcox intimately at any time, and during the war they had served in separate corps until Wilcox came to the newly organized Third Corps as a brigadier in the division, Anderson's, transferred from Longstreet's corps.

Prior to his promotion on succeeding Pender, Wilcox, making
brigadier as early as October, 1861, had been repeatedly passed over
at promotion time. This slowness in advance need not imply lack of
ability. Assuming the absence of one of those conspicuous performances that attracted the army's attention, failure to advance could
mean only a lack of personal supporters or the chance of serving in
a unit where no changes were made, or both. Before the losses in
general officers at Gettysburg, Lee preferred to make promotions
within a division, and Longstreet's divisions suffered the fewest losses
among general officers in the army. Lee's selection of forthright
Wilcox from Anderson's division to command four brigades strange
to him indicated a recognition of the old pro's sound qualities. Also,
as state-consciousness was always a consideration with a parochial
people, his North Carolina birthplace made him palatable to a division dominated by Tarheels.

Coming up behind Heth in the area of Lee's informal command
post at the Tapp farm, sturdy Wilcox, his broad face broadened by
bushy side whiskers, was bringing to the field as tough a fighting
division as could be put into battle. The proud men across all ranks
had become proud soldiers, and there is no tougher breed.

Lee did not order Wilcox to hurry his troops forward to support
Heth, whose last regiments were then disappearing into the green
brush off the Plank Road. In the unsettled situation caused by that
troublesome gap to the north, Lee must wait for rather than force
developments, with only the two divisions available for the right
wing of the army. He considered anything else too precipitate with
Hill's 3rd Division a day's march away.

This was the division of Major General Richard H. Anderson,
transferred out of Longstreet's First Corps. From the beginning no
warmth of accord existed between Hill and the reserved South
Carolinian. Probably Anderson never liked the shift away from
Longstreet, his friend since they were classmates at West Point, and
he may have been influenced by his friend's ill-feeling toward
Powell Hill. After the bitter clash between Hill and Longstreet in
'62, Hill, no grudge-holder, later established surface civilities, but
Longstreet carried the rancor to the end of his life. Then, neither
Hill nor Anderson were men to develop close relationships easily;
Hill never established another close military relationship after Pen-

der's death. Certainly unassertive Dick Anderson was not a type to feel at ease in the comparatively casual order with which Hill operated his corps, in contrast to Longstreet's familiar tight rein.

The two reserved men, one warm of manner, one low-keyed, got off to an unsatisfactory start in the first major action they shared, at Gettysburg, when General Lee placed Anderson between his new corps commander and his former commander in an ambiguous command situation. Anderson was subject to the orders of both Hill and Longstreet, with neither of them responsible for his division. Under the circumstances his performance was understandably inadequate, though two of his brigadiers (who performed well despite the situation) blamed him for a supineness they found inexcusable under any circumstances.

General Lee did not reproach Anderson. Long regarding him as a "capital officer," his highest praise, Lee had Dick Anderson tabbed for possible corps command. But courteous, colorless Anderson made no partisans in the Third Corps. His friends were in the old First Corps, where he was missed, and he seemed on something like a temporary assignment with Hill's new corps.

Of his five veteran brigades, one quite small, none was led by a professional soldier, though three brigadiers held dates of rank going back to '61 and '62. These were "Billy" Mahone, the Virginia bantam from V.M.I., "Rans" Wright, a thirty-eight-year-old Georgia lawyer, and Edward A. Perry, the Massachusetts-born Yale man, who left his law practice in Pensacola and led three Florida regiments. On Wilcox's promotion to major general, his Alabamians went to Abner Perrin, upped to brigadier for his superb handling of MacGowan's brigade at Gettysburg. On the Mississippi brigade, the fallen Carnot Posey was replaced by newly promoted Nathaniel Harris, a Natchez lawyer just under thirty, an aggressive leader and an able man.

In numbers, Anderson's division was only slightly smaller than Heth's and Wilcox's, not enough to account for Hill's selecting his division to remain as rear guard. Heth and Wilcox might not offer all that Little Powell wished of companions, but they were familiar, and Anderson remained behind, with the corps' reserve artillery.

The Third Corps' glory was its artillery, beginning with its chief of artillery. Colonel Lindsay Walker was physically perhaps the most impressive officer in an army of men superbly developed by outdoor life. He stood six feet four on an immense frame, with a great spread of shoulders, and, very handsome, his looks were given a boldness by a sweeping black mustache and imperial and dark hair worn long above a massive brow. A superb rider (though he must have experienced some difficulty in finding horses up to his weight in 1864), Walker made a spectacular figure riding among his guns.

Thirty-seven-year-old Walker, a V.M.I. graduate and peacetime civil engineer, began in the army as captain of a Richmond-raised volunteer battery, and from the first he demonstrated his great gift for organization. Only Armistead Long, with regular army training, was possibly his equal. As an artillerist he lacked Long's tactical proficiency and the intuitiveness of the First Corps' young Alexander. Walker's leadership was characterized by his strong will, with its readily communicated determination, and by the handling of his battalion commanders, three of whom were among the very best in the army. These were twenty-three-year-old Willie Pegram, the shy scholar from Richmond, his brother-in-law, David McIntosh of South Carolina, and twenty-eight-year-old William Poague, a Washington College graduate, whose guns were unlimbering in the Tapp farm clearing.

Taken as a whole, the brigades and gun batteries of the Third Corps gave General Lee every reason for confidence "in the men's ability to maintain themselves successfully against heavy odds." However, the lack of contact between the two wings of the army on the field restrained Lee from placing the decision in the fighting power of his soldiers. Instead, while the commanding general was waiting for Heth's division to form in position, something happened to make that intervening space of sudden and desperate urgency. General Lee was nearly captured.

3

Lee, Hill and Stuart were sitting quietly under a tree, physically relaxed in the indolent warmth of the afternoon sun, when a line of Federal soldiers popped out of a nearby field of pines on their left, to the north. The enemy troops did not appear to be lost, which they were, for they headed straight for the little group of Confederate generals under the tree.

With one rush, those unidentified soldiers of Meade could have brought a quick finish to the war right then, on May 5th, 1864. Lee jumped up first, turning to call to AAG Walter Taylor an unrecorded order. Stuart arose slowly, as Hill's chief of staff said, "looking the danger straight in the face." Hill never moved at all. Without changing position, he surveyed the situation with what a contemporary described as "the wonderful gentleness" of his eyes.

The Federal officer was as startled as his potential bag of prisoners. Himself lost in the trackless brush, and not recognizing the generals or their rank, he was aware only of having stumbled into the Confederate lines. With a quick order, he turned his men about. As suddenly as they had appeared, the Federal soldiers vanished back into the Wilderness.

The effect on Lee as a general was immediate. Heth was in position then, with the fire growing heavier between him and the enemy, and Lee wanted the Brock Road as passionately as Meade wanted to defend it. But, as Wilcox's division came up, instead of sending his brigades in to support Heth, Lee directed the troops off to the left of the road with orders to probe toward Ewell's right and develop the enemy's strength in the woods between the two roads. After Wilcox's brigades began groping their way northward, stirring up no more than light bursts of fire and sending back small bodies of prisoners, Lee turned his attention back to the Plank Road action. It was then nearing four o'clock and the General seemed to be of a more divided mind than when he halted.

With Ewell's battle unresolved as far as he knew, Lee was unwilling to be drawn into a second large action with only the troops at hand. Yet he was equally unwilling to pass the opportunity of striking for the Brock Road. He resolved the dilemma by a compromise. He wrote a note to Harry Heth and asked him if he believed he could carry the Brock Road intersection without bringing on a "general engagement."

Heth sent back an honest answer which was no help at all. He reported that the enemy was gathered in force along the Brock Road, and he could not determine the extent to which an assault would spread the action. If the General wished him to find out, he was ready to attack. While Lee pondered over this back at the farm clearing, the issue suddenly was taken out of his hands. The enemy lunged forward in overwhelming force.

While Getty's division had, after its full deployment, pressed hard against Heth's lines, Hancock's corps had gradually come up into position on either side of Getty. Winfield Scott Hancock might be a close friend of many Southerners from the old army, but no general in the Federal armies surpassed him in the skill and combativeness with which he fought Southern troops. The tall professional soldier also held a respect for their fighting qualities. As he aligned his twenty-five-thousand-man corps along Brock Road, he prudently built a breastworks of logs and earth before preparing his assault. During the afternoon, Meade and Grant had grown overanxious to mount an assault led by Getty, and around four o'clock Hancock was ordered to go in before he completed the careful disposition of his troops.

This was no business of developing Lee's strength. In their familiarity with one another's armies, Meade knew that Lee had no troops at hand to support Heth along the road and Wilcox in the gap. His orders were to drive Hill back to Parker's Store, chewing up his two divisions, and clear the north-south passage once and for all.

Hurried out, as with the earlier attack on Ewell, the assaulting units did not move simultaneously and bring the full force of their numbers to the point of contact. If they had, Heth's men could not have maintained themselves against the power. As it was, Heth's men could not have held as long as they did against the weight in the successive waves on any other field except the Wilderness.

4

Getty's division had worked its way forward in the concealing thickets to within one hundred yards of Heth's lines before his men opened the attack on both sides of the road, heavier on the Confederate right than left. Soon after Getty's division opened its close-range fire around four in the afternoon, Birney's division on the Federal right and Mott's division on the Federal left began to advance with deep-chested shouts. At four-thirty, their advance was supported by two fresh brigades from Gibbon's division, one north of the road and one on the road, bulging out to the south. By five o'clock, heavy-jawed Hancock had sent upwards of thirty thousand soldiers driving through the entangled woods at the line that, in the beginning, contained only Heth's seven thousand.

Harry Heth was at his soundly competent best. On the right of the road, he had drawn his line along a heavily wooded elevation which overlooked a swampy hollow in his immediate front. A stand of the wiry saplings climbed the rise from the swamp to his line. Using the time of Lee's indecision to build a low breastwork, he placed his men prone behind a log embankment, in a position like a fort with hidden firing holes.

With the shooting of both sides guided mostly by smoke and sound, the attacking forces fired at estimated targets about four feet from the ground. The virtually solid sheets of lead slashed off the tops of the saplings in a breast-high swath so complete that not a standing man could have survived the fire. But not a man was standing.

Heth's soldiers, prone behind their logworks, had the proper elevation in their fire into the masses floundering toward them, and did not need to pause to aim. The fastest men with those muzzle-loaders could get off three shots a minute under these conditions. At an average of two shots a minute, in ten minutes seven thousand men, with low casualties, could pour more than a hundred thousand leaden slugs into massed units at close range. Even this deadly fire power, with the relatively protected position of most of Heth's division, could not indefinitely contain the weight of successive waves manned by fresh troops.

For the early stages, Heth's brigades on the right of the road were helped in holding the major portion of line by the boggy ground the attacking troops were forced to cover. On both sides of the road, the Federal regiments were hampered in advancing the solid lines by the density of the vines that caused units to lose direction and alignment. They groped forward as they fired, mostly at sound and flashes. As the smoke thickened like fog in the woods and the sound began to scatter in all directions, both sides were fighting blind. The stationary troops, however, could hold their alignment. Then, as Hancock continually fed in fresh units, late in the afternoon the unrelenting pressure took its toll of Heth's brigades. The killed were low in numbers, for the intensity of the fighting, but the loss from wounded, though running high in slight wounds that would not list the men as casualties for long, opened gaps in the solidity of the defense.

On the left, Kirkland's brigade became almost enveloped by more than a full division of the enemy. The line of the other brigades, with the men nearly fought out, became interspersed with loose bodies of enemy troops, until the front as such began to dissolve.

Only all-veteran troops would have fought on, and not they had the Wilderness not hidden what was happening on their right flank. Extending Hancock's line to the south, two fresh brigades of Barlow's division pushed their way unopposed westward from the Brock Road to a space beyond the last man on the right of Heth's shattered line.

At the opening of the assault on Heth's division, General Lee had estimated at once the weight of the attacking force and hastily dispatched a courier to recall Wilcox's division. Whatever *might* happen in the gap between Hill and Ewell, unless Heth was helped, disaster on the Plank Road was a certainty.

5

When the courier went searching for Wilcox, General Wilcox had just completed his assignment of locating Ewell's right. Cadmus Wilcox had ridden, he judged, about a mile and a half, partly through the dense woods adjoining the Plank Road, then across a wide field on which stood a farmhouse, and then through more woods, when he found John B. Gordon, flushed with victory, holding Ewell's right flank.

On the ride, Wilcox had left two brigades in the woods between the Plank Road and the open field, and sent the other two forward across the field to the facing woods on the east. Wilcox had hardly more than greeted Gordon when he heard the sudden rattle of musketry in the woods east of the clearing. Spinning his white horse around, Wilcox started riding as fast as possible though the woods toward the firing. When he broke out into the clearing, Lee's courier spied him and galloped up with the urgent message to return his dispersed division to the Plank Road. Heth was in peril.

Wilcox quickly discovered that his two advanced brigades were no more seriously involved than a collision fight with a stray force of Federals wandering about between the two battles. Little time was required to disengage his brigades. They withdrew with two hundred or so prisoners, and the remnants of the enemy troops seemed relieved enough to start back to their own lines.

Wilcox, leaving not a soldier south of Gordon's brigade, ordered Thomas and Lane to hurry toward the Plank Road. Then he galloped across the wide field to the woods where he had left his other two brigades nearer the road. Pulling in his horse to push into the screen of vine-shrouded trees, the new division commander discovered that his men had already been sent in. Whether Lee or Hill had moved the brigade, Wilcox did not ask. In his first big test in command of the bulk of the old Light Division, forthright Cadmus Wilcox showed himself to be a cooperative and energetic soldier.

Moving on ahead of his two following brigades, he learned that Sam MacGowan had thrown his South Carolinians in across the road where Kirkland connected with John Cooke. MacGowan's veterans had gone in charging with their high scream and struck the enemy where the Federal units, their drive spent, were fighting in the confusion of Heth's disordered lines. This first Confederate counterattack, rolling forward in solid lines, drove the dispersed Federals before them, back toward the Brock Road.

Scales's North Carolinians had crossed to the south of the road and hastily formed in the gaps of Heth's line back of the swampy hollow. By the time Wilcox learned of the disposition of these two of his brigades, which he could not see at all, Thomas came up with his Georgians on the left.

There Kirkland's flank was engulfed by swarms of the enemy, some then working around to the rear. With whatever shortcomings the North Carolinians found in their new brigadier, unshaken Kirkland held his regiments steadily to their work and the men were too embroiled in the melee to be aware of the danger to their rear. The density of the saplings and the underbrush in that area prevented the loosely grouped Federal units from forming a perpendicular line for enfilade fire on Heth's flank, and for a moment they did not seem to recognize their advantage. In that moment of grace, Thomas's four Georgia regiments crashed their way toward Kirkland's rescue.

Wilcox saw that Thomas's brigade could not make their way through the thrashing Federal units to establish contact with Kirkland. Instead, the enemy troops who had been pushing toward Heth's rear turned on Thomas's fresh regiments.

Disordered, the panting men of both sides merged in a violent, personal, formless action, like, a Union officer said, "bushwhacking on a grand scale." Thomas's men were fighting at right angles to one another and even back to back. Where even officers, drawing back from the milling mobs, could not see twenty yards in any direction, such military objectives as flanks ceased to be a factor. The single absorbing purpose of Hill's men, from privates to Wilcox, was to refuse to break backward.

In his urgency, sturdy Wilcox grew a little excited. As Jim Lane came out of the woods on the left with the last brigade, Wilcox directed him to a position and then went galloping down the road on his white horse. He wanted to pull MacGowan back from the advanced position to which the brigade's impetuous charge had carried it.

By that time, troops on MacGowan's right had moved forward with the impetus of his drive. As their advance had been made more or less spontaneously, no one had informed Wilcox and he could not see them. In turn, he failed to inform anyone that he was withdrawing MacGowan.

Soon after Wilcox took off down the road, Colonel Palmer, Hill's young chief of staff, came riding up to Jim Lane. General Hill wanted Lane's brigade to hurry at once to the right. As a change of orders should be cleared through his division commander, the thirty-one-year-old college professor hesitated. Lane had taught military tactics at V.M.I. when Stonewall Jackson was there, and had been teaching tactics at the North Carolina Military Institute when war came, but nothing in his classroom experience prepared the brigadier general for emergency military etiquette on the battlefield. Lane, however, had served with Little Powell a long time, and accepted the orders brought by his chief of staff.

He pushed his North Carolina regiments across the road to the south, where A. P. Hill personally directed Lane to the support of Scales's shaken brigade. When his last squad moved about one hundred yards beyond the road, Lane faced the brigade to the front and sent the regiments rushing forward with, as he said, "their usual battle yell."

The troops bore right in moving forward, passing clumps of Heth's bewildered survivors and spreading to include the less battered regiments of Scales's brigade. Little resembling a battle line existed for Lane to align on. Light was falling then, smoke hung in the thickets like fog, and the musket crackle all around roared, one of the soldiers said, "like fire in a canebrake."

At some point, after MacGowan's thrust up the road relieved the pressure on Heth's brigades, Harry Heth had ordered a limited counterattack. The sudden loss of the initiative by the stalemated Federals in Heth's front caused them to fall back. Veterans rushed away from the bedlam in which, a South Carolina private said, "every man was his own general."

Heth's men exultantly followed to the Brock Road, passing Mac-Gowan without seeing that his brigade was drawing back on Wilcox's orders. Lane's men with some of Scales's, stumbling ahead in the wake of Heth, were uncovered on their left by MacGowan's withdrawal. Of this they also were ignorant.

In the general confusion, the Lane-Scales advance was slowed by passage through the swamp which had hampered the earlier Federal thrusts. They were climbing up the eastern slope, falling over dead logs, when a galling fire opened on their left flank and in front of the left regiment. The 7th North Carolina had been holding its fire to avoid shooting into what the men supposed to be MacGowan's South Carolinians, and the enemy's lead rained into them from a distance of only seventy-five yards.

Before Lane could move to help the 7th on his left, his right suddenly confronted a huge flanking movement wheeling out of the dusky woods to threaten their rear. These were the two fresh brigades of Barlow's division, the last wave, the fifth, sent in by aggressive Hancock.

Using his tactical studies as coolly as if at blackboard, Jim Lane broke back two companies to face the wheeling movement, and then changed the front of his whole right regiment. The regiment could not contain the weight pressing on them in the dusk, and the men were forced backward.

During Lane's action, some of Heth's men had made it all the way to the Brock Road. There martial-looking Hancock rallied troops behind the log breastwork he had prudently built before Grant hurried his assault. Against these works, Heth's disordered units fell back into the then familiar protectiveness of the Wilderness. Immediately the Federals came on after them.

Back toward the swamp went Heth's tired men, many of them not making it. In the gathering darkness, some of Heth's fragments recrossed the swamp, mingling with the separately engaged units of Lane and Scales. By this time, Lane's right and left were both pressed back, the 7th North Carolina breaking out of nearly total envelopment. Having no superior to communicate with, Lane withdrew his two center regiments to the works where Heth had made his stand at the beginning.

Surveying the broken patchwork of his front after his counterattack, Heth said, "I should have let well enough alone." This was indeed a sound after-the-fact judgment.

The inexhaustible enemy still crowded forward, rifle fire streaking through the shadowed woods.

Colonel Venable, of Lee's staff, and Jeb Stuart had ridden to the lines to study the chances of Hill's men holding on until full darkness. Venable expressed the sentiment of every Confederate on the field when he murmured, "If night would only come."

At this point, when it seemed that flesh and spirit could endure no more, an excited courier told A. P. Hill that the enemy at last was pushing troops — a whole division of them — into the gap between his left and Ewell's right. Hill knew that not one fought-out regiment could disengage itself. Slightly in the rear one battalion of 125 Alabamians guarded the swelling crowd of Federal prisoners. This 5th Alabama Battalion, the provost guard of the Third Corps, must do the job.

Turning over the prisoners to any noncombatants at hand, Hill formed the provost guard into a skirmish line and pointed their direction into the murky brush. He told them to rush ahead firing and give the Rebel Yell, as though they were followed by brigades.

The 125 men, led by a major, crashed into the gloomy thickets, firing as fast as they could load, and shrieking like banshees. The division floundering toward Hill's exposed left was Wadsworth's, of Warren's corps, the same division that had lost direction in moving out on Griffin's flank in the noon action against Ewell. This was not the day for Wadsworth, the white-maned Hudson River patroon. The screams of the unseen enemy in that chartless jungle were enough for him. His division's movement stumbled to a halt, as night came at last, and firing dwindled off across the jagged front.

6

At the clearing of Widow Tapp's farm, where Poague had posted his sixteen guns, a fire was built beside the wheels of the piece nearest the road. There a spent and exultant Hill set up temporary headquarters.

Little Powell had experienced his greatest day as a corps commander. With corps command at the executive level assumed by Lee, Hill had reverted to that type of personal direction of combat in which he had excelled at division command. His hollow cheeks pale above his well-brushed fox-red beard, he had ridden recklessly back and forth behind the lines, directing units and exhorting his men.

As with Ewell on the Turnpike, Hill led troops on that field in the area of command for which nature fitted him. His two divisions contained only three more brigades than had his old division, and numbered no more than its peak strength. Unburdened of those responsibilities of surveying the whole field, of forming a correlative decision before acting, A. P. Hill had once again released his emotional tension in the direct action of combat. Once again the rush of the intensity of his spirit communicated itself to his men, and Hill's corps fought on that long afternoon in the great tradition of Hill's Light Division.

Similar to other non-political-minded Southerners with strong Union ties, Hill became during the war a most devoted Confederate; he was one of the men who suffered personal hurt from what he called "the cloven hoof" shown by his former comrades in the vindictiveness of the war they carried into his homeland. But Hill was proud, and the pride of a sensitive man was gratified by holding his troops to their ground that day.

Fought into exhaustion, with their lines split into broken fragments without form or order, his fourteen thousand had contained more than twice their number, not counting the 125 Alabamians against Wadsworth's division, and the waves kept coming in the power and determination that characterized Hancock's troops in action. Not one enemy regiment fought poorly; no alignments had been faulty and no enemy flanks had hung in the air. The Third Corps divisions had stood up to the best there was, and high-strung Hill's heart overflowed with pride for every man in the corps.

With the crises of the exhausting day behind him, a reaction set in. Around nine o'clock, huddled in the flickering light of the campfire, he looked sick. Hill was not then too ill to get about; it was two days more before he gave up and took to an ambulance. However, Harry Heth believed that Powell Hill was sick enough that night not to be wholly responsible for his actions, and used this in building something of a case against his commanding officer.

The issue concerned the lack of any effort to straighten the lines in Heth's and Wilcox's fragmented divisions during the night. The men were allowed to sleep where they were when night came, and the disordered units were in no position to receive attack the following morning. Heth, with his awareness of his army record, was acutely self-conscious about the exposed condition in which the morning found his division. In writing about the incident after the war (not in his official report), he was motivated by a lingering need of self-vindication.

Though the soul of honor in social relations, Heth, like many another general on both sides, inclined toward a somewhat heavy editing of even his official reports. In Heth's unofficial account of the night of May 5th, his omissions are at variance with three other accounts by at least equally competent witnesses — including especially Wilcox, whose division was also involved. Heth's version has usually been accepted for one simple reason: in shifting all blame from himself to A. P. Hill, it also removed all responsibility for the disordered lines from Lee.

Here recurs the influence of that statuesque image of Lee, which caused his admirers to remove from the man the effects of tension, of strain and relief, of anxiety and excited confidence, of all the rise and fall of man's tidal flows of inner energies.

At all times the proper alignment of regiments in routine preparation against attack is the responsibility of the whole organization, from corporals to commanding general. On the specific lapse in Hill's corps on the night of May 5th, to single out anyone as the culprit — as history has followed Heth in singling out A. P. Hill — is to go in the face of general custom and the surrounding facts of that night.

No one has ever discovered where the initial order originated, but, after the shock of battle began to wear off the officers, generals began to talk of the dangerous position in which the troops had fallen asleep. The largest units together were squads, whose men had stacked their six or seven rifles and dropped to the ground in exhaustion. No fires were built. Some men kept awake long enough to draw a short ration of bacon and hardtack that got to the front, and others fell into a drugged sleep without, for once, thinking of their hunger pangs.

Brigade units were scattered and intermingled with other brigades. The enemy lay close enough in some spots for the two lines to conduct conversations in a normal voice, if any one had known where the others were. Though the sky was clear and cloudless, the intermingling treetops, with the vines and creepers, shut out all night light, and close to the ground was as black as a cave. Spaces between units were such that one soldier, who blundered into Federal lines and ran, said that he ran all the way back to where Lee's tent was pitched without encountering a single Confederate.

Colonel Davidson, who so handsomely fought his 7th North Carolina out of their encirclement, crept to a small stream to cool his parched throat, and was as quietly gathered up by a group of Federals as if snatched by Indians. A short distance away, Colonel Baldwin, of the 1st Massachusetts, went to the same stream and suffered a like fate at the silent hands of a Confederate group.

Officers worked their way back to Heth and Wilcox to report that their lines were "very irregular and much broken." Both generals recognized the urgent need of alignment before morning brought a renewal of the attack. As then situated, "a skirmish line would drive both" divisions, Heth said. He and Wilcox went separately to A. P. Hill to inform him of the need of arousing the soldiers and moving them into an orderly line for receiving attack at daylight.

As Heth reported his visits to Hill, the corps commander told him, "Longstreet will be up in a few hours. He will form in your front. I don't purpose that you shall do any fighting tomorrow; the men have been marching and fighting all day and are tired. I don't wish them disturbed."

This solicitude of Hill's for his men was typical. The condition he managed to maintain in his troops was partly responsible for their endurance of the pressure from four o'clock until dark, past eight o'clock. Heth was not reassured by the promise of relief by Longstreet, and twice more sought out Hill. On the third visit, the naturally quiet voice of Little Powell rang with metal in it as he said, "Damn it, Heth, I don't want to hear any more about it. The men shall not be disturbed."

As far as this account goes, Hill alone would have been culpable of negligence. But Colonel Palmer, the chief of staff who remained beside Hill until after midnight, reported that General Hill told both Heth and Wilcox that "General Lee's orders were to let the men rest as they were." This is different from Hill's making the decision, and is borne out by Wilcox.

Wilcox, after his interview with A. P. Hill, went to Lee's tent with the purpose of bracing the Old Man directly. Before he spoke, General Lee told him that he had sent orders to Anderson and Longstreet to move forward. " 'He [Anderson] and Longstreet will be up,' Lee said, 'and the two divisions that have been so actively engaged will be relieved before day.' " Hearing from the commanding general that his division was to be replaced, Wilcox "made no suggestions about the line," and left. Since Wilcox did not inform Lee of the precise conditions of the lines, the General saw no reason to disturb the men before they withdrew from their positions. This fundamental misunderstanding occurred around ten o'clock.

However, A. P. Hill did not, as Heth inferred, dismiss the whole matter and give in to his illness. After ten o'clock, he began to grow nervous about Longstreet's arrival for the relief of his troops.

Around midnight, according to Colonel Palmer, Hill and his chief of staff rode to Lee's headquarters to learn what news General Lee had of the First Corps. Palmer wrote, "General Lee repeated his orders." After that, Palmer said, "The anxious night wore away slowly. . . . We could not sleep, but waited for news of Longstreet."

With the passage of time, soldiers tended to shape events to fit the design in which they wished to remember the past. Colonel Palmer may have been unconsciously motivated by a protectiveness toward the superior with whom he so closely associated, and missed accuracy in some details. In substance, he was verified by Wilcox and Colonel Venable, of Lee's staff, who stated that "It was [Lee's] intention to relieve Hill's two divisions with Longstreet's."

Without the corroboration, it is unlikely that even indulgent Hill would put his men's rest before their safety unless under orders from Lee to leave them until relieved before day. From the breaking of camp at Orange Court House, Hill had acted only under Lee's orders and initiated no action of his corps.

In a state of vigor similar to Heth and Wilcox, Hill might well have stirred himself to investigate the lines and then personally informed Lee of the dangerous condition of the front. Hill may have been speaking for himself as well as the troops when he said, "Let the tired men rest." To this extent, his physical ill-being and emotional exhaustion showed their effects in his following of Lee's order without informing the commanding general of the condition of his lines.

Yet vigorous Wilcox, who moved restlessly about most of the night, did not mention the lines to Lee after the General assured him that Longstreet would relieve his division. And Heth, apparently the most anxious of all, made no report to Lee, with whom he was on intimate terms. He said that he could not find headquarters, though Lee's accessible tent was pitched only a few hundred yards from the rear lines.

Heth alone, in trying to place the blame on Hill, omitted from Hill's reported remarks the words that "*General Lee said* Longstreet would be up by morning to relieve the troops." Heth alone seemed burdened by a need of self-vindication. Late in the war he talked to General Lee in an effort to shift the responsibility entirely on Hill, and Lee said to him, "A division commander should always have his division ready to receive attack."

Wilcox and Hill's chief of staff, both of whom wrote without knowledge of Heth's version, were not trying to place the blame on anyone. Feeling no personal guilt, they, like Colonel Venable, wrote their record of a lapse in command. This lapse was a general misunderstanding, a crack across the whole command structure.

The condition of the divisions' front should have been stressed to Lee, but the General revealed, by committing himself to the uncertainty of a daylight appearance by slow-moving Longstreet, that the critical day had affected him according to his nature as A. P. Hill was affected according to his. Where Hill's tensions had exhausted him, Lee was stimulated.

By ten o'clock that night Lee knew that Longstreet, with his van camped ten miles away, would not move out before one in the morning. By then General Lee had thrown off the anxious caution which restrained him during the day's separate battles. Exhilarated by his men's performance and the poor tactics of the overconfident enemy, the General returned to his original strategy and his thoughts raced ahead to the next day's counteroffensive. He planned to gather all available troops on the next morning for the tactical execution of his basic strategy. With his mind beyond the details of gathering the army, he was thinking of their strike toward a decision when the units *were* gathered.

General Lee and Powell Hill reacted differently to the stresses of the day, and the effects were clearly visible on hollow-eyed Hill, frail and spent as he relaxed by the campfire beside the wheel of the gun carriage. Outwardly Lee reacted as the historic figure of the legend, an immutable abstraction of command. Composed and apparently tireless, he sat erectly at the camp table in the candlelit tent and gave orders in a voice of quiet assurance. It is those orders which showed the effect of the day on him.

7

Lee appeared changeless because of the composure of his impressive presence, because of the harmonious character he created on a self-image instilled in his impressionable years, and because he never acted "out of character." All of his disparities were resolved within, as well as all of his decisions.

In the anguish of making the decision to resign his army commission, for hours Lee paced the floor of his bedroom. His wife heard him there, and that was how his ordeal became known, as he consulted no one. The anguish cut so deeply that in his brief letter of resignation to his superior and friend, General Scott, he could not suppress a reference to "the struggle it has cost me to separate myself from a service in which I have devoted all the best years of my life." That the struggle was resolved entirely within could only have made it the more painful, with the effect a lasting influence on his commitment to the success of the cause for which he made the sacrifice.

In his tent after the battles of May 5th, Lee, as habitually, did not trace for his staff or visiting generals the progression of his thoughts. The course went from the apprehensions of the night before, when Davis's wires distracted him, through the uncertainties of the day, with corps commanders in whom he lacked full confidence and the dangerous gap between his columns, to the vitalizing effect of success in a perilous action. The change was traced in his orders.

With all other fronts and insoluble problems forgotten for the time, his mind concentrated on the opportunities in the field before him for winning a victory which would disrupt all "the enemies' preconceived arrangements." He could not have been less mindful than other generals with him of the vulnerable position to which Grant had exposed the Army of the Potomac, nor of the clumsy direction of its battle.

In the beginning, Grant acted neither with the considered boldness of rushing his combat troops through the Wilderness nor with the rudimentary caution of keeping the army compactly grouped until his wagon train was well started southward. Instead the new commander in chief moved his groups on a timetable as if Lee's army was merely another item in the schedule, inherently harmless and with no initiative of its own. As in the West, Lee's army was there merely to be acted upon, according to Grant's initiative.

After a smartly done river crossing, the combat units rested in the Wilderness the night of the 4th. On the 5th, allowing the full day for the crossing of the wagons, the infantry was dispersed in four separate movements in a model of logistics that, however, virtually ignored the existence of an enemy army.

When Lee's army appeared in two columns on the flank of the march, its potential threat was underestimated and two separate attacks were made so hastily that the available power was dissipated in the first assault and not fully utilized in the second. Discounting Wadsworth's late, abortive blundering off to the north of Hill's flank, no advantage was taken of the gap between Lee's columns. Even the heavily armed, superbly mounted cavalry, using its weight in forcing tactics against Stuart's lighter troopers, were fought off and achieved no practical purpose.

Lee, then, could find every reason in the enemy's careless under-estimation of the Army of Northern Virginia to support his confidence in the ability of his fully gathered army to exploit the advantages of the Wilderness.

This confidence began to soar as early as six o'clock in the afternoon. This was two hours before Hill's divisions had proven that they could sustain themselves against the waves of the attack. Even as Jim Lane hurried his, the last available, brigade to support the collapsing right, Lee sent his first message to Ewell about plans for the next day. Before A. P. Hill sent the Alabama battalion in with a yell against the encroaching division in the gap, Lee sent Major Mc-Clellan, Stuart's chief of staff, riding off to Longstreet with a guide to lead his two divisions forward in a change of plans. By eight o'clock, when officers were praying that the slow-falling night would save the men, Lee had matured his plans for the morning's offensive and sent his second, detailed message to Ewell.

This surge of confidence reflected the rise of adrenalin that came to Lee in battle. Then he threw off those crippling, nagging worries over areas outside his control and matched his powers with a single opponent.

Rare were the commanding generals in personally led armies who fought as well as they planned, or vice versa, and among those rarities Lee was one whose mental processes were quickened by combat. Not a cold fighter, Lee was stirred in his deepest instincts by the ultimate contest of battle. On that night of the 5th, in reacting from the restricting apprehensions, he became an aroused old battler. Having taken the measure of a younger opponent, he was flushed with the urge to close with him.

8

For the next day, Lee planned to execute his offensive strategy with offensive tactics. Grant had led and now Lee would counter. Recognizing that Hill's two divisions would have little to bring to another battle on the following day, he planned to shift them into the troublesome gap, connecting solidly with Ewell's right. Longstreet and Anderson, a fresh fifteen thousand, would carry the attack.

In simplest design, those three divisions would wheel from the Plank Road to the south and roll up Grant's flank. Once Lee's men gained the Brock Road passageway, driving northward toward the river, Grant would be forced to retire toward the fords with little alternative except to recross the Rapidan.

Concurrent with this flanking movement, Ewell might be able to swing past the Federal right. Reports indicated that Grant was weakening his right, and a sharp thrust by the Second Corps veteran assault troops could possibly cut the Army of the Potomac off from Germanna Ford. Then the Federal army would be crowded into a more chaotic state than Hooker was caught in on the May of the past year.

Ewell's message at the end of his day's battle sounded confident and even belligerent. He seemed very gratified by his "rough handling" of Warren's corps. Reporting that his lines were intact and strongly fortified, he mentioned the possibility of attacking the enemy if the commanding general so advised. General Lee had sent him the two messages, which crossed Ewell's, advising him that he should attack if the enemy withdrew troops from the Wilderness area. Otherwise, he was to support the movement from the right. In either case, Ramseur's brigade was to be withdrawn from its picket duty westward along the river, and be brought forward in readiness for daylight action.

Apparently Lee did not reflect on the possible effect that this choice of a decision might exert on Dick Ewell. With his own blood up, it would seem that he expected his subordinates to share the aggressive will toward exploiting the opportunities offered by the present positions in the Wilderness. As the terrain nullified the superior Union guns, Ewell's battle had shown that the very mass of the Federal infantry worked against sharp movements and concert of action. In any event, the major blow was planned to come from Lee's right, delivered by Longstreet, his old reliable.

In his eagerness to carry the battle to the heart of the enemy's multiple offensive, Lee also took no heed of the possibility of Longstreet's divisions arriving late enough to disrupt his arrangements. Even after he was informed that Longstreet's van could not possibly come up before daylight, the General appeared unconcerned.

Everybody in the army knew that Lee's "Old War Horse" was slow to move. Congenitally resistant to hurry himself, as a general Longstreet was very methodical and disliked to extend his men. In two campaigns, Second Manassas and Gettysburg, his slowness in coming to action was the cause of considerable later-day talk over dead bivouacs.

On the 4th and 5th of May, Longstreet's two rested divisions of veterans were ordered to cover forty miles and be up by the morning of the 6th. In the timetable, Lee expected Longstreet to cover thirty miles by noon of the 5th, average marching time for fresh troops moving on uncontested roads. From there the divisions, allowing ample time for rest, could reach the field by midnight.

In Longstreet's original orders, he was to come up beyond Hill's right flank, on the Catharpin Road paralleling the Plank on the south. Sometime after six o'clock, Lee sent orders changing Longstreet's march to the Plank Road, to come up in relief of Hill. When those orders were sent, midnight was the assumed time of Longstreet's arrival.

Longstreet's van, however, had not made the thirty miles by noon, as Longstreet had reported to Lee it would, but not until five o'clock in the afternoon. Under no orders to hurry, though five hours behind schedule, Longstreet put his men in camp and gave his division commanders orders to move out at one in the morning. He was then cutting the time extremely close for an arrival early in the morning, and making no allowance for any emergency that might have developed with Lee's scant forces.

When Lee learned that Longstreet was camped ten miles away,

he then sent the cavalry's Major McClellan with a guide to lead the First Corps across country to the Plank Road and with verbal orders for the leading division to move out at once. It happened that the commander of the leading division was Charles Field, a newly promoted major general who had previously been a stranger to the First Corps, and complications developed.

Charlie Field had distinguished himself as a brigadier with Hill's original Light Division and, when he was wounded out with a leg amputation, his replacement in brigade command was one of the most difficult the army experienced. By the time Field was ready to return to duty, with a promotion to major general, Hood's old division in Longstreet's corps was in trouble over Hood's replacement. Longstreet disliked the brigadier who was scheduled to replace Hood, but was blocked in trying to promote his favorite over him. To resolve the issue one-legged Charlie Field, was assigned by the war office, over Longstreet's violent protests, to assume command of the division.

Probably not at ease with his new corps commander under the circumstances, and on his best behavior, usually jovial Field became stiff-necked about army protocol when Major McClellan, a young Philadelphian, brought him Lee's order. A thirty-eight-year-old Kentuckian of Virginia background, Charlie Field was regular army cavalry and had been an instructor at West Point when war came. Becoming every inch old army, Field refused to accept verbal orders which conflicted with existing orders from his corps commander. He told the fuming McClellan that he would march out at one o'clock and not before.

At ten o'clock, McClellan indignantly reported the episode to Lee and asked for a written order to take back to the regulations-bound General Field. Lee was undisturbed. Pointing out that it would be nearly one o'clock before the cavalry staff officer could ride back in the dark, the General said that Field would be moving out his division by the time McClellan reached him.

Lee's equable acceptance of the leading division's arrival after daylight could be explained only by the resurgence of his natural aggressive spirit, after throwing off the earlier distasteful caution, and by his lack of knowledge about Hill's disordered lines. When he said that Hill's men should not be disturbed until relieved, Lee obviously assumed some order in the division's front. Hill and Wilcox, in not advising him of the contrary, assumed that Longstreet would be up before daylight. Neither knew that the supporting troops were starting cross-country, as late as one o'clock, when Hill and Wilcox were already growing nervous, and could not possibly reach the field by daylight. It was one of those misunderstandings, and not an isolated one, inevitable in an army which sustained itself and the weakening country behind it on the personal leadership of one aging man, undermined with a heart condition.

On four hours sleep the night before, he had fought his mental battles alone from daylight until after midnight. Not once during the long day did the image of the legend falter, and this changeless image of calm resolution was part of the leadership to his men. No matter what was happening on the field, there sat the Old Man on Traveler, a statue rising out of the smoke, immutable and indestructible. This was Lee to his army.

The destruction was taking place inside the man. Some time after midnight, General Lee lay down on his cot for another four hours sleep before his day of decision.

CHAPTER SIX

"There Are No Ifs"

A S HABITUAL with Longstreet, his troops had been slow to move out when they broke their temporary camp at Gordonsville on May 4th. No half-cooked dough or raw meal went into his men's haversacks. The columns were not formed until three days' Confederate rations, mostly corn pone, had been cooked and distributed. Then the men were put on the road methodically, and walked steadily without pressing.

Though thirty miles in a day and a half was a Confederate average for fresh troops, not regarded as a forced march, some of the troops felt pushed when they went into bivouac at five o'clock on the afternoon of May 5th. As their work showed the next day, this was not lack of conditioning. It was loss of the practice customary with Lee's army.

After an eight-hour rest, the two divisions moved out around one o'clock in the morning. This was the time when Hill, Heth and Wilcox were growing nervous over Longstreet's approach. If they had known that he was *then* beginning a ten-mile night march across country — by woods' lanes and cowpaths, and not a single road — Hill's men might have been disturbed in their sleep of exhaustion along their unformed lines in the Wilderness.

As it happened, Longstreet's men made one of their best marches that night. It is not known if division commander Field told his corps commander about Major McClellan's verbal order to move out earlier. But Longstreet did know their destination had been changed, to support an action in which Hill was heavily engaged. For the troops, when a guide led them through a roadless, black countryside, a sense of urgency kept the men stumbling ahead on a march remembered in detail long after major battles were forgotten.

The two divisions pushing through the night formed scarcely more than a remnant of the once powerful First Corps that acted as the Dependables in the great days of the Army of Northern Virginia. With Pickett's rebuilding division detached, ten thousand was the highest estimate of the troops with Longstreet. This number was reached by the return of recuperated sick and wounded from furloughs, with a scattering of recently turned eighteen-year-olds as conscripts, and all were in hard case from the winter in the Tennessee mountains. Through no fault of Longstreet's careful husbandry during his independent command, his supply system had run afoul of the administration's bureaucratic agencies and the men's suffering had been extreme even for Confederates.

On their return to Virginia in April, the men worked all hours to make a presentable appearance when the corps was reviewed by Lee. Buttons, belt buckles, rifles and bayonets, everything that could be made bright, were polished to shine against the carefully darned and patched tatters. At the sight of the men, Lee wept; at the sight of him, the men wept.

After this moving reunion, no troops with Lee were more eager than Longstreet's divisions to be the pride of the army. Fortunately for their morale, the soldiers were untouched by the discords in high command. Most of the men were unaware of their commanding general's vendettas with subordinates during his disappointments in independent command and his consequent low status with the war office. Then, despite the lasting bitterness created by the changes in general officers, the units were well served by all of their leaders, new and old.

Hood's old division, leading the way across the black countryside under Charles Field, had been the bone of greatest contention. At basis, when John B. Hood was wounded out at Chickamauga (and slated for corps command with the Western army), his choice of successor was Brigadier General Evander Law, a romantic-looking young South Carolina educator. Law and Longstreet were antithetical types, and Longstreet, a man who leaned strongly to favorites, wished the division to go to Micah Jenkins, another South Carolina educator.

Jenkins's large South Carolina brigade had been withheld from Pickett's division in the Gettysburg campaign and, in fine condition, was transferred to Hood's division when Longstreet went west. There was no question about the ability of Micah Jenkins, one of the most admired brigadiers in the army. But it happened that he and Law, both brilliant scholars of privileged backgrounds, had been bitter rivals since their days at the Citadel.

When Longstreet tried to override opposition in giving the division to Jenkins, dreamy-eyed Law revealed such a talent for behind-the-scenes Machiavellian tactics that Longstreet was never quite certain what happened. In brief, exploiting Hood's cozy relations with the war office, Law maneuvered Longstreet into a losing contest with a Richmond cabal that had none of Lee's long-suffering patience with the Dutchman's stubbornness. When Field, whose reputation had been made with the hated A. P. Hill, was given the division, Longstreet tried to vent his rage on Law, whom he vaguely recognized as the author of his frustrations.

Even as Law's crack Alabama brigade was marching through the early morning hours of May 6th, papers from Longstreet were with Lee, demanding that he intercede with the war office and force the Adjutant General to hold the young South Carolinian under arrest. Time took care of all these personality difficulties and, in moving toward Hill's relief, the division was favored by having two of its brigades led by ambitious young men of division-command caliber.

A third brigade, forever famed as "Hood's Texans," had also been involved in Longstreet's personality troubles. Hood's successor, Dr. Jerome Robertson, had been hounded out of the army because of some spite of the corps commander, and replaced by John Gregg. Thirty-five-year-old Gregg, an Alabama native who practiced law in Texas, had served as a brigadier under Longstreet's general command at Chickamauga. When Gregg's brigade was separated in one of the administration's troop dispositions, Longstreet snatched up the tough combat soldier and landed a man who satisfied him as well as the hard-bitten Texans.

The other two brigades, both Georgian, were led by a pair of furious fighters called "Tige" and "Rock." Tige was forty-year-old George T. Anderson, with Mexican War and some regular army experience, and Rock was fifty-year-old Judge Henry Lewis Benning, an associate justice of the Georgia Supreme Court.

Charlie Field, despite Longstreet's opposition and the war office's motives in giving him the division, was a good man to command these seasoned, self-confident and aggressive brigadiers. Though he might lean a little heavily on old army protocol where his superior was involved, the usually good-natured professional quickly established himself in his own division. He was a rather rough-looking customer, thick-necked and big in the chest; even with his new wooden leg, there was a physically formidable quality about him.

The division following Field's was yet another unit which had survived one of Longstreet's personal feuds. In this case, Lafayette McLaws had been cleared by a court-martial of some trumped-up charges precisely on May 4th, the day the First Corps moved out. However, to avoid further dissension, Lee transferred McLaws out of the army and continued the division in the temporary command of its senior brigadier, Joseph Kershaw.

Though Lafayette McLaws suffered a personal injustice, Joe Kershaw, at that stage in his development, was a better Confederate division commander than McLaws at that stage of his career. McLaws had been a competent professional long at division command. Passed-over officers, lacking incentive, could become set in their ways and bring little inspiration to the troops. Forty-two-year-old Kershaw, eager to prove himself at the temporarily higher command, brought an infectious enthusiasm to the whole division.

A lawyer and state legislator from Camden, South Carolina, of which his father had been mayor, Kershaw possessed in his personal authority the native qualities of leadership. Applying a literate intelligence to the techniques of warfare and absorbing the lessons of considerable firsthand experience, Joe Kershaw was ready for the big jump in responsibility and he looked it. Except for a droopy mustache, he was clean-shaven, with a broad brow and fine features, and his expression reflected his strong resolution. Standing at the middle height, he moved well, was a notably graceful rider, and his impetuous confidence in action made him appear a "hotspur" to his men.

With Kershaw in command, the division became the first one in Lee's army without a single professional soldier among its general officers. Of these, only William Wofford, forty-year-old Georgia lawyer and anti-secessionist state legislator, was a pre-Gettysburg brigadier. The two replacements of Gettysburg casualties seemed a little long in the tooth to be making general officer. Benjamin Humphreys, a Mississippi planter and another of the lawyer-state legislators, was fifty-five, and Goode Bryan, a Georgia planter and militia organizer, was approaching fifty-three. The nearest to a professional, Bryan had briefly attended West Point, served in the Mexican War, and was one of the brigadiers who had not reached the top of his potential.

Except for the colonel in temporary command of Kershaw's South Carolinians, the new brigadiers had served together in the West, the regiments were familiar with one another from long association, and McLaws's administration left a soundly operated division for Kershaw's highly spirited leadership.

During the night march across country, as the men at the head of the column continually lost their way on the overgrown footpaths, Kershaw's division began to parallel Field's in the course toward the Plank Road. Pushing through the unseen twining thickets and stumbling over fallow fields covered by briers, the vanguards of both divisions approached the Plank Road in the area of Parker's Store just at daylight. Not until five o'clock did the lead regiments reach the road about two miles back of Hill's rear lines. With daylight, the men realized that their wagons and guns were left far behind. That meant no breakfast, and no Alexander, the very best artillerist in the Confederacy and probably in the war.

Twenty-seven-year-old Porter Alexander was something fairly close to the elusive category of genius. The Georgia aristocrat, with his protean gifts and self-confident energy, would have excelled wherever placed. Only two years out of West Point when the war came, he was one of the younger Southerners most urged to remain in the old army and had been sought on all sides when he arrived in Virginia, coming from a California post, just before Manassas. Successively staff officer with Beauregard, ordnance officer, commander of an artillery battalion, Alexander won his fame and command of First Corps artillery at Gettysburg by an incredible display of judgment, coolness and imperturbable effectiveness during the confusion in command when Longstreet lost his self-control. (Later he wrote a classic account of the battle which has become one of the most sought-after books on the war.) He was promoted to brigadier general during the Tennessee campaign, and before the first corps returned to Virginia, Joe Johnston tried to get him as chief of artillery for his army.

Alexander's single most distinguishing quality as an artillery commander was his extraordinary quickness of perception. His vision seemed to encompass everything at a glance. With no delay between observation and decision, he would have his guns firing on the target while most commanders would still be studying the situation. He did everything fast, with no waste of motion, and he expected the same of his subordinates. As with other gifted perfectionists, the young Georgian sometimes expected too much of others and he could be blunt in criticism of fellow officers and superiors.

Personally, Alexander was not one of the more engaging of Lee's general officers. Though amiable enough, and courteous, he was a driver. Of average size, he was wiry, quick in his movements and as inexhaustible as Jeb Stuart. Without good features, he wore, as did many of the younger officers of both sides, a beard to disguise his youthfulness. It was a curving mustache and chin affair, black and "scraggly," and gave something like a touch of harshness to his bony face. With dark and intense eyes, it was his restless, commanding gaze that characterized his appearance. Men felt in the presence of a personage around Alexander. With nothing of arrogance or vanity, he was, as he looked, one of the most completely self-assured men with Lee.

The corps artillery had been scattered during the winter, and Alexander had only three battalions, totaling fifty-seven guns, following in the wake of the infantry divisions. The way Confederate gunners served their pieces, numbers were not so important. The enemy always had more guns and mostly better, longer in range, more accurate, and firing heavier weight of metal. The cannoneers made the difference.

Alexander's men typified the artillerists in Lee's army in that the average of their personnel came of background superior to the average volunteer in the other services (there were no conscripts), and at equal rank the average artillery officers were superior to the general average. The roll call of the famous young gunners who had served with Lee — Pelham, Pegram, Poague, Breathed, Chew,

Latimer, and many another — came in a service that numbered less than a single infantry division.

Alexander would get pieces to the Plank Road during the day, but when the vanguard of the infantry came out of the brush, the soldiers started down the road toward the enemy without their familiar supporting weapons.

It was then something after five o'clock, full light, and from two miles down the road the soldiers heard the sudden crackle of infantry firing in great force. Longstreet was nowhere at hand. He had ridden ahead to report to Lee the approach of his two divisions.

2

General Longstreet and his staff, passing through Hill's hospital stations, reached the Tapp farm clearing while the radiant May morning was disturbed by no more than the usual sounds of a stirring camp. As burly Old Pete turned his horse off the road into the clearing, Colonel Palmer hurried toward him.

Hill's chief-of-staff was acquainted with Longstreet from the early days of the war, and he exclaimed, "Ah, General, we have been looking for you since twelve o'clock last night. We expect to be attacked at any moment, and are not in any shape to resist."

"My troops are not up," Longstreet said, "I've ridden ahead —"

Whatever else the General intended to say was lost in a heavy crackle of rifle fire that roared in the woods across their entire front.

Hancock had struck with about a full corps on a narrow front across both sides of the road, along with Wadsworth driving his division forward from the gap at an angle on Wilcox's flank. Longstreet was slightly deaf, but he had no difficulty in gauging that volume of fire or in judging the intent behind it. Without a question, Old Pete swung his horse around, pushed out of the clearing and galloped down the road to bring his troops into action.

As Longstreet left the clearing, A. P. Hill rode in from the north. He had gone out at daylight to make a personal reconnaissance of the gap between his flank and Ewell, and the roar of sudden, full-scale battle brought him galloping back to the clearing. Hill had no sooner joined Colonel Palmer than the first of Wilcox's men emerged from the brush in falling back, and the din of musketry crept closer.

A curious blank exists about responsibility for the unpreparedness of Wilcox's and Heth's divisions for receiving attack. With all the versions of and the apologies about leaving the men "undisturbed" during the night, there is total silence regarding the failure to arouse them at first light. Though it was manifest by then that Longstreet's divisions were not on hand for relief, no order was given to alert the troops. Some slept on, rifles stacked. The only protection against the enemy was an unconnected line drawn by corps engineers during the last hours of darkness. On these segments of slices through the brush, with the debris piled toward the enemy, the troops could form and throw up works. Few, if any, did. In a curious awakening lethargy, from captains to colonels, from brigadiers to Heth and Wilcox, no officer seemed to *do* anything except wait on Longstreet.

As there is a blank about this laxity, so is there a confusion about the details of the action. No one stood with a watch to record the passage of time nor were instruments used for clocking the distance. Honest Hancock believed he drove Hill's men "about a mile and a half." Equally honest Wilcox believed his men were driven "about 300 yards." The precise distance from the Brock Road passageway to the Tapp farm clearing is one and one-fifth miles, and the opposing lines ran at all angles somewhere about midway between the clearing and the Brock Road. Some of Heth's men were closer to the Brock Road than to the clearing, though not appreciably more than three fourths of a mile from the Tapp farm. Some of Wilcox's lines, as where Jim Lane's brigade was bent back in the last dusk attack on their right flank, were closer to the clearing. None was so close as Wilcox's three hundred yards. About a thousand yards was probably the average distance from the clearing to the lines first hit by Hancock.

The distances were uncertain to men of both sides because nobody could see twenty yards in front of him, and the confusion over the details of the action was caused by the varying emphases placed by participants in that chartless wasteland. When things went awry in any battle, the tendency of each side was to attribute the failure to some breakdown in their own organization rather than to the performance of the enemy. On the contrary, a successful action was likely to be attributed to the strength of one's own side rather than to a breakdown in the enemy's organization.

In Hancock's early morning attack on Hill's two disordered divisions, the tall Pennsylvanian achieved that "concert of action" which had not been possible with the hastily thrown-in troops of the day before. Some twenty-five thousand soundly organized men were compressed on a one-mile front, plus Wadsworth's division supporting the right flank, and it seems hardly possible that, under the best circumstances, Hill's two fought-out divisions could have contained them. Heth and Wilcox combined numbered only fourteen thousand before the heavy casualties of the day before, and both their flanks were overlapped. As it happened that they were in the worst possible circumstances to receive attack, the battle opened with both of those elements of one side's organized strength and the other side's organizational breakdown.

Hill's men reacted largely as individuals. At the first crashing of the masses toward them, most grabbed up their rifles and fired. In some sectors the veterans immediately perceived that the enemy was overwhelming their unprotected lines, and their resistance was — according to Federal reports — "short." Experienced soldiers, they began to fall back out of reach of the solid waves, taking the cover of the trees and brush. On other sectors, where their lines were by chance in better order, their resistance was — according to Federal reports — "desperate." Then they too were forced back by the weight of the assaulting force, and also took cover as they gave ground.

No orders controlled their movements. Some fought until they were killed or overrun. Some never turned to look back once they started for safety. In the early phases, most would seem to have fired, fallen back and fired again. As the pressure continued across their whole front, and as islands of resistance were engulfed, more men ceased firing and some of the retreaters began to hurry a little. There was no running, but neither were they standing on the order of their going.

In an open field, Hill's troops would soon have been routed. But the assaulting troops could get little momentum in pushing through

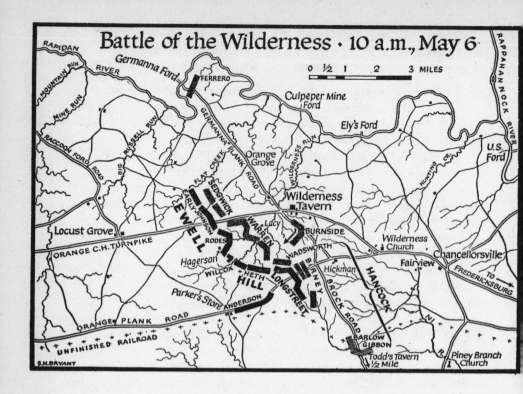

Battle of the Wilderness · 10 a.m., May 6

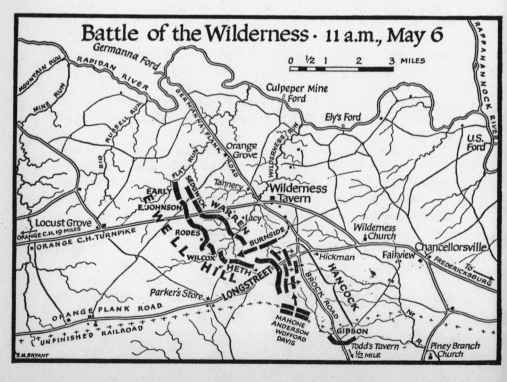

Battle of the Wilderness · 11 a.m., May 6

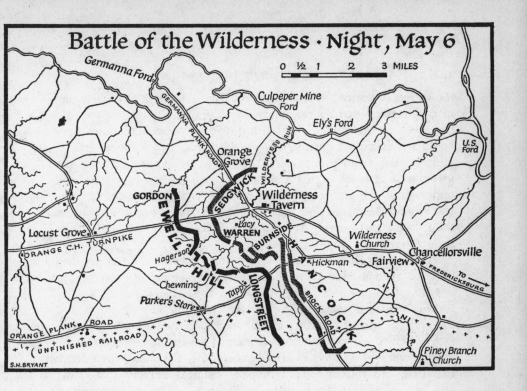

Battle of the Wilderness · Night, May 6

0 ½ 1 2 3 MILES

Germanna Ford
Culpeper Mine Ford
Ely's Ford
U.S. Ford
GERMANNA PLANK ROAD
WILDERNESS RUN
Orange Grove
GORDON
SEDGWICK
Wilderness Tavern
EWELL
Lacy
WARREN
BURNSIDE
Wilderness Church
Chancellorsville
Locust Grove
ORANGE C.H. TURNPIKE
Hagerson
HILL
Hickman
Fairview
TO FREDERICKSBURG
Chewning
Tapp
LONGSTREET
HANCOCK
Parker's Store
BROCK ROAD
ORANGE PLANK ROAD
(UNFINISHED RAILROAD)
NI
Piney Branch Church
S.H.BRYANT

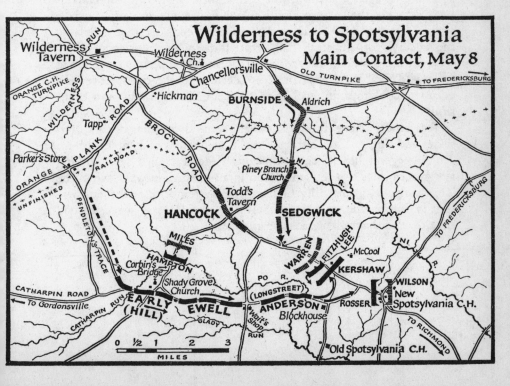

Wilderness to Spotsylvania
Main Contact, May 8

Wilderness Tavern
WILDERNESS RUN
Wilderness Ch.
ORANGE C.H. TURNPIKE
Chancellorsville
OLD TURNPIKE
TO FREDERICKSBURG
WILDERNESS
Hickman
BURNSIDE
Aldrich
Tapp
PLANK ROAD
BROCK ROAD
Parker's Store
ORANGE
RAILROAD
Piney Branch Church
NI R.
UNFINISHED
Todd's Tavern
SEDGWICK
PENDLETON'S TRACE
HANCOCK
WARREN
FITZHUGH LEE
McCool
NI R.
MILES
HAMPTON
KERSHAW
TO FREDERICKSBURG
Corbin's Bridge
CATHARPIN ROAD
Shady Grove Church
(LONGSTREET)
WILSON
New Spotsylvania C.H.
To Gordonsville
CATHARPIN RUN
EARLY (HILL)
EWELL
PO R.
ANDERSON
Blockhouse
Watt's Shop
ROSSER
GLADY RUN
TO RICHMOND
Old Spotsylvania C.H.

0 ½ 1 2 3
MILES

the screen of matted brush and heavy vines. Though the advancing men felt the force of resistance steadily diminishing, they could not see the condition of the withdrawing troops. Sometimes they could not know an enemy was nearby until, as a Federal general said, a burst from gunmuzzles "cut lurid windows" through the green wall in front of them. One hundred yards was a long way under those conditions, with streams of brush fires beginning to run around their feet, and the wounded of both sides screaming on the ground and lunging to pull themselves away from the flames and suffocation.

By the unclocked time, at least an hour, used in the step-by-step advance of approximately a thousand yards — more in some places, less in others — order began to go in the attacking forces. The units advanced unevenly, some drifted and some lost direction, and the very weight of numbers compressed into the narrow area with little visibility worked against the order of advancing troops.

However, while their order became loose, the men's confidence mounted, and this introduced a psychological element that could also be used against them. In the exhilaration of driving divisions of Lee's army, in the very ease with which they were moving toward a sizable victory, the Federal troops did not consider that a flaw in the enemy's organization had created the weak resistance. They were aware only of the collapse of the old opponent who had frustrated them so many times, as recently as the day before, and even Hancock joyfully exclaimed, "We are driving them most beautifully."

This set the stage for the dramatic arrival of Longstreet's divisions, and for one of history's most poignant oversimplifications. As the legend has it, the victorious Federal troops were rolling along both sides of the Plank Road in an irresistible wave when the Texas brigade, inspired by General Lee's attempt to lead them personally into battle, threw themselves at the Federal wave, turned the tide, and then rolled back the attackers.

3

Before Longstreet's first regiment neared the field, the advancing troops along the road had been checked at the clearing of the Tapp farm. The men who checked the advance, and whose great hour was sacrificed to the legend, were Colonel William Poague and the cannoneers who served the sixteen guns of the artillery battalion attached to Heth's divisions.

Poague was a twenty-eight-year-old Virginian of farm, rather than plantation, background. He came of that substantial rural middle class, the existence of which in the South is denied by many historians and other more outright writers of fiction. A lawyer and graduate of Washington College, Poague had enlisted in that famous Rockbridge (County) artillery battery first commanded by the Reverend W. N. Pendleton who became chief of artillery. Quickly learning the rudiments of the work of artillery, Poague revealed himself to be a natural and driving leader with high organizational talents. A friend said that usually mild-eyed Poague was "stern" in action, and one of his devoted cannoneers said his men whispered that he fought them so hard because he "wanted to get the starch out of our shirts."

Poague had placed his guns in the clearing around the widow's farm on the day before and, against any eventualities, he put his idle gunners to cutting logs and gathering fence rails for a rude breastwork. As with most other cannoneers in both armies, Poague had taken no part in the fighting in the Wilderness, and his batteries were at full strength with rested men when Hill's divisions began to fall back before Hancock's assault.

When Powell Hill saw his men being driven, and knew that Longstreet's troops would not get up in time, he directed Poague to load his guns with anti-personnel ammunition and open up along the road as soon as he could clear the heads of their own retreating infantry.

Firing obliquely at point-blank range, Poague shaved the heads of his infantrymen so narrowly that probably some of them were struck. But where the Federal troops were bunched along the road, his bursting cannister was deadlier than the fire of a full brigade.

The advancing troops piled up in the road and to the north of it, and confusion began to develop in the troops pushing on from behind.

In the woods immediately facing the clearing, fragments of Hill's men were still firing. When enemy units sliced between or overran them, they too came under point-blank fire from Poague's guns behind their works. No Federals as a unit entered into the cleared ground. Though this center of action covered no more than several hundred yards of the front, it was the center and on the road of direction.

Poague's men stood to their guns without infantry support and without line of retreat, with cannoneers dropping from rifle fire, as if serving pieces in a fort. To their right, south of the road, Federal infantry floundered through the brush to a point on Poague's flank. Starting from their advanced position on the Confederate flank the night before, these Federals had the shortest distance to cover, and resistance was about gone in their front. Poague directed two guns turned in their direction and his men kept firing.

General Lee stood in the clearing behind Poague's guns, with the smoke from the sixteen pieces drifting over his head. No legend should obscure the performance of young Poague and the scant three hundred men serving his guns. For, so steady was their work that Lee took them for granted, a finger in the dike, as he cast about behind his breaking lines for help to hold back the tide.

Lee made a personal appeal to Brigadier General MacGowan, whose impetuous counterattack had cleared the road the day before. "Is this the splendid brigade of yours running like a flock of geese?"

Sam MacGowan, a broad-faced man with a strong mouth and hot eyes, had taken many wounds by leading his troops in the Hill tradition. He called back forthrightly enough, "General, these men are not whipped. They only want a place to form and they will fight as well as they ever did."

MacGowan had spoken truly for his men, at least one of whom felt that the commanding general had "expressed himself rather roughly" to them. This private soldier said that the brigade was not at all in panic. "The men seemed to fall back upon a deliberate conviction that it was impossible to hold the ground and, of course, foolish to attempt it. It was mortifying, but it was only what every veteran has experienced."

Though MacGowan had given a sound enough explanation for the men's withdrawal, it did nothing to stabilize the dissolving front. There was no place on which they *could* form. The men who drifted back along the road tended to gather behind Poague's guns. But the Federals on the right of the road, on the line of Poague's flank, were pushing westward to turn his rear.

General Lee was facing the wreckage of his counteroffensive in the first battle. More immediately he faced the rout of one of the two wings of his army, which would expose the other wing to precipitate retreat. Outwardly he remained composed. The only order he gave, which admitted the imminence of losing the field, was to prepare his wagons for immediate withdrawal. His inner agitation was revealed by his reaction to the arrival of Longstreet's troops at the clearing.

4

The first troops of Longstreet that came up, Tige Anderson's Georgians of Field's division, were deployed in a break-line across the road below the clearing. Then Joe Kershaw, riding at the head of McLaws's old division, sent in two brigades to the right of the road to check the overlapping flank movement. Kershaw's brigades were the first to establish contact and under conditions to shake any except the stoutest troops.

As Kershaw's own brigade and Humphrey's began to grope through the brush to form a line, the last resistance went from Hill's troops on the right of the road. Though some continued to fire as they fell back, the great masses began to break to the rear. Only a few ran and the break was not a rout, but the units were fragmented and the men were quitting the field. Longstreet's chief of staff, Colonel Sorrel, was riding along that part of the road when the men from Heth's and Wilcox's divisions streamed toward Kershaw's forming brigades, and Sorrel regarded the steadiness of Kershaw's troops as one of the First Corps' supreme achievements. The men opened their ranks to let the fugitives through and, reforming, moved ahead to close with the confident enemy.

Kershaw's troops had the intangibles going for them. Along with the rivalry between corps, they were returning from detachment in a dismal campaign, and on their first appearance on the field they were given the opportunity of saving the Army of Northern Virginia. As with the Federals, Kershaw's men knew nothing of the reason for the break. They gleefully jeered at the Third Corps troops that they "were worse than Bragg's men," and some yelled in sarcasm, "Is *this* Lee's army?"

Though their fun was short-lived, the tawny men, fresh to battle, took the shock of the advancing masses with a surging sense of invincibility that magnified the weight of their numbers. Kershaw apparently had already secured the command of the division in his own mind, for he addressed his brigade as though he had already advanced beyond it. "Now, my old brigade," he shouted to his men, and placed his own pride in the spirits of those twelve hundred fellow South Carolinians.

On Kershaw's brigade, Colonel Henagan was also temporarily in command. Henagan, a forty-one-year-old farmer, sometime sheriff and state legislator, was distinguished by a great spade-shaped beard which grew wider at the bottom. A conscientious rather than brilliant soldier, his way with his regiment had been to lead them like a line captain, and he knew no other way to lead the brigade. In that jungle clash, no other way could have been more effective. The two lines met, and the neat tunics of blue and the ragged motley called gray intermingled in the maze, and the advance of each was violently halted. That happened to the right of the road, out of sight of the group around General Lee in the farm clearing, and this action also remained outside the legend. What was visible in the cleared area were the troops of Hood's old Texas Brigade, led by newcomer John Gregg, swinging along the Plank Road at double time.

While Kershaw's two brigades were halting the farthest Federal advance in the brush to the south of the road, and while Anderson's brigade had deployed across the road as a break-line, the last organized resistance went from Hill's troops on the north side of the road in the area of the Tapp farm. With the front of infantry in effect dissolved, exposing the gun battalion which represented the last line, the situation had deteriorated too far for the deployment of break-lines on which Hill's men could retire. The only hope lay in a quick counterattack delivered along the road and across the clearing, where Poague's hard-worked gunners were on the verge of envelopment. To meet this crisis, Longstreet rushed orders to Charlie Field to hurry his second and third brigades to the front without waiting to deploy or to form lines.

Thus it happened that in a moment of ultimate danger black-bearded John Gregg and the Texans appeared at the one open site in the Wilderness fighting. As the three Texas and one Arkansas regiments veered from the road to the clearing, the experienced soldiers formed into battle lines without losing stride. The men were running at a trot when they came into Lee's anxious vision.

The General pushed his gray horse toward the guide of the line and shouted, "What troops are you, my boys?"

"The Texans," the men yelled.

The Texans had been among Lee's favorite shock troops since they broke the Union line at Gaines's Mill in Lee's first campaign as commanding general and won him his first victory with the Confederacy. In his excitement, Lee took off his wide-brimmed gray hat and waved the men on. Traveler kept moving forward alongside the advancing line of infantry.

More than a dozen supposedly firsthand reports were written of this tense moment, when the beloved commanding general appeared to be leading an infantry charge, mounted, across open ground. Various interpretations of the episode tend to imply that Lee actually intended to lead the Texans into the action. It seems more probable that Lee, forgetting himself, had no intention of any kind. It was the gravest crisis his army had ever faced. In snatching at the last-minute hope of salvation represented by the Texans, he was unaware of continuing his own forward movement as his whole being concentrated on *willing* his favorite troops forward.

Lee's unawareness of his own movements was indicated by his slowness to react to the importunities of the soldiers. "Go back, General Lee, go back," the men called. A sergeant grabbed the bridle, halting the horse. John Gregg, though unacquainted with his new army commander, rode to Lee's side and urged him to return to safety. Lee did not come out of his unrelating state until Colonel Venable approached him. This quick-thinking staff officer said, "General, you've been looking for General Longstreet. There he is over yonder."

General Lee's gaze followed the pointing finger, and then he slowly turned his horse about. A monument there reads, "'Lee to the rear,' cried the Texans," and this shining moment, demonstrating the devotion of Lee's men for their general, entered folklore with the finest traditions of a people's past.

As the true part of the Lee legend, the Texans threw themselves at the walls of the enemy as if life had no meaning. Numbering less than a thousand, they gave up half their numbers without losing the impetuosity of their attack. For those men loved Lee as he loved them, and in all the war there was no such single isolated example of troops literally giving their lives to protect the life and the work of a leader. Here again is essentially the effect that the image of Lee had on his men. When his self-control broke within, the outward composure never faltered.

Poague said that, except for Lee's being uncovered, the only change the General showed was a certain grimness of determination. Colonel Palmer saw the General as so unchanged that he did not regard the incident as "remarkable, at the time." This classic composure contributed to the belief that Lee was acting purposefully in committing himself to a definite intent. It is more in the character of man, if less in the character of a legend, that in the crisis Lee simply lost himself in the desperation of the moment. On that assumption, and with the fact of the effect of his desperation on the Texas troops, the whole thing becomes more life-sized when placed in proportion to all the elements of the battle.

The less than one thousand Texans did not alone "turn the tide" of thirty thousand enemy troops spreading on both sides of the little clearing. First, the momentum of the Federal advance had passed and order was going from the attack. Next, Poague's guns had provided a perceptible brake in the center, increasing the confusion of the crowded troops. Then Kershaw, going in on the right, halted the deepest penetration. Finally, the Texans were supported immediately by Benning's Georgians and then on the flank by Laws's Alabama brigade.

"Rock" Benning was personally fuming when he ran forward with his troops. One soldier, who had taken himself out of the battle, called to the ex-judge, "Go it, Rock," and, referring to General Anderson, added, "Tige's treed."

On the opposite flank, Kershaw got up a third brigade, Goode Byran's. Fighting stationary, Kershaw's division probably held the most compact line in the Wilderness at that time.

The Texas Brigade took the center of the stage, as did Pickett's division at Gettysburg. But Hill's unformed lines had held up the advance for more than an hour and the Federals were open for counterattack when *six* (not one) fresh brigades struck with everything they had on a narrow front.

5

When Longstreet's brigades collided with the loosely ordered advancing lines, the Federals suffered a psychological setback from the overconfidence engendered by the relative ease of their drive. They had been in sight of Lee's white-topped wagons. As far as the Federals knew, Longstreet's divisions were not coming up on the Plank Road, and the Federals were unprepared for meeting fresh reserves. Then, though Longstreet's counterattack was also halted by the collision which ground the Federal drive to a full stop, the initiative passed to Longstreet's troops.

Along with this shift in balance between the interlocked lines, a faulty element in the Federal organization became exposed. Before Longstreet's troops were identified on the field, around seven o'clock, Hancock's information placed the advance of the two divisions on the Catharpin Road, paralleling the Plank Road four miles to the south. To receive Longstreet, Hancock had detached a reserve force under General Gibbon, with Sheridan's cavalry working out in front. This pugnacious Sheridan was an ex-infantry officer and what he brought to the Union cavalry was a desire to fight the enemy cavalry into the ground. At that stage and under the conditions, Stuart's troopers were able to contain his heavily armed numbers, and Sheridan received no hint of Longstreet's night march across country to the Plank Road.

Instead, various movements of not readily identified bodies of troops, in the area from which Longstreet was expected, kept Hancock uneasy, and kept Gibbon's reserve force waiting there long after Kershaw and Field were engaged on the Plank Road. As a consequence, not only was the advancing line struck in a counterattack by troops supposedly elsewhere, but a gap was left between the flank of the assault force and Gibbon isolated off to their left.

From the beginning, the attack had been delivered on too narrow a front. In the early drive against Heth and Wilcox, the compact weight was well organized to overrun a smaller force behind works. As Hill's division had thrown up no works of consequence, the rapidness of the blind advance through the jungle caused an inevitable disorder in the troops massed in depth. When the front was covered by Longstreet's six brigades, though in no depth at all, the confusion grew behind the lines of contact.

The first direct toll of this came north of the road, in that gap between Hill and Ewell, where the screeches of the 125 Alabamians had brought Wadsworth's division to a halt in the darkness of the night before. In the morning drive, Wadsworth's own momentum caused his division once again to lose direction. A turned-about brigade caught the deadly fire of Poague's guns in flank, and crowded into the masses already milling about along the road. Turned about again, Cutler's brigade was exposed to the Confederate counterattack, delivered on the flank by Law's Alabamians. Cutler's people broke out to the north, seeking safety in the woods away from the Plank Road bedlam.

Doughty Hancock had kept throwing in reinforcements from all over the field. General Meade had staked the whole battle on the Plank Road fight, and Hancock drew on the V Corps and VI Corps, as well as shifting about his own units. Striving to regain the initiative, he moved three brigades from his then unthreatened left to bolster Wadsworth's right and carry the fight to Longstreet's troops. Movement was of necessity slow. In the shifting tide, Hancock began to suffer from organizational breakdowns.

Hancock ordered troops from Gibbon's reserve to cover his shortened left, against Kershaw on the south of the road. Gibbon later claimed no messages had reached him and Hancock blamed his subordinates. During the battle, however, his mind was really on the north of the road, at the gap between Hill and Ewell. Concentrated on regaining the initiative, Hancock was not too meticulous about protective measures on his own flank as he gave his attention to exploiting the exposed Confederate flank.

By eight in the morning, Burnside's IX Corps, the last to cross the river, was due to come up in support of Wadsworth's division in the gap. With a fresh corps going in on the Confederate left, Hancock would have the weight for a new assault which could not be contained even by Longstreet's fresh men. But Burnside's men were then taking their turn at solving the mazes through the Wilderness and had not reached the field.

While Hancock was trying to hurry Burnside forward for an attack north of the road, Kershaw struck from his position on the extreme south of the road. The Federals there had made the farthest early advance, floundering over marshy ground, and the disordered lines had an open flank in the direction of Gibbon's reserve. As Gibbon never came, the Federal left was in the air.

Kershaw's three brigades lacked the numbers to turn the flank, but, as his troops had fought in more or less stationary lines, their alignment had suffered none of the disorder which came with movement in the Wilderness. When his confident men attacked, they moved forward in a cohesiveness possible in the beginning of a drive. Hancock's confused units gave ground. Kershaw's compact brigades kept nudging them, pushing them back on a line with the Federal pile-up in the area of the Tapp farm.

When Kershaw came abreast of the Confederate line north of the road, Field's division drove forward. With his drive, the Federals began to give ground across the whole front. Slowly at first, the formerly advancing troops began to fall back.

As the bitter fighting in the foggy brush continued to seesaw through the long morning, sections of the Federal line gave way. Before a Federal break, Hancock finally got in three reserve brigades on Wadsworth's right, and they drove hard in a counterattack against troops of Field's division. There in the woods north of the road, Evander Law, the young Machiavelli of Field's division, enacted a sped-up version of the whole fight with Webb's brigade. First one rushed forward, took works, then reeled back just as fast. Then the other charged and soon, as Law said, "advanced rapidly backwards." Then both did it all over again.

During this more or less private fight, Wadsworth evidently broke under the strain. The old man was unwell, and probably should have reported himself sick. Inexplicably he shifted around some of Webb's troops and forced a regiment to leave their works at an angle to expose themselves to cross fire. Webb's tough line was broken in an instant and, he said, "swept off as by a whirlwind." Poor Wadsworth rode forward as an example to the men and was toppled from his horse by a bullet in his head. By the time his body struck the ground, only Confederates were near him.

In that age, the men of both armies held respect for rank and constituted authority, and the vast wealth of the New Yorker was known even among the Confederates. Litter-bearers carried the white-haired patroon back to their own officers' field hospital, and the nearby soldiers regarded the Northern millionaire with frank curiosity. One grizzled soldier philosophized over the fate of a man who, commanding "more wealth than the treasury of the Confederate government," was dying among enemies away from all loved ones. Yet, the Confederate reasoned, Wadsworth, like all good soldiers, could take the comfort of dying for what he believed was right.

Nearby a different kind of exchange occurred between enemies.

Hill's men, as MacGowan had promised, quickly reformed when given a breathing space. Reflecting their basic morale under A. P. Hill's leadership, and their own pride as soldiers, the two divisions showed no effects of their humiliating experience. Within two hours, they moved again toward the enemy. Whatever the stage of Hill's illness, he was able to ride out ahead of his troops when they pushed into the gap toward Ewell. Though Powell Hill could not know it, his corps was racing Burnside's fresh IX Corps for occupancy of that nether land between the two roads.

Midway between the Plank Road and the Old Turnpike, Hill and his staff reached the large clearing of the Chewning farm, a silent little island around the deserted house in the midst of the roaring crackle in the brush on either side. Hill dismounted in the farmyard to reconnoiter the ground for the disposition of his troops, the van of which was, out of sight, slowly approaching several hundred yards away. Apparently not feeling well, A. P. Hill sat down on a box on the eastern edge of the clearing.

While the General was surveying the woods in front of him, he and his staff were startled by the sound of a breaking fence on the edge of the woods nearest them. Hill and his staff turned to see a solid line of Federal infantry preparing to enter the clearing. This was no small lost band as of the day before.

For a moment no one moved. Then Hill, in a quiet voice, said, "Mount, walk your horses, and do not look back."

With steeled nerves, Hill's group, with their backs to a line of enemy infantry, held their horses to a walk until they reached the woods toward the Plank Road. Then, escaping capture for the second time in two days, Hill hurried his troops toward the clearing.

Burnside's bewildered men were quickly contained, and Hill's two divisions at last closed the gap between the Plank Road and Ewell. Some of the Federal soldiers who had approached the clearing were captured, and herded into the crowds of prisoners being sent to the rear along the road. One of their officers saw Colonel Palmer there, and said to him, "Were you not at that house in the clearing a short time ago?"

When Palmer admitted it, the smoldering Federal let loose with a blast of curses at his superiors. "I wanted to fire on you, but my colonel said you were farmers riding from the house."

Most of these actions, large and small, could have happened all in a few morning hours only in the Wilderness. Then another thing happened because of the Wilderness.

6

General Lee quickly recovered from his brush with disaster, and his mind reverted to the counteroffensive plan of the morning. In the violent shift of fortunes, Lee did not try to include Ewell's troops in the movement. His last orders had been for Old Baldhead either to attack the enemy's right, near the river, or to reinforce Lee for the attack in the Plank Road area. Ewell, doing neither, had stoutly resisted localized attacks designed to get him to do just that.

Presumably Lee had heard the firing and, as soon as the Plank Road front was saved, thought first of protecting the gap between the two roads. After Hill's reformed divisions at last connected the two lines, Lee had no time to divert attention to Ewell. He was concentrated on mounting a counteroffensive with the troops on the Plank Road front.

While Kershaw and Field were driving the Federals back to and beyond the temporary works from which Hancock had delivered his daylight attack, the vanguard of Anderson's division, Hill's corps, had come up behind Longstreet's rear-guard brigades. There were no reports on what orders were given. Evidently in some verbal exchange Lee turned Anderson's fresh division over to Longstreet. With Hill and his other two battered divisions in the gap, Longstreet seemed to assume command of the Plank Road front. Lee relinquished the field to Old Pete as he had not with A. P. Hill.

Their last engagement together had been at Gettysburg, and nothing suggests that Lee ever analyzed Longstreet's intransigent behavior there. Most likely Lee regarded his "War Horse" as experiencing a bad day at Gettysburg in general collapse of command, for in the Wilderness no previous events had shaken his confidence in the First Corps commander's ability to fight troops. Unanalytical though Lee was, and without knowledge of Longstreet's total record, by instinct Lee was sound. Longstreet had few superiors when he was right, and he was at his combative best when he took control of the field along the Plank Road.

When General Lee returned to his plan of a counteroffensive, he first sent Longstreet his new chief of engineers. Brigadier General Martin Smith, a clean-shaven man with strong features and an authoritarian expression, was sent to discover the enemy's flank south of the Plank Road. Though the sequence becomes a little uncertain at this point, Smith and his staff did discover Hancock's flank to be short and in the air. Somebody discovered or knew that, concealed by the brush, the cut of an unfinished railroad ran in the gap between Hancock's flank and Gibbon's reserve. This cut, which before the war had been laid for a railroad to run from Fredericksburg to Gordonsville, was shown on no maps and was invisible in the Wilderness unless an observer stood over it.

According to some accounts, Kershaw's Brigadier General Wofford knew about the railroad cut and suggested a flanking movement along it. Planter-lawyer William Wofford had been around as a general officer for a long time and would have stood on no ceremony with his former fellow brigadier, Joe Kershaw, then in temporary command of the division. Kershaw said it was Wofford's suggestion.

Whoever conceived the plan in the confused group of officers on the road, one certainty is that Smith had reconnoitered the flank and said it could be turned. Somewhere between chief engineer Smith and Brigadier Wofford, division commander Kershaw and corps commander Longstreet, with the commanding general's approval, the flank attack evolved as a group extemporization.

In its spontaneity, the move was smaller than Stonewall Jackson's great maneuver, made with his full corps, at Chancellorsville the year before. Also, Longstreet personally was occupied with the unresolved front across the Plank Road and he could do no more than assemble a makeshift force and send it off with his blessings.

At hand were Wofford's Georgia brigade of Kershaw's division and "Tige" Anderson's Georgia brigade of Field's division. From Dick Anderson's division, most of which was to support the Plank Road front, Longstreet selected Mahone's Virginia brigade.

Mahone's selection, whether or not by chance, caused a personality change in the promising brigadier who had been a long disappointment. Billy Mahone was a small man with a large ego, very assertive, self-aware and a flamboyant hypochondriac. He carried his own milk cow attached to brigade headquarters' wagon. A V.M.I. graduate and prewar success as a civil engineer and railroad executive, Mahone had jumped to brigadier in the fall of '61, and there he remained. Outside the circles of "cousins" from the heraldic families in Lee's army, he was close to Dick Anderson, and would seem to have reflected his division commander's lackluster attitude during the past year. Apparently one of those men stimulated only by a chance to excel, by authority and responsibility, the bantam Mahone at last came bursting out of his shell during the flanking movement.

Before the movement started out, a fourth brigade was volunteered by Colonel Stone, temporarily in command of Brigadier General Joseph Davis's Mississipians in Heth's division. These were the troops, commanded by Davis's lawyer nephew, whom the President had foisted off on Lee at Gettysburg. Having performed poorly in that first campaign with the army despite individual heroism, and then caught in the break of Heth's troops during the morning in the Wilderness, Colonel Stone requested that the Mississippians be given the chance to show their mettle in the flanking movement.

Only in the Wilderness would such a maneuver have been entrusted to four brigades from four divisions and two corps, without a professional soldier among their generals. To complete the non-professional nature of the force, Longstreet gave the command to his twenty-five-year-old chief of staff, Colonel Moxley Sorrel, who had never before led troops in battle.

Sorrel was one of the most attractive men in the army in looks, in manner and in the warmth of his nature. He was also one of the most literate and intelligent. A native of Georgia, he was Virginian on his mother's side and French on his father's; his grandfather had been a colonel in the engineers of the French army. Though active in the fashionable militia organizations before the war, his work had been in the sedentary quiet of a railroad's banking department. In the First Corps, he obviously enjoyed the vantage point of observation offered to an AAG but, as with other valuable staff officers, he wanted his chance at the true glory. It came to him some time after ten o'clock in the morning on May 6th.

Mounted, he formed the four brigades beyond their own flank in the first move that introduced tactics into two days of stand-up slugging in the green fog. Where the brushy tunnel of the railroad cut passed Kershaw's flank, it loosely paralleled the Plank Road, bearing southward. Near the Brock Road, the cut bent to the south and east, and almost paralleled the Brock Road. The silent soldiers halted to form their battle lines in this bend of the cut. The unfought brigades of Wofford and Mahone came first, with Tige Anderson and Colonel Stone in support. As the unobserved brigades prepared to spring from their covered way, they faced north, with their line of attack at right angles to the Federal lines facing west.

By chance, the furthermost Federal brigade, temporarily withdrawn from the fighting, was taking its ease while its units were re-formed. When Colonel Sorrel led the makeshift force screaming and shooting out of the thickets, Frank's brigade was even more helplessly placed for receiving attack than Hill's divisions had been at daylight. Hill's troops had at least been facing the enemy. The Federal soldiers, with no position to defend from the direction of the attack, could only save themselves. Like sensible men, they got out of there.

McAllister's brigade on their right was alerted and turned front to face the flank assault. Too many of their own people came running toward them and the Confederates were too close behind. In a fulfillment of the dream of military leaders, the enemy flank was literally "rolled up."

In his great moment, young Sorrel led at the front like a line officer, paying no heed to his horse floundering hock-deep in the marshy ground. At his side, a small color-bearer, Benjamin May of the 12th Virginia, Mahone's brigade, was also stumbling in the bog and trying to lift his battle flag above the thickets. Sorrel, in his excitement, reached for the flagstaff and said he would carry the colors. Little May indignantly jerked his regimental flag away and shouted, "We'll follow *you!*"

They followed him all the way to the Plank Road, crossing their own front and veering eastward to the Brock Road. At around noon, south of the Plank Road, there ceased to be an organized force of Hancock's corps between the Confederates and the vital Brock Road passageway for the Union army.

North of the Plank Road, the already shaken Federal lines began to break. When Sorrel rode out on the Plank Road, as far as he could see in both directions, this line of march to the Brock Road intersection was filled with Confederates.

In front of the advancing troops, the staff colonel espied the blocky figure of General Longstreet, and he put his horse at a gallop to take to his hero the news of the First Corps' shining opportunity.

7

Old Pete recognized his moment with destiny. Every failure and frustration could be obliterated, the longest aspirations realized, on this terrain where his dead rival climaxed his fame. But Stonewall Jackson's victory had been only partial. The enemy, though beaten on the field, had managed to hold off the attackers and make an orderly withdrawal across the river. Longstreet saw the opportunity of driving the Federal army away from the river crossings in rout.

With effective resistance gone south of the Plank Road, the Federal front north of the road began to dissolve. In a reversal of the withdrawal of Hill's troops, Union soldiers quit the fight and walked to the rear. As with Heth's and Wilcox's men earlier, few ran and no general panic set in. Simply a growing volume of soldiers turned from the enemy and left the field. Obviously a continued advance could carry all the way to the Brock Road. Longstreet saw beyond that.

He had troops at hand for executing a second, wider flanking movement to *cross* the Brock Road, face north, and turn Hancock's reserve line of log breastworks along the road. While Longstreet's main assault forces followed the broken enemy to the works from the west, a flank drive from the south would leave Hancock's men no choice save to abandon their last line. As the four brigades from the railroad cut had rolled up the flank of one wing, Longstreet conceived of a larger force rolling up the flank of the whole Federal army.

At the moment, it all seemed possible. The way was open to the Brock Road and, with Hancock's force in disorder, no organized resistance could be arranged soon enough to defend the works or contain the flanking movement beyond them.

If everything worked, as Hancock was rolled up to the north, Meade's troops facing Hill would be outflanked, uncovering Hill's front for his two divisions to strike ahead. Then the troops against Ewell would be forced to pull back, Ewell's full corps would be free to drive ahead to the narrow roads which led to the river fords, cutting the broken units off from the crossings. Thousands of wagons, impeding the retreat, would have to be abandoned, with equipment beyond the dreams of the Confederate soldiers. Gibbon's reserve force and Sheridan's cavalry, cut off to the south, could do no more than find their way to the line of rout westward to Fredericksburg. Fredericksburg would be the terminal Longstreet envisioned for the wrecked army of his old friend Sam Grant, and the concept for creating the disaster was entirely his own.

The counteroffensive which exploited the railroad cut had been a group affair. Though Longstreet's aggressiveness would have led him to deliver some finishing blow to a shaken enemy, Lee had sent his chief engineer, General Smith, to reconnoiter the Federal flank. Now the battle was his and the size of the victory would be designed and executed by him.

Since his arrival on the disordered scene around the Tapp farm clearing, Old Pete had been relaxed and even cheerful in his confidence in his troops to restore order. Totally unaffected by the atmosphere of ruin, his bluff presence was like an act of reassurance on the field. When he rode forward on the cleared Plank Road, his heartiness expanded and a mood of exhilaration swept over the group of generals and staff officers gathering around the corps commander on the cleared road.

All had reason for personal elation — Sorrel, Wofford, Kershaw, and, in a different way, Micah Jenkins. His South Carolina brigade was assigned the key role in Longstreet's plan. This favorite of Old Pete, for all his personal rivalry with Evander Law, had been outside Longstreet's squabble over giving him division command. However, ambitious and a brilliant soldier, Jenkins had chafed under the opportunities that passed him by. As one of the most intense Confederates, part of his chafing came from the opportunities lost for using his gifts and those of others like him. Now, at the prospect of making a strike in a decisive movement, he grew so excited that he impetuously blurted out his feelings to Longstreet.

"I am happy," he said. "I have felt despair for the cause for some months, but I am relieved now, and feel assured that we will put the enemy back across the Rapidan before night."

Then Jenkins was joined by fellow South Carolinian Joe Kershaw, who was to give him the detailed assignment. They dropped back to the head of Jenkins's column. Longstreet had told Kershaw that he was to drive straight ahead through the woods on their right of the road, gathering up the troops from the railroad-cut movement as he went, and go on over the breastworks on the Brock Road. Young Jenkins, with his fresh brigade, was to move by the flank down the Plank Road to form the pivot on which Kershaw would swing northward in the flanking movement. Kershaw explained that Longstreet's plan was to drive the enemy east of, away from, the Brock Road and on "toward Fredericksburg."

Micah Jenkins, after receiving his orders, threw his arm around Sorrel, congratulated him, and said, "We will smash them now."

The enormity of the plan in itself generated an excited confidence in young generals already exultant at having saved the field and then driven the enemy from it. In the cavalcade riding toward the Brock Road, the stroke was as good as delivered. Only the details remained for the First Corps, completing the triumphant return to Lee's army, to become the heroes of the war.

Suddenly, from the woods to the right, several rifles crackled almost in their faces. Combative Longstreet instinctively whirled his horse in the direction of the shots, and the mounted men nearest moved ahead with him. At this rapid movement in the road, a heavier volley rattled from the woods and three men pitched from their horses. Courier Baum and Captain Dobie, Kershaw's AAG, were killed instantly. Enthusiastic young Jenkins took a mortal wound and never regained clear consciousness.

Kershaw, hearing the hammers click on the rifles of Jenkins's leading squads, galloped down the road in front of the woods yelling at the top of his voice, "Friends! Friends! We are friends!" After a startled cry in answer, a dead silence settled momentarily over the thickets from which the firing had come. When breathless Kershaw spun his horse around after the dash, he saw the worst. Longstreet's staff was helping the General from the saddle.

The big man, riding with a firm seat, had been lifted straight up by the bullet and came down hard, but he held on. The bullet had torn his coat high in the chest, entering his body near the shoulder and passing close to the throat. He was almost choked with blood when they laid him down at the foot of a leafy tree by the roadside.

Dr. Cullen, corps medical director, hurried beside the General and started removing his clothes. With his hat off, his forehead, not weather-stained, looked, an observer said, "white and domelike." Under his coat and shirt, a fine gauze undervest was stained with blood. The blood drained out of his face, and artillerist Stiles, who had never liked him, wrote that "its somewhat gross aspect was gone. . . . [Seeing him] calm and entirely master of the situation, he is both greater and more attractive than I have hitherto thought him."

Longstreet remained silent against the pain, but his mind was clear. He told Colonel Sorrel to turn the movement over to Field, the ranking officer nearby, and tell him to drive straight on. Then he told Sorrel to hurry to General Lee and inform him of their success, and urge him to continue the great flanking movement.

An ambulance came up and they lifted in the heavy man, his lids then closing and leaving only a faint line of blue beneath the lashes. When Longstreet was carried from the field, he left believing that the wound alone prevented him from driving a routed army to Fredericksburg.

8

That a lieutenant general's mounted party could be fired into by its own men on a cleared road at high noon indicated the confusion of the fighting in the Wilderness. As Hancock's troops had lost order in their early morning drive, it was inevitable that Longstreet's push should suffer the fate of any prolonged movement through those briery screens over marshy ground. There was simply not enough visibility for the officers, and the men inevitably shifted direction for footing and clearance.

Where Longstreet's party was fired into, Wofford's brigade had shortly before crossed the Plank Road without Mahone's brigade knowing it. As Longstreet's group approached, stragglers from Wofford's Georgians, themselves lost, ran back across the road. Several of Mahone's Virginians, on the south side of the road, fired rather tentatively at this movement. When Longstreet and some of his party then moved toward Mahone's troops, more of the Virginians fired in earnest.

After Kershaw's yell of "Friends" brought a baffled pause to Mahone's soldiers, everybody began running about apologizing and expressing regrets. At that moment no order had been issued for Longstreet's projected movement. Kershaw and Jenkins had merely been given their assignments. What was done when stocky Field and General Lee came up would have needed to be done first by Longstreet and Kershaw.

Field, whose fight against Hancock's main objective north of the Plank Road had kept him out of the exultant group with Long-

street, saw the situation without their excitement. He saw one disordered column parallel to the Plank Road (some on one side and
most on the other) while his men, in driving the enemy toward the
Brock Road came up perpendicularly to the Plank Road. At that
moment, Longstreet's assault forces stood at right angles to one another.

Longstreet and his younger officers, in their swelling confidence,
had simply assumed the straightening out of the four brigades
which had attacked from the railroad cut. With experienced soldier
Field and General Lee certainly no less eager than Longstreet, several hours were required to form the troops in an attacking alignment while driving the last of Hancock's men back on the Brock
Road. For, again like Hill's troops earlier in the morning, the many
brigades under Hancock did not cease resistance all at once.

Somebody once said there are no "ifs" in war. Longstreet, who
did not believe that Jackson would have driven Hooker across the
river even if he had not been wounded, believed that he would
have driven Grant beyond the river crossings if he had not been
wounded. Probably the result would have been the same in either
case, though not the details.

Longstreet would have moved some brigades, in whatever order
the troops may have been in, against Hancock's logworks along the
Brock Road. A line of the works would probably have been taken,
and Kershaw might have gotten some troops beyond the works in
the beginning of his flanking movement. But, just as Longstreet's
late arrival made him the rescuer of Hill's fought-out troops, so the
late arrival of Burnside's corps gave Hancock reserves with which
to check an envelopment movement.

Burnside had fresh conscripts among his troops and, by 1864
standards, his corps was not among the fearsome forces. Sorrel
said, "Burnside would and could fight troops, even if he didn't
know how." But twenty thousand men with guns in their hands, as
supports of half the Federal army, would be far from useless against
a scattered force that numbered only two brigades more than ten
thousand to start with.

The Wilderness was a force of checks and balances. By adroit use
of the Wilderness, Lee had checked Grant. The balances were there
to check him too. In the beginning, Hancock profited by Confed-

erate mistakes, in the middle Longstreet profited by Federal mistakes, and in the end it all balanced out.

It was four o'clock before Lee sufficiently straightened out Longstreet's divisions, with some brigades from Anderson, to deliver an orderly attack. The men had not been inactive during the re-forming. They had been firing, maneuvering, and edging forward. When they drove, the assault forces made it all the way to the burning logs of Hancock's breastworks along the Brock Road. By then Hancock had reformed his fugitives, thrown in some of Burnside's undependables, and they were enough to halt the drive. The Brock Road passageway remained in the possession of Meade's army.

In the post-mortems of after years, it was believed that Lee could have taken the road *if* he had possessed the additional weight of Pickett's detached division. The absence of Pickett, of Hoke and the detached brigades, did not constitute an *if*. Their detachment was controlled by the commander in chief of all the Confederate armies, and the incompletion of the Army of Northern Virginia was a factor which influenced Lee during the two days' fighting. The whole battle would have been fought differently with the presence of his full army. Lee tried with what he had and, as he had warned, it was not enough.

As it was, the post-mortems produced another *if*, in the parallel action on the Old Turnpike. The belief still persists that Ewell let destiny slip through his fingers on the Old Turnpike, while the Federal forces were concentrated on saving the Brock Road to the south.

9

Long before noon, before Sorrel formed the makeshift force for the flank movement through the railroad cut, Ewell was advised that the enemy's flank was short and unanchored. He was not informed by a headquarters engineer but by one of his two most enterprising brigadiers. This was John B. Gordon, the thin-faced non-professional who looked more like a spit-and-polish martinet than most West Pointers.

Gordon's division commander was saturnine Jubal Early, mean-tempered under pressure, and probably jealous of the impressive-looking Georgia civilian. Refusing to give credence to the findings of Gordon's scouts, Old Jube advised Ewell against an attack on the enemy's flank.

When Ewell was not under the influence of his new wife, he was under Early's. So Dick Ewell, who was satisfied to beat off the manifestly local attacks thrown against his dug-in lines, did nothing during the long afternoon while, over on the Plank Road, opportunity came and went. At the end of the day, General Lee rode across the then safe gap from the Tapp farm to discover why nothing had been done by Ewell to relieve the enemy's accumulations in the Plank Road area.

By then, Longstreet's drive, directed by Field, had fallen short of taking the Brock Road, and Lee could scarcely have hoped to salvage the day at that hour (half-past five) on the Turnpike. His problem during the whole battle was that he could not be on both fields, and the emergencies on the Plank Road, beginning with Hancock's daylight attack, kept him there until nothing more was to be feared from the enemy. In his first relatively free moment, Lee rode to the Old Turnpike primarily to investigate Ewell's inaction.

When the commanding general reached the Second Corps field headquarters, he and Ewell played a curious re-enactment of the dusk scene on the first day at Gettysburg. As the year before, a dismal conference, which included Gordon and Jubal Early, revealed that Old Baldhead had suffered paralysis of the will at the necessity of making a decision, and divorced his corps from the actions of the army. Once again Lee listened with little comment, as he learned that Ewell had heeded Early and overridden Gordon's importunities to attack the enemy's exposed flank. At the end, Lee simply ordered Ewell to send Gordon on the attack, as late as it was.

Lee could not have expected much from a dusk attack in that terrain, and his order seemed merely the last act of initiative possible to make. Yet a big *if* grew around Gordon's attack between the Old Turnpike and the river.

Leading a weak force, the Georgia brigadier managed to creep undetected past the enemy's flank and, in a limited version of Longstreet's assault from the railroad cut, his troops came storming out of the dusky woods. The surprise of the attack rolled up a Federal

brigade and created considerable confusion, during which two brigadier generals were captured and a number of startled soldiers gathered up. Gordon lacked the weight to achieve any more with night
falling.

The *ifs* concerned the possibilities of an earlier attack. According
to optimistic Confederates, an attack delivered simultaneously with
Longstreet's drive would have created havoc. Jubal Early, naturally
defensive about having advised against the attack, contended that
in a daylight attack the Federals would have discovered the skimpi-
ness of Gordon's force and murdered him. On the other hand, under resolute action, the attack need not have been skimpy. But
Ewell was not a resolute commander. Being what he was, the action
became inevitably what it was.

The element of *ifs* loomed large at the Wilderness because the
Grant-Meade combination fought one of the worst battles ever in
Virginia. Burnside at Fredericksburg and Hooker at Chancellorsville are regarded as milestones of Union ineptitude. Grant lost
more men in the Wilderness than Burnside at Fredericksburg and
at least as many as Hooker at Chancellorsville. More Federal mistakes were made at the Wilderness than in any battle at the river.

But Lee had less men at the Wilderness than in any major battle
he had fought before. Against Burnside, Lee's army was at its physical peak. Against Hooker, with Stonewall Jackson executing the
flank maneuver, the army was at its command peak, and Stuart
dominated the cavalry action. Against Grant at the Wilderness, Lee
brought forty-five thousand infantry against a hundred thousand,
with cavalry domination passing to the enemy.

In casualties, the Federal army sustained more than seventeen
thousand — killed, wounded and missing — nearly one third the
number of men of all arms Lee had on the field. In losing at the
outside not more than eight thousand, Lee's army had by any measure outfought the enemy. In Grant's first clash in the East, he had,
as Meade predicted, found Lee and the Army of Northern Virginia a different proposition from Bragg and the Army of Tennessee.

The Federal army had been rocked back on its heels, forced to a
desperate defense of its passageway. Most of the casualties were suffered in the veteran units which Grant inherited, some of which

were never again the same. Grant was acutely aware of his poorly fought battle, of a sense of failure.

Much mention has been made of his apparent coolness during the battle. With his black hat planted squarely on his head, no tilt to front or side, his plain face expressionless, he puffed away at his cigars and appeared to devote his whole attention to whittling. There was really nothing else he could do. Having exposed Meade's army on the march, and ordered attacks before the units were prepared, he could only leave the fighting in the hands of the men on the field.

Fortunately for him, there were sufficiently able men to hold the Brock Road, at whatever cost to the army. Grant knew the cost and the nearness of the thing. After the battle, with the need past for an appearance of stoical calm, he became extremely agitated and broke down on his cot. That was on the night of May 6th, in reaction to his first battle in Virginia.

But Grant, the uncomplex product of the evolved policy of total war, had been appointed commander in chief with the assignment of carrying the all-out war to the finish. Unlike Hooker and Burnside, he did not have to explain his losses or his failure. Nor, like them, did he have to withdraw his bleeding army across the river. Lee, having neither the manpower nor the command personnel which Grant's predecessors faced, could not, after the buffeting his army had taken, mount an attack to drive him to the river. Even in the aftermath of his decisive repulse, Grant must have known that he was safe from counterattack.

The formerly all-conquering Grant inevitably reacted to the bungling of his first performance against the Confederacy's hero. But he was not a man to do any repining. He knew the power he had at his command and he knew the limitations of the army he had tangled with. The Army of Northern Virginia had been bolder, more skillful and much fiercer than he had anticipated. Yet Lee's men, catching him at a disadvantage, lacked the strength to drive him from the field, or to impair the effectiveness of the vast and complex organism that was the Army of the Potomac.

After the reaction passed, Grant could look coldly at the physical potentials of the two armies and his natural pugnacity asserted itself. To support his determination to go at Lee again, there was the secondary army under Butler then threatening Richmond from the south. Lee would of necessity be concerned about his capital with an enemy at its back gate. With any success from Butler, Lee would be caught in a pincer between him and Grant, a hammer and anvil situation.

Though this was elementary sound reasoning, it still required confident aggressiveness to make it in the chaos of the Wilderness after Grant's introduction to Lee's army. It was this trait of a stubborn man, determined to do the job which had been given him, that decided Grant on his course of action.

He could rest his army, re-form its units, and move away from the pitfalls of the Wilderness. Moving fast, at least he would draw Lee out of the works his men had dug and fight in terrain more favorable to his numbers. At best, he could pass Lee's front and get between him and Richmond.

When this decision took form in his mind, Grant won the fundamental victory of the clash: he retained the initiative. Lee had failed to establish dominance over his opponent's mind. Shaken but intact, Meade's army possessed the physical strength and Grant the clarity of purpose to make the next move.

Tactically, Grant had lost a battle, in that he could not drive a weaker opponent. Strategically, his total offensive was unaffected.

10

The extent to which General Lee perceived the full implications of his clash with Grant would be anybody's guess. At the end of the day of the 6th, most likely Lee thought only of the immediate scene. On both sides of the Plank Road, from the Tapp farm clearing to the Brock Road, his disordered units were scattered in one of the most gruesome battle aftermaths of the war.

The absence of a front west of the Brock Road turned the square mile of darkening entanglements into a lost land for thousands of individual soldiers of both sides. The exhausted and bewildered groped their way toward groups of their own. The slightly wounded struggled to crawl away from the underbrush fires that sizzled and flared in the deepening shadows. The seriously wounded floundered and moaned, some calling for help. Cries of "Water" came continuously. In something like an area disaster, the soldiers of both armies thought first of helping their suffering fellow men. South Carolinian Frank Mixson, a three-year veteran at eighteen, said, "All we cared for was that he was a human being and brother, though we had fought him hard all day."

As the day ended the fighting across the Plank Road, none of Lee's generals needed to make a decision over whether or not the troops should be disturbed. With no unfought troops on the field, and no reserves within days of the army, the urgent problem was to collect the units, clear the woods of wounded, and form lines against a possible daylight attack. Strategic plans were gone. Around sunset General Field started his men digging in as soon as regiments began to regather. That part of the army on the Plank Road shifted itself to defense.

By accepting this condition, General Lee revealed his acceptance of the incompletion of his assault along the Plank Road. His last flickering hope for a conclusive attack in the Wilderness died with Gordon's belated effort on the Old Turnpike. When Lee returned to his tent beside the Plank Road, with night settling over the woods, he must have accepted the failure of his plan to wreck Grant's interrelated offensive at the center.

As an instinctive fighter, since his army held its field of action, the General could hope, however faintly, that the enemy would attack his entrenched men the next day. With one more decisive repulse, Grant might follow the course of Burnside and Hooker and withdraw across the river. As a realist, Lee could not place much foundation under such a wan hope. By entrenching his men and preparing to repel attack, Lee, as a professional soldier, was only doing what the existing situation indicated. Beyond that, whatever he recognized during that night in the Wilderness, thoughts of immediate offensive were gone. His counteroffensive had failed of its objective. With that failure went the initiative.

It seems unlikely that Lee would receive the full impact of this significance in the fatigue and disappointment following fourteen hours of crises. It also seems likely that his unconquerable spirit, transcending as it must a logical appraisal, refused to accept the final reality of loss of the power to initiate action.

Then, too, a larger perspective would have been difficult to achieve through the pressing urgency of details. Though his losses did not exceed eight thousand infantry, his one dependable lieutenant general, Longstreet, was lost for the foreseeable future. His most intense fighting lieutenant general, Hill, was coming down sick, and his third corps commander, Ewell, was manifestly unfit for high command.

Moving up Dick Anderson for Longstreet, and Jubal Early temporarily for Hill, placed two more divisions under untried brigadiers and, with their transfer, two more untried colonels at brigade command. In addition, three brigadiers were gone from Ewell's corps, along with the second-in-command of corps artillery. The wound-prone MacGowan was temporarily lost from Hill's corps, and in Longstreet's corps the brilliant young Jenkins was gone, along with the temporary loss of Charlie Field and Rock Benning from slight wounds. In Kershaw's old brigade, temporarily commanded by the ex-sheriff Henagan, the deaths of Colonels Gaillard and Nance depressed the men who had known those distinguished South Carolinians and devoted Confederates since the pre-Sumter days.

Of necessity, Lee's attention was directed that night to the solution of the immediate problems of command. In doing this, he was left with no time nor mental energy to look beyond the next day.

It has often been pointed out that, as Burnside and Hooker had withdrawn across the river after their defeats, Lee expected Grant to do the same. Nothing in Lee's actions or words indicates that he expected this. By aligning his men in defense, though he could not seriously hope the enemy would try works in the Wilderness, Lee showed that he did not anticipate a withdrawal. He recognized as clearly as Grant how much the Army of Northern Virginia had accomplished and how much it had failed to accomplish, and why. He also knew about Butler at Richmond; he had known it before Butler got there, which was one reason for the urgency in striking at the center of the enemy's invasion.

Having brought on the battle along the lines of his choice, though not under the conditions he would have wished, his army had been forced to survive a succession of hairbreadth escapes. It had survived the shocks, held its ground, and accomplishing that extended the ultimate limit of its potential.

Grant would be less carelessly confident in his next move, and he would certainly get out of the Wilderness. But the move would be up to Grant. There was nothing Lee could do except wait for it. With one of Early's absent brigades coming up, Lee could wait with perhaps thirty-eight thousand infantry.

As for his cavalry, though no figures had come in, the mounted troops had suffered under the hard fighting and already losses in irreplaceable horses were heavy. Jeb Stuart could do no more than guard the flanks and, as galling as it was to his combative spirit, watch for signs that would indicate the enemy's intention. There was nothing more any of them could do when night came on that warm Friday of May 6th.

Those who fought with him and against him, and those who came after, regarded the two-day battle as the opening of a campaign. The Wilderness was a campaign in itself, as were Second Manassas and Chancellorsville. After Second Manassas (where Pope had first been maneuvered northward) and after Chancellorsville, Lee was free to strike on counterinvasions in the enemy's land against an opponent with the offensive taken from him. After the Wilderness, the offensive was gone from Lee.

PART TWO

"To Command Is To Wear Out"

CHAPTER SEVEN

"If It Takes All Summer"

DURING THE restless Saturday of May the 7th, General Lee began his first defensive campaign of the war. He did not acknowledge this to himself. Yet, as the General pieced together the bits of information that came to him in the Wilderness, he studied Grant's intentions for the purpose of thwarting him, and not of defeating him.

In Lee's natural will to win, he would consider that any defensive stand could offer his army the opportunity to deliver a decisive blow; but, by acceptance of this role, Lee tacitly limited himself to anticipating the enemy. Confident in his generalship, Lee could also hope that successful anticipation of the enemy might develop opportunities for counterblows; but this shift to dependence on opportunism in battle was a tacit admission of the loss of initiative.

In looking for evidences of Grant's intention, Lee discovered early Saturday morning that the enemy did not propose to continue the battle in the Wilderness. The Confederate skirmishers in the charred thickets fired at any blurred movement ahead of them, sniped at any unwary blue figure that exposed itself, and huddled close to the ground against return fire. With every sense alert to detect movement coming in their direction, they *felt* the absence of aggressiveness in the enemy.

To Lee, at his informal field headquarters in the little farm clearing, it was evident that the two past days had convinced Grant of the ineffectiveness of numbers in the briery, blinding, then smoking brush. With the Confederates fortified and inviting attack, even such a free-swinging opponent as Grant would back off and try to get at the Army of Northern Virginia from another angle, in a more favorable terrain. From the way in which he had come pouring into the Wilderness, and with his large and efficient supporting services, Grant was not likely to delay in putting his well-conditioned army in movement again.

To counter the move, Lee would have to work with his incomplete army. All available units were in the irregular north-south line, facing east. The individuals out of line, working in burial details and assisting the understaffed medical corps with the wounded, would be ready on short notice to rejoin their regiments. Also, an unusually large proportion of the casualties consisted of lightly wounded men who, in the seesaw action in the area of their positions, had escaped capture while temporarily incapacitated. These hundreds, not listed on the casualty rolls, would also be ready to rejoin their fellows. Lee needed every man of them, for his absent brigades were not coming.

Pickett's division and Hoke's old brigade would be held at Richmond, now that Butler's army had gone into action on the south side of the James River. Already Kautz's cavalry, with Butler, had cut the life-line railroad from Petersburg to Weldon, North Carolina, which connected there with the railroad to the open port of Wilmington.

Lee did not divert his attention to the possible fall of Richmond behind him. He had warned Davis and suggested protective measures, and the city's fate was as out of his hands as was Atlanta's fate, five hundred miles away. To Lee, the danger primarily meant that for the present he must operate against Grant without replacements.

Of more immediate concern was the strain placed on the cavalry's poorly conditioned horses by Sheridan's pressing tactics. The Federals' new cavalry chief seemed bent only on fighting Stuart's numerically weaker force into the ground. In subordinating the traditional reconnaissance service of the mounted arm to cavalry-against-cavalry combat, Sheridan reflected Grant's policy of subordinating finesse to the application of might. Though this might seem a clumsy use of relatively inexhaustible manpower, nonetheless this cold pragmatism represented a constant potential of danger against Lee's smaller force, with supporting manpower almost non-existent. If he were caught off balance or out of position just once, the machine would roll over his men, and that would be the last of them all.

Looking squarely at the enemy's command policy in the changed war, as revealed by May 7th, Lee used fragments of information to deduce the move Grant would make — not Meade, not just any general, but specifically Grant.

When Ewell's scouts reported that the enemy's right flank had severed connections with the Germanna Ford crossing, cutting off retreat, Lee knew for a certainty that Grant was preparing for a move to another line of advance on Richmond. The question was where? Cavalry reports indicated that heavy wagons were in movement to the east, and Lee thought briefly that Grant might be shifting to Fredericksburg. There he would be closer to the supply base at Belle Plain, and on Lincoln's old favorite highway (the present Route 1) for an "On to Richmond."

Against this, personal reports from Jeb Stuart indicated heavy activity by Sheridan's cavalry around Todd's Tavern, on the road south from Grant's position to Spotsylvania Court House. As it seemed more in Grant's character to cross his front and try by a quick move to get between his army and Richmond, Lee soon discarded the Fredericksburg possibility and shifted to the little courthouse village of Spotsylvania County as Grant's more likely objective.

To anticipate Grant without committing himself, Lee gave General Pendleton the responsibility for cutting a road through the pinewoods from his right flank in the direction of Spotsylvania. (The enemy would have the use of the much-disputed Brock Road and another farther east.) It is not known precisely why the General selected his nominal chief of artillery to supervise an engineering job. In the informality of his total staff, Lee employed his clergyman friend in various capacities which used his conscientiousness and urgent attention to small details.

Late in the afternoon, after making another personal check with Ewell's headquarters on the Turnpike, Lee stopped at A. P. Hill's headquarters on his way back to the Tapp farm. Hill had taken over an abandoned house between the Old Turnpike and the Plank Road, and the General joined him there on the porch. As they conversed, Colonel Palmer was passing the time by looking through a marine glass at what he believed to be Grant's headquarters. Some shingles had been broken out of the roof to make an observation post of the attic, and Hill's staff took turns at the small opening.

While General Lee was still on the porch, young Palmer hurried downstairs and reported that a large park of heavy guns had started moving out of a field behind the enemy's headquarters. The guns were moving south, the direction that led to Spotsylvania.

That was enough for General Lee. He rode back to his own tent and issued orders for his staff to deliver. At that time, as far as Lee knew, not one Federal soldier had moved out of the facing lines, except on the Confederates' far left, near the river. Such was his confidence in his deductions that orders went to Longstreet's corps to pull out of the lines at dark. Exposing the whole right flank, the two divisions were to prepare to move by three o'clock in the morning to Spotsylvania.

In sending this order, Lee disregarded the element of uncertainty in having a new man in command of the corps formed by Longstreet. Only that day had he shifted Major General Richard H. Anderson from division command in Hill's corps to succeed Old Pete in command of the First Corps.

Lee's choice for the corps command was probably Jubal Early as the better soldier. Always considering personalities in a people's army, he first conferred with Longstreet's chief of staff. Forthright young Moxley Sorrel told the commanding general that Early's harshness and criticism of others would make him unpalatable to the old-timers in the First Corps. On the other hand, Dick Anderson was warmly remembered for his service with the corps, before his division was transferred in the formation of Hill's Third Corps. He would be welcomed. On that Lee made the decision, despite Anderson's lackluster career with Hill.

On that decision, very probably the war was prolonged in Virginia. Among all the *ifs*, it is almost a certainty that if Longstreet had been in command, Grant would have won the race to Spotsylvania Court House. From there, between Lee and Richmond, with Butler at the city's back door, Grant would have been well on his way toward a quick and complete victory in the opening battle of the new campaign.

Lee's anticipation would not have been enough to save the situation. By the relative conditions of the roads traveled by the two forces, the Brock Road and Pendleton's poor trace cut through the woods, Lee's men needed the elements of chance on their side.

2

The first element of chance was the burning woods in the area where Anderson pulled the two divisions out of line. The flames ran along the ground brush, climbing up the vines, and some of the dry trees caught, "burning furiously," Dick Anderson recorded.

Anderson himself was the second element of chance. Advancement and opportunity came simultaneously and suddenly to the reserved South Carolinian, who spent one ill-adjusted year in Hill's new corps. When under Longstreet's familiar control, unassertive Anderson had built a record of high competence, and General Lee evidently believed corps command would bring out the qualities Anderson had displayed at his best. Then he had been sound of judgment, quick to decision, energetic in movement, and in combat had that urge, which Lee so much admired in his generals, of staying right with the enemy. As it happened, the opportunity of moving out against the enemy, within a few hours of assuming command, caused a reaction in Anderson beyond anything Lee could have expected.

Around nine o'clock Anderson started withdrawing the troops of his new command from their positions. When they fell back to the area for their rest, before moving out on Lee's orders by three in the morning, Anderson discovered he would have to move some distance to clear the burning woods. At the same time, he discovered the wretched condition of the "road" Pendleton had cut. Consulting no one, he abandoned the allotted period of rest and put the two divisions into motion without sleep.

The day had been quiet and easy on the men, with less than a dozen wounded in the corps from picket fire, and during the evening hours some had probably dozed off as they rested. Nevertheless, Longstreet would have given his men sleep until the three o'clock outside hour allotted in Lee's orders and only then started them out. Anderson had the two divisions actually on the road by eleven o'clock. Those four hours determined the course of the war's history in Virginia.

Walking fifty minutes of each hour, stumbling in the first miles over tree stumps protruding from the ground, Anderson's men required more than six hours to cover eight miles. Their march on the trace was almost due south to the Catharpin Road, where they turned almost due east toward the courthouse. Sometime after five in the morning, in first light, the two divisions emerged from the woods into an open clearing with a nearby stream. There they were three miles west of Spotsylvania Court House with no enemy visible in the early light of Sunday morning. The new commander then allowed the troops a full rest of an hour, during which the men cooked and ate their breakfasts.

A chunk of fattish bacon and a hardtack was all they had, washed down by a tin cup of substitute coffee made from sweet potatoes or peanuts. Yet the hot liquid was cheering and, as the soldiers pointed out, they always stood up better to marching and fighting when fortified in the morning by a piece of meat. However small, it was all their bodies were accustomed to. Federal medical officers reported that shock and "the depression of vital powers" was much greater among the wounded who had gone into action without breakfast than among those who had eaten something.

While Anderson's men were fortifying themselves, Warren's V Corps (newly organized for the spring campaign under a hero of Gettysburg) was wearing itself out on a forced night march along the Brock Road. Two elements, not of chance, contributed to the frazzled condition of the troops in Warren's four divisions. As frequently in the war, one element was malfunctioning in their own organization and the other a sharp performance in the opponent. On Warren's night march, the elements were interactive.

In the Army of the Potomac, the subsurface conflict had not been resolved between Meade's old-liners and the new men who came with Grant. Though General Meade gracefully accepted his awkward status of executing Grant's decisions, he still regarded himself as commander of the army in its field operations. Grant's man Sheridan, who was neither by training nor nature a cavalryman, wanted essentially to fight his mounted troops as an independent combat force and resented Meade's attempts to restrict him to cavalry's traditional uses in support of infantry. This situation would soon be resolved by the reduction of Meade's authority and

Sheridan's ascendancy in power directly under Grant. But on the night march along the narrow, winding Brock Road cooperative communication broke down between Meade and the new cavalry chief.

Sheridan, whose mounted troops were badly mismanaged, acted more as if the infantry followed along to support him. In Merritt's division, preceding Warren's corps, the men and horses were tired from all their forced fighting, and clogged the roads for miles. The foot soldiers, for whom the cavalry was supposed to provide a screen and clear the road, spent the long night hours shuffling a few steps behind the horsemen and then halting. They never halted long enough to break ranks and rest, and never marched far enough to gain any momentum. They were exhausted by daylight, when the first firing broke out ahead.

This firing represented, on the opposite side, the outstanding performance which Jeb Stuart provided Lee's army that unseasonably hot Sunday morning. In a clear-cut victory, his services would have overshadowed his gaudiest adventures. As it was, though less spectacular than his exploits of the early days, Spotsylvania was probably Stuart's most solid contribution to the Army of Northern Virginia. The fate of the campaign depended on him there. With no chance for the glory which he had vainly chased at Gettysburg, Major General Stuart fought his forces and cooperated with the infantry in an action which could serve as a model for the function of mounted troops in relation to an army.

Unlike Sheridan, Jeb Stuart was the apogee of the cavalryman. As a Confederate, the young and golden quality of his image, even his flamboyant uniforms with the plume and red-lined cape, evoked the chivalric tradition. Whether dancing at parties or riding in battle, laughing in camp or singing on the march, he was, a staff officer said, "always in character," and that character expressed the spirit of the age for which the South was fighting.

The physical decline of his troops, forcing him on the defensive against increased strength of the Federal cavalry, did not affect Stuart's character in the least. Instead, he adroitly shifted tactics to compensate for his weak horses in contending with Sheridan's aggressively applied power. Fighting dismounted whenever possible, he endured the gall of watching his regiments barely hold their own, and not always that, in a series of running actions, while he adhered steadfastly to his assignment of screening the infantry. Liking to win more than most fighters, General Stuart never concentrated his units in order to make a good fight against the enemy cavalry.

His organization was then in what might be called a "fluid" stage. Before Gettysburg, the summer before, Stuart's cavalry had consisted of one division composed of five large brigades. To permit promotion of talented, spirited young officers, Stuart petitioned Lee for permission to change his organization into a corps, consisting of two divisions and six brigades. One of Lee's thoughtful soldiers observed after the war that the single most grievous weakness in the army was the lack of incentive of field promotion, caused by the administration's bureaucratic control. As Lee himself suffered from his lack of authority to promote general officers in his own army, he willingly assisted his young friend in changing the cavalry's organization to serve the end of morale.

Then in the spring, Lee's middle son, Brigadier General W. H. F. Lee, the big fellow called "Rooney," returned recuperated from a Northern prison. His capture had aroused a good deal of feeling, as he had been snatched out of his wife's home, where he was in bed wounded, and his wife died during his imprisonment. While he was away, John Chambliss, a West Point-educated young planter, had done too well on Lee's brigade to be demoted. Stuart solved that situation by reorganizing again. W. H. F. Lee was promoted to major general and, with various shifts in and combinations of regimental units, the corps was divided into three divisions of two brigades each.

Rooney's cousin, Fitzhugh Lee, commanded a division with the Virginia brigades of Lomax and Wickham, and W. H. F. Lee's division held his own old Virginia brigade under Chambliss and James Gordon's North Carolina brigade. Wade Hampton, the herculean South Carolina grandee, commanded Tom Rosser's Virginia brigade and Butler's makeshift small brigade of Carolinians and Georgians.

Hampton also had a problem over promotions. Calbraith Butler had lost a foot at Brandy Station the year before and, during his long absence, his undermanned brigade was commanded very ably by an elegant young Carolinian named Pierce Young. Like Chambliss, Young was a West Point graduate without regular army service. It happened that three finely equipped South Carolina cavalry regiments had enjoyed thoroughly that segment of Davis's troop dispositions which kept them near home, disporting themselves in all the regalia of war without the danger of a shot or the discomfort of missing a meal. These gallants were ordered on to Richmond, to meet Calbraith Butler on his return to duty. Though these expedients solved Hampton's command problems, on the 8th of May these regiments and Butler were more than a fortnight away from their destination. Also a couple of odd units, ordered up from Georgia to fill out Pierce Young's weak brigade, had not arrived.

At Spotsylvania, then, Stuart's cavalry corps consisted, in fact, of five brigades, numbering on the average approximately fifteen hundred each, plus the several hundred troopers with Pierce Young. With no very young officers to pull the age level down, and with middle-aged Hampton to bring it up, the general officers averaged less than thirty-five years of age, with Stuart at thirty-one.

Against this cavalry corps, Sheridan's well-mounted three divisions mustered around forty-five hundred effectives each, and his corps outnumbered Stuart's by about fifty per cent. Prior to May 8th, Sheridan's reports of fighting the enemy's cavalry read so consistently of "routing the rebels" and "driving the enemy handsomely" that he gave the impression of the woods full of Stuart's fleeing people, leaving wounded and prisoners in their incontinent panic. In the race for the crucial crossroads at Spotsylvania, Sheridan had two of his divisions riding around looking for more rebels to chase, while Merritt's division, on spent horses, impeded the progress of the infantry whose front they were supposed to screen.

At the same time, Stuart so disposed his units as to cover all approaches for his own infantry, posted one brigade to guard the courthouse, and gave the assignment of slowing down the enemy's advance to the commanding general's high-living nephew, Fitzhugh Lee. Stuart himself was out with his staff long before daylight, waiting for developments in the clearing near the courthouse village.

As seen in the first light, General Stuart, with all his vain display, "looked like work." When it came to work, he never rode big horses as part of making a show. He liked middle-sized animals, quick and nimble, and he handled them with no awareness of the horse at all. He was also totally unaware of personal danger. A devout Episcopalian, like many another old-fashioned Christian in Lee's army, the days of his life were as implicitly in God's hands as the days of a happy child are in his parents'.

During the early morning, he apprised General Anderson of the progress of the Federal infantry along the Brock Road. Well before dawn, Fitz Lee's two-brigade division had placed obstructions in the Brock Road passageway. For lightly equipped cavalry, the troopers did a pretty good job of pulling branches and logs across the road. In any event, the obstructions slowed Sheridan's tired men and provided more obstacles for Warren's miserable foot soldiers.

Near daylight, when Merritt's cavalry division established contact, Fitz Lee's dismounted troopers fought in the woods as if they had come there to stay. The two brigades numbered less than three thousand, with one in every four of those pulled out of line as horse-holders. Yet, firing with single-shot carbines from behind trees on both sides of the obstructed road, the cavalrymen gave no indication of their awareness of the full infantry corps behind Merritt. Though the troopers did not know it, their stand allowed Anderson's men the period of full rest and food.

3

The cavalry fight in the woods began beyond the Wilderness, with its matted screens and stands of saplings, but Spotsylvania's second-growth woods were laced with typical Virginia vines and the ground thick with underbrush. It was favorable terrain for defense of cavalry against cavalry, and Merritt's division could not drive Fitz Lee. Under the pressure of numbers and heavier fire power from the repeating carbines, Lee's two brigades gave ground very slowly. After about an hour of daylight, his men had not yet been pushed out of the woods into the open clearing.

Though it made Sheridan boil to do it, and he tried to throw the blame on Meade, by six o'clock he had to call on Warren's infantry to come up and drive Confederate cavalry. Warren was slow in getting his lead division deployed. This thirty-four-year-old professional soldier had been seized with ambition after his heroic hour at Gettysburg. Regarding the war as a means to the big fame, he was understandably cautious about another pell-mell attack after the rough handling his corps suffered from Ewell on the Old Turnpike. Also, his troops were exhausted by then, and they began wearily forming their lines in the woods while Anderson's two divisions were stretching themselves after breakfast.

Warren's road, running southeast, debouched from the woods about one and a half miles northwest from Spotsylvania Court House. Anderson's resting field was three miles about due west of the village by the Shady Grove Church Road. By the time, around seven o'clock, that Robinson's lead division of Warren's corps had deployed and finally pushed Fitz Lee's troopers out of the woods, the lead brigades of Kershaw's division had marched one and a half miles closer to Spotsylvania. This spot was locally designated as the Block House, from a curious dwelling structure owned by a man named Perry. At this point, Kershaw and Robinson were about the same distance from the village, but, across the open clearing of the Spindler farm, the two forces were only one mile directly from each other.

The importance of the village, a cluster of modest buildings dominated by an imposing new courthouse, existed entirely in its location. The north-south road was intersected there by the east-west road. In point of fact, a road to Fredericksburg terminated at the village from the east, and the westward road which led eventually to Orange began several hundred yards north of town, but to all military intents Spotsylvania Court House was a crossroads junction. The roads changed names at intervals, according to the light in which the various communities regarded the destinations, though none of this concerned troops hurrying into a meeting engagement.

The place where the opposing infantry met was determined by a line of light works which some of Stuart's busy people had thrown together, from dismantled fence rails, as protection in the clearing south of the woods. Fitz Lee's by then cut-up regiments could not have withstood one push of an infantry brigade. Around six o'clock Lee had sent word of his danger, in opposing an infantry corps. When his troopers fell back to the fence rails, supported by

Breathed's battery of horse artillery, he sent Anderson an urgent appeal to race his men to the flimsy works before the Federal infantry got there.

At the same time, to the right and rear of Lee, and east of Anderson, Rosser's cavalry brigade was being forced back to the courthouse town by Wilson's division of Sheridan's corps. Though the woods to the north and west of the town obscured the details of the action there, the spat of carbines identified the fight as between cavalry. Dick Anderson, without hesitating between the courthouse and the enemy infantry in his front, turned his two lead brigades off the road to Spotsylvania and sent the men running to Fitz Lee's line about a mile to the north.

By the chance of march, the two brigades ran along a farmer's road through a clearing which was screened from the enemy by a light stand of woods behind the cavalry's fence rails. That would be the last run the unslept men would have in them for the day. However, due to that bacon for breakfast, they had it when they needed it.

On the other side, Robinson's worn-out lead brigade, weakened by stragglers, had waited for the second brigade to clear the woods before attacking the partially protected troopers across an open stretch of ground. During their wait, the two brigades of Kershaw's division made their run. The last of Kershaw's men reached the works when the first line of advancing Federals was less than one hundred yards away. It was that close.

By then the time had passed for a hastily thrown-in Federal assault. The Confederate veteran brigades were Humphrey's Georgians and Kershaw's South Carolinians, led by ex-sheriff Colonel Henagan. Along with the advantage of defense, these troops possessed the moral lift of having checked the Federal breakthrough two days before and then rolling up the enemy. Two batteries of Haskell's battalion were giving them good support very close up.

The attacking Federals, along with being tired and unfed, had not yet recovered from the disastrous effects of being sent in too fast against Ewell in the Wilderness. Besides, the officers, with no information from Sheridan, told the men they were only attacking cavalry, who could offer no defense against bayonets. Some of the soldiers in the first line found out different when they stumbled close enough to get a good look. But the other lines pushed on from behind, all losing heavily from the rifle fire in their sleepwalking pace over the rough ground. When they finally closed with the bayonets, it was no contest.

The Confederate infantry held the advantages of surprise, of some protection from the works, and for that moment the men were fresher. The experienced survivors of the assault force, recognizing that this was not their day, ran away as fast as their leaden legs could carry them. Warren got Robinson to try again with other units, and they fared as badly. In a morning hour or so, the division was wrecked beyond repair, and its remnants were later scattered among other units.

This meeting engagement, causing the First Corps very light losses, turned out to be the crucial action in the battle for Spotsylvania Court House. Yet before the field was clearly won, another urgent choice came to Dick Anderson, on his first day of corps command.

While his two brigades watched the beginning of the deployment of Warren's four divisions coming out of the woods across their front, and his other two brigades at the Block House were about to come up in support, a message arrived from Jeb Stuart. Rosser's brigade had been driven from the courthouse village, and Wilson's big cavalry division occupied the crossroads. Stuart had sent a horse battery there, and fragments of Wickham's brigade with Fitz Lee temporarily occupied the Federal division's attention. However, if Wilson formed lines for dismounted troopers and held for his infantry to come up in support, it would be all over. As it was, Rosser was in danger of being gobbled up.

Again Anderson took first things first. He rerouted the brigades of Wofford and Bryan on a hurried circuitous march to the courthouse. Again the Confederates received timely help from Sheridan. In another confusion in command, the cavalry chief ordered Wilson's division to abandon Spotsylvania at the approach of Kershaw's two strung-out brigades. Without his infantry engaged in the town, Anderson had secured the crossroads by working in spontaneous harmony with Stuart.

Jeb Stuart never left the scene. While Anderson was deploying his brigades as they came on the field, the cavalry chief remained in the almost exact center of things, personally extending the infantry line to the left with the reduced force of dismounted troopers in Lomax's brigade. The firing was so heavy around him that he sent his staff officers off, sometime with needless messages, to keep them out of danger. One of them remembered Stuart alone, sitting quietly on his horse in a picture of relaxed alertness, as he surveyed the action swirling around him.

When the Georgia brigades of Wofford and Bryan passed through the town, Anderson hurried them on northward to extend the right of the line of Kershaw's other two brigades, then digging in behind the fence rails. For a time on the left, while Warren's full corps unfolded in their front, only the dismounted troopers of Lomax's brigade extended the line, with the support of the gun batteries.

When Warren's four divisions got seriously down to business, Field's division, following Kershaw, began to deploy on the left in good defensive ground. It was still four divisions to two, but Warren could mount no sustained attack against the heavy fire spurting from behind works, and a couple of Field's angled counterattacks in the woods prevented him from throwing forward his full weight at one thrust.

In terms of the military purpose for which the armies met, the first battle of the new campaign was over then. Grant had not passed Lee's front. Lee stood squarely in the way of the road to Richmond.

During the afternoon, Lee and Grant came on the field, as their armies converged, and the fighting extended. The decision had already been won, by Jeb Stuart's last contribution to his cause and by Richard H. Anderson enjoying the greatest day he was ever to know with the Army of Northern Virginia.

For Anderson, it was like one inspired hour in a capable, contained man. Released from an unstimulating situation and offered sudden opportunity, he was seized with a fire in the spirit which briefly blended each of his talents at the top of their potential.

Well before the day was over, General Lee assumed control of the widening field. When the fighting faded off at dusk, Lee expected Grant, finding his move checked, next to try to overrun him by force. Though Grant had the potential strength, Lee did not fear him in a straight-on action. He did fear draining his own manpower in an inconclusive defense.

To avoid exposing his irreplaceable manpower, the General put his tired men to digging entrenchments on the ground they must hold. He would not attempt a counterattack unless Grant grew careless in his confidence in numbers and exposed segments of Meade's army. That possibility, existing in the realm of hope when night fell on May the 8th, must wait on the immediate details of preparing his own army against making any mistakes themselves.

4

On Monday, May the 9th, one week from the day when the generals gathered on Clark's Mountain, Lee left his tent shortly after three o'clock in the morning. In that one week, Lee faced the beginning of the collapse of his command organization around him.

With Longstreet lost on the 6th, two days later, while the army raced to support Anderson at Spotsylvania, A. P. Hill reported sick. He followed behind his troops in an ambulance, too ill to give orders, while Lee hastily summoned Jubal Early from his division in the Second Corps to assume temporary command of Hill's corps. Despite the unpopularity which Early's bitter harshness won for him, Lee held Old Jube's soldierly qualities in great respect. Still, he was untried in corps command, and the Third Corps had in Mahone, Anderson's successor, a long-time brigadier only two days in division command. Lee came onto the dark field Monday morning to prepare to meet Grant's rushes with new men on two of his corps and demonstrably undependable Ewell on the third.

With no announcement of it, and perhaps no conscious awareness, Lee began that day to direct his army on the compact field of Spotsylvania at a more personal level of field command. The semiautonomous status of the three corps was retained in the field of administration, but for combat Lee shifted about their division units, and even brigades, according to his single view of the action. Frequently he operated directly with subordinates without clearing through their superior. Occasionally there simply wasn't time. Primarily, Lee's increasing urgency caused him to do the things himself when he needed to be sure they were done the way he wanted. He became more like a field commander, and headquarters (though the headquarters tent was maintained) became wherever the General could be found on his horse.

In this shift to the direction of combat units, General Lee, in order to get men of his choice where he wanted them, displayed an impatient pragmatism in evading Davis's tables of organization. Usually, after giving proper consideration to the canons governing seniority and to the President's sensitivity over the state-consciousness of troops and constituents, Lee could only submit names to Richmond for approval. At Spotsylvania Court House, the General violated the principle without doing violence to the form of his superior's policy.

The man he wanted to replace the transferred Early in division command was John B. Gordon. This highly spirited Georgian had twice been overruled by Early and Ewell (at the Wilderness and earlier in a crucial hour at Gettysburg) when his initiative attracted Lee's attention. Gordon was one of those men encountered in any field who never stopped thinking about his work. To his vigilance he brought intelligence and self-confidence. When not restrained, he was energetic and clear-minded in action, very quick to perceive and exploit an opportunity offered by the enemy. With his ramrod carriage and proud tilt of his head, he presented such an inspiring image in battle that one of his soldiers said, "He's so purty, it'd put fight in a whupped chicken just to look at him."

To elevate this untrained soldier who had become a favorite of his, General Lee was forced to evade the seniority law with Harry Hays, senior brigadier in Early's division, himself a good man whom Lee would not wish to offend. It happened that both Hays's Louisiana brigade (the former "Tigers" famed in Jackson's valley campaign) and Stafford's Louisiana brigade, in Edward Johnson's division, were below average in numbers when Leroy Stafford was killed at the Wilderness. Lee removed Hays from Gordon's path by combining the two Louisiana brigades and giving Hays command of the new, large, home-state brigade — with the combined unit in Johnson's division.

However, since Hoke's old brigade had not yet been released by Davis, the division commanded by Gordon would then contain only two brigades. But R. D. Johnston's brigade, of Rodes's division, had just been released from its guard duty and, as Rodes commanded four other brigades, Johnston was shifted to Gordon's division. In proving "there's more than one way to skin a cat," General Lee made a move which, like his decision to go with Dick Anderson, was to have a vital affect on a crucial action.

These shifts in command structure occupied little of Lee's time. When he rode along the lines before daylight, his mind was concentrated on building fieldworks stronger than any previously used in the war. Though both armies (and those in the West also) dug in immediately on taking a position, at Spotsylvania Lee developed a more complicated system of entrenchments which, extended further by both sides later, introduced what became modern trench warfare. Meade's chief of staff reported that the nature and extent of Lee's entrenchments were "unknown to European war [and] new to warfare in our country."

In preparing these defenses Lee had the advantage of his long experience as an engineer in the peacetime regular army. He was as brilliant in that field as he was in army command. As a young lieutenant in the old army, he completed the fortifications at Fort Monroe, on the tip of the Virginia peninsula, and this was the only major United States installment in the South which remained in Union possession throughout the war. Similarly, Savannah and the works around Richmond, the two defensive positions which he erected in the first year of the war, remained impregnable to attack. (Savannah was taken from the land side after the military collapse in Georgia.)

In all his fieldworks, Lee's eye caught the natural roll of ground. His entrenchments rose with the earth as part of nature's conformations. (Viewed in their unoccupied condition today, it is difficult without study to distinguish works dug by Lee's men from the contours of the ground.)

At Spotsylvania, he was forced to work with three unavoidable disadvantages in designing his field fortifications. First, he must build approximately along the existing lines, formed haphazardly by the circumstance of battle. Then woods of varying degrees of density covered more than half of his front, offering the enemy both concealment and some protection in advancing. Finally Rodes's and

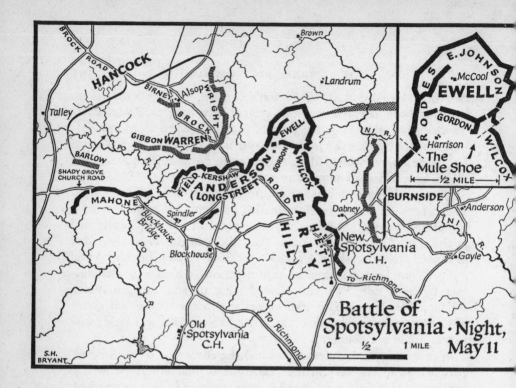

Battle of
Spotsylvania · Night,
May 11

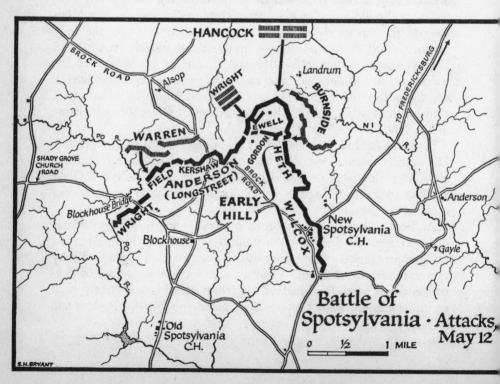

Battle of
Spotsylvania · Attacks,
May 12

Johnson's divisions of Ewell's corps joined in a triangular salient which projected northward nearly one mile from the lines sloping to the southeast and southwest. Ewell had made the last section of this extension deliberately, in order to occupy ground which offered the enemy a good artillery position.

Lee regarded this projection — "Mule Shoe," as the soldiers called it — dubiously from the beginning. Anxious to fortify his position before the aggressive Grant attacked, Lee put his men at unprecedentedly hard labor along the lines more or less as he found them. In turn, the soldiers were impressed with the way this new fellow, Grant, had come at them so quickly after his going-over in the Wilderness. They spent themselves uncomplainingly in building three miles of intricate works in a semicircle, with flanks resting on sharply banked streams.

Short of shovels, spades and pickaxes, the men dug with sharpened sticks and scooped up the earth with flattened canteens, tin cups, or anything at hand. Others cut down trees in their front, the logs were covered with earth, and traverses (cross-lines within the works) were built to protect the gunners from cross fire. For a distance of two hundred yards in their front, where picket lines were established, the men "slashed the woods" and immediately in front of the works erected timber barriers with sharp-pointed sticks, called abatis. The "toe" of the "Mule Shoe," not truly an angle as it came to be called, was fortified under the personal supervision of General Martin Smith, chief of engineers, and eight guns placed there. Two artillery battalions were posted within the one curving mile of the salient.

This extensive operation continued for three days (May 9th to 11th) while Grant unaccountably permitted these field fortifications to take form. He said that he left the Wilderness because Lee's men were waiting to be attacked in their strong works. The fortification at Spotsylvania became immeasurably stronger.

Like all generals in the Civil War, Grant was slow to adjust to the changed conditions presented by the magnified fire power of the rifle in conjunction with the relatively protected position of defensive troops behind works. All the professionals had studied tactics on the principles of the Napoleonic wars, which presumed an average effective range of about sixty yards in musket fire. Then, with the defensive line standing to receive the attack, everything else being equal, the advantage lay entirely with the larger force. With an effective rifle range of closer to three hundred yards, and the defensive line protected until the assault line got in close, a numerical superiority in the attacking force must be overwhelming to achieve a calculable advantage.

For the three unseasonably hot days that Lee's men doubled as day laborers, Grant probed here and there, made reconnaissances in force, tried a flank movement to the west beyond the Po River flank, and mounted several limited attacks. Nowhere did Meade's army assault with a concentration of force. In the continuous fighting, the well-protected Confederate artillery was very effective and Federal casualties ran high.

Late in the afternoon of May 10th, a sharp attack delivered against a segment of Ewell's line on the western side of the Mule Shoe effected the first break. Quick counteraction restored the breech when Federal reinforcements failed to arrive, but the unexplored local success convinced Grant that Lee's lines could be broken in that projecting salient. The next day, the 11th, a heavy rain began to fall, and during the afternoon Meade's staff evolved the details for Grant's delayed big push.

It was on this day that Grant, in a wire to Washington, wrote the widely misinterpreted phrase, "I propose to fight it out on this line if it takes all summer." The "this line" referred to what came to be called his "hammering" tactics. However, as he wrote in the same wire, "I am satisfied that the enemy are very shaky," he obviously did not expect to take all summer, nor had he anticipated that hammering would be required for long. When he planned his concentrated assault for the next morning, Grant would seem to have been convinced that Lee's Army was falling apart under his blows right then, and he intended to keep hitting until his famous opponent was broken. Grant underestimated his own casualties and overestimated Lee's which, through the fourth day at Spotsylvania, the 11th, had been comparatively light.

However, on that rainy afternoon, General Lee set in motion a little chain of incidents which brought to the Army of Northern Virginia an overdue slip in its organizational operations.

5

Between four and five o'clock on the afternoon of the 11th, General Lee received two messages from his son Rooney. Called "too big to be a man and not big enough to be a horse," W. H. F. Lee was operating on the enemy's flank with his division of Stuart's cavalry. The message, addressed to "General" and signed "Respectfully, W. H. F. Lee, major-general," mentioned that reconnaissance parties had discovered enemy trains moving to Fredericksburg, enemy wounded being moved to the Belle Plain base, and columns in motion. Cavalryman Lee concluded, "There is evidently a general move going on."

Commanding General Lee, keyed to anticipate Grant, evidently expected his opponent to move again rather than to attack his by then forbidding position. During that day, he had been notified of what appeared to be withdrawals in his front. Also, the Federals had made what Lee considered to be a feint on his left, beyond the Po River. But the right, where his son was patrolling, seemed the logical direction for the enemy's next move. Except through Spotsylvania, that was the way to the roads to Richmond.

On such slight evidence as Rooney's report, along with vaguer reports that some Federal troops were withdrawing from the front, General Lee would not pull his exhausted men out of line on a rainy night. Preparing for a possible morning move, he directed the advanced artillery to withdraw before dark to be ready for quick movement. The details covered by the word "directed," as in Colonel Venable's account, are vague and suggest a vagueness in command.

Chief of artillery Pendleton reported that Lee gave him the order to withdraw the advanced batteries, and implied that he gave the order to Alexander and Long, First and Second Corps artillery commanders. Ewell reported that he himself gave the order to Armistead Long. Ewell's son-in-law, staff officer Campbell Brown, wrote that he "heard General R. E. Lee give the order to General Long in person in General Ewell's presence." Later, in verifying this report, Brown recalled that the three generals were gathered at the Harris house shortly before sunset. Neither Long nor Alexander mentioned who gave them the orders, and neither they nor Ewell mentioned Pendleton in any way. This confusion is important in that it indicates the lack of a communication system of direct lines connecting with general headquarters.

As Lee had been getting up at three in the morning since the army reached Spotsylvania, he retired to his tent for the night around ten. The artillery corps commanders interpreted their orders according to their circumstances and natures. Being nearer the road, confident young Alexander, with his usual initiative, prepared his ammunition chests for moving out and brought the gun carriages up near the pieces, for instant withdrawal, but left the guns in line. Meticulous Long observed that the rainy night would be black and his batteries in the salient must cover a mile and a half by a difficult passage in the woods. Leaving only two batteries of Cutshaw's battalion scattered in the Mule Shoe, and none at the toe, Armistead Long withdrew the two battalions to the camp of corps reserve artillery around the courthouse.

In all this activity, nobody explained to Major General Johnson why his division's guns had been removed. His four brigades covered most of the works in the salient — three brigades on the eastern side and in the blunt toe, and one brigade from the apex down on the western side. Toward midnight his pickets on the eastern face of the salient reported heavy movement from the enemy in their wooded front. As a matter of fact, the Federals did everything except send over a flag-of-truce messenger announcing their intentions. Their bands playing all hours of the damp night, apparently designed to deaden the sounds of infantry movement, would have aroused anyone's suspicions. "Allegheny" Johnson sent off a report of these goings-on to General Ewell, and asked for the return of his guns.

There is no doubt that Dick Ewell, and no one else, endorsed Johnson's message and sent it as an order to Long. There is doubt about when he sent the order. Ewell received Old Allegheny's message, delivered by Major Hunter, Johnson's AAG, around midnight. Ewell implied that he sent on the order to his dapper artillery chief without delay. Major Hunter, however, reported that Ewell refused to countermand Lee's orders about the artillery, and he made a second trip back with General Johnson to persuade him.

Though neither Johnson nor Ewell mentioned this, the order was unconscionably long in reaching the corps artillery chief. Armistead Long reported that he receivèd it at three-thirty in the morning. This hour was verified by Major Page, who was immediately ordered to move forward the fourteen available guns of his battalion.

Aside from Ewell's endorsing Johnson's request for the return of his guns, and sending it on as an order to Long, no further attention was given Johnson's report of the enemy massing in his front. Old Baldhead would seem to have gone back to bed.

Except for one unsubstantiated personal account, no evidence indicates that Lee was informed. Colonel Venable stated specifically that he was not. The General had his breakfast by candlelight at three-thirty, when Johnson's guns were started back to the salient without his knowledge, and by all evidence the General was startled at the heavy gunfire that swept along the Mule Shoe shortly before daybreak.

Allegheny Johnson, left to his own devices, had alerted his men and manned the trenches some while before Hancock struck with his full corps. The roughhewn eccentric claimed that he would have repelled the assault except for the missing guns. Page's batteries had unlimbered in the dripping night woods, but by the time the cannoneers were in position to serve the pieces, guns and gunners were overrun by stampeding thousands of an enemy emerging out of the misty blackness. Only two pieces of twenty-two guns got off two shots each, and only two of Page's guns were brought out. Twenty were lost. The enemy broke over the works so quickly in such masses that a bewildered corporal asked a dying artillery officer which way to shoot. "At the Yankees," the artillerist said with his last breath.

Honest, forthright Johnson unquestionably told the truth as he saw it, and his viewpoint has been generally accepted. Most of his division had been technically alerted and physically moved into the trenches. This should not necessarily imply that the men were alertly manning the trenches.

Following on the hard fight in the Wilderness, the soldiers were underfed for three days of heavy manual labor in unseasonable heat, under the strain of constant exposure to danger, and with sleep broken by night picket duty. On that night what sleep they could get was snatched in the discomfort of the wet ground and the drifting veils of cold fog. It was an "uneasy night" anyway, as one soldier said, and some time in the early morning the men had been shuffled forward to the trenches. No breakfast, with hot coffee, had been brought forward to arouse them. It seems likely that the exhaustion which weakened Warren's corps for the first day's fight at Spotsylvania affected units of Johnson's division in the pre-daylight hour of the fifth day.

Because the spirit was emphasized where the soldiers were forced to endure so much on so little, Confederate officers had a tendency to minimize the factor of physical depletion. Fatigue was entered as an element in the performance of Grant's well-fed army more frequently than in Confederate reports, though Lee's soldiers dwelt ceaselessly on the subject of their hunger, their poor diet, and their stratagems to obtain mouthfuls of food. This factor was largely ignored where officers' reports of command failures usually read like a defense of personal honor. Unless the officer could find something outside his unit to blame, like the removed guns, his honor required him to prove that he had been vigilant and his men valorous. Saying that his men were "tired" might reflect on his abilities in administration and in sustaining morale.

Against this background, it must be considered that in the dead hour before a clammy dawn many of Johnson's men were half asleep when the enemy came swarming out of the fog. The men, having heard Federal troop movements for hours, did not expect an attack before daylight — as neither, by his own report, did General Johnson. By the time the awesome masses were heard rather than seen outside their works, doubtless few of Johnson's troops were aroused to their full powers of vigor and coordination.

In this consideration, there is also the factor of numbers. Johnson's division did not number appreciably more than five thousand effectives in camp, and the three-quarter mile of their curving narrow front was struck on three sides by four solid divisions of the best troops in the Federal army.

Because plain Old Allegheny was a notably brave man and selfless soldier, with an honorable career in both armies, his subordinates were anxious to clear the debacle from his record by placing the blame entirely on the removal of the artillery. Magnanimous Lee, as at Gettysburg, assumed the full blame himself in exonerating Johnson. But there were many factors. Though Lee made a wrong guess on Grant, a command flaw was exposed in an informal system which, that night, happened to operate around the pivot of Lizinka Ewell's physically failing and morally irresolute new husband.

The factor of the guns has been overemphasized. Gun support may well have given the men some chance to get set, and rounds fired from thirty-odd pieces, especially the eight in the blunt angle, could have given a different character to the clash. Yet scholarly, soundly trained artillerist Long, whose guns had been moved on a superior's orders, stressed the element of the fog in reporting that the result "might" have been different with all batteries in place. All observers stressed the obscuring fog, out of which the enemy appeared, and this would have affected the gunners as well as the infantry. Cutshaw's two guns that got off only two rounds were in position all night. Most of all, the impartial observers emphasized the quickness with which it was all over.

In the lack of serious check given the dense masses of assault troops, another factor mentioned was the wet powder in the paper-cartridges in the Stonewall Brigade. Brigadier General James A. Walker, holding the western works closest to the toe, emphasized the disheartening *plops* of rifle hammers striking on uninflammable powder. Yet properly alerted troops, sleeping in drippy woods after an afternoon of heavy rain, would have made sure their cartridges were serviceable.

Private Casler, one of the Stonewall Brigade's most case-hardened soldiers, made no mention of the wet powder. He said that the break at the toe exposed their own segment of line. "Before we knew it they [the enemy] were coming over the works of the second brigade of our division in solid numbers. They filed out to the right and left, firing at us behind our breastworks." A soldier in the 2nd Brigade, posted in the blunt toe of the salient, said *they* were doing all right when their left was exposed by a break in Walker's line.

It was known that the once-crack 2nd Brigade had been rebuilding under Jones, with a fairly large proportion of conscripts, when their likable brigadier was killed and the regiments shaken in the opening clash at the Wilderness. Ewell regarded Jones's "loss as an irreparable one to the brigade." His replacement, doing nothing to restore the men's morale, also seemed incompetent. At the time of Hancock's attack, the 21st Virginia Regiment, originally formed around proud, prewar militia outfits, was wandering off in the wet blackness between their works and their picket lines. In all the confusion, the regiment suddenly found itself *behind* Hancock's assault waves, and the men continued going until they came out in front of Hill's lines, east of the salient. The 2nd Brigade, low enough in numbers without missing regiments, had too few men in line to make a stout defense unless very well led and fighting at the top of their potential. As soldiers outside of the division seemed to assume the break began with the 2nd Brigade, most likely as a unit the troops in the toe were quickly overrun.

To their right, on the eastern face, it would look as if the recently combined Louisiana brigades also offered little resistance. Before their regiments had become accustomed to operating as a single unit, Harry Hays was wounded out on May 10th, and the colonel in command of the new outfit did not have them ready at four thirty-five A.M.

With all the blame and self-vindications, and all the other factors, the unmentioned factor of exhaustion, affecting the psychological preparedness of the units as units, was indicated by the nature of the division's undeniably feeble defenses.

The veteran division had been formed by Stonewall Jackson, around the nucleus of the proud and tough Stonewall Brigade, and contained the well-commanded Virginia brigade of "Maryland" Steuart. Yet these famous combat soldiers surrendered in droves, many without firing a shot. Uncounted numbers of men trained by bayonet-minded Stonewall Jackson were killed and wounded with bayonet thrusts inside their own lines.

Major General Johnson, angrily waving his hickory club up near the front lines, was swallowed up in the shadowy hordes of the enemy, and regular army "Maryland" Steuart vanished from sight. Both were hustled off as prisoners.

Walker, Jackson's onetime student at V.M.I., went down with wounds but made it out. The two colonels came out unscathed with the disordered remnants who escaped by fleeing before the onslaught. Major Hunter had picked up a black "rain overcoat," which bore no insignia, and by this chance threaded his way through crowds of the enemy until he found a stray artillery horse. When he spurred the horse away, swarms of bullets followed him. The staff officers at division headquarters back at the McCool house also made it out, including Henry Kyd Douglas, who had finally replaced his white mule with the sleek horse of a captured New York colonel.

Nobody knows how many were lost in the disaster. Ewell admitted two thousand prisoners and Hancock claimed "nearly 4000." The exact figure lay somewhere between. Killed and wounded ran into uncounted hundreds, and two brigades were later formed of the survivors of the five thousand-man division.

With a combination of all factors and no single villain, the breakthrough was, despite all the explanations invariably advanced in both armies after such disasters, one of those things that happen in war. In the Civil War particularly, battles were seldom won by the winner; the loser lost them.

For the dripping gloom of daylight on the 12th, the only point was that Stonewall Jackson's old division had ceased to exist and an enemy corps was pouring through the section of line it occupied in the center of Lee's position. The army was cut in two.

6

General Lee galloped up to the open end of the salient before first light, when the chilly fog blurred all except the closest objects. The wave of Hancock's corps had swept over the fortified lines so quickly that escaping Major Hunter reached the half-mile-wide base of the salient at the same time as Lee. Hunter blurted out the news. The General did not pause for any details. He spun wellrested Traveler around and started for General Gordon.

This brigadier, for whom Lee had used so many stratagems in order to give him a division, had been assigned the trusted place of reserve with orders from Lee to move immediately to any threatened point of the salient. The soldier of Lee's choice vindicated his judgment. As Lee rode to find Gordon, R. D. Johnston's brigade had already hurried forward, its whole strength deployed by Gordon in a line of skirmishers. Pegram's Virginia brigade, temporarily under a colonel, and Gordon's own Georgia brigade, commanded by Colonel Clement Evans, were forming battle lines to follow Johnston's North Carolinians when General Lee found Gordon, riding in front of his troops.

Here occurred another "Lee to the rear," less publicized than the Wilderness incident with the Texans. Happening in the murky predawn dimness, it was observed by few, and its retelling lacked the dramatic impact of the last-minute arrival of Longstreet's returning veterans loping across the clearing in the Wilderness. Yet with the Virginia and Georgia brigades forming behind the magnetic Gordon, General Lee seemed more purposeful about leading them into action than he had in the dazed state at the Tapp farm.

In front of Gordon's troops, when their lines prepared to move forward, General Lee showed agitation as he waved his gray hat, pointing ahead. The emergency was incomparably more complicated than in the Wilderness. There, however critical, the known situation was remediable by the straight-on advance of reinforcements to a given observable position. With Gordon, Lee could not even see the enemy.

All he and Gordon knew was that oncoming hordes were sweeping unchecked through the blurred woods in their front. Lee could presume that enemy forces would turn right and left to enfilade his lines adjoining the wrecked salient. Before developing countermeasures against their intentions, first he had to find them. He certainly could not wait until they found him.

In contrast to the Wilderness, when his horse carried him forward beside a line of trotting men, Lee prepared to move forward with the soldiers when their lines started toward the base of the Mule Shoe. This would seem the ultimate extension of his personal leadership in the compact position at Spotsylvania, where the size of the field and the narrow front enabled him to assume command like a field officer personally commanding a sector.

Another difference was that Gordon's men did not rouse him out of a trance, as did Gregg and his soldiers, and finally Colonel Venable, at the Tapp farm. While a Virginia sergeant grabbed the bridle to halt Traveler, Gordon argued Lee out of moving forward with them. His younger favorite assured the General that if he would go back, the troops — "these are Virginians and Georgians," Gordon said — would drive back the enemy. On that assurance, Lee moved aside, but he did not go "to the rear." He remained where he was, even when cannon fire began to break all around him, retaining direct command of all units on the field.

Though the episode was less glamorized, Gordon's men reacted with the same inspired fighting by which Gregg's Texans were remembered. Again, however, nobody saw them, except the enemy, though the behavior of Hancock's onrushing troops provided the greatest compliment Gordon could have received.

The homely British aphorism, "What you lose on the swings, you make up on the roundabouts," applied to the freak break of a veteran division of Lee's army. Hancock's units had not been in the best order from their night maneuvering to the point of attack. When the assaulting lines zoomed over the dark works, the men in the supporting lines grew excited and pressed in behind them. The fog had not lifted and daylight had not come when the three lines bunched together, one pushing on the other in the murky wet woods.

The muddy ground was sliced by gullies and strewn with the debris of battle. The poor visibility, which had played its part in Johnson's debacle, now took its toll of the attackers. In the elation of victory, where was there to go? The troops crowding from behind sent the forward elements stumbling ahead into the soggy woods, but not as lines of battle. Halfway down the inside of the salient, the victors became a mob.

At this point they were struck first by R. D. Johnston's North Carolina brigade, attacking in a skirmish line. Johnston fell wounded. His regiments could not stretch to cover the front of the enemy and his units grew confused. But so did Hancock's disorderly crowd. Some had then veered off, to the right and left, guided by officers trying to exploit the Confederate lines which they flanked. Where the presses in the woods of the salient milled uncertainly, Gordon's Virginia and Georgia brigades came charging out of the shadows with their high Rebel yells.

None of their rifles missed fire and, shooting at a four-foot level into those milling masses, few missed a target. They kept on coming, to close with the bayonet, their high-pitched screams echoing through the dripping woods to sound like ten times their number.

Gordon was a brigadier, in his first fight in command of a division, and each of his brigades was led by a colonel newly in command. The enemy knew nothing of this or what troops were behind the assault line. Soon the front ranks of the mob began pressing on the back ranks. By half-past six, in one of war's strange reversals, victorious units of four divisions began to give ground before two brigades and a broken part of a third.

7

Gordon's men did not, any more than had the Texans at the Wilderness, do it all alone. From the opening crash of the breakthrough, younger generals (outstandingly Ramseur in Rodes's division and Rodes himself) and the officers and men of several brigades rose to the emergency in one of the completest expressions of individual responsibility in a family army. They showed the other face of a personally commanded army, the antithesis of the breakdown, caused in part by a weak link, in the informal chain of command. They also gave the most convincing refutation to Grant's conviction that Lee's army was "shaky."

On the Confederate right, sloping southeastward from the projecting salient, Wilcox's division of Hill's corps held a powerful section of line, strongly supported by artillery. Their danger was enfilade fire from the enemy streaming toward their flank from inside the works of the salient.

Reacting quickly, Jim Lane, the professor from tidewater Virginia, broke back half of his North Carolina brigade to protect the flank. Those two regiments were ready to take the first shock. Their fire into the Federal masses brought the advancing troops to an uncertain pause. By the time the crowds pushed on again, energetic Wilcox had reduced his front to a skirmish line, with blasting fieldpieces, and rushed parts of Scales's and Thomas's brigades over in support of Lane. These brigades, though without replacements since their heavy casualties in rescuing Heth on the first day in the Wilderness, poured in too much fire for the unsettled condition of the Federal troops in the woods. Early in the morning, they fell back on the fringe of the mob retreating before Gordon.

On the western side of the salient, things were more serious.

There the disappearance of Walker's brigade, from whatever cause, immediately exposed the flank and rear of the troops in the lower section of the salient itself. These troops belonged to Ramseur's brigade of Rodes's division.

Twenty-seven-year-old Ramseur, with gentle, trusting eyes, covered his unusually youthful face with a ferocious beard. In battle, the professional soldier from North Carolina was more like his beard than his eyes. Reacting as quickly as Lane, Ramseur formed his troops about and, instead of waiting for the shock, charged. His lines almost bounced back when they hit the solid masses but the advancing troops halted too, for a moment. Then Junius Daniels, another North Carolina professional, brought in his brigade on Ramseur's left. Daniels fell, mortally wounded, leading them into line, but the men held steady.

At full daylight, through the mist, division commander Rodes saw that his lines were the target for the enemy's main thrust. Sedgwick's VI Corps was coming up as reinforcements on Hancock's right, and Rodes had not another man. On Rodes's left, Warren's V Corps was driving at Dick Anderson's front to keep his two divisions pinned down. Rodes, on his nervous black horse, rode to General Lee to report his danger.

With Heth holding the right of the works in front of the courthouse, Lee had only one division out of the lines. That was Anderson's former division, in Hill's corps, over across the Po River on the left, guarding against the enemy's threats there. There was no help for it. Lee sent Colonel Venable galloping off with orders to leave one of Mahone's brigades across the river, and hurry the other three forward. Then he told Rodes to hold on.

The big, tawny-haired Rodes had enjoyed a good day at the Wilderness as a balance for his first inconclusive action in division command, at Gettysburg, but he had never come up to the performance at Chancellorsville which won him his promotion. He did that drizzly Thursday of May 12th. He rode up and down his tattered lines, humming to himself, as he watched everything and held the desperately fighting men to their work. Even aggressive Ramseur sent word that he could hold on little longer without reinforcements against the weight increasing on his front.

General Lee rode back personally, alone, to hurry forward his only reinforcements. The first brigade from Mahone's division to arrive on the field was Nat Harris's Mississippians. The mist had then turned into a fine rain and the brigade, having hurried through the mud from across the river, had halted briefly on the courthouse road directly behind the open base of the salient. General Lee rode to the head of the column on his gray horse and called to Harris to move his men rapidly to Rodes's assistance. Here occurred yet another "Lee to the rear!"

This time there was no suggestion that the General intended to lead the troops into battle. In his urgency to hurry the men, he was riding at the head of the column beside General Harris, when their line of march came under suddenly heavy artillery fire. Traveler reared. At the one instant while his forefeet clawed the air, a solid shot passed under the horse's belly and barely missed taking off Lee's stirrup. Though Lee frequently commanded in a dangerous field of fire, it was the only recorded incident when he was known to have just missed death or maiming.

The scared soldiers yelled, "Go back, General Lee! For God's sake, go back!"

Completely composed, he said, "If you will promise to drive those people from our works, I will go back."

The troops shouted their promise. Colonel Venable, who guided them forward, likened their inspired reaction to Lee's danger to that of the Texans at the Wilderness. The regiments deployed from columns of fours running. The martial-looking Rodes, a strange division commander in a different corps, was waiting for them by a spring in the woods. General Rodes had just received a second message from Ramseur saying that he was done unless help arrived at once. Under Rodes's urgings, the Mississippians formed in the sloppy woods under a galling fire. When they plunged ahead to relieve the weight on the right of Ramseur's fought-out Carolinians, the soldiers needed their added inspiration.

An unidentified staff officer, serving as guide, led them in a direction to expose their flank to raking fire from the shrouded woods. When General Harris went toward the guide to complain of their course, this nameless staff officer took off. He outraced Harris' best-mounted courier in an impromptu point-to-point through the woods, and vanished literally in a cloud of smoke. From their awkward, exposed angle, Harris's men had to fight their way to Ramseur's right. They kept pushing forward, with heavy losses, until they reached the area of the toe of the salient. Harris later protested in his report that, after leaving Rodes, he saw no one from Ewell's corps except the men of Ramseur's pinned-down regiments on his left.

Without knowing these details, around nine o'clock General Lee felt satisfied the western section of the salient was safe from the enemy inside the works. To their left, Anderson's lines were more than holding steady under Warren's attack. The searching fire of Alexander's guns was giving the unhappy V Corps troops a bad going-over.

On the eastern face of the Mule Shoe, Gordon with the supporting regiments from Wilcox had pushed the enemy outside the works. There the Federal troops took position and refused to be dislodged. Lee then decided that if the enemy could be driven away from the heavily fortified toe, cutting their disordered forces in the middle, the entire salient could be cleared of the Federals.

There was no perceptible shift in the action to indicate this next phase of the strange struggle. Chiefly it was a decision of Lee to send in fresh troops with an objective beyond clearing the Federals out of the inside of the salient.

8

The second brigade to arrive from Mahone's division was given the brutal assignment of following Harris and going all the way to the apex. This was Wilcox's old Alabama brigade, commanded by South Carolinian Abner Perrin, who had been given command of troops of a different state on his performance at Gettysburg. In the misty rain, the Alabamians plunged into the then cluttered woods, slipping and stumbling over the churned mud. They fought their way to the works where Perrin, a prewar volunteer in an elegant militia unit, was shot dead from his horse while leading the charge to the outer parapet. His regiments were soon swallowed up in the sickening debris inside the works at the blunt apex.

One of their sharpshooters was found all alone by the 21st Regiment of Johnson's Second Brigade. Having toured around the outside of the salient behind Hancock's troops and into Hill's line, the Virginians were returning to their works from the inside. The young Alabamian, firing with deliberation from behind a tree, was astonished to learn that the lines of his own regiment no longer stretched on either side of him.

In response to Lee's nine o'clock order, around ten o'clock MacGowan's South Carolinians came swinging along the road just below the base of the salient. The last brigade pulled out of Wilcox's line on the right, they were directed by Lee toward the apex under Rodes's guidance. At that time Lee, without clearing through corps commanders, was personally directing the movements of brigades from five divisions of two different corps in the fight for the salient.

When Sam MacGowan's veterans reached the woods, Rodes showed that his inspired performance brought out unexpected gifts of timely flattery. Not recognizing the South Carolinians from Hill's corps, he was compelled to ask the leading officers what troops were with them. When told, Rodes turned to his staff and shouted, "There are no better soldiers in the world than these."

MacGowan's brigade chronicler recorded, "We hurried forward, thinking more of him and of ourselves than ever before."

It was perhaps well they received this extra boost to their morale, for, on reaching the contested fortification, the honest recorder wrote, "It was not a sight calculated to encourage us."

The rain had filled the ditch with bloody muddy water, on which corpses floated. Groaning and struggling wounded nearly covered the ground. The enemy, pressed up against the outside wall of the works, fired between chinks and occasionally threw over bayoneted rifles like harpoons. To look over the parapet to get in a shot was certain disaster.

Wound-prone Sam MacGowan was led off with a Minié ball in his arm and the senior colonel was carried out wounded by volunteers eager to serve as stretcher-bearers. The soldiers fought as individuals in the weird hand-to-hand battle which changed the name of the Mule Shoe's toe to the "Bloody Angle."

Under Lee's orders, the men, caught in the ghastliest fight of the war for them, kept trying to break the deadlock. The Federal troops were equally determined not to be pried loose from the outside of the fortifications, to which they clung as if to life itself. In a way, their perch on the works was life. To retire toward their own lines was to expose themselves to rifle fire from what remained of ten brigades and to the artillery fire of batteries moved up into the base of the salient.

Some of the lost twenty guns had been temporarily recaptured, and Second Corps cannoneers poured canister into the presses from close up. Later, in the confusion after dark, these guns, which could have been removed, were lost — in effect, abandoned.

9

As the fearful afternoon wore on, Lee's men went through the familiar motions of combat, half-drugged with weariness and shock, with no purpose beyond holding to their side of the works. In a curious way, the fight at the Bloody Angle returned the armies to the situation which existed before the break of Johnson's division. Militarily, it was as if Johnson's disaster had never occurred, for Grant's grand assault was stalemated at the works of the salient.

During the afternoon, Grant tried to break the stalemate by throwing Burnside's IX Corps in on the extreme right of Lee's position. This commitment of the last troops of the Federal army was made against Heth's sector northeast of the courthouse. By the chance of two regiments of sharpshooters being outside the works on their way to a local counterattack, and by the deadly effectiveness of the guns of Poague's and Willie Pegram's battalions firing into the dense attacking masses at point-blank range, Burnside's assault dissolved with extremely heavy losses.

This slaughter produced by the Third Corps guns on the right and Alexander's on the left strengthened argument about the fatal absence of Long's guns in the salient. All seemed to ignore the misty blackness at 4:35 A.M. when Hancock attacked. Some critics even attributed to the brilliance of First and Third Corps cannoneers the opportunity presented them when Grant repeated in the daylight the mass assault tactics that had worked in a night fog under special Confederate conditions. Instead, the nature of the daylong fighting was determined by Grant's ignorance of those conditions existing in the salient, and caused him to attribute the break in the lines to the effectiveness of his tactics.

As the day ended the battle, it was apparent that the tactics had changed nothing in the relative positions of the armies. The assault by Meade's whole army on the 12th only climaxed another heavy toll in losses, which ran to more than seventeen thousand casualties in the fights at Spotsylvania. Nearly fifteen thousand of these again came from the largely veteran Army of the Potomac. Sustaining approximately thirty-five thousand casualties in two prolonged engagements with Lee, Grant had lost one third of the infantry of the army he inherited.

Lee must have sustained close to ten thousand, largely through losses in Johnson's division. Federal estimates placed this figure higher, some considerably higher. Lee would have had no effective force to field had his losses reached a twenty thousand total in the Wilderness and Spotsylvania. If the claims of individual Federal commanders were added together, Lee would have lost more than one half his infantry, which manifestly he did not. The point was that for Lee's losses, proportionately somewhat higher than Grant's, there were no more where those lost came from.

Even so, there has been a tendency to apply a hindsight strategy to Grant's tactics. This reasoning professes to find in Grant's hammering a conscious policy of attrition. Actually, the attrition evolved from the tactics when many other factors, beyond the control of both Lee and Grant, affected the course of the war.

By Grant's own statement, his objectives were Lee's army and Richmond. There was no implication of a policy of attrition in his determined words: "if it takes all summer." Far from articulating a plan which contemplated the eventual wearing down of Lee's army, Grant expressed confidence in adhering to the "line" which led immediately to his objectives.

Within his fundamental purpose of hammering, Grant became an improviser. On May 12th, he revised the opinion that his blows had made Lee's army "shaky." This opinion, when voiced on the 11th, expressed an expectation rather than a judgment: from experience in the West, he expected his strokes to shatter an opponent. It was true enough that Lee was forced to protect his force by fighting from behind works, and obviously lacked the strength to try a crushing counterblow. Nonetheless, behind these works Lee could cut Meade's army to pieces before he was overrun.

The one weakness in the works at Spotsylvania had been corrected by midnight. Lee held his somnambulistic men at the grisly parapet until a new line was completed along the base of the salient. Lee had planned this line from the beginning. Chief of engineers Smith, perhaps because of the poor physical condition of the soldiers, had delayed until the other works were completed. During that endless day of the 12th, men were put to work as long as they could stand.

Brigade pioneers were usually a small group composed of the stronger-backed soldiers and the well-conditioned conscripts who might desert if put in the infantry. The commanding officer was likely to be an educated man who could learn the rudiments of civil engineering from the scattering of trained engineers who had not, like Rodes and many others, insisted on serving with combat troops. The pioneers did little more than lay out the lines on which the works were to be built. Most were willing enough, but there were not enough of them to construct heavy works in a hurry.

For the rush job on the new line across the base of the salient, connecting with Hill's corps on the right and the southwest segment of Rodes's line on the left, Lee collected during the afternoon all detached units and all the men from engaged units who were out of the lines for one reason or another. Some had stumbled out in partial shock, some with temporarily incapacitating injuries or what they thought to be an injury. Some got turned about in the confusion and, of course, some turned themselves about and headed for the rear. During the salient fight, a provost line was formed to welcome all who came out for whatever reason, and they built up the work force with which Lee completed the straight line by midnight.

Then the shattered, half-conscious men along the parapet were allowed to lurch their way back to the new works, where they fell out on the muddy ground, nearer dead than alive.

Grant's men also withdrew, and the unmanned fortifications of the old Mule Shoe embraced only a triangular section of the ghostly woods.

Though the armies remained facing one another for eight more days, the battle for those crossroads to Richmond was over. Lee had accomplished his immediate purpose: he checked Grant. His battered army had stood off the Army of the Potomac and blocked its way to Richmond.

While the secondary battle for the city raged behind his back as a separate operation, Lee continued the ceaseless speculation on the next move of the enemy in his front. With his own detached units and potential reinforcements engaged with Butler south of the James, without replacement for his losses, Lee could entertain no immediate purpose beyond another check.

This was a depressing business to him, the way to ultimate defeat. Yet, with the hope inherent in his strong spirit and his gift of leaving the future to God, General Lee projected his full faculties into doing those things which the moment indicated.

CHAPTER EIGHT

"The Picture Presented Is One
of Ultimate Starvation"

AFTER THE BLOODY ANGLE, Grant waited eight days at Spotsylvania, while "Beast" Butler's battle at Richmond's back door reached its climax. This delay had a profound effect on Lee's Richmond campaign against Grant, which has been curiously neglected by history. For, if Grant had been wrong about Lee's army being "shaky" on the 11th, it was physically shaken on the 12th, and needed time to recover.

Though new works had been built across the base of the abandoned salient, the troops occupying the center of Lee's lines were in a state of exhaustion, their command personnel shattered and the structure of the Second Corps a shambles. Only seven of the corps' generals remained, and the most experienced of those, Jubal Early, was detached on temporary command of Hill's corps.

The remnants of the three Virginia brigades in Johnson's division were reorganized into one brigade, with the old Stonewall Brigade losing its proud identity, and the recently combined Louisiana regiments continued as one small rather than one large brigade. Both commanded by temporary colonels, they existed for the moment as unattached units. Colonels also commanded four of the other seven brigades in the division, nearly all of which had been severely cut up in the salient, and a number of regiments had lost their commanders. Corps artillery, losing twenty guns and heavily in cannoneers, including able officers, also reorganized remnants.

At corps headquarters, poor Dick Ewell could do little more than bemoan the low estate to which Stonewall Jackson's once great Second Corps had been brought. Numbers were estimated at from eight thousand to nine thousand. As he opened with approximately fourteen thousand, and his Wilderness losses were made up by the return of Johnston's North Carolina brigade, he had lost approximately fifty-five hundred men at Spotsylvania, mostly in one day. Though Allegheny Johnson's division bore the brunt, the losses cut through all brigades, very heavily on Ramseur.

Physically spent, underfed troops, with dubious leadership at the top and untried men temporarily in command across all the units, could not recover from forty per cent casualties in men and more than fifty per cent in general officers without time and replacements. The replacements were held at Richmond, in the desperate action against Butler's army. Grant gave them the time.

The time was needed almost as urgently by the other two hard-fought corps of hungry men, especially the brigades of Hill's corps which fought at the Bloody Angle, for their replacements were also held in at the capital. Five brigades belonging to Lee's army were fighting there, and batteries from his army artillery, along with all the troops rushed from Davis's reluctantly denuded garrisons for the containment of Butler. During this distant action, Lee's men soaked up the rest, and absorbed the shock of the personal loss of leaders.

Grant's losses in general officers were also heavy, the most serious of which was the death of corps commander Sedgwick. While assuring his staff that, at a half-mile's distance from the enemy's skirmish lines, they were safely out of range, General Sedgwick was hit by a Georgia sharpshooter using one of the imported Whitworth rifles with telescopic sights. Grant said Sedgwick's loss was worse than the loss of a division.

With Lee, corps commander Longstreet topped the list of more than a dozen general officers lost, some temporarily, along with a division too, and then came the new loss which was beyond any comparatives. This was Jeb Stuart. Of him, Lee might have said as of Stonewall Jackson, lost the year before, "I know not how I shall replace him." As with Jackson, Lee did not try.

The blow fell, of all times, on May 12th, in a message delivered to Lee during the fight for the fateful salient. He did not announce it to the army for several days, when things had quieted down, and details came in.

2

As in General Stuart's great hour at Spotsylvania, the action in which he took his mortal wound had its genesis in the conflict between Meade and Sheridan. After the Federal cavalry's poor performance at Spotsylvania, Sheridan and Meade clashed in a personal argument, during which the new cavalry chief came out with what he really wanted. With no interest in providing reconnaissance or screens for moving columns, his one purpose was to defeat "the rebel cavalry." As he said, "Our cavalry ought to fight the enemy's cavalry and our infantry ought to fight the enemy's infantry."

Only recently promoted from command of an infantry division, Sheridan saw in his weaker opponent the opportunity both for advancement and for the expression of his pugnacious assertiveness. Of him it could never be said, "It's how the game is played that counts." Winning was everything to him; he wanted to beat people, to dominate by will or authority or physical force. A bully-boy with the weapons and the sanction of power behind him, he personally hated Southerners of a privileged background.

He hated the ritualistic manners, the formalized customs, the pride and the inviolable personal dignity in the class with which Meade felt at home and into which his wife's sister was married. Sheridan was goaded to destroy the very symbols against which the Meades could not bring themselves to make total war. "I do not believe war to be simply that lines should engage each other in battle," he wrote, "as that is but the duello part."

First of all, the primary project was to prove that his cavalry corps could whip the rebel cavalry. Though Jeb Stuart still had an aura about his name, Sheridan knew from continuous contact that the best days were behind Stuart's cavalry. Incredibly, in view of official reports, Sheridan stated after the war he "was led to believe, on information derived from the most reliable sources, that the enemy's cavalry was superior to ours in numbers." He attributed his success to "spirit." This was a part of the winner's complex, to have overcome odds in humbling his enemy and to withhold from the foe respect for his valor.

Along with denying his fifty per cent numerical superiority,

Sheridan attributed nothing to the new repeating carbines or to a flow of horses so inexhaustible that when some of his mounts temporarily broke down it was simpler to shoot them than to husband them along with the spares until reconditioned. In admitting that he shot broken-down horses to prevent them falling into the enemy's hands, by inference he acknowledged the acuteness of the enemy's need. He also acknowledged this by his complaint of the leanness of the enemy's countryside, which worked a hardship on his men and horses when they lived off the people.

Here was the no-holds-barred, winner-take-all prototype of the hatchet man of the new policy of total war. When Grant heard that Sheridan claimed, in his argument with Meade, he could whip Jeb Stuart's cavalry, the commander in chief gave the cocky little man the chance he wanted.

That was on May 9th, the day after Grant lost the race to Spotsylvania, and when he was beginning to grope around for ways to overrun Lee's lines. As Lee's infantry was intrenched in works in plain view, and the heavily wooded country was not conducive to cavalry maneuver, Grant gave Sheridan verbal permission "to cut loose from the infantry." Maybe in the open Sheridan could bring some finality to these "routs" he constantly inflicted on the rebel cavalry.

Leaving little more than a regiment for routine patrol, Sheridan started thirteen thousand mounted men in solid columns that reached thirteen miles on a raid to Richmond. They circled wide around Lee's right and were on their way before the heavy movement was discovered.

Grant, on the grounds that his wagons were not attacked, claimed that Sheridan achieved his purpose of drawing off all of Stuart's cavalry. Sheridan, for his part, rarely specified individual units encountered. He always fought "the rebel cavalry," giving the impression that even detachments could be the full cavalry corps of the Army of Northern Virginia. Yet, even with the size of Sheridan's threat, Jeb Stuart did not denude the infantry of cavalry support.

Rooney Lee reconnoitered with Chambliss's brigade on Lee's right flank, and Wade Hampton extended the left flank with Tom Rosser's brigade and Pierce Young's slim command. Stuart sent first only his brigade farthest to the right and closest to Sheridan's line of march, James Gordon's North Carolinians. Gordon's troopers drove into Sheridan's rear guard, and did what they could to slow down a force ten times their number. One of Gordon's companies cut its way in like a blade in a cotton bale and the men were engulfed, never to be seen again.

Jeb Stuart led Fitzhugh Lee's division, with Lomax's and Wickham's brigades reduced in numbers from their clash with Warren's infantry. A few miles north of Richmond, in a field rolling away from the main highway to the city, Stuart collected his forces for a stand near a public place called Yellow Tavern. He numbered something over four thousand before the losses sustained in Gordon's reckless charges designed to entangle the heavy rear guard.

Personally led by Stuart, his three brigades made a hard fight of it across the rolling ground near the Telegraph Road, but they could not contain the numbers and the fire power. Stuart fell mortally wounded, his staff barely getting him away in an ambulance, and Sheridan had the satisfaction of whipping Stuart's cavalry — or, at least, the half of it which opposed him.

While Stuart lay dying in a house in Richmond, clear-mindedly waiting for his wife and son, and stricken friends and government officials hurried to the bedside, Sheridan's corps drove over the outer fortifications of the city. This was an accomplishment that sounded more decisive than in actuality it was.

The fortifications to the north of the city were not permanently manned and only a scattering of militia offered a token resistance until all the militia units could be formed in the middle lines. The militia was composed of over-age men and under-aged boys, men unfit for active service in the field and semi-crippled veterans invalided out of the army into government clerical work. General Kemper, partially recovering from the wound sustained in the charge of Pickett's division at Gettysburg, was one of the commanders. All regular units in and around the city were south of the river fighting off Butler's army from the other side. In the middle works, however, some second-line artillerists worked several gun batteries. They were old guns, without enough good horses to perform at any distance from the works, but they could nullify Sheridan's batteries and drop some shells among his troops.

Sheridan moved off during the drizzly night, making much of "repulsing" two infantry brigades which were hurried over from Drewry's Bluff to speed the raiders' departure. He made no mention of hanging the civilian who, impressed as a guide, lost his own way in the wet blackness and failed to lead Sheridan where he wanted to go. Followed by a few observation parties, the triumphant cavalry corps moved on to a landing twenty miles down on the James River, where the regiments rested and refitted from supplies provided by gunboats operating in support of Butler's army.

Militarily, Sheridan's only accomplishment belonged in the field of raiding. In tearing up some railroad tracks, which were soon repaired, his men fell upon a large train of meat and bread rations for Lee's army, and the loss of this food was a sizable blow.

In proving that he had the manpower to defeat Stuart's cavalry in an open fight, Sheridan changed nothing at all in the traditional operation with which Lee employed his cavalry for reconnaissance. On the other hand, the great raid left Grant practically without cavalry against an opponent who consistently outguessed him. Sheridan was a favorite of the commander in chief and Grant, at least by record, never seemed to recognize the handicap of trying to outmaneuver Lee with a cavalry chief who so concentrated on whipping the enemy's horsemen that finally he took off from the army altogether.

The by-product of the glamorized "raid on Richmond" was beyond anything Sheridan's greatest boasts could have envisioned, though, from several references in his reports to General Stuart's being "killed," he obviously regarded this act of battle as an achievement of his venture. He relished those parts of the duello aspects of war where the enemy's legendary chieftain was brought down, like an opposing knight on the field of honor.

Jeb Stuart, in his close-up leadership, had cheated death too often by the chance of battle for Sheridan to take any personal credit for the snap-shot fired by one of his unhorsed troopers. Stuart had had his mustache singed, felt the buzz of bullets and shell fragments that struck friends and staff officers standing beside him, taken ditches like a steeplechase rider when his followers could almost see the swarm of bullets chasing him. But when the usually voluble Stuart was riding on the way to Richmond to head off Sheridan, his quiet manner suggested to Major McClellan that the General sensed the running out of his string.

As the other staff officers had been killed off, wounded out or transferred, the twenty-three-year-old chief of staff became the dependable man to the cavalry's commanding general. Stuart's had been the most cosmopolitan of all staffs. It was natural that his young intimate was a native Philadelphian, a militarily untrained graduate of Williams College, and a first cousin of the Union's General McClellan with four brothers in the Federal armies — one an adjutant general with Meade's chief of staff. Henry McClellan had been a tutor in Virginia when war came and enlisted as a private in a Virginia cavalry regiment. On that ride which ended at Yellow Tavern, McClellan said that Stuart was "softer than usual, and more communicative. It seems now that the shadow of the near future was already upon him."

Early in the evening of May 12th, saying that "I would like to see my wife, but God's will be done," James Ewell Brown Stuart died of the wound in his stomach.

When General Lee received the news, he knew that something had died in the army too. The message of the mortal wound was brought to Lee during the afternoon while the fight for the salient raged. Visibly affected when he told his staff, his first comment was "He never brought me a piece of false information."

When the message of the death came that night, Lee could not speak at all. Unable to control his grief, for he loved the bright soul who had been one of his cadets at West Point, the General went into his tent to be alone. Later, when a staff officer came in, Lee murmured, "I can scarcely think of him without weeping."

When Lee announced the news, the army felt the same way. Colonel Sorrel said, ". . . his devotion to Lee was so thoroughly appreciated . . . his disposition so happy and sunny, his enterprise so untiring, his soul so valiant . . . our sense of security against surprise with him in the saddle . . . that deep was our grief."

In General Order 44, Lee made one prophetic statement: "His achievements form a conspicuous part of the history of this Army, with which his name and services will be forever associated."

3

There was no time for grief. Already overburdened by the breakdown in infantry command, Lee ordered the cavalry division commanders to report directly to him, and went on pondering each little sign for indications of Grant's next move.

For the first three days after the salient fight and the death of Jeb Stuart, the rain continued and this understandably slowed down the Federal army. Indeed, the rain mired a flank movement that would have been dangerous to Lee. During those days, enemy infantry units kept shifting to Lee's right, beyond the semicircle of entrenchments. Lee shifted his rebuilding men, interrupting their rest to put them at more digging. By the 16th, when the roads began to dry, Lee expected that Grant, having enough of hitting entrenchments, would try another flanking maneuver. Grant just kept shifting the weight.

To meet the shift, Lee brought Anderson's two-division corps over from the left to form a new right line. Hill's corps, in front of the courthouse, then became the center and Ewell's Second Corps the left of the line. The 17th, a day of hot sun, passed, and still the enemy continued to do nothing. What Lee did not then know was that Grant was waiting for thirty thousand fresh troops, which he had ordered up as replacements for his losses.

While waiting, early on the 18th, Grant took one more swipe at Lee's works. Reasoning that Lee's shift to the right might have weakened the left, held by Ewell's corps, the commander in chief tried a repeat of Hancock's pre-dawn attack at the salient. The movement out was bungled on the second try, and Hancock's people did not begin climbing over the deserted works until eight in the morning. Back at the new line, Colonel Cutshaw, who had lost eight of his battalion's guns in the other attack, said that the Confederates "could not believe a serious attempt would be made to assail such a line as Ewell had, in the open day, at such a distance . . . [but] when it was found that a real assault was to be made, it was welcomed by the Confederates as a chance to pay off old scores."

None welcomed it more than corps artillery chief Armistead

Long and the cannoneers he ordered on the twenty-nine guns placed in line. Maybe some of the belief in what Long's guns might have accomplished in the before-daylight attack on the salient was buttressed by the murderous work done when the massed enemy came on for nearly a mile to the base of the salient. The fire was literally so devastating that no troops climbed through the abatis outside Ewell's lines, and Ewell's infantry was scarcely engaged.

After this futile and costly assault receded, Lee was convinced that Grant would move out. On that day, he learned that Grant had been waiting for reinforcements. When Grant moved, Lee expected him to shift to the right, to maintain contact with supply bases which the Navy set up on Virginia's network of rivers. As it was, Grant had established a behind-the-lines community of hospitals, supply services and transportation, reaching back to the sacked city of Fredericksburg and on to the Potomac, which in immensity and complexity was unlike anything ever before seen in the South. Yet, to check every report and avoid risks where possible, on the 19th General Lee sent Ewell on a reconnaissance in force to the left.

Dick Ewell, going along personally, acted with poor judgment and lost even his skill in fundamental tactics. Going with only six guns, he managed to get a division entangled with a sizable body of the enemy, who were aching for such a crack at some of Lee's soldiers outside their works. The "reconnaissance" lost several hundred more men from the Second Corps, and Ewell needed the help of Wade Hampton's horse guns and dismounted sharpshooters in order to break off the engagement. If, as Grant claimed, Stuart had removed all his cavalry to go after Sheridan, Ewell's corps could have suffered a minor version of the salient breakthrough. Old Baldhead was simply no longer fit to command troops.

Though again it was something Lee could not know, Ewell's battle on the left served the purpose of delaying Grant's move out for another day. Instead of moving out before daylight on the 20th, during that day Grant made the preparations which alerted Lee to the possibility of a move sometime during the night. At the end of the day, Lee ordered Ewell to be ready to put his corps in motion at daybreak of the 21st. But, though Lee's mind raced through the hours in balancing all the factors, his men were given a full day of rest. When that peaceful day ended, the stretch of eight days of relative freedom from exertion and stress had given Lee's troops the time to recover even on their sub-subsistence diet.

4

Of equal importance, the situation at Richmond had then changed drastically. Sheridan's threat from the north, while adding strain to the defenders' nerves, had diverted little strength and no attention from the main threat of Butler to the south. Finding himself the object of the enemy's undivided concentration, political general Butler, always at his best against civilians in occupied cities, lost the opportunity to hasten the end of the war. Instead, he bungled himself into a position where his army was immobilized and Confederate troops were free to join Lee.

At the same time, the third prong of Grant's multiple offensive broke off in the Shenandoah Valley, partly due to the inadvertent assistance given by another of the Federals' poor generals. The Germanic Sigel ("I goes to fight mitt Sigel," as the song had it) called it a day when 225 teen-aged cadets of the Virginia Military Institute, at the Valley town of New Market, joined a scratch force of two infantry brigades and Imboden's cavalry brigade, all commanded by the imposing Kentuckian, John Breckinridge.

With the fertile Shenandoah Valley safe as a supply source, a threat to the salt works in Virginia's southwestern corner was also turned back. John Morgan, imprisoned in Ohio's state penitentiary when his Confederate cavalry raided in the North, had escaped in time to collect a force to fight off Averill's heavy raiding party. Not only were these distracting and potentially crippling threats removed, but former U.S. Vice-President Breckinridge put his 2250 men on the still-operating Virginia Central and started for Lee's army.

Lee had been able only to check Grant's main force, Meade's army, at the center of the enemy's operation. But around this stalemate, Grant's total offensive had collapsed within two weeks. With the collapse went Grant's chance to grind Lee's army between Meade and Butler, and to threaten Richmond from the rear.

Recognizing that the decision had become reduced to the Army of the Potomac and to Lee's army, Grant planned to draw troops from Butler's helpless army to Meade's for the purpose of overpowering Lee's reduced forces in the open. For Butler's troops, while bottled up from the land side, could be moved about Virginia's conveniently placed rivers by transports escorted by the U.S. Navy.

To Lee, the changed situation meant incomparably and basically more than it did to Grant. To Grant, the accretion of more numbers was similar to the acquisition of more money by a millionaire; to Lee, a potential of manpower was like paying off the mortgage. For the first time since the summer of 1862, Lee was offered the opportunity of concentrating forces in Virginia against a single enemy.

However, there was another fundamental difference between Grant and Lee. The added numbers to Grant were a certainty: as commander in chief, he needed only to speak a sentence to a staff officer, directing him to send an order for the troops. For Lee, as an army general, the manpower which offered a potential of concentration existed in the realm of uncertainties. Though Lee anticipated Grant's call for troops from Butler's army by days before Grant sent the formal order, instead of making a countering move, the General first must open another campaign of diplomatic maneuver with his commander in chief.

For submitting to these crippling restrictions, Lee has been criticized for not "doing something" about Davis. This criticism is based largely on the thoughtless assumption of a type of irregular movement evoked by the image of the word "Rebel." Though Unionists emphasized the use of the word as part of the policy which denied a dignified status to the self-determinist Confederate States of America, and Southerners liked the word for different reasons, no government in world history adhered more rigidly to the letter of a formal establishment. In such an organized government, there is nothing any army officer can do about his superior's orders except obey them.

Where Lincoln fired generals (especially Democrats) right and left, Davis, with less available manpower (and a one-party system), banished those who lost his favor into regions which offered slight opportunities for either power or glory. Lee, for his part, wrung more compromises from his commander in chief than any other army general won from either Davis or Lincoln. As Confederate territory and Lee's department shrunk, Davis encroached more on Lee's domain. By 1864 he exerted a much tighter control than when Lee assumed command, and Lee could only try for compromises in detail.

It is true that Lee himself should have been commander in chief. He was on the wrong side for receiving such recognition and it certainly never occurred to the conservative gentleman, any more than it did to his model, George Washington, to seize power from the constituted authority.

With all the loss of faith in Davis as a leader and the bitter antagonisms to him personally, no internal revolutionary movement was seriously proposed. States, counties and sections carried on separatist movements, officers resigned from the army, and individuals stormily washed their hands of the whole administration. All these publicly aired agitations were essentially the assertions of an individualistic people. Though some may have disrupted the South's efforts to maintain its independence, none was designed to overthrow the Davis government. In May of 1864 the Confederate President was more securely in office than was Lincoln.

With Davis's tenure went his unchangeable system of departments, and, at the basis of the relationship between Davis and Lee, the concentrations desired by the field general were antithetical to the principles of the system. During the days of his greatest power, in all the compromises Lee ever gained from the President, not one violated the principle of his system of defense. This had been true from the earliest days, when Lee served in the ignominious post of military adviser. In March of 1862, Lee wrote, "It is impossible to place at every point which is threatened a force which shall prove equal to every emergency." Davis was committed to precisely the opposite of this proposition, and his principles were expressed in his departmentalized defense.

This policy represented a projection of Davis himself, rather than an intellectual process, and until the 1864 campaigns the various Confederate failures could always be explained away by other factors. The other factors always existed, as they did in 1864. But, beginning with the sixth "On to Richmond" campaign, which Grant opened on May 4th simultaneously with the drive on Atlanta, the central system affected all the military factors in the Confederacy, especially in Virginia, more directly than in the preceding years.

Because of the multiple effects of the departmental system, the custom has been to view the various actions of the spring of 1864 as separate, and even peripheral, affairs, unrelated to the main campaign. To Grant in his planning, all the actions in the Virginia-Carolina theater were aspects of a single purpose; and to Lee, it was a single purpose he was trying to thwart. The Confederates were forced to defend their points separately only because the attacks came in different departments in Davis's system. These separate defenses were such hairbreadth, last-minute escapes from disaster that history has studied these isolated heroics for themselves, when all the events were determined by the departmental policy with which Davis countered Grant's interrelated offensive.

During the two weeks beginning May 5th, the threats came so fast from so many sides that Davis was hard put to maintain his bureaucratic structure. That he tried at all under the circumstances of the enveloping emergencies indicated that his preoccupation with departments had become an obsession. By retreating from the realities, by ignoring the larger pattern and concentrating on details, by working himself half-sick into the late hours of the night, the President managed to keep his departments intact during the chaos of the defense of Richmond.

5

Prior to Butler's threat at Richmond's back door, the departments embracing the territory from the south bank of the James River to north of Charleston operated largely in reaction to the enemy's movements. Thus, the Federal objective of the port of Wilmington became the Department of Cape Fear, commanded by Major General W. H. C. Whiting, disassociated from Charleston to the south or the inland coast of North Carolina to the north. As North Carolina's inland coast was the scene of constant peripheral action, while the area of Virginia south of the James River was usually quiescent, this total section was loosely embraced in the Department of North Carolina. Though this territory existed in a half-world of military-naval operations, its significance on the Richmond campaign has never been sufficiently stressed.

A factor in its influence lay in the Federal occupation of Fort Monroe, the naval base on Hampton Roads a hundred miles due east of Richmond on the tip of the Virginia peninsula. It was from Fort Monroe that the *Monitor* took off to challenge the sea supremacy of the *Virginia-Merrimac* when the Confederates still occupied Norfolk. Ultimately it was the Union control of Fort Monroe which caused the evacuation of Norfolk, and made possible McClellan's naval-supported invasion up the peninsula to Richmond in 1862. Also in 1862, from Fort Monroe Burnside launched the successful amphibious expedition against Roanoke Island, a pivotal position in North Carolina's inland waters. Until coastal positions were secured in the Carolinas, the Federal blockading fleet operated from Fort Monroe, and it continued to serve as a base for the gunboats and transports which turned Virginia's rivers into something like an interlocking Federal canal system.

It is difficult to explain the curious neglect of the advantages the Federal forces enjoyed by occupying this fort. Perhaps the possession of this knife in the Confederacy's side did not fit history's demands for heroes who, personifying the might of the Union, could give color to the stress on the puissance of the moral forces.

Then, the associations of Fort Monroe were very Southern. The oldest fortified position in the United States, the original fort was erected in 1609 as an outpost for Jamestown. The modern fort had been started during the administration of a Virginia president, James Monroe, under the direction of General Walker Armistead, whose son was killed in the charge of Pickett's division at Gettysburg. It was completed by First Lieutenant R. E. Lee, whose first son was born there. The old Hygeia Hotel adjoining the grounds was a favorite Virginia spa, and Captain George E. Pickett had met his future wife on the beach there. Naturally the fort's war use was a touchy subject to Southerners.

It was not until Grant became commander in chief that the various Federal activities, spreading through the area dominated by Fort Monroe, were coordinated in a single drive south of the James River. This move shifted the threats on the life-line Weldon Railroad from distant points to a concentration at Richmond's doorstep. At the same time, the second army provided a potential pincer movement with Grant against the capital.

When Lee first advised his commander in chief what was in the wind, the nebulous Department of North Carolina was nominally in command of Major General Pickett. Since the wreckage of three of his brigades at Gettysburg, Pickett's division had been scattered. Jenkins's big brigade had been transferred to what became Field's division, and Corse's Virginia brigade, also held back from Gettysburg by Davis, remained the only sound unit. The three chewed-up brigades had spent the winter rebuilding with returned wounded, returned prisoners and a thick sprinkling of conscripts. None of the brigades was with Pickett. Two brigades had been garrisoned around Richmond and, as they were north of the James River, outside his department. The other two were among the half dozen or more brigades in North Carolina. As Pickett was not commanding the coastal operations theoretically within his department, those also were his in name only. Pickett had commanded some of his brigades in a hodgepodge force in North Carolina during the early winter, but his performance was so unsatisfactory that Bragg "promoted" him to the office job of department commander.

As commander of the Department of North Carolina, General Pickett had headquarters pleasantly established in Petersburg, Virginia. A thirty-eight-year-old widower at Gettysburg, Pickett had recently married the young girl who had loved him since as a child she had met the gallantly caparisoned officer at Fort Monroe. As military appearances in the charming small city were maintained with a staff, a regiment, and an assortment of cavalrymen scattered for forage, newlywed Pickett had found his innocuous employment as department head a thoroughly agreeable assignment.

After Lee had advised Davis to transfer troops from the Carolinas to meet Butler's threat, and to bring Beauregard on in command, Davis first rearranged his departments in order to accommodate the shift of Beauregard. When the new Department of Southern Virginia and North Carolina was organized on paper, Beauregard's area embraced Pickett's department at Petersburg and Whiting's department at Wilmington, and included Hoke's semi-independent North Carolina operations in Pickett's department. Since no troops were immediately shifted toward Richmond and no urgency expressed, self-interested Beauregard took up quarters at the centrally located point of Weldon, North Carolina, and busied himself defining the areas of his new authority.

On May 5th, the day that Lee tangled with Grant in the Wilderness, Beauregard sent out a general order from Weldon clarifying the new departmental situation. Pickett, Whiting and Hoke were to command "districts" within the grand department. However, the day before, on May 4th, Pickett had received orders from the War Department to report to Hanover Junction. There he was to meet with his two brigades from Richmond, and report to General Lee. These were among the detached troops which Davis had advised Lee, on the night before the Wilderness, were four days away.

On May 5th, before either General Pickett or his brigades had started for the depot, and before Pickett had received Beauregard's definition of his status as a district commander, Pickett received information from a signal station that Butler was disembarking an army at Bermuda Hundred about twelve miles away. An unusually accurate estimate was made of the force gathering on the shores of the undefended Department. Butler would field as "effectives present and equipped" about twenty-two thousand infantry, three thousand cavalry and heavy artillery. His "aggregate" would approach forty thousand.

Pickett's one regiment of a few hundred was scattered into small patrolling units, and, along with a city battalion of local militia, in a hurry he could gather in thirty-six hours about fifty troopers of the dispersed cavalry brigade. By chance, the horses of the Washington Artillery Battalion, belonging to Alexander's First Corps artillery, had not then fattened sufficiently to return to Lee's army, and this circumstance placed twenty-one guns at Pickett's disposal. In addition, outside his jurisdiction, a garrison manned fixed guns at the river fort of Drewry's Bluff, with the support of fifty Confederate Marines and a major. Across the James, General Robert Ransom commanded two brigades, fixed artillery garrisons and the local defense troops, but they were in a different department altogether — the Department of Richmond. Under his authority, Pickett's "aggregate" numbered something less than a thousand.

Of these, Pickett coolheadedly refrained from gathering the units

of the infantry regiments scattered east and southeast of Petersburg. There the detachments could guard the city and the railroad
south of it from raiding parties of Kautz's cavalry division, where as
a regiment the few hundred second-line troops would be useless
against Butler's infantry. The enemy's main force concentrated
within a great loop formed by the "curls" in the James River where
it entered into the Appomattox. Butler's base at Bermuda Hundred
occupied the site of America's first city and first university, both
abandoned after the Indian massacre of 1622. From Bermuda Hundred Butler was only six miles from the Richmond-Petersburg railroad which eventually ran to Wilmington. At the railroad Butler
could turn south seven miles to Petersburg behind the barrier of
the Appomattox River, or north six miles to Richmond's protecting
river fort at Drewry's Bluff, and on to Richmond across the James.

If Pickett could have anticipated Butler's move to the yard, there
was nothing he could do about it. In fact, by orders, he wasn't even
supposed to be there. It seems a safe guess that Pickett, with all
his heart, wished he had taken an earlier train to Hanover Junction.
If he had, Richmond would have been cut off from the South while
Lee was fighting in the Wilderness.

In one of the curious twists of the war, George Pickett is remembered for a charge that failed in a glory-seeking hour, and unknown
for his key part in saving Richmond by unheroic actions performed
in a bureaucratic chaos which shook his nerves beyond the breaking point.

6

Pickett had suffered something like a traumatic experience at
Gettysburg. He was a dramatic man, theatrically good-looking,
dandified about his dress and, in the old army, had demonstrated a
flair for the spectacular. In the Confederate army he advanced rapidly, partly due to the influence of his close friend Longstreet, but
by the chance of battle Major General Pickett had never enjoyed a
great moment. At Gettysburg his natural ambition was intensified
by his middle-life passion for his young fiancée, and he led his troops
down Seminary Ridge in the belief that his belated rendezvous with

destiny had come at last. In a somber way it had, though at the time Pickett was unaware of the immortality the future would bring to what to him was the disastrous blow to his ambitions.

For all his vanity, Pickett was a man of feeling, and his emotions were profoundly disturbed by the destruction that swept through his brigades of Virginia volunteers. He was almost out of self-control when he rode back among the shattered men who numbered scarcely one third of the forty-five hundred who had marched out forty minutes before. Pickett filed a bitter report, which was suppressed by Lee on the grounds that it would create inter-army dissension. Beyond that, the records are unrevealing, and it can only be assumed that something went out of George Pickett.

When Longstreet was wounded, Lee never considered him for First Corps command, though Pickett was a personal favorite of Old Pete, nor expressed any need of his services during the May crises in general command. Yet Pickett, born to privilege in a Virginia family (his home was on the other side of the James River from Butler's landing base), was a soldier at heart. He had never wanted to be anything else. Whatever his emotional state, when Butler's army came swarming from their transports, Pickett reacted as a professional soldier.

First, he wired the information to and called for help from his immediate superior, Beauregard. Then he began a steady flow of wires to the war office, giving precise details of the hourly developments. None of the wires to the War Department was acknowledged.

From Beauregard Pickett received an answer around one-thirty in the afternoon. In this the department commander generously tendered him the authority to "remain in command of your present district until further orders, and assume command of all troops that may arrive therein." One brigade was on its way from South Carolina, by trains which carried three hundred troops a load, and the first train was a day away. When Pickett received this intelligence from his superior, Butler's troops had been disembarking from fifty transports for two hours.

Beauregard then sent a message to the President's Military Adviser, Braxton Bragg, announcing that he was too sick to come on immediately. In private correspondence, the department commander made it clear that he had no intention of burning his own fingers by trying to pull Davis's chestnuts out of the fire. Manifestly he believed that with Butler's army already landing, the Richmond-Petersburg situation was beyond saving, and the practical-minded Creole wanted his record clear of involvement with a decisive action that was foredoomed to disaster.

Trapped on the scene, Pickett had no choice. By three o'clock in the afternoon, when he had received no answer to any of the seven wires sent the war office, Pickett understandably began to grow frantic. He then sent a courier by the still-functioning railroad to deliver a message in person to Adjutant General Samuel Cooper.

After the courier left the war office, General Cooper endorsed the message over to Braxton Bragg, and the next day Bragg returned the message to Cooper, marked "Seen." On the day when no one in the War Department answered Pickett, the Adjutant General's office issued Special Order 105, in which Article XXVII proclaimed that "in all matters relating to command, military police and operations, the Departments of Henrico [County] and Richmond are hereby consolidated." At the same time, Bragg wired Beauregard that he had "directed Pickett to communicate directly with you." Beauregard wired Pickett to "call directly on the war department."

Fortunately for his sanity, Pickett did not know, when night fell on the 5th, that both of these ambitious men had refused to assume personal responsibility for the military crisis created by the President's obsession with departmentalization. Evidently Bragg had not even informed the commander in chief of the details.

The next day Davis sent Beauregard a wire in which, mentioning that the department commander was "no doubt well informed of events in this direction," he casually expressed the hope that at Petersburg Beauregard could "direct operations both before and behind" him — i.e. the whole department. At that moment, except for Lee battling for his army's life in the second day of the Wilderness, the only important point in the Eastern Confederacy was Petersburg.

Without any question, under any Federal general officer of more than average competence the area from Drewry's Bluff to Petersburg would have been militarily occupied by nightfall of the 6th. A dozen brigadiers from Meade's army would have done the job inexplicably entrusted to a sadistic, thieving Boston political adventurer of proven military ineptitude.

Butler wasted eleven daylight hours of May 6th in bullying civilians, as he advanced six miles across a flat farm country with scarcely an armed man in sight. In the area of a dilapidated junction-point of a short spur with the main line (grandly named Port Walthall Junction), his men had torn up only a few sections of track when, at four in the afternoon, Pickett rushed the first troops in line. These were six hundred men, the first two regiments of Hagood's South Carolina brigade to arrive. Supported by one battery and well placed on a narrow front by unsung Colonel Graham, of the 21st South Carolina, this line halted the advance of Butler's army. Around six o'clock, when a more serious advance developed to overlap Graham's narrow protected front, Pickett received unexpected support that arrived like manna from Heaven.

In all of Davis's shuttling around of troops, by the sheerest chance a Tennessee brigade, which had served with Longstreet, turned up in Richmond during the 6th. Bushrod Johnson's small brigade, slightly under twelve hundred, was designated for the Department of Richmond, as replacements for Pickett's brigades which were under orders to join Lee.

The new commander of the Richmond Department, Major General Robert Ransom, was a soundly trained professional from North Carolina, who was too much an old army martinet ever to get along well with Confederate troops. Perhaps having abandoned hope for personal advancement, on May 6th, the second day of Pickett's mounting frenzy, Ransom acted as if he had never heard of Davis's departments. He sent the Tennessee brigade from one train in Richmond to protect another railroad near Petersburg so fast that Bushrod Johnson reported the order was the first he had heard of an enemy threatening any railroad. Johnson's brigade came up on Graham's flank just before Butler's people got there, and Butler's second and last movement of the day sputtered out.

For the third day of Pickett's ordeal, May 7th, the other regiments of Hagood's brigade arrived to be sent running from the train across the flat countryside. The South Carolinians then totaled fifteen hundred. With them, Pickett fielded a force a little more than one tenth of Butler's infantry. The two brigades, strange to Virginia and to each other, were placed under the command of a stray major general who appeared on the scene on his own.

This was D. H. Hill, another North Carolina professional, and as good a combat soldier as the war produced. A learned, literate man, Harvey Hill simply could not help finding fault with other generals. What made his carping criticisms harder to bear was that they were usually right. Lee had to transfer him out of the Army of Northern Virginia in the interest of personnel harmony. In the Army of Tennessee, after Hill signed the petition which declared Braxton Bragg unfit for command, Davis, in small spitefulness, sent him home to wait for a new assignment that was never coming. As soon as Hill heard, indirectly, of the threat at Petersburg, he patriotically offered his services to Beauregard in any capacity.

The department commander seized on this opportunity of giving the impression of directing operations from his sick bed. In Special Order 3, he appointed the major general as volunteer aide-de-camp, "especially charged with communicating to . . . Pickett the views of the commanding general." Whatever these views may have been on a field Beauregard had never seen, under conditions of which he held only the vaguest general idea, Pickett sensibly gave the good soldier Hill command of the troops in line with authority to fight them as he saw fit.

The reports generally credited Harvey Hill's direction of the two brigades and supporting artillery with holding off Butler's heavier lunges on the second day. Hill fought so skillfully that by the next day, the 8th, Butler was something of a baffled "Beast." He spent the day brooding on some easier way of getting the railroad and/or Drewry's Bluff than by taking on two brigades with his own two corps.

The division of his cavalry to the south of Petersburg had drawn no attention from him. Kautz's three thousand troopers, held partially in hand by detachments of Pickett's original regiment, had managed to burn a wooden trestle on the railroad and cause a break in the flow of troop traffic from the Carolinas which could not be immediately repaired. Pickett, though breaking under the strain, left that logistical problem to the absent department commander and concentrated on the immediate problem of containing Butler.

Again he received unexpected help from Robert Ransom. The usually stiff-necked Ransom had kicked over the traces once he started crossing departmental boundaries. When the second brigade ticketed for the Richmond Department arrived from the West, he sent Gracie's sixteen hundred Alabamians to join Bushrod Johnson and Hagood in Pickett's district of Beauregard's department. Then he denuded the Richmond Department and sent Pickett's two brigades to the Drewry's Bluff fort-garrison. Finally, Ransom went all the way. He crossed the James River in person and took control of the Drewry's Bluff sector.

By then, May 9th, Pickett cracked. He began sending contradictory orders, which the solid pros in the field had the discretion to disregard. After all, no one was really in command. Harvey Hill, the Bragg-Davis castoff, and Robert Ransom, without permanent assignment, collaborated with George Pickett, in his nebulous status, to exercise their skills with a selfless concert of action in a desperate hour in the life of their country. Probably such harmony would not have long endured. For that hour they had braced the back door against the pack. Like Lee at Spotsylvania, the three soldiers kept Davis's system propped up through one more emergency.

By May 10th the troops from the Carolinas, sent after Butler had made his landing, began to pour into Petersburg in a steady stream. Hoke's old brigade, detached from Lee's army, came first, then the big brigade of political general Wise, prewar governor of Virginia, then the brigade of Ransom's brother Mat, a handsome peacetime lawyer who was as popular as the West Pointer was disliked. Pickett's other two brigades finally came along, then the brigade of Colquitt, an earlier failure with Lee, brigades led by "One Wing" Martin, a professional who had served briefly in Virginia in '62, and former U.S. Senator Clingman of North Carolina. Numbering well over twelve thousand, these late arrivals could have been gathered there, without endangering a spot of Southern soil, to greet Butler on May 5th.

With the units already at Richmond, the combined Confederate force would have approximated twenty thousand infantry. Not one moment of the last-ditch heroics had been necessary. On the basis of Butler's maladroit performance, a force of practically numerical equality held the potential of inflicting a serious defeat on Grant's secondary army.

With the crisis passed and fresh troops arriving by the hour, the magnificent Beauregard, looking every inch the French marshal, appeared on May 10th. The department commander no more than established headquarters before he assumed that he would inflict the might-have-been defeat on Butler's army. Observing how few troops, unorganized, had reduced "The Tyrant of New Orleans" to a state of brooding frustration, Beauregard looked beyond disposing of him to a collaboration with the great Lee.

Now that he was back in the main theater, where he had begun, Old Bory intended to make the most of it. Orders were dashed off for organization of the brigades into four divisions. Beauregard showed his appreciation of Major General Hill by offering him the opportunity of remaining as his volunteer aide-de-camp. Harvey Hill, still hoping for a command, threw in his lot with Beauregard for a while before going on back home. Pickett was offered one of the newly formed divisions. Since the brigades of Pickett's division continued at that phase in different departments, no one suggested giving him his own division and he declined the new command.

As soon as Beauregard got off the train in Petersburg, Pickett reported himself sick. He suffered a nervous collapse, which Beauregard called "fever." Pickett wished, when he got well, to obey that old order of reporting to Hanover Junction. He'd had all he wanted of the Department of Southern Virginia and North Carolina.

That department had not yet done its worst in affecting the defense of Richmond. With Beauregard on the scene, its effects became more insidious and far-reaching, intertwining with Lee's area of responsibility. For the final effect of the creation of the new department was to create for Lee a new problem, in Beauregard.

7

It had been the fate of Pierre Toutant Gustave Beauregard to begin in the Confederacy at the top, as its first military hero, almost entirely through circumstance. The first circumstance was his Louisiana birthplace.

The seven states of the lower South which formed the original

Confederacy, with its capital at Montgomery, produced few West Point trained professional soldiers in comparison to Virginia and, to a less extent, North Carolina. Many of those, such as Albert Sidney Johnston and Longstreet, were at distant posts and did not come home until after Lincoln resorted to armed force as a practical measure for resolving the abstract rights of a state to secede. Jefferson Davis, a recently powerful U. S. Secretary of War, was regarded as the Lower South's greatest military leader, and the President was to exercise overall leadership as commander in chief.

Beauregard, West Point class of 1838, was a regular army captain, the average line-rank held by men five and ten years behind him at the Point. During the unresolved stage of the secession movement, Beauregard had, probably for his reputation, served briefly in the impossible position of a Southern superintendent of West Point. When, as a secessionist, he was soon forced to resign from the U. S. Military Academy, the incident gave him publicity and also availability.

A shrewdly practical Creole, Beauregard secured the support of Louisiana political powers, notably John Slidell, a Columbia man from New York City, before he "offered his services" to the newly formed Confederacy. The sectional impasse was then centering on the issue of Fort Sumter, and President Davis selected Slidell's candidate to represent the fledgling nation militarily at this danger spot. To dignify his position, the military representative was commissioned brigadier general, and thus P. T. G. Beauregard became the Confederacy's first general officer.

The to-do at Charleston was political rather than military, a pawn in the manuevers between Lincoln and Davis. But it was a focal point of international attention, and the resplendent brigadier cut quite a figure as leader of the militia units composed of South Carolina's hot bloods. When Lincoln outmaneuvered Davis in provoking the Southerner to "fire the first shot," Beauregard militarily accomplished nothing. The shore batteries banged shots off the fort's walls until Major Anderson, Sumter's unhappy commander, felt the honor of the United States Army had been satisfied, and marched his garrison out with colors flying and bands playing, all in the finest Old World traditions.

In all the excitement, with the long cold war at last resolved and the emotional Southerners looking no further than the finality of their separation (a Declaration of Independence), Beauregard became the personification of the historic hour. When Lincoln's declaration of war brought powerful border states into the Confederacy, with an array of professional military talent, Beauregard, already the toast of the country, was given the key assignment of defending the Manassas line against the first "On to Richmond."

Though the Battle of First Manassas was won almost in spite of him, his glory grew to the extent that he was appointed one of the Confederacy's five full generals. Old Samuel Cooper, the Adjutant General from the Hudson River country, Albert Sidney Johnston, R. E. Lee, and Joseph E. Johnston were the other four, who ranked him.

While chance may have given the people's hero this eminence, Old Bory, accepting the adulation as his due, began to believe himself the South's Napoleon. He did have a French cast to his features, brooding eyes, a skin of dusky pallor and, with a sharp black mustache above a firm mouth, he looked the part he essayed to play.

In a mixture of naïve effulgence and bad judgment, Beauregard took to writing letters of grandiose schemes to President Davis. Even his most fanciful suggestions contained some fundamentally sound concepts of the Confederacy's war needs, but they all concerned concentration and aggression. As this threatened the very foundation of Davis's system, the commander in chief dismissed the plans in their entirety on the grounds of their flaws in detail. Inevitably he developed a reversal of feeling toward the onetime hero.

Soon after the foolish battle of the two armed mobs at First Manassas, Beauregard's star began to dim. He was treated shabbily by Davis, who was never more petty than in his dealings with Beauregard, and finally shunted into the mundane assignment of commanding the Department of the South Atlantic. With this imposing title, Beauregard was little more than administrative head of coastal defenses in the Charleston area, an anticlimactic completion of his career cycle.

The ambitious Creole was not unmindful of this comedown, which he attributed to Davis's being "too egotistical and jealous" to allow the development of a genius who might save the country. Beyond his abiding personal hatred of Davis, Beauregard sincerely believed that all their misfortunes stemmed from the President's "inability and obstinacy." He wrote that "The curse of God must have been on our people when we chose him." Beauregard's own state was so low that he was on the point of resigning when he was offered the new department in mid-April (the formal commission came through on the 23rd).

In perceiving the opportunities for glory in a return to the main theater, especially as it involved the capital, Beauregard never lost sight of the problems which might affect his interests. At this stage of the war, he was wary of risking his reputation in a suddenly crucial area where, with nebulous departmental authority, he would suffer from the President's "hampering restrictions" and operate in the shadow of the great Lee. Joe Johnston had been reduced to futile supineness when placed in a similar departmental position the summer before, and Vicksburg had fallen to the enemy while three department heads were trapped in the bureaucratic maze.

From his acceptance of the department until Pickett's emergency message reached him, Beauregard moved with a caution that was close to inanition. As with Lee, Joe Johnston and the rest of them, he had endured his full share of Davis's troop manipulations. Soundly enough from the viewpoint of his personal self-protectiveness, Beauregard preferred some troops in the area, rather than on the commander in chief's charts, before he assumed command of a vacuum. After the Pickett-Ransom-Hill combine had halted Butler, Braxton Bragg, with the President's approval, went into a frenzy of ordering idle troops up from all over the east coast. That was when Old Bory decided to take the risk for the recapture of the big glory.

With this background, the vain general did not come to Petersburg with any such modest purpose as to cooperate with Lee. Before he even felt out Butler's position, Beauregard proposed a plan in which Lee would cooperate with *him*. In essence, Lee was to fall back toward Richmond and, avoiding all except rear-guard actions, send Beauregard ten thousand men. Ransom's troops, which had been returned to the Richmond Department, would recross the James River and bring Beauregard's strength to approximately thirty thousand. With this force, Beauregard would fall upon the wretched Butler, cut him off from his river base, and obliterate his army. With this threat removed, Beauregard would then move up as a wing to Lee's army and together — *together* — they would finish off Grant. Of his scheme, Beauregard said, "I felt sure of defeating Grant and probably open the way to Washington where we might dictate *Peace!!*"

He sent an aide to Richmond to lay this plan in person before the commander in chief. When the President sent word that he was too sick to appear, Colonel Stevens delivered the message to Bragg. According to Beauregard's memory of the event, nine years later, the Military Adviser came to see him in the lines. There Bragg said he agreed with the plan, but refused to disturb Davis to obtain his approval for issuing the order. Beauregard recalled saying, "Bragg, circumstances have thrown the fate of the Confederacy in your hands and mine. Let us play our parts boldly and fearlessly. Issue those orders . . . and I'll guarantee success."

It sounds like one of those after-the-fact recollections of a scene. In any event, Bragg was not stirred to play his part boldly and fearlessly. Also, while Beauregard was spinning his grand strategy, with Ransom's troops moved from Drewry's Bluff back to their own department, Butler broke his fix. He attacked the river fort and effected a lodgment in the outer works.

The President at least returned Ransom's troops and gave Beauregard permission to employ his full force in a movement to cut Butler off from his base. At this time, to his twenty thousand infantry, Beauregard had added three artillery battalions; and Dearing's cavalry brigade had finally gathered most of its sixteen hundred troopers. He had the force and the position to inflict a decisive defeat on Butler's awkwardly disposed troops. As the Federals on the outer works of the fort were marooned there, the enemy disposition invited a pincer movement. Beauregard, as nearly always, planned with imaginative and skillful strategy. Tactics were something else.

Unexplainably, unless by reason of jealousy, Beauregard did not assign one of the four hastily collected divisions to D. H. Hill, the best soldier on the field. Ransom and Hoke were legitimate enough choices, but Colquitt was regarded by Beauregard himself as a weak commander and Whiting was hurried up from Wilmington as a personal friend. When Beauregard attempted a complicated maneuver, which involved coordination between separated bodies of these assembled strangers, one of the parts was almost certain to fail. The culprit was friend Whiting. Forty-year-old professional soldier Whiting was one of the finest military engineers on either side, and in 1862 Lee had transferred him out of the army in the belief that his forte was not in the field.

At the moment for him to move forward in conjunction with Ransom, who had a segment of the enemy pinned down and in trouble, Whiting went into something like a trance. Because of a dense fog, highly favorable for attacking troops, the generals waiting for Whiting had no notion of what had happened to him. Harvey Hill, the "volunteer aide" who was near Whiting, could only look on helplessly. Later he defended Beauregard's friend from charges of drunkenness. If Beauregard had given the engineer a chance to prove Lee was wrong in his judgment of him as a field commander, it was a costly method of vindicating the Old Man.

Though the disjointed, incomplete attack (May 16th) did not cut Butler off from his base, the aggressive blow shook him. He hurried back to his river base within the sheltering wings of the loops of the river on either flank. Butler forgot that the distance across the open end of the squat peninsula was little more than three miles. When Beauregard constructed lines between the James and the Appomattox River, and manned the works with guns, the Beast's base became a cage. By May 20th he had managed to immobilize the army provided for him.

Before Butler was bottled up, Beauregard advanced (May 19th) another plan for collaborating with Lee. Again Lee was to fall back toward Richmond and this time Beauregard, slipping away from Butler, would lead fifteen thousand men in a flank attack that would render "Grant's defeat certain and decisive." After Grant was sent reeling back, it would be simple to return and dispose of Butler. Despite the airiness of this scheme, and the motives behind it, General Beauregard made one sound prediction: "Without such concentration . . . General Lee must eventually fall back before Grant's heavy reenforcements . . . and the picture presented is one of ultimate starvation."

On this fundamental of strategy, Beauregard and Lee were in

complete accord. Yet, by operating as separate department heads through the commander in chief, the two generals were placed in conflict to one another.

8

Davis rejected the very notion of concentration, and continued to regard troop units as elements to be shifted in the various departments according to the most pressing local emergency. When Butler was threatening from the outer lines of Drewry's Bluff, brigades from Lee's army (promised him within four days on May 4th) were held with Beauregard to meet the nearest threat. With that threat contained, the brigades officially on the roster of the Army of Northern Virginia were to be returned to Lee, precisely those and none other.

Both generals looked beyond this emergency shuttling. Even with Pickett's division and Hoke's old brigade scheduled to leave the Richmond area, Beauregard and Lee recognized that the remaining troops were more than needed to protect the lines which penned up Butler. Lee saw the troops as the key to maneuver; Beauregard saw them as the lever to his bid for glory. Potentially and actually Lee and Beauregard were unequal collaborators, but because of Beauregard's ambition and the opportunities provided by the departmental system, he became in effect Lee's rival. The conflict between them began over which general would get the use of the spare troops.

When Beauregard sent his plan of leading fifteen thousand troops in a flank movement in support of Lee, Davis could not repress his ill will in the manner of rejecting the General's plan. In returning the plan to Bragg, he wrote, "If 15,000 men can be spared for the flank movement, certainly 10,000 may be sent to reinforce General Lee."

Davis had no intention of sending ten thousand men to Lee, though he recognized, when he ordered Pickett and Hoke's brigade to start toward Lee on the 20th, that Lee needed more reinforcements. The gratuitous slap alerted Beauregard to his true status. He perceived that his force was regarded merely as a potential reserve for Lee, with himself excluded from the consequential actions. Beyond that, Davis belittled him personally to an extent that a war office official recorded: "In the midst of these great events, one has no heart to chronicle the petty bickerings which tease Beauregard."

Old Bory, himself not a large man, was less attentive to the accustomed slights than to the guidance they provided his course of self-interest. He was determined to escape an assignment which reduced him to the role of observing the quiescent Butler. While that worthy improved his time by directing gunboat shells into Pickett's family home across the river, until the house caught fire and burned to the ground, Beauregard reorganized the units with him into a more compact force.

With D. H. Hill temporarily remaining as volunteer aide, deflated Whiting was returned to his post at Wilmington, and Robert Ransom, somehow getting on the wrong side of Beauregard, was returned to the Richmond Department with one brigade. One more brigade was released from coastal garrisons to come to the Richmond area. Though no one agreed on the numbers of all the troops which passed through in May, the force left with Beauregard would not have totaled less than thirteen thousand infantry. These Beauregard divided into two divisions, one under Bushrod Johnson and the other under Robert Hoke.

What the droopy-eyed Creole prepared to do with these two divisions, larger than Ewell's Second Corps, plus artillery and cavalry, was probably not clear even to him. But his immediate intention was certain: he was not going to let Lee have them if he could help it.

On the 21st of May, Beauregard received another cutting letter from Davis which hardened the lines between the two departments on the day that Grant moved from Spotsylvania in a wide flanking movement toward Richmond. As Beauregard was to be denied a conspicuous part in acting with Lee, on that day he began to emphasize to Davis the dangers from Butler on his own front.

The President, having satisfied himself by putting Beauregard in his place, did not conceive of the additional problem he had created for Lee. At this period, Davis gave Lee warm moral support in assuring him that he recognized the General's need of "reinforcements."

While to Lee reinforcements meant the possibility of maneuver which could *change* the situation, to the President reinforcements meant only units shifted to support an *existing* situation, usually after the situation began to deteriorate. Then, as Davis balanced troops between two departments without giving strategic preferment to either, he was influenced in his natural defensiveness by Beauregard's stress on the imaginary dangers from Butler. Thus, he did not send reinforcements to Lee even in his own restricted meaning of the word. Davis was perhaps shaken by Richmond's close call, and Lee's situation had not reached emergency proportions.

Beginning with May 18th, Lee had begun to stress his need for more troops. That was the day he became convinced that Grant waited at Spotsylvania for replacements, and he mentioned this repeatedly to Davis. He also reiterated the dread possibility of falling back closer to Richmond. But the tone of the brief messages, though lacking in warmth, was quietly insistent rather than urgent. As accustomed as he was to working around Davis's fixations, Lee never guessed that the new element of the South's Napoleon had been added.

When released from Richmond, Pickett's division and Hoke's brigade would merely complete the complement of Lee's army, minus their losses at Drewry's Bluff. Their variously estimated total was probably around six thousand effectives. Many estimates of Lee's strength have counted these troops twice — on the roster and again when they reported after Spotsylvania. The only reinforcements ticketed for the Army of Northern Virginia were the two pick-up brigades with Breckinridge, about 2250, and a large regiment of green troops on their way to Kershaw's old brigade. In terms of his losses, the total of all troops on their way to Lee's army constituted something over 40 per cent replacements. Grant replaced 85 per cent of his losses.

When the Spotsylvania-south of Richmond period ended on May 21st, two known elements had changed — one favorable to Lee, and one unfavorable. As a positive element, the Virginia struggle had been reduced to the two main armies. As a negative element, Grant's next move would edge Lee closer to Richmond; the distance in which maneuver would be possible was closing in. There was yet a third element unknown to Lee at the time: the additional troops, which would enlarge the possibilities of a counterstroke, would be, withheld from him. For all his anticipation of Grant's plans, he would be denied the use of the force of potential cooperation.

More than at any time in his career, Lee, with his ablest subordinates gone or ailing, was caught between the enemy in his front and the system behind him. Though Lee had no premonition of it, when his headquarters tent was struck on May 21st, his own physical organism was about to break under the strain.

CHAPTER NINE

"Good Health Is Indispensable in War . . ."

WHEN LEE'S TROOPS withdrew from their field fortifications around Spotsylvania Court House on Saturday, May 21st, the General's antipathy to giving up the heavily wooded ground was eased by his hope for striking a counterblow. He was always stimulated by movement, with its suggested possibilities of the unexpected, and the approaching return of his troops encouraged him. Though their number was small, even eight thousand, with an artillery battalion, relieved his anxiety over continuing without replacements, and he expected more. Then, along with relief and hope, the movement away from Spotsylvania held none of the desperate urgency of the race from the Wilderness.

Grant's Virginia tactics have been usually described as a series of flanking movements, a crabwise advance toward Richmond. This is not strictly true. Grant opened the campaign with an aggressive march due south and was halted in the Wilderness by Lee's offensive operation against his flank. In disengaging his army, Grant crossed Lee's front in resuming a southward movement via Spotsylvania. When Lee raced around in front of him, Grant first tried to smash through the roadblock to get to the road south.

Until that drive failed, Grant had sought battle wherever he found it, whether Lee was on his flank or behind works. At that stage, according to his own orders, the objective was Lee's army. Later, from retrospect, he wrote that Richmond was the objective, and his movements interrelated with Butler in a far-reaching plan. Actually Grant, like Lincoln in the political sphere, was improvising.

On the night of May 20th-21st, he swung in a quarter-circle outside Lee's eastern flank with the immediate objective of moving southward *around* the roadblock. In this phase, Grant began to seek favorable conditions for bringing Lee to battle. By circling Lee's flank in moving away from Spotsylvania's discouraging works, Grant forced Lee to fall back in order to keep between the Federal army and Richmond. Yet when Grant completed his quarter-circular march, he returned approximately to the same north-south line on which he began in crossing the Rapidan on May 4th. By then he was thirty-odd miles closer to Richmond by the direct route, and he seemed to be playing off the capital and Lee's army as alternate objectives.

The distances were not great for all the movement involved. The direct line by highway and railroad from Richmond to Fredericksburg was fifty-five miles. From where Grant first crossed the Rapidan ten miles west of Fredericksburg, the battle lines extended five miles due south. From the end of these lines to Spotsylvania Court House was barely ten miles southward, bearing east. From the courthouse, the highway and the railroad were about six miles to the east on a direct line. Grant's quarter-circle movement crossed the highway, swung in an arc to the east of that, and then returned to the highway twenty-three miles north of Richmond.

Since Lee needed only travel by the chord of this arc in order to get in front of the Federal army again, Grant evidently hoped the concealment provided by the thickly wooded country would sufficiently baffle Lee about his intentions to bring on a meeting battle in the open. At least he could catch Lee, even if in his path, outside heavy works. But the rivers on which Grant depended for supply also provided Lee with a clue to his movements.

In marching southward, Grant moved out of the supply area of Belle Plain on the Potomac, and the next river supply base was at Port Royal on the Rappahannock. By the time Lee knew that Grant was moving out on the morning of the 21st, he knew the Federal army would make for Milford and Bowling Green, because a road connected these towns with Port Royal. From the Milford-Bowling Green area, a logical move was the swing back to the highway at Hanover Junction. There the railroad from Richmond to Fredericksburg connected with the Virginia Central, from Richmond to the Valley.

By such mental processes, Lee nullified the screening effects of the country and planned to fall back on Hanover Junction with as much certainty as if he had read Grant's orders. In this certainty, the General was protected against the intangibles by the patrolling of his cavalry, while Grant, as a result of Sheridan's raid, was stripped of the cavalry necessary to provide a screen for his march. When the Federal infantry moved out, Sheridan was four days away from rejoining the army.

Through Grant's maneuver was far from brilliant, it would serve the purpose of moving him closer to Richmond, unless Lee caught him in motion. With the troops Lee had at hand, Grant welcomed an attack; in fact, he hoped to induce Lee to attack Hancock's separated lead corps. Had Lee possessed the troops he wanted, there is no doubt that he would have struck the moving columns of the Federal army. Because Lee could not attack Grant in passage with what he had, a certain grimness of resolution formed under Lee's acceptance of the necessity of retreating to cover Richmond. He was like an old fighter goaded when his waning strength prevented him from taking advantage of the openings offered by a less skillful younger opponent, who kept boring in with aggressive confidence in his physical powers.

2

Under this subsurface goad, General Lee rode most of the night of the 21st-22nd southward from the abandoned works on which so much toil had been spent. His army had moved out during the 21st by corps, with Ewell's stout marchers leading the way around noon and Hill's corps, as rear guard, leaving at nine that night. Lee, with his staff and a young cavalryman from the neighborhood as guide, left an hour or so before Hill's troops. Moving through the night on Telegraph Road, at times Lee's small cavalcade was only one mile across country from Federal flankers to the east.

Hancock's corps had started its swing east at eleven the night before, crossing the railroad at the telegraph station at Guiney's, by the house where Stonewall Jackson had died. The other three corps left at intervals during the day, Sedgwick's corps, then commanded by Wright, leaving after dark and considerable rear-guard skirmishing. Though Hancock's corps had a twelve-hour start on

Ewell, the last troops of the two armies left around the same time.
Lee's men had not only the shorter way but for most of it the
better road.

As Grant moved without cavalry in force, Lee had no fear of a
quick mounted thrust (as was possible at Spotsylvania) taking Hanover Junction before his infantry arrived. Against a forced march
of a mobile column, Lee had ordered Breckinridge's two brigades to
detrain at the Junction and remain there. Wade Hampton's cavalry
fanned out to the north.

Another element here was the network of small rivers, flowing
into the large tidal rivers which emptied into Chesapeake Bay. The
streams in the Spotsylvania countryside formed into the middle-
sized Mattaponi River east of the Telegraph Road and west of
Grant's line of march. The river flowed almost due south along
Grant's line of march as far as Milford, where it bent sharply to
the southeast. The parallel North Anna River flowed southeast
about two miles north of Hanover Junction. Shortly beyond Hanover Junction, in another merger of streams, the North Anna became the Pamunkey, and the loosely parallel southeasterly rivers —
Pamunkey and Mattaponi — would form a double water barrier
between Lee's army and the enemy, unless Grant crossed the
Mattaponi back to the west near Milford. This Lee expected him
to do.

On this assumption, Lee determined to protect Hanover Junction
from the North Anna. However, beyond choosing the position on
the hill rising steeply from the river, his plans were fluid. After
leaving Spotsylvania, the General suffered a conflict between the
necessity of falling back to protect Richmond and the desire to
catch Grant in motion, and he resisted committing his army to a
strictly defensive stance. This inner agitation caused Lee to neglect
himself physically on that night ride.

With only one brief rest, he was in the saddle from around eight
at night until three in the morning, covering seventeen miles. This
was only one mile less than the superbly conditioned Federal cavalry allotted for a full day's march. Then, resting barely two hours,
with a nap and a scanty breakfast, Lee rode on six more miles to
the North Anna. Some time after seven in the morning he halted
briefly on the south bank of the river to issue orders, as the van of

Ewell's corps shuffled down the opposite hill toward the river crossing.

These dependable marchers had covered twenty-three miles since noon of the day before, with little sleep, and the survivors demonstrated their physical recovery from the Bloody Angle disaster. Assured that his army was coming up, General Lee rode on the two miles to Hanover Junction. There his headquarters tent was pitched in a hollow in the angle where the two railroads crossed. By nine-thirty in the morning of the 22nd, a little more than twelve hours after leaving Spotsylvania twenty-five miles away, he was sending telegraphic messages to Richmond.

Among routine duties, the General was again put to the necessity of providing a division for John Gordon — this time permanently, as the Georgian's promotion to major general was going through. A. P. Hill reported for duty when his corps moved out the day before, thus returning Jubal Early to his division, which Gordon had commanded at Spotsylvania. Lee formed a division with Gordon's Georgia brigade, commanded by Colonel Clement Evans, and the two brigades, one Virginian and one Louisianian, salvaged from the wreck of Johnson's division, and at last Gordon had his own division.

Hoke's old brigade, then commanded by Colonel Lewis, fortuitously arrived from Beauregard, and Lee returned this unit to its regular place in Early's division. Though Early's and Gordon's divisions contained only three brigades each, the Second Corps was returned to a sound command structure, considering the number of unproved colonels in temporary brigade command.

Only three brigades of Pickett's division had then arrived, apparently without their division commander, and these troops were attached temporarily to Hill's corps. At Hanover Junction the bourbon-flavored Breckinridge reported directly to teetotaler Lee.

During this quiet day of the gathering and rebuilding of his army, away from the unremitting pressure of the enemy, Lee's resistance to a defensive battle intensified. Judging from the disposition of his troops, he prepared his army to move against the enemy rather than to receive attack. Evidently not expecting Grant to try to force the river crossing, Lee spread his corps in anticipation of moving by the right or left.

The railroad bridge and the highway bridge, crossing the North Anna one half mile apart, were left intact, with small detachments posted at the bridges on the northern bank. South of the river, Ewell's corps was shifted to the east of the bridges and Anderson's two divisions faced the crossings. Besides light trenches overlooking the bridgeheads, no works were dug. When Hill's corps started arriving after noon by a westerly road with the wagon train, the Third Corps troops went into camp a mile back from the river, several miles west of the bridges. Only a regiment was posted along the river bank on picket duty. It was the first day since May 5th that the army was out of contact with the enemy, and the General allowed the men to enjoy a quiet Sabbath in the pleasant countryside.

The army had then moved out of the densely wooded area of Spotsylvania and crossed into the more fertile region of Hanover County. This was the county of Henry Clay and Patrick Henry, a land locally famed for its prosperous farms, its melons and vegetables, especially bright red tomatoes. Outside the area damaged during the Seven Days Battle in 1862, except for the casual vandalism of transient raiders, the large country, without cities, had been spared the ordeals which devastated the Fredericksburg region. The houses, from the humblest to the stately red-brick Georgian mansions, were set in groves of shade trees, fences still lined private property and sweet-smelling vines bordered the roadsides. Few of the homes were deserted. Lee's young cavalry guide, after leaving the General, had ridden to his mother's house for a square meal.

The respite given the soldiers was not shared by General Lee. Resting his army for possible movement (at Hanover Junction, Breckinridge was under specific orders to "be prepared to move"), Lee was preparing a forthright message to Davis on the subject of concentration for counteroffense. In the dispatch, sent the next morning, Lee revealed that, in his hardening determination to hit Grant, he shared Beauregard's general concept.

"Whatever route he [Grant] pursues, I am in a position to move against him, and shall endeavor to engage him while in motion. I shall also be near enough Richmond, I think, to combine the operations of this army with that under General Beauregard." Then, mentioning that Butler was entrenched and saying that no more troops were needed than to "retain the enemy in his entrench-ments," Lee came to the point. "On the contrary, General Grant's army will be in the field . . . and it seems to me our best policy to unite upon it and endeavor to crush it."

When this message was sent on the morning of the 23rd, Lee had no notion that Beauregard had advanced in substance the same plan. To clear the way for cooperation between himself and the other general, and to remove any impression that he sought only the troops with Beauregard, Lee added, "I shall be very glad to have the aid of General Beauregard in such a blow, and, if it is possible to combine, I think it will succeed."

On the same day, Beauregard wired Davis that reports indicated reinforcements were coming to Butler. "If this be true, he may take the offensive soon. Then I shall require assistance."

The fact was, on the day before, May 22nd, Grant had ordered Smith's XVIII Corps to leave Bermuda Hundred and reinforce Meade's army.

Without knowledge that Beauregard, having failed to win the share of glory he lusted for, was working then on Davis against a combination, Lee must have been undermined by a sense of frus-tration at trying to achieve his objectives through the commander in chief. He had physically overtaxed himself and, as the day wore on, the General began to come down sick and grew unprecedent-edly irritable.

3

There is uncertainty about the beginning of Lee's illness. His precise condition on the 23rd is clouded by the curious obscurity which overhung the actions of both armies that day. It was as though everyone was too tired to remember or record details.

Anderson's and Ewell's corps seemed apathetic after the complete relaxation which followed their night march, and Hill's men, com-ing by a longer, rougher route, after skirmishing until the last min-ute, were done in. The Federal army suffered from straggling in its roundabout journey to the North Anna. Hundreds of exhausted men arrived in division ambulances and more than four thousand sick from the Army of the Potomac had already been shipped to Washington. It was a period when individuals in each army believed the other army was beginning to collapse, and maybe all of them were partially right.

In the forenoon, when the blue groups gathered on the opposite hill and guns were unlimbered, General Lee appeared to be his usual composed self. He stood in the front yard of a large red-brick house on the crest of the hill near the Telegraph Road and watched the smoke puff from the muzzles of the Federal cannon as the gunners sought the range of the two bridges. Lee's cannoneers answered without orders, and the small detachments left on the opposite shore huddled a little closer in their bridgehead trench. Grant, instead of making another pell-mell rush, was feeling out Lee's position, and these uninspired preliminaries evidently convinced Lee that his opponent did not intend to force a crossing. In any event, the General sent no orders for his soldiers to build works. Later in the afternoon Federals were reported massing opposite Ox Ford, two miles upriver from the road bridge, and heavy artillery fire opened to the west of that. General Lee decided to make his own reconnaissance, and it was then he first revealed that he did not feel well.

Turning Traveler over to an orderly, the General rode in a borrowed carriage along a country road which ran beside the Virginia Central tracks and paralleled the river, about one mile to the south of it. Near the firing, Lee's carriage cut across the field, and the General stepped out beside a battery of horse artillery. He made only a brief study through his field glasses. After satisfying himself that the movement was only a feint, Lee returned to the carriage and apparently went to his headquarters at Hanover Junction. Nothing appears to be known about his relation to the action which followed his leaving the field, and little about the action.

The section where Lee made his observation west of Ox Ford was occupied by A. P. Hill's corps. The resting men were mostly in camp in open country along the Virginia Cental tracks in the area of Anderson's Station, about one mile back from Ox Ford. West of Ox Ford, the course of the river cut to the north, forming a sharp angle three miles northwest at a bad crossing beside a neighborhood gristmill, called Jericho Mills. While the country was mostly cultivated between the flag stop of Anderson's Station and Jericho Mills, near the mill crossing heavy woods blocked the river from view of the Third Corps. Whether in routine precaution or from cavalry reports, before Lee's reconnaissance A. P. Hill had ordered Major General Wilcox to reconnoiter the region with MacGowan's brigade.

Nobody seems to know what happened to the cavalry or what reports were made. Rosser's brigade had stayed in front of Warren's V Corps all the way to the North Anna in the Jericho Mills area. Also, Orr's rifles, of MacGowan's brigade, had skirmished with Federal infantry in the early afternoon along the Virginia Central one mile south of the river crossing at the mill. Yet at three o'clock, when Wilcox rode his white horse back to Hill's headquarters, he gave as news the information that enemy infantry had crossed the river and were pushing toward them through the woods. For one certainty, Hill ordered Wilcox to attack with his division. At this point, the mystery becomes complete.

Lee had left for Hanover Junction before Wilcox brought the news. Powell Hill, having returned to duty less than forty-eight hours before, did not feel well enough to assume command of the field, and Wilcox commanded the assault. At some time after Hill ordered Wilcox forward, he sent Heth's division in support on orders no one will ever know. Whether Heth was sent late or moved slowly, his division arrived when the attack had failed, or was failing, and his troops hovered uncertainly in the dusk. Colonel Venable mentions Mahone's division getting in on the edge of the attack, and perhaps some of his troops came in at the tail end when light was failing. Clearly no one knew, until contact was established, that they were taking on Warren's V Corps.

Warren's troops had started crossing the steep-banked stream at noon, some wading over and some using the bridges the engineers built for the guns and wagons. At six o'clock, when Wilcox attacked with his division, all four of Warren's divisions were over, most of the troops in position and guns posted. Wilcox had not been slow. His brigades were put from camp onto the road in columns of fours, marched three miles along the narrow road beside the railroad track, then deployed in lines of battle and advanced across a wheat-field, over a railroad cut, and another wheatfield before entering the woods.

From the point of contact on, the fight was one of which no-body on either side seemed at all proud. The battle opened with Thomas's brigade by chance striking Cutler's division, the last on the field, before it was fully formed on the right of the line. Cutler's troops were driven back, exposing the Federal battle line to a flank-ing movement. After this brief success, with MacGowan and Lane pressing against the main Federal line, and Scales coming up on their right in reserve, coherence disappeared from Wilcox's divi-sion. Whatever one unit did, its fellow did the opposite.

Considering that the four brigades, operating at odds with one another, were attacking four divisions, Warren's corps could not have been very sharp in merely repulsing the bungled assault. Wil-cox's men were forced to fall back but, despite leaving a number of prisoners within Union lines, the losses were even, and no resolute pursuit was made. Heth relieved Wilcox at dark, and Warren's peo-ple, abandoning their advance, dug in against Hill.

As an action, the so-called Battle of Jericho Mills would seem to indicate that neither army had fully recovered psychologically from the shock of the sustained fighting from May 5th through the 21st. Cadmus Wilcox lost control of the action and of his intelli-gence. Neither Thomas nor Scales gave a representative perform-ance, and one of Jim Lane's finest North Carolina regiments broke and, when re-formed, broke again.

How and when a report of this action reached Lee is among the mysteries. As Colonel Venable mentioned that Lee "hoped much" from the attack, it can be presumed the General was aware of the movement before Wilcox met the enemy. When Lee learned the de-tails the next morning, the 24th, he grew enraged at Hill for at-tacking with only Wilcox. Though sick, Lee had ridden over to Third Corps lines and he turned on Powell Hill with a sharp re-buke. "Why did you not do as Jackson would have done — thrown your whole force upon those people and driven them back?"

This flash of ill temper at a lieutenant general, in the presence of subordinates, revealed Lee's exacerbated condition rather than serv-ing as a considered judgment of Hill's battle.

Hill did not know until three o'clock that the enemy was moving toward him on the same side of the river, nor in what strength. He acted soundly enough, as did Lee himself on the Orange Plank Road on the first day of the Wilderness, in sending Wilcox forward and then Heth and Mahone in support. Though tactically the movement was not closely supervised by Hill, Wilcox's surprisingly poor performance lost the field in the center before the other divisions came up. From the reticence of Heth, quick enough to blame Hill in support of his own record, he could not have displayed any noticeable celerity or decisiveness with his division — though the approach of dusk may have restrained him.

Had the movement begun two hours before, scarcely half the enemy would have been formed. With two hours of daylight, Heth and Mahone would have come up before Warren's last division crossed the river. This "lost opportunity," for such it was, was caused by the time element and not because Hill failed to behave like Stonewall Jackson (though he certainly did not). And the time lag was caused by the failure of the cavalry to report the approach of an enemy infantry corps.

Rosser's brigade, of Hampton's division, operated independently in covering Warren's advance, and communications broke down somewhere. Along with the tentative system, since Stuart's death, in which division commanders reported directly to Lee, the cavalry units were scattered in patrol and in rebuilding. Pierce Young, of Hampton's division, had gone to Richmond to form the odd units coming up from the South, and General Hampton seemed to have only one regiment with him east of the Telegraph Road. James Gordon's North Carolinians, of Rooney Lee's division, had been badly cut up and lost their brigade leader in Sheridan's Richmond raid, and, temporarily leaderless, were spread out along the rivers north of the capital.

Shortly after Stuart's death, Lee said to an aide, "If I had my poor Stuart with me, I would know what those people are up to." As was said of Lee during the Gettysburg campaign, it was not that he lacked cavalry, but that he lacked Jeb Stuart. Without Stuart to control and channel the reconnaissance of all units, Lee was failed by his cavalry in the movements around Jericho Mills. In another one of these multiple-factored breakdowns, no one had distinguished himself at Jericho Mills, and Powell Hill was the obvious and handiest object for the frustrations of the sick man.

Lee had probably suffered an attack of diarrhea the night before, similar to the attack on the second night at Gettysburg. As the day wore on, he grew increasingly ill, and that night, the 24th, was confined to his tent by acute intestinal inflammation.

Any illness irritated Lee. It was the only predictable circumstance in which he lost control of his temper. Lee's composure did not derive from a lack of strong feelings within his normally equable disposition. The majestic element in the composure resulted from the symmetrical whole he formed of a powerful nature. When he was struck by a debilitating malady at this stage of his struggle against the array of forces, his emotional nature resented most powerfully his body's betrayal, and he was not under his habitual control.

Lee, the man, had so concentrated on delivering an offensive blow that Lee, the general, refused to recognize the extent to which his army had been bled. In turning on A. P. Hill, he was striking out at all the uncontrollable turns of fate — the hindrance of Davis, the want of physical support for his army, the collapse of the human organisms which comprised the army and, finally, the collapse of his own physical powers in an hour of opportunity.

For on that morning, before the weakness and sickness overcame him, General Lee extemporized the most fascinating trap for an enemy devised by anyone during the war. A saint would have rebelled at being thwarted in springing the trap on an opponent who regarded him as too feeble to strike a telling blow.

4

By nature, Lee, like Grant and Sherman, was a military opportunist. With the restrictions imposed by Davis's system and his need to defend Richmond, Lee's flashes of his usually restrained opportunism were limited to battlefield extemporizations. At the North Anna River, by an imaginative use of the terrain, he turned a crisis into a tactical stroke of genius.

Manifestly Lee had not expected the crossing of an enemy corps five miles up the river. If he had, Hill would have been prepared for Warren — not to prevent the crossing, but to catch the corps in motion. Once Warren's V Corps was over and dug in, as the men were thoroughly by morning of the 24th, this threat to his left could only be accepted as an accomplished fact.

Also, at dark of the day before, troops from Hancock's corps had rushed the small detachments at the bridgeheads, and gobbled up the one hundred or so Confederates who could not escape across the bridge. No small loss ever served Lee a more useful purpose. Lee was warned that Hancock was coming over in the morning against what had been his center, or right center. This would indicate that Grant did intend to force a crossing. As concerned Hancock's expected push, necessity and the terrain combined to form Lee's spontaneous plan.

In the bridge area, the north bank hills were higher than those on the south bank, giving domination to the heavier Federal artillery. Lee's troops would have been hard put to it, at best, to defend against a crossing. Though the wooden bridges had been burned on the southern bank, the river was low enough to be waded (as Warren's corps had shown) and the efficient Federal engineering corps caused bridges to appear as if by magic. At worst, Lee would be defending a river crossing against Hancock while fighting Warren on the same side of the river six miles to the west, with a dangerous gap between his two wings. A Federal river crossing between the two would cut Lee's army in half.

It happened that at the only good crossing between Lee's right and left, Ox Ford, the higher ground on the southern bank gave his gunners domination. Also, the way the river dipped, Ox Ford was at the bottom of a loop, with Hancock's crossing two miles to the northeast and Warren's three miles to the northwest. On the pivot of Ox Ford, all the factors fell into a single pattern.

The Ox Ford crossing would be defended as Lee's center. Since Warren was already across to the west, Hancock would be permitted an uncontested crossing to the east. Then, to the right and left of Ox Ford, Lee's wings changed front. From running parallel to the river, facing north, the lines were bent back at a 45-degree angle, and the right and left at this slant faced to the east and west, instead of north. In another way, the continuous line was changed into a triangular fort, with the apex at the river front, and the ob-

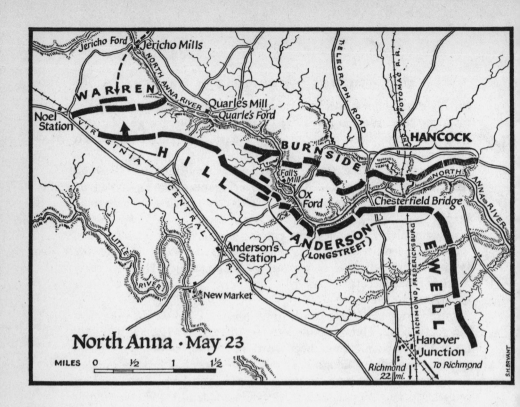

North Anna · May 23

MILES 0   ½   1   1½

Richmond 22 mi.   To Richmond

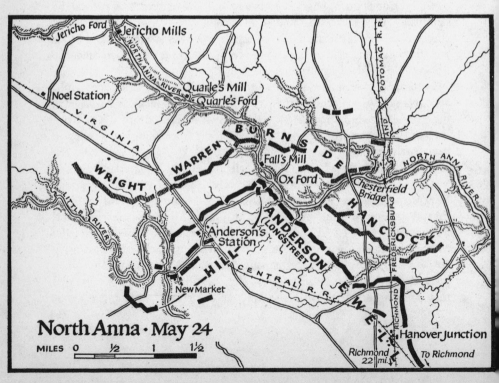

North Anna · May 24

MILES 0   ½   1   1½

Richmond 22 mi.   To Richmond

lique sides as bastions against land attack from their side of the river.

With this change, Lee's dangerously spread army contracted along a four-mile base. The western side, facing Warren, was barely two miles wide, with flanks anchored on the North Anna at Ox Ford and on the Little River, a loop of which came to within one half mile of the Virginia Central. The eastern face, where Hancock was to cross, covered slightly over three miles. One flank rested on the North Anna and the other curved about the Richmond, Fredericksburg & Potomac Railroad track on the edge of the swampy ground about a half-mile from Hanover Junction.

In the center, from Ox Ford east along the North Anna until the river bent to the northeast, Anderson's two divisions covered the Ox Ford crossing and formed the flank of the right wing. On the right, Ewell's corps, numbering at least nine thousand with the return of Hoke's old brigade, had moved during the night of the 23rd-24th. With forty hours' rest, without serious contact with the enemy, the refreshed troops of these two corps threw up lines almost as tough as Spotsylvania's works, and sliced traverses back from the parapets to protect men and gunners from cross fire from the river.

After Lee's unanswered rebuke of Powell Hill early in the morning, the Third Corps withdrew two miles from Warren's front to their drawn lines from Ox Ford to Little River. Hill's men had not shared the hiatus with the other two corps, and they needed a little rest before they started digging. Probably the men were helped in the heavy work by Pickett's three brigades, of whom little was recorded. They came up separately, one did not behave well in a brush encounter with light enemy cavalry, and evidently they were held in a general reserve, attached to Hill, until the division completed its reforming. It is not likely that some thirty-five hundred soldiers would have been allowed to stand around idly in the emergency.

The men were allowed all day to dig. Despite the reproach Hill received for his piecemeal attack on the 23rd, Warren spent the 24th strengthening his lines, while Wright's VI Corps crossed at Jericho Mills and formed on Warren's right. That was half of Grant's army on one side of Lee.

Burnside's IX Corps, the army's weakest unit, was given the assignment of crossing the river at Ox Ford. This must have been considered a routine assignment in the Federal army's assumption that Lee's two wings, Hill and Ewell, were separated by six miles. Between Alexander's handsomely served guns and well-protected sharpshooters, Burnside was not able to mount a serious threat at crossing the river.

The key Federal unit became Hancock's corps. Its heavy losses at the Wilderness and Spotsylvania had been made up by the replacements, and the II Corps was probably the best outfit in the Army of the Potomac. Certainly it was the best led. Hancock pushed across the river on the morning of the 24th, with veterans and recruits full of drive, only to discover a deserted hill where he had observed the enemy's line at sundown the day before. Not even a straggler was in sight.

Hancock's most detailed reports were scarcely subjective, but his anticlimactic bafflement was revealed here by classic understatement. He had written glowingly of capturing the small bridgehead-detachments of the night before, saying "this affair was very spirited and brilliant." But, after his morning rush to the Confederate side of the river, he summed up his situation by saying only, "This day was spent in reconnoitering."

It was while Hancock's "reconnoitering" strung out his corps, from the river to two miles to the southeast, that Lee finally caught the enemy in a position where one fourth of the Federal army could be destroyed. The V and VI Corps, facing Hill, would have to cross the river twice and march close to ten miles to come to Hancock's rescue. If Burnside withdrew from Ox Ford, Anderson could cross to the Federal side. Overnight Lee had turned the threat of separation of his own army into a tactical *coup* which divided the enemy's army. On the same side of the river with him, the Federal units were cut off from one another, with one fourth wide open.

General Humphreys, Meade's chief of staff, conceded that "for two or three hours" Lee had the chance to overwhelm Hancock. The consensus of critical military opinion points to this division of Grant's army as Lee's great opportunity.

Lee probably had read Napoleon's statements that "Good health is indispensable in war, and nothing can take its place." If the General had not read it, he proved it. He was too ill personally to direct an attack on Hancock's isolated, strung-out corps.

With his troops behind the powerful lines of his ingenious "fort," Lee could have pulled out at least a full division from Hill and a division from Anderson to join Ewell. With Breckinridge's two brigades free to march up from Hanover Junction, on the edge of Ewell's flank, some twenty thousand men would have been concentrated. Though combined this force would scarcely equal Hancock, his II Corps would have been caught in an irretrievably awkward position for defending itself, with the river across its line of retreat. But who would command such a crucial movement?

The army had come upon a time when what Lee could not direct personally could not be attempted. Napoleon also said, "To command is to wear out." And Lee was not the only general of whom the prolonged struggle against odds was taking its toll. While Hill, just returned from a two-weeks sick leave, was not fully recovered, Ewell was breaking rapidly and would report himself sick within the week. Lee, of course, left no record of the painful thoughts which resulted in his watching his long-desired moment come and go. His actions revealed the anguish of his disappointment and frustration.

When illness forced him back to his tent, he could still hope that Hancock or the two corps on his left would attack his lines. But not even aggressive Hancock had the humor for assaulting any more of Lee's lines. Hancock had quickly turned to digging himself in. As for Grant, this pugnacious driver seemed nonplused at finding himself, the hunter, suddenly the hunted. He, too, with a tendency to rationalize his actions, came up with a guarded understatement about the fix in which he found his separated army. "Finding the enemy's position on the North Anna stronger than either of his previous ones, I withdrew." Grant remained in position for two days, probing here and there, before pulling out. Maybe he hoped that Lee would attack his by then well-fortified lines.

Lee was desperately ill and never left his tent. He grew so irascible that he provoked even hero-worshiping Venable into a violent outburst at the commanding general. Lying on his cot, the Old Man murmured over and over, "We must strike them a blow. We must not let them pass us again. . . . We must strike them a blow." Lee must have sensed that more than the opportunity at the North Anna was slipping away. As sick and as disagreeable as he felt, before daylight of the 25th he composed one more appeal to Davis for a combination with Beauregard.

A dispatch from Grant to Burnside had been captured, which outlined the accretion of reinforcements to the Army of the Potomac. Mentioning this concentration, Lee wrote, "This makes it necessary for us to do likewise, and I have no doubt that your Excellency will do all in your power to meet the present emergency. If General Beauregard is in position to unite with me in any operation against General Grant, I should like to know it, and at what point a combination of the troops could be made most advantageously to him."

Beauregard never learned that Lee actively sought his personal cooperation. Almost daily, Old Bory nudged the commander in chief with some small alarum on his front, in his determination not to relinquish troops, as he said, "for the purpose of reinforcing Lee."

With communication blocked between the two generals, Lee had not abandoned hope, however unrealistically held, for a combination of their forces, when, on the morning of the 27th, he awakened to find Grant gone from his front. The Federal army had recrossed the North Anna during the night, and was marching southeast along the north bank of the river. When Lee sent orders to his generals to move out toward another interception of Grant, he clung to his purpose of trying with Beauregard's help to catch Grant in motion.

In Lee's weakened, sick condition, his tenaciously held purpose was perhaps supported more by will than by reason. Yet, once reason triumphed over that indomitable will to win, the wellspring of hope would dry. Without that, the field general would have only the mechanics of a professional technique to employ within a system which doomed itself in an arithmetically impossible struggle. With the will, there could be another North Anna opportunity, when he was well.

5

It was after the strange "battle" of the North Anna, the greatest unfought repulse of the war, that Grant began what was called his "sidling movement." It was only here, not before, that Grant gave up trying to overrun and/or get around Lee on the direct passage to Richmond. Despite Grant's later rationale about his far-reaching plans, involving Butler, for placing Richmond under siege, his march on May 27th certainly looked like an attempt to turn Lee and drive on to the capital from a new angle.

Though he was anxious to catch Lee in the open, a duality of purpose merged the two objectives into a pugnacious stubbornness to keep hitting until something fell. Neither Lee's army nor Richmond seemed to hold preferment any more. A gunner in Chew's horse artillery battery probably summed it up as well as anybody. "General Grant is still searching and hunting for a weak place whereby he may butt his way through and onward to Richmond."

His refusal of battle at the North Anna showed the respect of his military judgment for Lee's army in position, but his stubbornness refused to admit that his blows had not finished the Army of Northern Virginia. On the day before he moved away from the North Anna, he wrote Washington, "Lee's army is really whipped. . . . I may be mistaken but I feel that our success over Lee's army is already assured. . . . A battle with them outside of intrenchments can not be had."

Grant grew very fretful about Lee fighting behind works. From the opening clash, he assigned defeatism rather than intelligence for Lee's refusal to fight in the open against odds of two to one. Yet Grant's most combative generals instantly threw up works against Lee, and no troops ever dug in more quickly than Hancock's and Warren's south of the North Anna River.

Grant seemed to resent encountering a general who would not fight the way he wanted him to. In the West, the Confederates invariably fought according to Grant's plans. Against Lee, though Grant held the initiative, he could not bring the enemy to fight along his "lines." The fact was that Grant, representing a new policy of total war, which hitherto had swept everything before it, failed to recognize that the weakening traditionalists against him had introduced a new compensating tactic in warfare with field fortifications.

On the 27th and 28th, in his expressed conviction that the morale of his troops rose as Lee's men fell, Grant marched the men hard some thirty-odd miles over indifferent roads, very dusty, along the north bank of the river which soon became the Pamunkey. His line of march along the Pamunkey was southeast to Hanovertown, on the base of a triangle whose sides were roads to Richmond. On one side ran the direct north-south road from Hanover Junction, twenty-three miles from Richmond. On the other, from the river crossing at Hanovertown, roads fanned out in all directions to Richmond only fifteen miles away.

Hanovertown was barely a ghost of a once thriving river port, which grew around the long-since abandoned warehouse and shipping operations of the Page family. The muddy Pamunkey was narrow there, with steep banks and marshy approaches, but this crossing offered Grant three choices to the capital. Also, from the river crossings between Hanovertown and Hanover Junction, a network of roads leading to Richmond were joined by crisscrossing country roads.

Grant's swift march along the north bank of the Pamunkey was potentially his most effective maneuver against Lee, and the movement from the North Anna to Hanovertown was an extremely efficient operation. His troops had recrossed the North Anna and the last infantry column was on the road before daylight of the 27th. By noon of the 28th the first troops began to cross the Pamunkey at Hanovertown and thereabouts. Sheridan's cavalry corps had then rejoined the army. With the river between the Federals and Lee's men, in a country of heavy foliage, only the vaguest information had reached General Lee.

By midafternoon of the 28th, Grant had three infantry corps across the river, with no Confederate infantry beyond his immediate front. He had three fourths of his infantry and two thirds of his cavalry (the total outnumbering Lee three to two) on Lee's side of the river, with a wide choice of movement across flat country screened by walls of foliage. Though the land was more cultivated than timbered, and its second-growth woods held none of the density of the Wilderness, the intervals of woods and groves, of tree-bordered drives and vine-bordered roads, prevented any open view for any distance at all. In even the lightest pinewoods, the interlacing vines and creepers cut visibility to a matter of yards. Up to this stage, Grant had exercised the advantage of initiative to the fullest.

Yet, once across the river, he acted with none of the boldness that might be expected against an enemy he believed to be "really whipped." With no enemy in sight, he started his troops digging entrenchments to secure the roads which led from Hanovertown, while two of Sheridan's divisions worked out ahead four miles to learn what Lee was doing. With this cautious action, his advantage was lost.

6

On the 27th, General Lee, still too ill to ride his horse, rode in a carriage with the Second Corps for about fifteen miles due south on the Telegraph Road. Near the end of the day, Lee and the troops went into camp near Atlee, a station on the Virginia Central only nine miles from Richmond.

The General was so depressed by his physical disability in the approaching crisis over Richmond that he said, "I am not fit to command this army." Then, in camp, he learned that another general had been too ill to ride a horse. Corps commander Ewell had made the trip in an ambulance. That night, suffering acutely from diarrhea, Old Baldhead reported himself sick and said he had turned the corps temporarily over to Jubal Early.

Aside from his sadness at the collapse of Stonewall Jackson's formerly faithful lieutenant and the army's "character," Lee was doubtless relieved at having Early replace Ewell in command. For the General did not regard Jubal Early's command as "temporary." Two days later when Ewell, still feeble, reported that he would be ready to resume command in two more days, Lee ordered him to extend his sick leave. Two weeks later, Dick Ewell was permanently removed from command. To save his face and to salve his wife's outrage, Lee appointed him commander of the Richmond defenses. Black-bearded Robert Ransom, who could not get along with anybody, was shunted off once more, making a place for the broken lieutenant general.

In his new command, Ewell would have as a subordinate another lieutenant general, the Pemberton who surrendered Vicksburg. Since no army wanted this martinet friend of Davis, the old army Pennsylvanian showed a deeper and more selfless loyalty to his adopted land than did many a native-born. He served as a volunteer lieutenant colonel of a battalion of stationary artillery.

Though Dick Ewell did not know it on that Friday night at camp in the warm countryside near Atlee, he was then unceremoniously terminating his career with the Army of Northern Virginia. Having contributed as much as any except the very greatest to making that army what it was in its good days, one-legged Ewell was a victim of the necessity which pushed Confederate leaders beyond their capacities and demanded more than their weakened organisims could endure.

Lee had no time to think of the constant changes in his army — Longstreet, Stuart, and Ewell gone in less than three weeks — in concentrating, from his sick bed, on anticipating Grant. On the morning of May 28th, no definite information had been brought him as to the enemy's whereabouts. Though Lee consistently considered Grant's dependence on naval-supported river bases, as the armies approached Richmond he could not dismiss the possibility that Grant would cut loose and strike at the Virginia Central. After all, Grant's sick and wounded had been removed by the Federal supporting services, his sixty-five-mile wagon train freshly supplied, and the severance of Richmond from the Valley would be the most damaging blow Grant could deliver against both Richmond and Lee's army.

As Lee's army gathered at Atlee, during Saturday the 28th, he was slightly south of the Federal army, ten miles to the east at Hanovertown. As at the North Anna, he was ready to move either to his left, to protect the railroad, or to his right to intercept Grant. Sick as he was, Lee still planned to catch Grant in movement. On that morning, he wrote Davis, "I shall endeavor to engage him as soon as possible, and will be near enough Richmond for General Beauregard to unite with me if practical." Apparently trying to reach Beauregard, he added, "Should any field nearer to Richmond

be more convenient to him and he will designate it, I will endeavor
to deliver battle there."

Davis passed this letter on to Beauregard. However, Old Bory
knew, as Lee did not, that the commander in chief had no plans for
him personally beyond guarding Butler and using his force as a
feeder for Lee. He held out that he was almost *in extremis* himself,
and the President answered Lee on the 28th by saying, "It is doubtful whether he [Beauregard] could be better employed at this time"
— than watching Butler.

Accepting this setback in his losing maneuver with the commander in chief, Lee still had to find Grant. For this he possessed
one clue. His detachments of cavalry patrols had encountered no enemy movements from the Pamunkey River to the northwest of
Hanovertown, the area that would be traversed in a push to the
Virginia Central. At river crossings between Hanovertown and
Hanover Junction, Federal cavalry had demonstrated fiercely, but
this did not fool the Confederates. Sheridan was too eager to
"drive the rebels pell mell" wherever he found them. In fact, he was
beginning to complain that the Confederate detachments "would
not stand and fight" his divisions.

But at Hanovertown, when Sheridan brushed aside a small patrol
in crossing the Pamunkey on the 27th, he could not resist pushing
on until he found a larger Confederate unit who might fight. This
happened to be the luckless North Carolina brigade of the recently
killed James Gordon, and those troopers saw no point in offering
a determined resistance to a division. Sheridan reported that the
rebel cavalry was so demoralized that he would have captured the
whole brigade (of probably a thousand at the outside) if his own
troops had not been so "fatigued." This was on his third day back
with the army after rebuilding from his Richmond raid.

As with Sheridan's fighting at Todd's Tavern before the shift to
Spotsylvania, his action against Gordon's North Carolinians pointed
to the Hanovertown area. To make certain, there was nothing Lee
could do except demand a forced reconnaissance from his out-
manned troopers.

The cavalry was failing physically so fast, detachments were so
scattered and changes of units so constant, that the brigades had
almost ceased to operate within the structure of a corps. No one

knew the exact status from day to day. Lee would have done better to choose between Wade Hampton and Fitzhugh Lee as Stuart's successor. As he grew accustomed to doing everything himself, Lee postponed this decision in his deepening concern over the physical superiority of the enemy's cavalry. Yet in the necessity of anticipating Grant, he depended upon reconnaissance. On the morning of the 28th, for the first time General Lee personally organized a cavalry force for the purpose of fighting Sheridan in order to obtain definite information.

Fitz Lee with his two brigades would command one wing and Wade Hampton the other. During the North Anna operations, Hampton had worked chiefly with only Rosser's brigade. Pierce Young was still in Richmond, gathering up oddments around the capital, and organizing the dismounted troopers, veterans whose personally owned horses had broken down or been killed in action.

This loss through mounts was a not insignificant drain on the cavalry's manpower. Also, the small detachments which Lee sent on patrol, while useful, continued to lose men through the inability of their poor horses to run out of the enemy's reach. What Sheridan referred to as their "demoralization," which he attributed to their fear of him, was chiefly the troopers' uncertainty over the performance of their mounts.

On the 28th, however, as Young was off rebuilding, the first half of the new brigade designated for Hampton's division arrived on the field. The 4th South Carolina Regiment and one half of the 5th, these were the finely conditioned troops which Lee had finally snatched from their agreeable idleness in one of the President's dispersals. The whole brigade, armed with rifles, would be commanded by Calbraith Butler on his return. For the immediate emergency the inexperienced troopers would be commanded by their own inexperienced colonels under the eye of General Hampton. The battle-innocent South Carolinians numbered eleven hundred, which probably equaled the effectives present for duty in any cavalry brigade then with Lee.

While young Fitz Lee brought a trained skill to his native, childlike pleasure in combat, middle-aged Hampton was a fearless man who brought intelligence and native leadership to a very cold determination. The two of them made a good balance, and the combined force rode off with some of the spirit which characterized Stuart's troopers in the early days. One of the reasons for this younger spirit was the presence of the green South Carolinians. The jeers of the ragged veterans at the pretty home-guards stung the formerly protected princelings, and they were going to show the derisive Virginians that South Carolinians knew how to die.

Their destination was Haw's Shop, a large blacksmith shop which served as a point of designation for a key crossroads in Grant's operations. Three country roads from Hanovertown, four miles to the northeast, here entered into or crossed a relatively major east-west road which connected with main highways to Richmond. Gregg's division of Sheridan's corps covered this crossroads in the Haw's Shop area. Behind Gregg, between the crossroads and the river, the three infantry corps were beginning to stretch for miles.

The Hampton-Fitz Lee force followed this crossroads as it angled northeast. Then, little more than one mile west of Haw's Shop, the road ran straight east and west, parallel to the Pamunkey and crossing the front of the gathering Federal infantry near the river. As soon as Gregg sighted the approaching Confederates, he formed to charge, which had then become routine against Rebel cavalry.

To remove the uncertainty over their mounts' behavior and to nullify the superior fire power of the enemy's repeating carbines, Hampton and Lee dismounted their men on either side of the road at a clearing around Enon Church. In a country as flat as a billiard table, a lane crossed the road by the little white frame country church, and the Confederates found some fence rails with which they quickly built a light line. When Gregg's men charged, Sheridan had no complaint about the enemy refusing "to stand up and fight."

The Federal division fell back in the first meeting of Sheridan's cavalry with even numbers, and Sheridan referred to it in his official report as "an unequal contest." As the day wore on and Gregg's division could not budge the three and a half slim brigades, Sheridan claimed that the enemy "appeared to be the rebel corps," plus the South Carolinians who were "reported to be 4000" of "mounted infantry." At least one general — A. A. Humphreys, Meade's chief of staff — publicly raised his eyebrows at this magnification of the obstacles Sheridan had to overcome on his glory road.

Finally, Sheridan brought over Torbert's division to help, and sent Custer's brigade in on a dismounted charge with a general attack. By then, after five hours, the superior fire power of the repeating carbines had taken too heavy a toll, and the Confederate troopers fell back from the fence rails to their horses. The only boast Sheridan could make about the green South Carolinians was that they left their dead at the works. There was no pursuit.

On the ride back to Lee's headquarters, there were no more jeers in the cavalry. South Carolinian Hampton had a new brigade of overnight veterans. They had a lot to learn about handling themselves in action, but they needed no lessons in courage. And the whole brigade, of two thousand when completely assembled, could have been with the cavalry since the opening skirmish.

When Hampton and Lee reported, they brought back what they were sent to get. They carried with them Federal infantry prisoners from the V and VI Corps. Lee knew where Grant was.

7

Before the information reached Lee, he had grown so ill that, for the first time during the war, he was forced to accept a room in a private house. From there General Lee had ordered a disposition of his troops to intercept either a swing west to the Virginia Central or a drive to Richmond from a river crossing.

The advanced Second Corps, commanded by tough-bitten Jubal Early, moved eastward to another of the crossroads, this one named for the Pole Green Presbyterian Church, the nearest public building. From here, Haw's Shop was about three air miles to the northeast, though the ground miles belonged in another calculation altogether. Between Early and Grant's advanced troops lay a swampy area formed by the marshy-banked fingers of Totopotomoi Creek. With no cavalry in force after the concentration against Sheridan, Lee depended on his Second Corps veterans to use the Totopotomoi as a barrier behind which their skirmish lines could reconnoiter in the primal method of contact.

Still not expecting Grant to make the obvious move of pushing straight ahead, Lee retained Hill's rear-guard corps within five miles of the railroad and the Telegraph Road. Between the Second and Third Corps and back from them, to be able to shift to immediate support of either, Lee placed Anderson's First Corps. By then, Longstreet's old corps was completed for the first time since before Gettysburg by the return of Pickett's division.

Newly reassembled, this once-crack unit was something of an unknown quantity. Only Montgomery Corse, whose brigade had been withheld from the Gettysburg campaign, was a holdover from the pre-Gettysburg days. Eppa Hunton, a forty-year-old lawyer, with a fine reputation as colonel in Garnett's brigade, had been promoted and succeeded to command after Garnett was killed at Gettysburg. Colonel William R. Terry, a former colonel in Kemper's brigade, had commanded since Kemper's wound at Gettysburg and, with the certainty that Kemper would not regain fitness for the field, Terry was soon to be promoted to brigadier. He also was an able man.

Armistead's old brigade was temporarily without a commander. Originally, Brigadier General Seth Barton had seemed a fine replacement. A West Pointer from Virginia, he had served in the West and, taken prisoner in the fall of Vicksburg, had come East after his exchange. During the winter, Barton had fallen afoul of Pickett who, though hot-tempered, was not a trouble-maker; then, in the fighting against Butler, Barton had clashed with his temporary commander, Robert Ransom. While inquiries were in progress, a colonel commanded, and Barton was never to come back.

Though three of the four brigades were led by proven men, the number of conscripts, along with the months when the units were separated and not under the command of their regular major general, had prevented the rebuilding of division morale to anything like its pre-Gettysburg peak. Early in the afternoon of the 28th, before marching out, Pickett sent an urgent message to corps chief of staff Sorrel: "The men are calling loudly for bread. . . . We must get something or the division will be worse than useless."

This was a strong admission for a major general whose troops had missed all the fighting, digging and marching from the Wilderness to the North Anna. It was made at a time when the troops who had endured the unending struggle, *as part of the army*, were as close to starvation as Lee's soldiers had ever been. Lee's men had never actively campaigned before when their sub-subsistence diet fell away to nothing. On reaching the area of the Totopotomoi, some units went for two days without receiving a single ration of food of any kind. After being issued three hard biscuits and a slice of fat pork (the "sidemeat" which at home they used for cooking greens), they went two more days. Then they received a single cracker.

One artillerist decided to hoard his cracker until night, when he could savor it quietly in camp. He was holding it in his hand when the bullet of a distant sharpshooter crushed the cracker to nothing in its course to the soldier's skull. The bullet ranged under his hatband to cut a swath as from a razor along the side of his head. The passing blow caused an intense headache but the gunner gave never a thought to his close call. Instead he philosophized. "If I had eaten that cracker half an hour ago, it would have been safe. I should have had none left for the next time, but I have none left as it is. That shows how foolish it is to save anything."

Another cannoneer, George Cary Eggleston, recorded that the word "hunger" was meaningless to persons who have never known starvation:

Hunger to starving men is wholly unrelated to the desire for food as that is commonly understood and felt. It is a great agony of the whole body and of the soul as well. It is unimaginable, all-pervading pain inflicted when the strength to endure pain is utterly gone. It is a great despairing cry of a wasting body — a cry of flesh and blood, marrow, nerves, bones, and faculties for strength with which to exist and to endure existence.

Yet the starving men in the Richmond Howitzers were capable of making a joke when they unlimbered their guns in camp. It was a running joke from the first gallant days of the war, when the private soldiers in the gun batteries had brought along their own trunks, some containing as many as a dozen face towels. When the batteries were mustered into the regular forces, an order went through eliminating trunks, and one of the privates immediately wrote a letter "resigning" his position in the Howitzers. His battery mates never forgot it. As the cannoneers took a look at one another in their rationless camp, as dirty and as emaciated soldiers as ever bore arms, one of the Howitzers yelled to the former dude, "Hey, Jim, don't you think it's about time for you to resign again?" And the once elegant urbanite, only a few miles from his threatened home city, could laugh with his fellows.

This basic morale remained uniform in the troops who had been sustained by the familiar group spirit. What Grant, some of his subordinates and private soldiers attributed to the "demoralization" of Lee's men was in large part physical weakness. Morale does not exist as an abstraction, and many elements contributed to their declining effectiveness under prolonged demands. But a failing of the spirit in the veterans was not among them. The men showed this in the heavy skirmishing against Grant's probing movements which began on May 29th.

8

The broad-fronted skirmishing along the Totopotomoi on May 29th was most succinctly described by General Humphreys, Meade's chief of staff. "While we were securing the roads from the Pamunkey to Richmond, upon which to advance against Lee, Lee was endeavoring to cover those roads." This Lee did. Burnside's rear-guard corps was across the river and deployed on the morning of the 29th, and the wagon train began its daylong crossing, but by then Grant's caution had lost him most of the advantage of the initiative. In an area where no battle was fought, the Federal fieldworks were as extensive as any thrown up anywhere in an equivalent period of time.

However, Lee was not yet convinced that Grant would not swing back to the northwest and the railroad, as most of the Federal weight seemed concentrated to the Confederate left. On the night of the 29th, while Lee puzzled over reports, he did finally learn there would be no combination with Beauregard. He learned this personally from Old Bory himself. The simulacrum of a French marshal came to Lee's headquarters in response to Lee's May 28th telegram, which Davis had relayed to him.

Neither general nor their staffs dwelt on what must have been a brief, formal and inconclusive interview in Lee's sickroom. Lee's

full record of the meeting is contained in an icy two-line telegram
he sent the commander in chief that night at nine o'clock.

"In conference with General Beauregard he states that he has only
twelve thousand infantry and can spare none. If General Grant advances tomorrow I will engage him with my present force."

On the next morning, after recovering from the sharpness of his
disappointment, Lee wrote more fully to Davis on his need of more
troops even for engaging Grant. All the Federal reinforcements had
then come into line, and the front was growing dangerously wide
for Lee to cover. He pointed out to the President that with one army
north and another army south of the James River, certainly troops
in the Richmond defenses could be spared. This appeal was not
acknowledged.

During that day of the 30th, with Lee unable to shake free of his
illness, Grant's heavy probings began to assume some form to Lee.
Having found all direct roads to Richmond blocked, Grant was not
going to move by his right toward the Virginia Central. His shift
instead to the Confederate right was indicated by Warren's crossing
of the Totopotomoi to the east, where the V Corps was stretched
as far as the Old Church Road. This main highway to Richmond
passed through the little town of Mechanicsville, where Lee opened
his first engagement just two years before, as commander of the
forces he welded into the Army of Northern Virginia.

Lee's first act as field general had been to open an offensive. With
his back being pressed toward the works of the citadel, the aging
General decided to attack again.

The suggestion really came from Jubal Early, and General Lee
endorsed it. From the lines his men dug south of the Totopotomoi,
tactically sound Early had cut cross-country traces to the Old
Church Road, which passed beyond his right flank. Originally
Early had cut the passageways against the event of having to move
to his right in a hurry. When cavalry pickets reported that Warren's
lines were extended to the Old Church Road, Early saw an opportunity to turn the V Corps flank. By using his cross-country passageways he could reach the Old Church Road behind the cavalry skirmishers and come up on Warren's left. He sent off a courier to Lee
with the proposal.

By then General Lee was convinced that Grant was, after all, shifting to the southeast, to the direction of communication with a naval supply base. The newest base was the White House landing on the Pamunkey. The White House property belonged to Lee's son, Rooney, coming to him through his ancestress, Martha Washington. When McClellan used the landing as his base in 1862, he issued orders for the protection of the house because of its associations with George Washington, but it was burned anyway.

Though Lee had grown certain that Grant retained a line of communications with the White House base, the steady Federal pushes across the Totopotomoi covered an expanding front which, if continued, would inevitably spread Lee's lines too thin. An assault on Grant's left flank would remove from him the unlimited local initiative and at least force some contraction of his own lines. Then, the possibility of inflicting serious damage was always inherent in any surprise attack on the end of a line.

Jubal Early, supported by distant Lee, took command of his first field as a lieutenant general. Like Anderson at Spotsylvania, Old Jube was full of fire in his new assignment. Up to a point, everything worked according to a well-conceived plan. In compliance with Early's request, Lee had ordered Anderson to shift troops over to Early's strong works and be ready to move up in support in the event the attack succeeded. With his lines secured, Early moved by his traces to the Old Church Road in the area of the Bethesda Church. There, behind the screen of a cavalry skirmish line, he deployed parallel to the road in position to roll up Warren's flank, which extended along a country crossroads and rested on the Old Church Road.

As with A. P. Hill at Jericho Mills, there is no precise information on what units Old Jube used or the manner of their deployment. Apparently Rodes's division bore the brunt of the assault, with at least parts of Early's own division in close reserve. Early's division was then commanded by young Dodson Ramseur, transferred on May 27th out of Rodes's division and soon to be promoted to major general. In the Bethesda Church action, it would appear that Early handled the troops himself almost as one command.

At the opening of the assault, the Second Corps regiments rushed forward in something like an old-fashioned charge of Lee's troops.

Brushing aside the enemy's skirmishers, they drove the blue soldiers at the end of Warren's line and began the movement of rolling up the flank.

Other Federal brigades were rushed quickly to the danger point, formed lines and got guns in position. Against their front Rodes's division ground to a halt. Early then brought up his own old brigade, whose commander, John Pegram, had been wounded out at the Wilderness. Its temporary commander, Colonel Edward Willis, was himself overdue for promotion to brigade command and widely esteemed in the army. A fair-haired young Georgian, just out of West Point at the outbreak of war, he was the only field officer mentioned for special praise by Stonewall Jackson during his fatal illness. The Federals had thrown up works by the time Colonel Willis led the brigade in a desperate charge, and in front of the works the young Georgian fell with a mortal wound.

Though Early's losses were comparatively light in this definite repulse, and the attack had its effect at least of contracting Grant's line, the death of Edward Willis in a futile attack gave a depressing note to another offensive which failed. Lee gave Early no rebuke for not being a second Jackson and throwing in his whole corps, and Early tried to shift the blame on Anderson. Dick Anderson, after his great hour at Spotsylvania, did seem to return to an uninspired competence and had not been at all cooperative with Early. But essentially the failure was merely another melancholy illustration of the army's inability to mount an offensive. No individual could be blamed.

With the physical weakness of the veterans, there were simply too many new men at regiment, brigade and division command. Most of the officers were at least adequate, and newly promoted Ramseur and Gordon held great promise, but they all lacked familiarity in working together as unit leaders. Early's old division, under Ramseur, was a sample.

R. D. Johnston's North Carolina brigade, which had not rejoined the army until the Wilderness campaign had opened, disliked being transferred out of Rodes's division to balance Early's division while Hoke's old brigade was held in North Carolina. Then the men, losing their brigadier, Johnston, at Spotsylvania, went temporarily under Gordon as division commander, then back to Early, whom they disliked, and finally to Ramseur — welcomed enough as a fellow North Carolinian but a total stranger. Hoke's old brigade, held away from the army, rejoined at Hanover Junction under a colonel. Not only was division *esprit* hurt by accommodating Davis's troop dispositions, but the units were not accustomed to operating together.

Finally, all the shifts made it impossible, as Ramseur pointed out, for general officers to retain sufficiently intimate knowledge of their regiments. In Early's old division, at Bethesda Church the 58th Virginia Regiment fought with sixty-eight men under a captain — and he was worried about his wife at home in the land crossed by Grant's army. Under these conditions, the determination of the ill commanding general to get off the defensive was remote from the potential of the army with him.

At the end of the day, information reached Lee which momentarily drove all thoughts of offensive from his mind. He learned that Smith's XVIII Corps, from Butler's army, was arriving at the White House landing. Baldy Smith, whose line of march would bring his sixteen thousand fresh troops up on the left of Grant's wide front, simply concentrated more strength than Lee could contain. The question became suddenly reduced to the defense of Richmond.

9

Before dark of May 30th, a grim commanding general defied the protocol of Davis's system. Ignoring the regular channels of the war office, he wired Beauregard directly for reinforcements. Since Lee exercised no authority in Beauregard's department, ten miles south of him, the message was a request, though a most urgent one. This was nothing about a combination of forces, or the assistance of General Beauregard: he simply asked for the newly formed division of Robert Hoke to be hurried across the river to meet the emergency presented by the addition of another corps to Grant's army.

Punctiliously Beauregard wired back: "War department must determine when and what troops to order from here."

General Lee did not ponder over this for a moment. His next

wire, sent at seven-thirty, went directly to His Excellency the President. "General Beauregard says the Department must determine what troops to send for him. He gives it all necessary information. The result of this delay will be disaster. Butler's troops [Smith's corps] will be with Grant tomorrow. Hoke's division, at least, should be with me by light tomorrow."

Lee had never before used such a word as "disaster." When the commander in chief read that, he was immediately on firm ground. There were no more alternatives. When the enemy was at the door, Davis always acted.

A messenger was sent to Braxton Bragg, presumably then at home, for the Military Adviser did not send a wire to Beauregard from the War Department until ten-thirty that night. Fifteen minutes before Bragg put his order for Hoke's division on the wires, Beauregard sent Bragg a telegram advising him that he felt "authorized by the President's letter of the 28th" to send Lee reinforcements.

By ten-fifteen, when Beauregard decided to send Hoke to Lee, he knew with relative certainty that Smith's corps had gone from his front. Smith had embarked the night of the 28th and the morning of the 29th, and by the 30th it seemed that everybody except Beauregard and Davis knew the Federal corps was headed for the White House. Recognizing that the game was up for him, Old Bory, some four hours after Lee's request, decided to do on his own what the War Department would eventually order him to do. This would appear better on his record. Also, he might have been partly motivated by the desperate need for defending Richmond, even if he would share no part in it.

With the long delay in his acting, there was no possibility of Hoke's division arriving at daylight, though with Braxton Bragg on the job the troops would be moved with dispatch. Such things he did well. However, with all of Bragg's administrative efficiency, the four brigades of Hoke's division reached Lee's army on the night of the 31st, instead of in the morning. This time difference was of considerable consequence.

As when the regiments were rushed up from the Carolinas, they arrived too late to be part of any plan; more critically in this case, the brigades were depended upon for cooperation with an army they had never seen — and they were not fighting Butler.

Lee's dependence on immediate cooperation from General Hoke could have been partly inspired by emergency thinking and partly by the gaudiness of Hoke's reputation. Lee's personal knowledge of the twenty-seven-year-old North Carolinian was as an able, promising brigadier in Jackson's old corps, who had been wounded out in the Chancellorsville campaign. After recovering from his wound, he was given the assignment of the surprise attack that worked so well on Plymouth during the late winter. Robert Hoke had nothing to do with planning this assault, nor with the cooperation of the ram which contributed greatly to its success, but the glory went to him. As the recapture of Plymouth was a bright turn in the dreary minor disasters which had characterized Carolina's coastal operations, his home state made a hero of him, and the good brigadier became reputation-conscious.

In his new glory, personally promoted by President Davis, Major General Hoke first commanded a division in the field in cooperation with other troops in Beauregard's mangled offensive against Butler. There, with Whiting's glaring failure and Beauregard turning against friendless Ransom, it went unnoticed that Hoke did not cooperate at all. On the contrary, the seven-thousand-man division became such a bone of contention that "Hoke" began to loom as a synonym for salvation.

Of his brigade, Hagood's South Carolinians had demonstrated their stoutness in the first desperate days below Drewry's Bluff. Less was known of Clingman's and Martin's North Carolinians, though James Martin personally was highly respected by Lee from his earlier service in Virginia, Martin was something of a character with his ruffled dignity at being called "One Wing," a result of an arm lost with the regular army in the Mexican War. Colquitt, though known not to be a strong brigadier, at least was experienced and devoted.

It is doubtful if Hoke or any of the men recognized the prominence of the role assigned them by Lee. Certainly Hoke acted more as if he wanted to preserve his Plymouth reputation rather than to enlarge it. It must be said that their opportunity was offered them before the officers or men hardly knew where they were. Again the unnecessary element of unfamiliarity became a factor.

10

During the 31st, while Hoke's regiments were being put on a succession of trains to Richmond, Grant more definitely shifted to Lee's right. Entrenchments were built across the Old Church Road near Bethesda Church (not the Old Church of the road's name), and a division of Sheridan's cavalry moved farther southeast to yet another of the crossroads at Old Cold Harbor.

Cold Harbor was a white-framed tavern in a triangular grove, and the name, deriving from the British usage, originally meant shelter without food. The east-west crossroad from Old Church Road to Cold Harbor connected at the tavern triangle with the road Smith's corps would use moving south from the White House. From the tavern on, no direct road led to Richmond. A circuitous road eastward entered the Old Church Road near Mechanicsville. From the Old Church Road eastward, the Chickahominy River, a series of swampy streams covering about half a mile, presented a formidable military barrier in front of Richmond.

It can only be presumed that Grant's purpose, in shifting to this unpromising eastward approach, was either to outstretch Lee's thin lines and expose a weak spot or, by restraining the eastward movement of Lee's troops, to concentrate an overwhelming number on his flank in the Cold Harbor area. This would have been an effective maneuver if begun purposefully by Grant immediately after he crossed the Pamunkey River on the 28th. As Grant more or less worked into the movement through the constant probing skirmishing of the 29th, 30th, and 31st, Lee anticipated it and planned to take advantage of his anticipation.

Physically he was improving by then. On the 31st, the General felt able to leave the private home and move by carriage to field headquarters at Shady Grove Church, nearer the shift of the armies. It was amazing how his aggressiveness rose with the least reinforcements. Having called on Hoke's division as a final emergency to support his right, since Hoke reached the Cold Harbor area before the enemy, Lee immediately devised a counterattack around the fresh unit.

On the night of the 31st, the General learned from Fitz Lee that his nephew's division had been forced away from the Cold Harbor crossroads by a division of Federal cavalry. In the fighting that went on into the dusk, the troopers had tried to fall back on Clingman's brigade, the first of Hoke's units to reach the field. These troops commanded by the fifty-two-year-old politician were not accustomed to forced marching, and the ten hurried miles from the train through the dusty heat brought them to the shadowy field in loose order. When Fitz Lee's two brigades tried to fall back on Clingman, the infantrymen were inclined to continue the backward movement. Fifty or so of them got lost in the confused movement along a belt of dark woods, and were gobbled up by the enemy.

Losing the crossroads to cavalry did not disturb Lee. Again using Sheridan's point of hardest fighting as the compass to Grant's line of direction, he was confirmed in his selection of the Cold Harbor Tavern as the area for a flank attack.

During the afternoon of the 31st, Lee had planned a larger version of Early's roll-up attempt. With all else in Early's failure, the assault lacked weight. Hours before Fitz Lee's fight, the General had sent orders to concentrate more than a corps on a line parallel to the road the Federal army was following toward the tavern. His purpose was to hit the head of the Federal advance in the vicinity of the crossroads and roll it back on the columns strung out in march. Though this move was not of the scale of the counteroffensive he felt goaded to deliver, it represented his first planned counteroffensive since the armies left the Wilderness.

His spirits rising with some returning energy and the prospect of striking a blow, Lee moved with a boldness characteristic of earlier campaigns. At three in the afternoon of the 31st, he pulled Anderson's corps out of its supporting connective line with Early and Hill, and ordered the three divisions to march eastward. Kershaw's leading division would turn northward to get into position for a daylight attack at the Federal army's crossroad to the left of the tavern intersection. The following divisions would come up on Kershaw's left, where they would connect with Early's right and form in position to support the attack. Already on the field, Hoke would form on Kershaw's right, aim directly at the tavern intersection, and move out with Kershaw at daylight.

Lee risked the pulling out of Anderson on the unlikelihood of heavy thrusts across the shifting front while Grant's army was in motion, and on the works his own men dug as they moved to their right. In turn, in the race for the crossroads, the Federal march toward Cold Harbor would be slowed by the constant digging of the Federal troops in Grant's sidling movement. From the crossing at the Pamunkey to Cold Harbor Tavern, the passage of the two armies could be traced by continuing earth mounds like a design of gigantic molehills.

The skirmishing continued heavily until darkness of the 31st, but Lee's calculations proved right. His men won the race to the point of the flank attack. When Hoke and Kershaw formed in position at daylight of a warm June 1st, the nearest Federal infantry was four hours away.

The road leading to the tavern and the intersection was held by two divisions of Sheridan's cavalry, dismounted behind light works, and supported by gun batteries. With every fourth man out of line with the horses, Sheridan fielded probably little more than sixty-five hundred men on the firing line. On the field, Kershaw and Hoke would have nearly twice that number, with almost ten thousand more coming up in Pickett's and Field's divisions.

Hoke's division was deployed across the road that led from the tavern circuitously southwest to Richmond. His front was generally flat land, either under cultivation or lightly wooded, with open ground around the big Garthright house on his right. On his left, a wide ravine sliced past his flank. On the other side of the ravine, Kershaw's brigades faced a vine-shrouded stand of woods between them and the crossroads.

Dick Anderson was in command of his first field since he shared the Sunday morning's fight at Spotsylvania with Jeb Stuart. In view of the lack of control Anderson exercised on the morning of June 1st, perspective suggests that the great cavalryman may have contributed more to the cooperation at Spotsylvania than did the new corps commander.

At Spotsylvania, Anderson had commanded a clearly defined,

limited action, however large the consequences, and in the emergency he reacted with cool decisiveness. Yet with the stimulating presence of Jeb Stuart, with whom he shared the emergency, no more than reaction was demanded of Anderson. In the following actions, under the tight control held by Lee from Spotsylvania to the North Anna, little more was demanded than the administration of two veteran divisions, both well led. Then on the 30th, under the generalized order for cooperating with Early, Anderson showed the same lack of initiative which characterized his behavior at Gettysburg under similar conditions. Judging off his resolute soundness as a division commander when strongly directed, Anderson's qualities were best revealed in reaction to a developed situation; in an undeveloped situation, he lacked the assertiveness to assume control and direct it.

In his modest character, Anderson had never sought advancement, never belonged to an army coterie, and never made excuses. By nature and habit, the major general in temporary command of Longstreet's corps was the last man to impose authority on glamorized Hoke, whose detached division was placed under his command for the assault. For his part, Robert Hoke was too mindful of those Plymouth laurels to risk an assault against an unknown force on his own and did nothing to establish cooperation with Anderson. Before the attack opened, the potential assault force was reduced from twelve thousand to five thousand.

Then, not knowing he was opposed only by cavalry, whose regular U. S. Army batteries fired like infantry guns, Anderson opened his action by a reconnaissance in force on the heavily vined woods in his front. In this movement, Anderson evidently gave Joe Kershaw the responsibility, and Kershaw made his contribution to the chain of command lapses.

Ever since Kershaw held division command, he showed a preference for using his old brigade as a spearhead, and at Cold Harbor his South Carolinians were strengthened by the largest regiment in the army. The recently arrived 20th South Carolina was so large in comparison with the veteran units that Kershaw's old-timers called it the "20th Army Corps." But the 20th Army Corps contained the seeds of disaster for the brigade movement.

These fine-looking young South Carolinians offered a tragic illustration of the effects of Davis's continued dispersal of troops to fit an 1861 chart of defense and the considerations of state-minded politicians. Well clothed, well shod and well fed, healthy from a regimented life in barracks or stout tents in outdoor garrison duty, the men were totally unsuited to and unprepared for war at this stage. Through no fault of their own they were parade-ground soldiers, thoroughly drilled by company but wholly unfamiliar with maneuver by brigade. One of their fellow South Carolinians, in a hardened field regiment, regarding the clear-eyed young men with pity, said, "If only they had come out two months earlier . . ."

The crux of the tragedy lay in the ill chance by which dates of rank made their commanding officer senior colonel in the brigade. Since Anderson had procrastinated in recommending a colonel for brigadier — sheriff Henagan, the temporary leader, was the men's and the obvious choice — the colonel of the sheltered 20th Regiment, by the laws of seniority, led the veteran brigade in the move out against the woods.

Lawrence Massillon Keitt, just shy of forty, a well-educated lawyer who had served in the U. S. Congress from the age of twenty-nine until secession, was esteemed in his region for his superior qualities. As the brigade chronicler wrote, when the line moved forward, every man "knew he was being led by one of the most gifted and gallant men in the South, but every old soldier . . . saw at a glance his inexperience and want of self control." Crossing an old field toward the heavy timber of oak and thick underbrush, "Keitt led his men like a knight of old . . . mounted upon his superb gray charger . . . preparing to cut his way through like a storm center." Here in the chivalric mood of 1861, this "martyr to the inexorable laws of army rank" rode ahead of his brigade, flashing his sword in the early morning light, a target for thousands of repeating carbines firing from behind works.

The doomed man fell before his tight-faced garrison troops reached the woods. As their leader toppled out of the saddle and the gale of 1864 fire power swept across their handsomely ordered ranks, the uniformed civilians broke. A gunner in a supporting battery described their flight as the "most abject rout ever committed by men in Confederate uniform. Some were so scared they could not run, but groveled on the ground, trying to burrow into the earth." It could have been here that the story was told about one green soldier trying to burrow under another, when the rigid one said to the burrower, "Man, don't get under me. I'm too high now."

Their break carried the veteran regiments helplessly along in the tide. The second brigade, its flank exposed and its line unanchored, could only retire out of range of the concentrated fire power of the carbines in the woods. This reconnaissance, which discovered nothing, comprised the daylight attack Lee designed as a flanking movement for two divisions.

Though Kershaw tried to mount another attack later in the morning, the day had been decided by the succession of details which placed Laurence M. Keitt in command of a reconnaissance in force. By the time Pickett was formed on Kershaw's left, with Field coming into line on his left, Wright's corps came panting to the tavern crossroads and the vast relief of Sheridan. This rebel-chaser made a big thing of holding on behind his "little works," as he called them, until the VI Corps arrived, but the danger existed only in his own mind.

Within nine days, the third of the corps commanders had failed in an offensive, reserved Anderson the most dismally of all. In a general deterioration in command, Anderson went unreproached. For those things he did well, and because of the men's respect for him, the South Carolinian was promoted permanently to lieutenant general. He was even less qualified for corps command than flighty Hill and no more than eccentric Ewell, whom necessity had advanced the year before. Dick Anderson was one of those middle-forties professionals of both armies (or any army) who performed at the top of a sizable potential only under supervision. As Ewell had been with Jackson, and Anderson himself with Longstreet, such men were designed to be superb lieutenants. The qualities they displayed in their proper employment gave an illusory promise for higher command; in the higher command, instead, their best qualities became dissipated.

For Anderson's puny attack was not the worst. During the probes and counterprobes of the day, while he turned his corps to throwing up powerful works against the enemy, Anderson established a weak liaison at the gap of the ravine between Kershaw's right and Hoke's left. This was exploited late in the day after the long-awaited arrival of Smith's XVIII Corps.

The Army of Northern Virginia had been offered some luck as a counterbalance for Lee's trouble in getting reinforcements from Beauregard. Butler had not been eager to let go of the three divisions Baldy Smith took with him, and perhaps counted on his political connections in procrastinating with Grant. When Smith was finally pried loose, two days before Hoke, the XVIII Corps fell afoul of an organizational breakdown at Grant's headquarters in moving from White House landing to Cold Harbor. The troops wasted time and sweat in a march in the wrong direction and, like Hoke's, accustomed to garrison duty, the troops tired in the hot march.

When the Confederates did nothing with their good fortune, General Meade, in field command in the Cold Harbor area, decided to use Smith in a counterassault on Lee's flank.

Smith and Wright's VI Corps attacked at half-past four on a front which extended from across the road from Cold Harbor westward toward the Old Church Road. The hard thrust was mostly contained, with moderately heavy losses in the attacking troops, but the weak link in the ravine parted like paper. In the marshy ground there, below a peach orchard, Clingman's brigade, without the excuse of unfamiliarity this day, broke on contact. Clingman gave up a load of prisoners and exposed Kershaw's flank brigade, Wofford's, across the ravine. Kershaw and Anderson hurried troops into the gap, built a new line, and dusk prevented the Federals from taking advantage of the breach.

When night fell on the shaken defensive line, at what in the morning had been the launching area of Lee's hoped-for counteroffensive, Anderson showed little command of the situation. Always punctilious in reporting, he sent Lee a message at ten o'clock, in which he explained the delay of his report on the grounds of trying to discover the condition of Hoke's lines. In this he admitted failure and stated, "Re-enforcements are necessary to enable us to hold this position."

By then General Lee, knowing the worst, had forced himself to ride to the Cold Harbor area to establish field headquarters. With the crisis approaching, well or not, he must assume personal command.

II

R. E. Lee gave little indication of a bent toward reflecting upon changes of fortune. Yet, on the sultry Wednesday morning of June 2nd, the least subjective of men must have been aware of the differences suggested by his new field headquarters at Gaines' Mill.

The road from Old Cold Harbor ran straight for only a mile. At a site called (for no known reason) New Cold Harbor, it turned at a right angle on a cross-country course which, after many circuitous windings, intersected the Old Church Road near Mechanicsville. On this cross-country road the General had led the army in his first command to New Cold Harbor (called the Battle of Gaines's Mill) in the second of the Seven Days Battle around Richmond, and there won his first victory.

Two years before, in approaching McClellan, the army Lee commanded attacked across the road from Old Cold Harbor to New Cold Harbor to drive the enemy eastward and break his hold on Richmond. From that successful counteroffensive, Lee had maneuvered the enemy north of the Rappahannock, caused the Federals twice to vacate Virginia in following him north, and prevented them seriously threatening Richmond again. Now, an army he commanded was formed on defense astride the Cold Harbor Road, awaiting the enemy's attack with their backs to the city.

Where the road from Mechanicsville entered Venable Street in Richmond was barely nine miles from Lee's lines, and no more than a mile from Venable Street the semi-invalided Mrs. Lee waited in a red-brick house near Capitol Square. In front of her house collapsing wagons creaked by at all hours bringing in the wounded and hurrying out supplies.

General Lee's field headquarters were established one and one-half miles from the tavern, on the crossroad leading from New Cold Harbor. His crossroad paralleled the road held by the Federals from Bethesda Church to the Cold Harbor Tavern, and across country would have been little more than one mile from their lines, within range of their heavier guns. Gaines's Mill — confusingly *not* the site of the battle of that name — was the site of a house and mill belonging to Dr. Gaines.

Having survived the period of McClellan's occupation of the area and of the Seven Days, the mill had been burnt by Sheridan a few weeks before when his cavalry was riding away from Richmond. The charred remains of the mill were on the narrow floor of a sharply hilled valley, where Powhite Creek spread into two mill-ponds. On the north side of the road, nearest the battle, where the least precipitous hill was open in its rises above the mill, half a dozen weather-beaten tents formed in a cluster. Nearby were parked a few army wagons, bearing a faded "U S" on the canvas, and picketed horses foraged for grass. Staff officers came and went to the tent over which an army headquarters flag drooped in the cloudy heat. Couriers lounged on the hillside indifferent to the intermittent crackle of rifles behind and the boom of cannon, sounding very close.

General Lee could not long remain in the headquarters tent. On the day before he had sent his, by then, routine appeals to Beauregard and Davis for reinforcements. With Smith's corps, Grant's total reinforcements approached forty-five thousand. With Hoke's division, Lee's reinforcements (including the return of his own units) went something over sixteen thousand infantry. In this total were the 20th South Carolina Regiment and two newly arrived Florida battalions, who had been briefly grabbed up by Beauregard as they passed through his department. A Georgia artillery battalion also got across the James to Lee, while various units were held by Old Bory. (It was difficult to get accurate estimates of the troops with Beauregard, as he gave different numbers according to the point he wanted to make. He certainly had more than the twelve thousand infantry he admitted to before relinquishing Hoke, and even had he tried Beauregard could not have kept count of all the detachments of artillery and cavalry which showed up.)

By the morning of the 2nd, Lee knew he must contain Grant with what he had. Grant's army then extended over a front of six miles, wide for a Civil War field, and as wide as Grant could extend his five corps and still bring a heavy concentration on Lee's flank. Lee's first order of the day was to suggest to Jubal Early that he look for an opportunity to get in a swipe at the columns shifting across his front toward the right of the Confederate line. Aggressive Old Jube could at least act on the discretionary orders which had paralyzed poor Dick Ewell. If nothing else, a local assault would tend to slow the heavy concentration building against the shaken right, where Anderson joined Hoke near the Cold Harbor Road.

Before Anderson had sent his ten o'clock appeal for help the night of June 1st, Lee had ordered a shuffling of the troops at hand to support the right. Early in the morning of the 2nd, Lee discovered that the new troops had not reached the position assigned them.

This was a return to the unsettled command conditions of two years before, when the loosely organized units inherited by Lee operated in unfamiliar combinations. In that other time, with Lee holding the initiative, mistakes could be made and men could be lost without checking the impetus of healthy troops commanded by officers trying to outdo one another in gallantry. Out of that hodgepodge, after judging the leaders on their performance, Lee constructed an organization, the Army of Northern Virginia, to fit his material. Now, that once undefeatable army was little more than a skeleton structure, its organization largely administrative. Odd units, such as Hoke and Breckinridge, were unconnected even with the army's administration, and must be handled personally by the commanding general.

After arriving in the Richmond area on May 27th, General Lee had remained the next four days quietly in his room, dispatching orders through his staff like the executive of a great military system. This worked well enough during Grant's indecisive probings. On the morning of June 2nd, with Lee expecting the climactic attack hourly, the enfeebled General was forced to leave his new headquarters in the hillside above the ruined mill. He made a most unmilitary appearance, wearing a sack linen coat in the breathless, humid heat that wore at men's nerves and intensified the strain of every effort. On well-rested Traveler, the Old Man of the army set out on an odd chore. He needed to find Breckinridge and his two-brigade unit.

Breckinridge's scratch force, with its own batteries, had not appeared at its designated slot beyond Hoke. Half-listening for the guns to announce the enemy's assault, the commanding general found the missing unit in Mechanicsville. There, with perfectly legitimate excuses, the former Vice-President and his troops were partaking of a leisurely breakfast. The General set the men on the proper course.

At the lines where Breckinridge was headed, Hoke had not shifted to his right as Lee had ordered Anderson to direct him. This was done. By the delay, the high ground needed by Lee was held by the enemy. Some men had to be sacrificed to drive off the Federals to get room for gun emplacements.

At three o'clock in the afternoon, Grant had not yet assaulted, and two of A. P. Hill's veteran divisions had completed the hot dusty march from the left of the line to the right. Grant had thrown local attacks at the far left, which Lee accepted as feints and was not diverted. In order to support his right, he left only Heth's division on the extreme left, its line of heavy works projecting forward at an angle and its flank covered by reconnoitering cavalry.

Beyond the troopers, a Federal cavalry division diverted itself by tearing up railroad tracks. They grew so careless that a detached brigade was caught by Tom Rosser who, with some help from Rooney Lee, enjoyed the momentary reversal of chasing Yankees. Sheridan had taken the two divisions who fought at the tavern to the Chickahominy to guard against strikes from that direction. Fitz Lee took his two brigades on the same briefly restful assignment. As the Federal infantry massed on Lee's right, and Lee moved over Hill's two divisions to meet the shift, cavalry ceased to play any active part in the approaching clash.

From left to right, from Heth's flank position came the three of Early's slim divisions, the right one, Ramseur's, astride the Old Church Road facing the Federal works at Bethesda Church. Across what would be the center was Anderson's corps, Field, Pickett and Kershaw, the last finally and firmly connected with Hoke. Except for Clingman's brigade, Hoke's division had stood up well to the Federal attack of the day before, and proved themselves willing workers in erecting powerful fortifications. Beyond Hoke, Breckinridge occupied the rise. The right flank was extended by Wilcox's division to the edge of the slope that ran down to the Chickahominy. Mahone moved over to the right in general support.

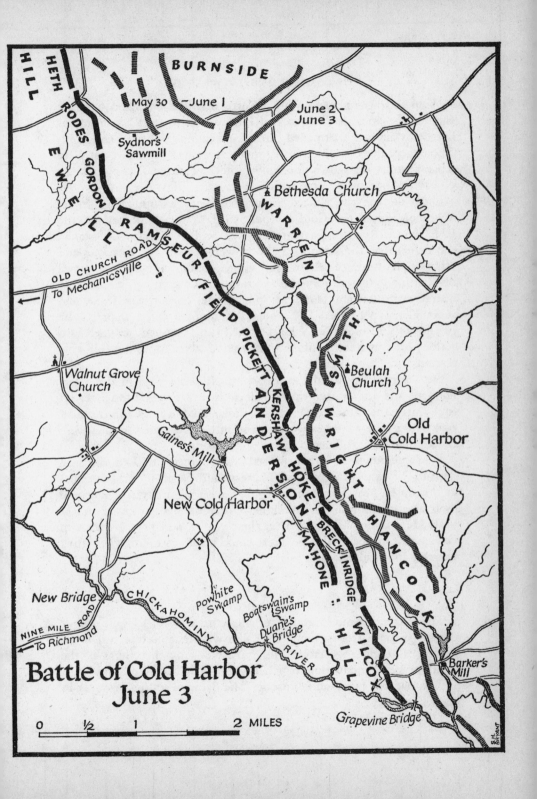

BURNSIDE

May 30 — June 1

HILL
HETH
RODES
EWELL
GORDON

June 2 —
June 3

Sydnor's
Sawmill

Bethesda Church

WARREN

RAMSEUR

FIELD

OLD CHURCH ROAD
To Mechanicsville
←

PICKETT

ANDERSON

SMITH

Beulah Church

WRIGHT

Walnut Grove
Church

KERSHAW

Old
Cold Harbor

Gaines's Mill

HOKE

New Cold Harbor

HANCOCK

BRECKINRIDGE

MAHONE

New Bridge

CHICKAHOMINY

Powhite
Swamp

Boatswain's
Swamp

WILCOX

NINE MILE ROAD
To Richmond
←

Duane's
Bridge

HILL

RIVER

Barker's
Mill

Battle of Cold Harbor
June 3

Grapevine Bridge

0   ½   1   2 MILES

S.H.
BRYANT

With this arrangement, Third Corps divisions occupied opposite ends of the line; the Second and First Corps formed a continuous line, with the two unattached forces connecting the center and right. These were not combinations formed for unified actions: they were separate units formed in connecting blocs of defense to meet what clearly had built to be a test of force.

Only on the overshifted right was there a supporting force, Mahone's. From the Cold Harbor Road to the flank beyond the Old Church Road not a regiment was held in reserve. Lee staked the defense of Richmond on the powerful field fortifications and "the steady valor of his troops" under conditions which required of them no extensive physical exertion nor of their leaders any co-operative maneuver. This was Spotsylvania on a wider front, and again Grant permitted Lee's men the time to build impregnable positions. Not since the Wilderness had Grant rushed pell-mell into action; he was very deliberate in committing troops to full-scale assault.

He originally planned the grand assault some time in the afternoon of the 2nd. After three o'clock it was already too late. At four-thirty the clouds opened and drenched the lines for the next two hours. The trenches were turned into mires, but the men were cooled off and the officers' tension was broken.

When darkness fell, from the rawest conscript to Lee, the men slept in the calm of certainty. There would be no hurried marches in the dusty heat, no frantic digging with their arms aching and their breaths labored, no wondering where the enemy might appear next. He was coming straight at their works, and not a veteran in Lee's army believed the Federals could overrun them when they were set and ready.

12

The Battle of Cold Harbor is usually conceived of as the daylight charge of June 3rd, in much the same way that Gettysburg is regarded as "Pickett's Charge." June 3rd was only the climax of the fighting and maneuvering which began on the night of May 31st, and at that was fairly anticlimactic. The decisive action was over in eight minutes.

The three-day battle for advantage and position was historically reduced to the general assault because the Federal troops sustained the heaviest losses of any army in any battle of the war in a comparative period of time. Nobody knows the exact figures of casualties in the first wave, but within less than an hour more than seven thousand men fell, killed or wounded, in moving against a fire power so uniform in its destructiveness that no living thing could advance in the face of it. The burden of the Federal assault was borne from the Confederate right westward by Hancock, Wright and Smith.

Only one weak Confederate spot was found, and this was negligence rather than weakness of fire power. Part of Breckinridge's front lay in low ground, which the rain turned into a swamp. Brigadier General Echols had just retired sick, and the colonel in command permitted the men to withdraw to high ground for rest. Only a picket line was left along the works. When the attack was delivered at four-thirty in the morning, the Federals overran the picket line before Echols's comforted soldiers were fully aroused, and they broke for safety.

In Mahone's supporting line, the nearest brigade was another patchwork affair. After Brigadier General Perry was wounded out, his three Florida regiments numbered too few to continue a separate existence without replacements and a brigade leader. In the last-ditch scraping of garrison forces after Butler was contained, Brigadier Finegan was called on to bring up an assortment of companies and battalions who had been idling in Florida. As it was feared that half the men would desert before they got out of Florida, Finegan brought along only two battalions of unspecified numbers, perhaps several hundred, to merge with the remnants of the three regiments shortly before Cold Harbor. Whether Mahone ordered them in or Finegan went on his own initiative, the isolated Federals of the narrow breakthrough were quickly driven out by this so-called brigade. Aside from this action, most of the Federal units took such shelter as they could find between thirty and fifty yards from the Confederate works. Those in the open retreated.

A curious, unplanned factor of the defense was the inward curve of the works where new lines had been built after the June 1st breakthrough between Hoke and Kershaw. The effect was that rifle and artillery fire partially enfiladed Hancock's right, Smith's left, and Wright on both flanks.

After the first wave receded, Grant's army headquarters ordered the three corps to attack on their immediate fronts without reference to the movements of the other units. The officers on the ground recognized the impossibility of executing such an order. They merely advanced the men who had formerly retreated to spots of shelter and ordered a heavy firing from the men already sheltered. Yet a third order came from general headquarters for a general advance. This time the officers only ordered a firing along the whole line. Not one man exposed himself by rising.

This was very baffling to the Confederates. The opening repulse had been made so easily and quickly that most of the men were still waiting for the main blow to fall. The soldiers would hear the enemy officers yelling out orders, the Federal soldiers would cheer with their loud hurrahs, rifles would crackle in volume, and nothing moved.

By six in the morning, generals sent messages back to Lee that it was all over. The commanding general was not as spry as usual in the early morning. Having planned the details for containing the attack precisely where it came, without placing undue burdens on the general officers, he had listened at his headquarters to a roar so violent that windowpanes rattled in Richmond. It was the only battle since the armies met in the Wilderness which General Lee did not command on the field.

13

This sputtering out of the climax of Grant's sustained one-month offensive brought no particular elation to Lee. He was relieved to have saved Richmond, for which he duly thanked God in his report to the commander in chief, but he recognized Cold Harbor to be only another check. It was a brutally decisive repulse, more than enough to have caused the removal of any Federal general previous to Grant. Yet, as the Union commander in chief had been given power to finish the job, Lee was the first to realize that Grant would not turn back.

The difficulty for Lee was that he could not take advantage of the shattering effect of the defeat on the Federal army. The total losses around Cold Harbor approached thirteen thousand, bringing Grant's campaign losses approximately to fifty thousand men, about the amount of infantry Lee started with. Federal soldiers spoke of the "butchering in the slaughter-pens" on the drive to the Chickahominy, and at Cold Harbor morning reports were no longer called for because "the country would not stand for it, if they knew." General officers reported a discouragement all through the ranks, in a reversal of the optimistic view that Lee's army was on the run and needed only one good lick to finish it off.

Even Grant, a hard man to convince and never one to admit that he had been outgeneraled, had enough of trying to get at Richmond through Lee's army. He quietly shelved his opening directive to Meade, that "Lee's army will be your objective." He did admit that Cold Harbor was a mistake, and the June 3rd assault was obviously a goaded act of frustration and obstinacy.

Perhaps he had been truly convinced that Lee's army was demoralized. Many Federal officers and men misread the meaning of the weak offensives attempted by units of Lee's army. The new men who came in with Grant wanted to believe that the legend of Lee's invincibility was only a myth which they exploded. The war-worn veterans wanted to believe that the great obstacle to their victory, to a return to their homes and normal life, was at last to be removed. Maybe hope also buttressed Grant in his wild lunge to force the weak opposing army to break under one blow delivered with all he had.

When Lee lost less than fifteen hundred men as Grant's army reeled back from the contact, disenchanted Meade said, "Grant had now discovered that Lee and the Army of Northern Virginia are not the same as Bragg and the Army of Tennessee." On the sudden quiet that followed the June 3rd debacle, Colonel Venable reflected that Grant's resolution "to fight it out on this line if it takes all summer" now seemed "to be sicklied o'er with the pale cast of thought."

Both observations were true enough. Yet there was nothing Lee could do about Grant's pause for thinking things over as long as the Federals remained in their works. For the fortifications against which Grant's soldiers had knocked themselves back would work the same way against Lee's men.

It probably never occurred to Lee that the crossing of the fields of his two victories — Gaines's Mill and Cold Harbor — represented a crossroads in world warfare. Gaines's Mill was a battle in the Napoleonic tradition, of masses rushing forward with bayoneted rifles to close with waiting lines, while mounted generals studied the action in classic groupings. Cold Harbor was modern war, at a stage when the defense more than compensated for increased fire power, and the genius of the Confederacy did not even witness the battle.

The old massed assaults from the Napoleonic wars, as Grant's standard technique, came to an end at Cold Harbor, over the graves of men whose leaders had used them successfully two years before in the same sultry heat. Cold Harbor would be the last set battle piece to be fought in the East.

In the endless conflict between maneuver and fixed position, between the fluid and the static, a pattern of circumstances caused one of the great exponents of maneuver, Lee, to improvise — what might be called — the mobile fixed position, the trench. While the new technique had saved his army, it also immobilized him. When both sides are in impregnable positions, with sufficient numbers in adequate condition to defend, to gain an advantage one side must move. Try as he might, General Lee could conceive of no way to move without uncovering Richmond. Since Grant could move in any direction except forward, the initiative remained with him.

As a guess, it must have first occurred to Lee then that the abandonment of Richmond would be militarily desirable. However, chained there, the General grew almost as goaded as Grant had been to break the stalemate with some sort, any sort, of offense. Yet, seeing what happened to Grant, he could not commit even a regiment to mass suicide. Knowing that Grant would try something else as soon as his army recovered, General Lee, with his great victory putting new heart in all the loyal, could only follow it up by restively waiting on his opponent, and continue the strain of anticipating his next move.

CHAPTER TEN

"My Idea Has Been to Beat Lee's Army North of Richmond"

I N THE DAYS FOLLOWING the grand assault at Cold Harbor, the hot, stinking trenches were remembered more vividly by the soldiers than was the fighting. In his reluctance to admit defeat, Grant was slow to ask for a truce for the burial of the dead, and that first week in June the damp heat which comes to the water-drained land of eastern Virginia lay over the ditches and mounds of freshly dug earth. The men's discomfort was intensified by the tireless vigilance of enemy sharpshooters.

Yet it was a period of mental relaxation for Lee's soldiers. With all the resolute confidence with which they had approached the campaign, there was nothing like the tonic of having taken the enemy's best and brought him to a dead halt. With this lift to the spirits came an overdue stimulant for their bodies. Blockade-run bacon came in from Nassau, and loads of onions were distributed as a specific against scurvy. The gaunt horses of the cavalry and the attenuated troopers were given a few days respite, and wagon-loads of corn came in for the animals' forage.

General Lee took to riding about the lines again, still wearing the linen sack for comfort, though otherwise he showed no outward effects from his ten-day illness. Beneath the familiar composure, the General was gnawed at by the need to get at the enemy before Grant moved again. His inner unquiet was reflected in his unusually brief, even curt, messages to the President.

In this period Davis's obsession with moving units about had destroyed all coherence of command in what had manifestly become the single Richmond-Petersburg front. The few hundred yards of the muddy James River, above which rose the streets of the capital, could have been an ocean barrier between rival powers as it affected cooperation between Beauregard and Lee. With their field headquarters less than thirty miles apart, every communication of their separate departments must clear through the mazes of the war office.

There Braxton Bragg had gradually assumed the duties and authority of War Secretary Seddon, and created a post as assistant commander in chief in charge of departmental coordination. Though Bragg was an able administrator, the clerks of all the bureaus together could not maintain a record of the units which came and went in the area from the south side of the James to south of Petersburg. Units never before heard of in Virginia appeared briefly on records and were seen no more. Infantry regiments, artillery battalions, cavalry legions were scattered over an area of thirty by ten miles in a fantasia of troop dispersal. The various departments of the war office were burdened down with sending directives appointing officers to new duties, new places to defend, new units that must first be found.

General Lee, struggling against his immobilized position, was helplessly trapped in the system of divided authority. His communications with Beauregard, mostly indirect, were reduced to such petty considerations as moving a brigade back and forth from Beauregard's department to the Department of Richmond. Gracie's Alabamians and Mat Ransom's North Carolinians played a game of musical chairs to the satisfaction of no one. Nobody seemed to know whether Hoke's division belonged with Lee or was on leave from Beauregard or yet belonged semi-independently back in what Beauregard designated as the Second Military District of Coastal North Carolina.

Along with precluding any unity of action, this bureaucratic control prevented Lee from forming any organization around his seriously reduced Army of Northern Virginia. In its command structure reliable George Doles of Rodes's division had been killed in the Cold Harbor fighting, leaving only one brigadier general in Early's Second Corps. Jim Lane was wounded out of Wilcox's division, and Evander Law in Field's division. After all his string-pulling to prevent Micah Jenkins's being promoted over him, Professor Law went home to recuperate and never returned to the army.

The new promotions came largely from colonels scarcely known beyond their own regiments, and few of them were ever to be heard from as brigadiers. As always, the cavalry had an able man to advance. Rufus Barringer, brother-in-law of Stonewall Jackson and D. H. Hill, succeeded James Gordon on the North Carolina brigade in Rooney Lee's division. Outside the cavalry, discounting several men of limited promise who never lived to reach it, the pool of general officer material had been drained.

Lee's army lost more than one third of its general officers from May 5th to June 3rd, and for the most part well-meaning adequacy was the best that could be hoped for in replacements. All too well did Lee know that even this modest demand would not be met with any consistency. With any bold maneuvers out of the question under those conditions, the Old Man could only survey the scattering of troop units, all of which could have been concentrated in Virginia at the opening of the campaign, and suffer the strain of waiting on the enemy's move.

2

Grant's first move was a reversion to offensives and diversionary attacks directed toward secondary objectives. In a tacit admission of his inability to defeat Lee and/or to take Richmond, Grant designed these movements primarily toward cutting the sources of supply of both Lee's army and the capital. Secondarily, diverse threats could disperse Confederate strength.

On June 6th, Lee learned that a new force in the Shenandoah Valley, led by David Hunter, had occupied the central Valley city of Staunton, western terminus of the Virginia Central Railroad. The next day, Lee learned that Sheridan had left Grant again and headed west, toward Hunter. Two days later, June 9th, Beauregard sent another of his alarums, this one immediate and urgent. Cavalry and infantry were attacking Petersburg.

As troops to meet these diversions were then with Lee's forces, the President permitted Lee to make the decisions regarding these three new threats. Lee ignored the "attack" of Petersburg as reconnaissance, and nothing came of it. Units from two divisions with Butler, one colored, were supposed to attack the lines in front of the city while Kautz's cavalry came in from the south. The infantry shuffled around for a while in front of the powerfully constructed lines, manned by one brigade and several gun batteries, and slunk away. Kautz fought a brief action locally known as "The Battle of the Patients and the Penitents." The hospitals and the prisons released their occupants to help the city battalion of over-aged and under-aged. This gathering, accompanied by the sprightly airs played by a Negro band, held off the Federal cavalry until a gun battery and Dearing's cavalry brigade came up.

For the Valley threat, Lee at first followed what had become standard procedure since his first counteroffensive in 1862 cleared the supply area of the enemy. He ordered a gathering of assorted units to act as a restraining and observation force until the enemy revealed his intentions.

After McClellan's regime, the enemy's western operations in the Shenandoah Valley had been conducted by third-raters, like Milroy and his "weary boys" (as fellow Federals called them), and nothing serious had developed. David Hunter, like Milroy, was distinguished more as an arsonist than as a soldier, though he did not run from noises as quickly as Milroy nor perform as ineptly as Sigel.

To deal with Hunter, Lee returned the two brigades of Breckinridge to the Valley. At twenty-one hundred infantry, the unit was minus only a hundred and fifty soldiers from its Cold Harbor experience, though their imposing leader was temporarily absent. Breckinridge had suffered considerable damage when his horse, struck by a solid shot, pinned him to the ground in the fall. For four brigades of western cavalry, "the wild ones," a slot was found for disciplinarian Robert Ransom, when he was removed from the Department of Richmond to give a post to Ewell.

Before this makeshift force was assembled, the enemy revealed the scope of his intentions. Brigadier General George Crook rode into the Valley from the western mountains with a large, rough party of mounted raiders, and on June 8th joined Hunter in Staunton. As Lee had learned the day before that Sheridan was on his way west with two divisions, the unfolding pattern showed the seriousness of Grant's purpose to destroy the Shenandoah Valley as a producing center for the army, along with a belated project to break Lee's communications with the Valley via the Virginia Central.

In one month, Sheridan's riders had shown themselves to be zealous wreckers of railroads and, left to themselves, these mobile demolishers could sever connections with the Valley beyond the Confederacy's hope of rebuilding. After the dual operations were completed in the Valley and on the railroads, the combined force could return to Grant as a powerful striking arm to be attached to the army. The Hunter-Sheridan combination presented a danger as grave as "Beast" Butler's southside threat had appeared to be — and, well led, would have been.

For that Lee sacrificed most of his cavalry. There was no alternative. The Virginia Central must operate and a juncture between Sheridan and Hunter must be prevented. Sending off five sevenths of his cavalry was a desperate measure.

Under Sheridan's policy of exterminating the enemy's cavalry, Lee's losses in his troopers had not been made up by the accretion of Calbraith Butler's South Carolina brigade, approaching two thousand, and the several hundred in the Georgia battalions or legions (more than one company and less than a regiment) which joined Pierce Young's sparse units. Also Calbraith Butler's no longer inexperienced mounted rifles had suffered heavily in sharing the brunt of the Cold Harbor fighting.

With no Confederate cavalry records for the period available but based on a composite estimate of something over seven thousand effectives operating as of June 8th, Lee's campaign losses until then must have amounted to well above three thousand. Surprisingly, in view of Sheridan's claims about the spineless ineffectuality of the enemy, Federal cavalry losses, by record, were approximately the same. Sheridan's replacements had been supplied by recruits shipped in.

On what started out to be a more destructive and militarily purposeful operation than the raid on Richmond, Sheridan's force numbered between eight thousand and nine thousand troopers, with four gun batteries of U.S. regulars, and the usual accompaniment of supporting services. Having experienced the leanness of the Virginia countryside, Sheridan took along his own herd of cattle.

(Grant ran something like a mobile meat-packing operation on the side.) The expedition was to be Sheridan's last major affair against the Army of Northern Virginia in the current phase of the war, and he was very evasive about it in reports.

He started out in high confidence, by leading the force to retrace Grant's march to Cold Harbor. Crossing the Pamunkey near Hanovertown, Sheridan swung west on a northward looping arc. He planned to set his wrecking crew to work on the railroad at Louisa Court House, and destroy westward to Charlottesville, where the Virginia Central connected with a railroad south to Lynchburg and on to Tennessee. Charlottesville was the seat of Albemarle County, the demesne of Thomas Jefferson, and natives remembered the tales from their parents of the time when the British cavalry raiders came through and Jefferson was forced to flee from his hilltop home of Monticello. A regional hero, Jack Jouett, had ridden across country at night, permanently scarring his face from the briers, to warn Virginia's governor and assembled dignitaries. In Sheridan's raid, the hero was Wade Hampton.

3

Lee gave Hampton command of the emergency expedition consisting of his own then three-brigade division and Fitz Lee's two-brigade division. The two divisions numbered about five thousand, with three batteries of horse artillery. The men carried three days' rations of one and a half pounds of hardtack and one-half pound of bacon, with ears of corn for the horses strung on the pommels of their saddles.

Starting on June 9th, two days after Sheridan, Hampton rode his men and horses hard on a chord below Sheridan's arc. At dusk of June 10th the two divisions reached Louisa Court House and, a few miles beyond, the depot called Trevilian's Station, twenty-eight miles east of Charlottesville. Between the courthouse town and the way station, the massive South Carolinian planned a split-force tactic for the reception of Sheridan the next morning.

Considering the small size of his force and the aggressiveness of the enemy, Hampton's tactics were not as brilliant as his admirers have claimed. They did have the advantage of boldness, against an enemy who underestimated the fight in the Confederate cavalry when combat was its assignment and the troops were properly prepared to make it. Chiefly, it was the personal leadership of Wade Hampton that caused the ambitious tactics to be supported by determined fighting.

Destined to replace Stuart in command of the cavalry corps, Hampton was totally unlike his predecessor and most of the younger leaders who looked on combat as a frolic. Dressed without ornamentation, he wore a plain, gray sack coat of civilian cut, a brown felt hat, and brass spurs on his large boots. His dark eyes were friendly and he rarely raised his low, sonorous voice. His weather-stained face was decorated by dark side whiskers and mustache, and his presence was characterized by a grave, simple courtesy. Like Lee, he held complete control over himself at all times. The plantation master, probably the richest man in the South, was never known to be overbearing with anyone. He required big horses to carry his weight, but he never rode a showy animal. Doing nothing to set himself apart, Hampton was impressive by the act of being, and his men recognized in their patrician leader a perfect flowering of their era.

To battle he brought the composed resolution of powerful convictions, and this force was communicated by his known lack of interest in warfare as an end in itself. He had watched one son killed in front of his eyes and seen another carried off the field wounded. He epitomized his approach to battle when he wrote, "I would not give peace for all the military glory won by Bonaparte." He prepared for action with a businesslike calm, but the heavy saber the General carried in his huge hand conveyed the idea, rather awesomely, that it was a very personal business.

Of the clash between the two cavalries, no battle in the war was recorded by such contradictory reports of the combatants, from commanding generals to brigadiers. Both sides insisted they opened the action with attack and, beyond that relatively simple disagreement, the details grow somewhat fantastic. The key to the confusion, in the fight and in the reports, was glory-minded Custer, who almost suffered his "Last Stand" in back of the country depot.

In the realm of certainties, while Calbraith Butler's brigade, dismounted in the woods, was fighting Torbert's division, Custer took his brigade on a side lane that brought him out by the station. There he found the horses of Butler's dismounted troopers being held, as the Confederates thought, out of harm's way. A couple of reserve guns and a few wagons were also around. With his eye on this booty, yellow-curled Custer never considered the reason why he had slid around Butler's flank so easily.

In Wade Hampton's ambitious plan, Fitz Lee was designed to close on Calbraith Butler from the east and catch Sheridan's men between the two divisions. But Gregg's division hit young Lee while he was coming up and drove his two brigades back from Butler. Custer had unknowingly slipped between this gap.

When Hampton learned that an enemy brigade behind him had captured his led horses, he ordered Butler to fall back. As always when Confederate cavalry gave ground, Sheridan's people described the backward movement as a "demoralized" rout. Butler's quickly bloodied South Carolinians had by no means become veteran campaigners in two weeks. Against two of Torbert's large brigades, the men became considerably confused in disengaging themselves, without their horses nearby, from the pressing enemy. While they were experiencing their troubles, Custer's began.

Rosser's brigade, mounted, had been working beyond Butler's left flank. All the Confederate units seemed to recognize Butler's danger at once. Rosser came charging in from the west, Fitz Lee from the east, and Butler's far from demoralized dismounted troopers from the north. Custer lost all his captures, along with his own headquarters wagon, in fighting on all sides to save his brigade until Torbert and Gregg came up. When those two Federal divisions arrived, everybody began to fight on all sides.

But there were too many Federals with too many shots in their repeating carbines for Hampton. After as hard a mounted cavalry fight as the war saw, he pulled his division out of the action. Though Sheridan and his officers made the usual claims about the miserable helplessness of the Confederates, Hampton was not followed. Fitz Lee withdrew around the Federal forces and joined Hampton in preparation for the renewal of the fight the next day.

Sheridan's two divisions held the railroad the few miles from Louisa to Trevilian's Station. The next afternoon, while some of Gregg's troopers tore up the tracks in that section, Torbert went at Butler again. Calbraith Butler, recently returned to action minus one foot, made no vainglorious claims for his stand. He said, in effect, that his men were fought to the last breath of their strength and courage in maintaining their position. They did hold their position, and Sheridan's attackers withdrew after nightfall. That is where the facts began again.

Among all the counterclaims, Sheridan showed by his action that he had enough. He abandoned the field to the "panic-stricken" rebels and abandoned his mission. Sheridan recorded that he turned back because Hunter had not come to Charlottesville. But commander in chief Grant specifically stated that the purpose of the raid was to break up communications between Richmond and the Valley. Beyond that, he "hoped" Sheridan would join Hunter and finish the job in the Valley, before the combined forces returned to him.

The Virginia Central ran unmenaced while Sheridan took a roundabout ride back to safety. Though he was only four days in coming up from outside Richmond, he used nine days in a circuitous course to reach the north bank of the Pamunkey across from the Federal base at White House landing. On those days, Hampton's people rode along the south bank of the Pamunkey, and never once could Sheridan complain that the enemy would not stand and fight. He never tried to cross to their side of the river and find out; he finally crossed under the protection of the gunboats to the Federal supply base.

Hampton and his men candidly admitted they had survived a severe and punishing action, which cost the division eight hundred casualties. Tom Rosser went out with a bad leg wound. Though Hampton's men bore by far the heaviest weight of the action, the combined force could not have lost less than one thousand men. Sheridan admitted to eight hundred-odd for his two divisions. Yet, though Trevilian's Station was his last major action against Lee's cavalry in 1864, he officially reported five thousand as his total losses in his campaigning against the enemy's cavalry. This represented more than 40 per cent of the effective force with which he crossed the Rapidan on May 4th.

There is another thing. After shepherding a wagon train across the Virginia peninsula from the Pamunkey to the James River, he reached the main army on June 26th. Then he needed the period from July 2nd to July 26th to rest and refit his cavalry, while Hampton remained continuously active. When ready for action again, after an inconclusive flurry, Sheridan went with two of his divisions to assume command of the operations in the Shenandoah Valley. There in the fall, with overwhelming physical superiority, he won the fame which retroactively colored his part in the 1864 campaign against Lee. It is undeniable that the cavalry of the Army of Northern Virginia, in sad physical decline when belligerent Sheridan came on the scene, could continue neither to function indefinitely under equivalent losses nor to maintain itself under such pressure without the periods of rest and refitting which Sheridan required. But that the Confederates could inflict at least equal losses, while serving Lee in reconnaissance as Sheridan never served Grant, is a denial of the boasts made by one of the few truly ungenerous foes Lee's men met in their ancient and respected antagonist, the Army of the Potomac.

During the campaign, a revealing exchange occurred between two professionals — a captured sergeant of the 5th U.S. regulars and Fitz Lee, who had served in that command. As the two old pros talked about the regiment, Lee asked the sergeant why the men of the 5th cavalry no longer "stood up better to their work." The sergeant explained that since they had lost Captain Ashe, killed at Spotsylvania, the men could not get a good leader.

This friendly, professional appraisal between two soldiers reduced the struggle between the cavalries to the realities of armed combat. Manifestly Sheridan's extermination policy was exterminating his own cavalry at the same rate. No all-conquering foe would need the protection of gunboats to cross a river against an enemy of half its numbers nor three weeks to recover from chasing a shadowy foe who, by Sheridan's count, had lost more in killed and captured than it started with.

Sheridan's vanity over his tactic of fighting the enemy's cavalry was maintained by replacements for men and horses, by rest and resources for constant renewals to top strength. At Trevilian's Station, Sheridan's cavalry had come upon a time when it needed rebuilding in order to re-establish physical superiority. Like Grant at Cold

Harbor, Sheridan had overestimated the effects of his pugnacity on the enemy.

As an extension of Grant's policy of supporting hammering by the uncounted expenditure of human life, Sheridan's method could not be maintained unless other factors affected the total situation. As factors remote from the armies in Virginia supported Sheridan's methods, his was the morale of ruthlessly applied might given glory (as an anti-slavery Virginian had predicted) by the banner of a crusade.

On the field where his hordes ranged, something ugly and vicious came into the war, and something of mutually shared respect for the individual went out. The sentimental song of beplumed Stuart, giving his life for his homeland, was replaced by the winner-take-all mechanics of the bully-boys.

4

Before Lee knew that Sheridan had been disposed of, he learned that General Hunter had turned south in the Valley and on June 11th reached Lexington. This charming post-Revolutionary town, the rural center of Rockbridge County, was distinguished as the site of V.M.I. and Washington College, and boasted some handsome homes. Hunter did not behave at all well in Lexington. He burned the college buildings of V.M.I. and the home of John Letcher, who had been Virginia's governor at the time of secession, allowed his men to remove all the books from the library and to steal generally from the townspeople.

Hunter's next stop was obviously Lynchburg, on the eastern foothills of the Blue Ridge. Though primarily a residential city, Lynchburg was a railroad junction, with scattered manufacturing plants and depots of military supplies. Not one of the large Confederate centers, Lynchburg held importance in Virginia operations, especially for its railroad connections with Richmond and Tennessee. Its loss would seriously affect the Eastern area. With only Breckinridge's leaderless brigades and the unruly cavalry brigades, which had already performed poorly, Lynchburg suffered from a command situation similar to Petersburg at Butler's appearance.

As at Bermuda Hundred in May, there was Robert Ransom, with the impossible task of making soldiers out of the collection of mounted raiders, and there again was D. H. Hill. Beauregard had decided that Lynchburg was included in his department, which he had named the Department of North Carolina and Southern Virginia, and sent out his volunteer aide to supervise a brigadier on the scene. The War Department would not have this for a minute. By chance, bristly Arnold Elzey, a Marylander in high favor with the administration because of his regularity, showed up in Richmond without a command. As the onetime commander of the Department of Richmond, General Elzey seemed the ideal man to assume charge of the Lynchburg defenses, which consisted mostly of generals.

Whether or not this duplication of Pickett's earlier trials influenced General Lee, while he possessed the authority he determined to be done with half-measures and finish off Hunter once and for all. To this end, on the 12th he ordered Early's Second Corps to make the roundabout train trip to Lynchburg. Had Sheridan wrecked the Virginia Central at Charlottesville and eastward, Early could not have moved to the rescue. By the morning of the 13th, Lee knew that Sheridan had been repulsed.

Though it is nowhere stated, Lee, for all the urge to maneuver which nagged at him, must have inwardly accepted the inevitability of defense when he detached his mobile striking corps. When the Second Corps with its artillery left Lee, the remnants of this once powerful force numbered no more than eight thousand infantry. Yet, while only the size of a Federal division, the veterans newly under Jubal Early represented one fourth of what was left of the infantry of the Army of Northern Virginia. Without any precise figures for the period, a composite of the estimates allows Lee approximately twenty-eight thousand foot soldiers after the Second Corps was detached.

Once Lee determined to rid the Valley of menaces' the like of Hunter, no less a number could be counted on to complete the job of destroying Hunter's force of some fifteen thousand. Then, since he must make so large a commitment from his own army (having no authority over any other troops), Lee looked beyond the mere countermeasures against Hunter. Early, combined with Breckinridge and a heavy force of artillery, would, counting the undependable Western cavalry, field a force approaching fifteen thousand. With this command, Early could not only drive Hunter all the way down the Valley but, after clearing the Valley for the farmers, he would be in a position to threaten the North in the Washington area.

It is not likely that Lee hoped at that stage of the war to duplicate the effects of Jackson's 1862 Valley campaign. Old Jack, arousing a fear for Washington, immobilized the fifty-thousand-man army at Fredericksburg on which McClellan had depended for his imaginative pincer movement on Richmond. Lee probably hoped to draw off some veteran troops from Grant and to divert reinforcements from him. With an aggressive fighter such as Early, any offensive opened possibilities. Of all things for Lee, it was an *offensive*. The extemporized plan, an overnight decision, broke the passive defensiveness of waiting on the enemy's every move. For General Lee, it broke the outraged frustration at being forced to permit the enemy's "prearrangements" to unfold according to plan. At least, in however small volume, the war would be carried to the enemy somewhere.

At the outset, Hunter crossed Lee. The arsonist had approached to the outskirts of Lynchburg and was feeling out the position when he learned that Early's corps was gathering there. Not only did Hunter make no fight at all, he did not even retreat down the Valley in an attempt to do damage on his way out. He fled into the Alleghenies and kept his army intact, even if his reputation was gone. Early, while saving Lynchburg and the Valley by his mere presence, did not accomplish the part of his assignment of destroying Hunter's army. By then the situation at Richmond had changed so drastically that Early was allowed to march on down the Valley, victualing his men along the way and presenting such threat to Washington as he could with his small force.

It was to meet this threat that Sheridan was sent to the Valley, later in the summer, to command a newly assembled army. This was composed of two of his cavalry divisions and the VI Corps of infantry, drawn off from Grant, the Federal army formerly commanded by David Hunter, and a fresh corps which had been scheduled for duty in the Lower South. Along with occupying these fifty thousand Union troops, Early's effect on the military pattern in Virginia was to establish the Valley as a separate front. In doing that, he preserved Lee's supply source and kept open communications with the West, which were the fundamental purposes in detaching Early. Grant was frustrated in his plan of getting at Lee's army indirectly by cutting off a source of supply. By detaching Early, Lee achieved what his army achieved directly against Grant — a stalemate.

5

When Hunter's force took to the hills on June 17th, this ended the second of Grant's multiple offensives within about six weeks. Of strategic importance in the collapse of the second plan was the failure to isolate Lee and Richmond from the productive areas north of the James River. By enemy gunboat control of the four waterways (Potomac, Rappahannock, York-Pamunkey, James), and by enemy occupancy of coastal and inland-coastal bases from Alexandria to Norfolk, tidewater Virginia was Federal territory to within twenty miles east of Richmond. Had the Virginia Central been put out of existence, the capital and its defending army would be reduced to dependence upon supplies from south of the James River.

All of Lee's thinking from the North Anna on was conditioned by his expectation of Grant's moving against the Virginia Central. As Meade said that the Army of Northern Virginia could never be defeated while that railroad operated, Lee simply could not believe Grant would continue to send no more than cavalry against his life line. But the Federal commander, unwilling to sever connections with river naval bases, would not commit the Army of the Potomac to a reverse swing to the west. Instead, Grant decided to isolate Richmond from the south by the capture of Petersburg.

Grant reached this decision before the Sheridan and Hunter threats were turned back. Shortly after Cold Harbor, he wrote Washington: "My idea from the start has been to beat Lee's army if possible north of Richmond." Then saying, "Without a greater sacrifice of human life than I am willing to make, all cannot be accomplished that I had designed outside the city," Grant outlined the new plan which shifted his objective from Lee's army to operation against the supply system of Lee's army and Richmond.

In this outline, the commander in chief could not bring himself to make the simple statement that he had failed to defeat Lee's army in the field. He again reproached the Confederates for fighting behind works and preserving their small numbers. Since Lee would not fight along lines to accommodate him (as the Confederates always had in the West), he devised the oblique approach which was designed to get Lee, one way or another, out of his entrenchments.

This substitute design led *eventually* to the wearing-down operation which Grant's admirers have praised as his policy of attrition. This is another of those convincing rationales after the fact. Any armed struggle in which the physically superior opponent retains the will to conquer the enemy, whom he cannot defeat in battle, becomes a war of attrition. The side with the fewer men, the leaner resources, must wear out if the aggressor remains determined. But Grant did not open his campaign with the purpose of wearing out Lee; by his own words, he began with the purpose of defeating Lee's army.

Nor did his hammering methods constitute an articulated policy of attrition. Where he outnumbered Lee two to one, where his replacements were inexhaustible and Lee's close to zero, Grant simply tried to overwhelm Lee with sheer might of numbers. As Lee feared, arithmetic would ultimately obliterate his army by subtraction, if the Army of the Potomac could itself survive the punishment. But Grant was not working on a long-range policy ("if it takes all summer" was as far ahead as he conceived), and the army he commanded could not withstand the punishment. Though Grant was not forthright about the morale in the army as he fought it, the troops remained badly shaken after Cold Harbor and their confidence did not return immediately, as he claimed.

He wanted to believe that his tactics had not shaken the army's morale and he planned his substitute operation against Petersburg on that assumption. Grant's own outlines make it very clear that his new plan was not devised, any more than his original plan, toward a long-range policy of attrition. His revised plan was aimed primarily at forcing Lee out of his entrenchments.

To that end, his plan of working against Richmond from the

south, by occupying Petersburg, was sound in all ways. In fact, it had been a sound plan since the beginning of the war, when Lee first considered the possibility. Grant only got around to it when, to his angry incredulity, he discovered that the Army of Northern Virginia *was* different from the setups in the West. It was true what they said about Lee.

The occupation of Petersburg was in a different realm of strategic importance from severing Richmond from the Shenandoah Valley. Where the loss of the Valley meant only supplies, grave though that was, Grant in Petersburg would cut off Richmond from the coastal South. Not only would the enemy lie across Lee's main line of communications, but the Federals would be in a position to disrupt other lines of supply and transportation. With Grant in occupation of Petersburg, Lee would be forced to come out of his works around Richmond.

Whether Lee tried to drive the Federals out of Petersburg or tried to maneuver to the west, it would be all one to Grant. He would have forced the battle-wise old lion out into the open. That was all he asked and, from the abortive attack on Petersburg on June 9th, Grant knew the city was lightly defended. On the night of June 12th, with most of Lee's cavalry off at the Trevilian's Station action, Grant made the next move with the main army.

CHAPTER ELEVEN

"It Will Be a Mere Question of Time"

ALL OF GRANT'S tactical orders involving troop movement were superbly executed by the supporting services in conjunction with the U.S. Navy and naval bases. None demonstrated a more complete mastery of the mechanics and logistics of moving a large, oversupplied army than the march which began secretly out of the Cold Harbor lines on the night of June 12-13th.

Leaving the malodorous works around midnight, the troops first marched east along the north bank of the Chickahominy, crossed that river on pontoons in the Long Bridge area (the bridges having been burned) and pushed southward into thickly brushed country. Much of this land had been exhausted by seventeenth- and eighteenth-century tobacco crops, and the second-growth woods, mostly pine, were draped with the usual vines and creepers. With only occasional hills, most of the breaks in the flatness were shadowed creeks or swampy ravines, and a damp heat hung over the shrouded passageways. Although as effective as a tunnel for screening purposes, it was poor terrain for forced marching in the summer. Pushing all day on the 13th, the van reached the James River, at the boat landing on the plantation wharf of Dr. Wilcox, by midday of the 14th. The first troops to arrive had covered about twenty-five miles; those coming on behind, following more circuitous routes, would march more than forty miles.

Wilcox's Landing had been selected as the first feasible crossing point beyond observation of the Confederate signal stations. There the broadening James was seven hundred yards wide, twelve fathoms deep, with swells of four feet in the tidal water. To prevent the approach of Confederate gunboats from Richmond (including the *Patrick Henry*, the training ship of the CSA Naval Academy), five vessels loaded with rocks were sunk to block the river channel at Trent's Reach. With the help of ferries sent up from Fort Monroe, a pontoon bridge was secured for men, guns and wagons by afternoon of the 14th. The heavier trains and the cattle herds, with their mounted drovers, would later cross the peninsula from the White House landing base.

The Army of the Potomac began crossing to the south side of the James below Bermuda Hundred at a landing called Windmill Point, sixteen miles by road from Petersburg. The first of the troops, Hancock's II Corps, approached the junction city during the afternoon of the 15th.

Ahead of Hancock's men, Smith's XVIII Corps was already deployed at the works two miles outside the city. These troops of Butler's army had left the Cold Harbor lines during the day of the 12th. Marching only to White House landing, they embarked there on ships. Down the Pamunkey into the York and around the tip of the peninsula past Fort Monroe, the transports entered the James at its mouth and on the 14th returned Smith's corps to Bermuda Hundred. There General Butler's engineers built a pontoon bridge across the Appomattox, one of the two watery arms which enclosed his base, and Smith's corps did what they could have done at any time before — crossed to the south bank of the Appomattox on the same side of the river as Petersburg. Following the course which he had earlier urged, Baldy Smith moved straight on to the city, accompanied by Kautz's ubiquitous cavalry.

On the morning of the 15th of June, with Petersburg defended by one infantry brigade, an assortment of field batteries and old guns in fixed position, a Federal corps and a cavalry division approached the city, with Hancock's redoubtable II Corps coming up in support. Logistically one of the great operations of the war had been completed.

2

On the morning of June 13th, as Early's corps was boarding the train to Lynchburg, Lee was informed that the enemy had vanished from his front. At his hillside headquarters tent, overlooking the millponds, the General listened to the details of the enemy's disappearance. Confederate skirmishers had advanced through the labyrinthine works so suddenly abandoned and a mile or so beyond without encountering a single straggler. The cavalry pickets out on the left, and across the Chickahominy to the right, had observed no movement in these directions. This indicated that Grant had neither turned to the northwest, toward the Virginia Central, nor over the nearby marshes of the Chickahominy for a quick thrust at Richmond from due east. Since Grant, then, could have only marched eastward along the north bank of the Chickahominy, obviously he planned to cross that river farther to the east, beyond the swamp, with the James River as his destination.

Lee was not surprised by this move. In a routine endorsement of a message to Davis on the 11th, he wrote that he expected Grant to shift his main force to the James River. From there Grant could have one of two objectives. He could establish a naval-supported base on the James, for a campaign at Richmond from the east, or he could cross the river for a move against Petersburg. This latter move seemed the likeliest. This possibility had been generally discussed around Richmond, and a newspaper had commented upon it.

On June 9th, Beauregard had also predicted this move, though he had been warning of dangers to his front since Grant was at the North Anna River. Later, however, Beauregard and his admirers used this bit of prescience as a base in building a highly doctored, highly flavored epic in which Lee played the dupe to Beauregard as Hero. As Old Bory's drama was supported in substance by claims of Grant's admirers, Lee's countering moves have been obscured by one of the war's most inextinguishable myths.

In this myth, when "Grant stole a march" on Lee, the commanding general of the Army of Northern Virginia remained in helpless befuddlement in his trenches for most of five days while Beauregard bombarded him with "urgent reports" of the presence of Grant's "whole army" at Petersburg. "I failed to convince him," Beauregard wrote, "that I was fighting Grant's whole army," and this statement has been endlessly repeated as a fact. Though any legend gains credence with repetition, it is incredible that Beauregard's misrepresentation has been accepted when standard records disprove it completely.

At best, it is often difficult to disassociate our hindsight from the position of an individual who, in the midst of events, could not possibly know anything of their unfolding. The effect of the Beauregard myth has been to imply that General Lee misused information which, in point of fact, he never had. For the first days, his only information was that gathered by his own reduced forces.

The myth, supported by the Grant version, also gives an impression of the Army of Northern Virginia as in its great days, when it was indeed a terrible host. But when Lee, at his field headquarters behind Cold Harbor, prepared to counter the latest move of Grant, his infantry numbered little more than a Federal corps.

With Early, the Second Corps artillery, and Breckinridge off to the Valley, the remaining First and Third Corps together numbered about 27,500 infantry. Hoke's temporarily attached division, mustering perhaps six thousand after casualties, did not belong to Lee's organization and was to be detached in two days. For cavalry, Lee was even worse off. On June 13th, the two divisions under Wade Hampton had just concluded the action at Trevilian's Station and were under orders to stay with Sheridan all the way, to keep his wreckers off the Virginia Central. With the army were only the two thinned brigades commanded by Lee's son, Rooney.

Against this small force, Grant's army numbered more than a hundred thousand, after sending back Smith's corps to Butler's army. Replacements counted for upwards of one third of the infantry, but the veterans still maintained their original ratio of about two to one over Lee's soldiers. With the infantry were one full cavalry division, all the artillery, and the mobile community formed of the supporting services.

Knowing the odds and Grant's two choices of movement, Lee immediately sent orders for his army to cross the Chickahominy near the Cold Harbor lines to be on the same side of the river which Grant would presumably cross farther east. Once south of the Chickahominy, the rudimentary problem was to select a point which covered the approaches to Richmond at a distance from its fortifications, where the miasmic flatlands could be reconnoitered.

When the headquarters tents were struck during the morning of June 13th, and the General prepared to ride Traveler again, there was no element of urgency as to Grant's whereabouts. Lee was incomparably less anxious than when Grant had moved away from the North Anna. At that time, Grant had more choices of movement, and Lee had been apprehensive about the Virginia Central. When Lee rode away from the camp overlooking the ruins of Dr. Gaines's Mill, he was beginning a routine operation.

Ahead of him, the soldiers moved out of the trenches in an apathetic state. To them, release from the trenches to meet another of Grant's "sidling" movements meant only more digging, and they were tired. The two weeks in the Cold Harbor trenches had been a prolonged physical strain, coming as an extension of the exhausting campaign. The intense heat of the sun beating down on the open works was broken by only enough rain to maintain the consistency of the muddy footing. After each shower, steam rose from the baked earth. The toll of the sharpshooters, though not high in numbers, was severe on the men's nerves. Their bounty of food, which halted the devastations of hunger, was insufficient to rebuild their strength. When the quartermasters tried to stretch out the hoard, the bacon turned rancid. It was eaten anyway. With no opportunity to bathe or wash their clothes, the men had to suffer the vermin which infested their rags. Diarrhea, dysentery, and slow fevers were wasting away a growing proportion of the soldiers.

The chronicler of MacGowan's South Carolina brigade recorded, "Our health was very bad. . . . A good many men had to be sent to the hospitals in Richmond, and some we did not and shall not see again." Their general attitude in the movement out after Grant was summarized by Major Stiles, the Yale man in the Richmond Howitzers. He wrote, "There was nothing about it calculated to make an impression . . . it seemed rather a slow, stupid affair."

As with the citizens in the city at their backs, the men around Lee reflected a letdown after the repulse of Grant as the climax to the fight for Richmond. Grant had become more of a bore, a "trial," than a menace. In those hazily hot June days, nobody seemed to care much where he was for the moment. This was the atmosphere in which Lee crossed his infantry and guns across the swampy Chickahominy, to place his army once more between Richmond and Grant.

3

Soon after the army crossed to the south side of the Chickahominy on June 13th, Lee received his first information about the
route of Grant's army. In addition to Rooney Lee's two cavalry
brigades, a small brigade recently up from South Carolina had been
picketing well out in front of the Richmond fortifications between
the Chickahominy and the James. Though these regiments of Colonel Gary belonged in the Department of Richmond, which was to
become the command of Dick Ewell, Colonel Gary passed directly
on to Lee the information of an encounter with Federal cavalry.

This had occurred in the brushy country in the area of the Long
Bridge crossing of the Chickahominy. Wilson's cavalry division was
screening the roads approaching the area from the west, and this
satisfied General Lee that he had located the vicinity of Grant's
army. He would have preferred more certainty, but he lacked the
cavalry to make a forced reconnaissance and, anyway, the Army of
the Potomac was in no present position to do any damage.

Moving east along the Williamsburg Stage Road (once the Indians' Pocahontas Trail), the army crossed to the south of the White
Oak Swamp, another of the marshy water barriers, to a crossroads
which commanded the approaches to Richmond from the east. This
was all standard procedure, with the cavalry skirmishing several
miles out on his front.

Toward dusk, Rooney Lee reported that his troopers had not
been able to find any gaps in the enemy's resistance, but the prisoners gathered were all cavalrymen and the blue troopers were not
using Sheridan's customary pushing tactics. They were merely
screening the passage of the army. After this information came in, a
camp was made placidly for that night at the road intersection
called Riddell's Shop. Lee was then twelve miles from Richmond,
and about fifteen miles straight across country from Grant's destination at Wilcox's Landing.

The next morning, the 14th, Lee ordered some of A. P. Hill's
infantry to put weight behind his lean mounted units and push into
the concealing brush to discover what Grant was up to. Hill's
tawny men moved forward with their skirmish lines spread out on

either side of the roads fanning northward from the old battle-
ground of Malvern Hill. The action varied in intensity along the different roads. In some places, when their own cavalry was driven
back on them, the foot soldiers stood off brief charges from the
enemy troopers. In the dense sections, the enemy cavalry sprayed
the foliage with jacketed bullets from their repeating carbines and
then fell back out of rifle range. Closer to the river, some of Hill's
soldiers made contact with enemy infantry and gathered some
prisoners from Warren's V Corps. Across the loose front the action
constituted a series of disconnected skirmishes. Against the light
units of Rooney Lee's two brigades, the enemy cavalry moved aggressively. Against Hill's infantry support, the enemy gave ground,
though never rapidly and never far out of range.

The frustrating action was a throwback to the Indian fighting on
this same land, two and a half centuries before, when the ancestors
of Lee and of many men with him were hacking out of the wilderness a strip of land along the James River for the founding of an
aristocratic domain. The great river plantations, patented before
Plymouth Rock, became New World baronies on which the fabled
mansions were erected in the early 1700s. Lee's advancing soldiers
moved along high ground to the north of these plantation houses,
the first of which had been a second home to Lee.

This was Shirley, of the dynastic Carter family, where Lee's
mother was born and where he played as a boy and visited with his
own family as an adult. A Carter cousin from Shirley commanded
one of Lee's artillery battalions. Next was Berkeley Hundred, site
of America's first Thanksgiving (1619) and birthplace of President
Harrison, with a river frontage so vast that all of McClellan's army
had camped there in 1862, when its private wharf (called Harrison's
Landing) was converted into the Federal naval base. Next came
Westover, the home of the elegant William Byrd, who had boasted
the largest library in America, and whose red-brick home was the
purest structure of classic Georgian on the continent. Beyond
Westover was Dr. Wilcox's less famous plantation, whose wharf
Grant's vanguard began reaching the middle of the day.

Hill's infantry, supporting the troopers, did not probe far enough
east to establish contact with the enemy's army. Since the summer
of 1862, no Confederate infantry had moved east of Berkeley Plan-

tation in the James River area, because of the exposure to the Union gunboats. However the reconnaissance in force moved far enough from Richmond to satisfy Lee that Grant was not trying a swing around his flank for a move against the capital. Near the river the marshy land was low and the old planters' road, very picturesque with its serpentine course through a wall of vines, was scarcely designed for the weight of armies. Around midday Lee sent a message to Davis, in which he wrote, "I think the enemy must be preparing to move south of the James River."

Leaving only his cavalry out in front, Lee began the concentration of his army at Riddell's Shop, and planned to detach Hoke's division for return to Beauregard. At four o'clock, Lee wrote the President a fuller message, in which he developed his reasons for believing Grant would cross the James. (At that time no Federal troops had crossed.) He advised Davis that he would move his army the next day to Chaffin's Bluff, where the permanent pontoon bridge was maintained to Drewry's Bluff on the south side of the river.

From Richmond the James River flows due south for about eight miles, where it bends sharply to the east before the great loops begin the course generally east. The bridge connecting the river forts at Chaffin's Bluff served as a depot for the passage of the troops by foot. With his army in this area, Lee, as at the North Anna and at Totopotomoi Creek, would be placed in position to move either of two ways — out against Grant, if he came on toward Richmond, or to cross the river.

In the evening of June 14th, before Lee ordered the movement of his troops, his mind was changed by his first messages from Beauregard. Sent at 6:45 and 8:10 in the evening of June 14th, both matter-of-factly relayed information from signalmen. On the day before, the 13th, enemy troop ships and transports had passed the Hampton Roads area, and on the present day a deserter from Butler's army reported that Smith's XVIII Corps had returned to Bermuda Hundred. This accurate information indicated a shift back to action on Butler's sector in the pattern of strikes with which Grant employed secondary forces.

In addition, an observation of pontoon-carriers suggested that pontoons had been transported up the Chickahominy, where

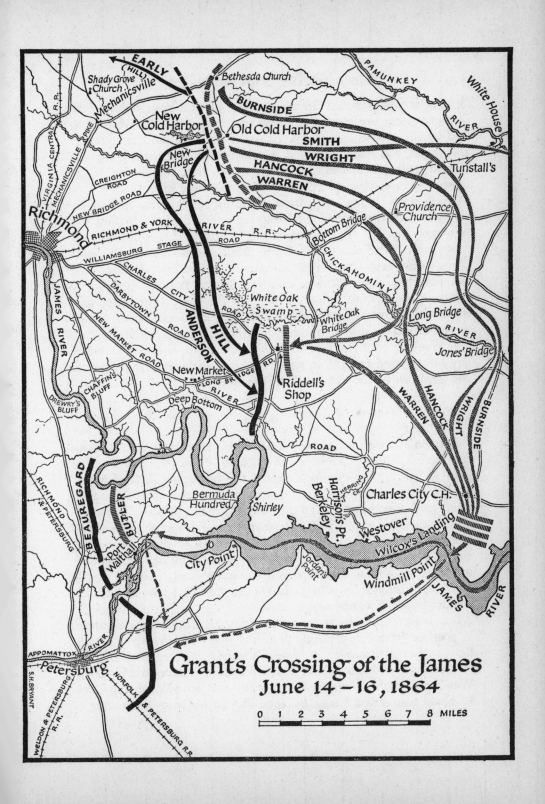

Grant's Crossing of the James
June 14–16, 1864

0 1 2 3 4 5 6 7 8 MILES

bridges would serve in Grant's crossing of that river only. These items together presented the possibility that Grant, like McClellan, had transferred his base across the peninsula from the Pamunkey to the James, and might, after all, not plan to cross to the south side immediately. (At that time, the night of the 14th, only Hancock's II Corps had crossed, and no Confederates anywhere knew this.)

With the possibility suggested by Beauregard's routine messages, Lee withheld the order for shifting his army to Chaffin's Bluff the next morning. If Grant did move on Richmond, Lee would be too close to the fortifications at Chaffin's Bluff. As the return of Smith's corps to Butler's army suggested renewed action on that front, Lee did detach Hoke's division, as planned, and ordered the glory-minded Carolinian to Drewry's Bluff. At the end of the second day of Grant's move away from the Cold Harbor works, Lee's troops were allowed the balm of another quiet night in camp.

It was not until the next morning, June 15th, that Lee received any information from Beauregard concerning the Petersburg front, and this made no mention at all of Grant's army.

4

Captain Paul, of Beauregard's staff, made a personal visit to General Lee's headquarters during the morning of the 15th, and Beauregard, in writing his epic, represented this communication as something of a climactic point in his appeals to Lee. Beauregard attributed to his staff officer knowledge that was not then available. The most significant information which Beauregard did not at the time have himself was that Smith's corps was then south of the Appomattox and Hancock's corps south of the James, both in his department and marching on his fortifications. What Captain Paul's visit did represent was Beauregard's turn to Lee when he failed to get what he wanted from the war office.

Beauregard, continuing to maintain his department as separately as possible from Lee's jurisdiction, had operated directly through Braxton Bragg. From his arrival in Virginia, Beauregard had tried to use the President's Military Adviser as an intercessor. Ignoring War Secretary Seddon as well as Lee, Beauregard seemed to believe he could manipulate Bragg by appealing to his sense of power. It was to "Headquarters, Confederate States Armies" that he had sent his June 9th prediction of Grant's imminent crossing, with an outline of his needs for a defense, and from then until the night of June 14th Beauregard continued to appeal to Bragg for a return of his troops.

Bragg evidently did not wish to intrude on the President over matters pertaining to the shift of troops from one department to another and did not want to brace General Lee directly. As a result, he did nothing. Sharing Davis's dislike of Beauregard, he was inclined to extend him the same type of incivility and simply left the message unanswered. It is also possible that he had ceased to pay attention to Beauregard's unending stream of desperate telegrams.

Since he first began his resistance to releasing troops to Lee, Beauregard had repeatedly alerted the war office to impending crises. As late as the night of June 10th, he wired Bragg: "Information just received that considerable column of the enemy's infantry has crossed this evening to the south side of the Appomattox, indicating another attack on Petersburg. Without immediate reenforcements we shall lose that city or our lines in front of Bermuda Hundred." The next day no further mention was made of this imaginary disaster. When, on June 14th, Bragg received a somewhat more specific telegram from Beauregard, he made no distinction between it and the routine calls for help. Beauregard wired, "Movement of Grant across Chickahominy and increase of Butler's force render my position here critical. Can not my troops sent to Lee be returned at once?"

Though the President's Military Adviser did not acknowledge this message directly, he did wire Beauregard at nine o'clock that night that General Lee had detached Hoke, sending the division to Drewry's Bluff, "with a view to re-enforce you should Petersburg be threatened." Beauregard was not satisfied with this conditional assurance. By the morning of the 15th, certain then that Smith's corps had returned to Butler, he wanted Hoke definitely assigned to him. After all the false alarms he had been sending, Beauregard had grown genuinely apprehensive when, with Grant in motion north of the James River, Smith's corps appeared again on his front. It was, however, only in this generalized apprehension that he sent Captain Paul to appeal to Lee to intercede with the War Department. To buttress his appeal, he sent along pages of figures to prove the weakness of his position.

When Paul appeared at Lee's tent during the morning of the 15th, the General was preoccupied and, with his dislike of paper work, brushed aside the pages of Beauregard's figures. The point of the message was that Beauregard wanted his troops back and Lee had already detached Hoke. Lee sent specific orders for Hoke, waiting at Drewry's Bluff, to be released to Beauregard's orders, and then requested Bragg to send Ransom's relatively large brigade on from the fortifications of the Department of Richmond.

Since Gracie's Alabama brigade had already been moved to strengthen Bushrod Johnson's division at Bermuda Hundred, the Richmond works were denuded of veterans, and Lee also asked Bragg to call out the local defense troops to man the lines. With these orders, Lee met Beauregard's requests promptly in detail.

The figures in Beauregard's department are inexact and the shifting composition of the units confusing. The Confederates agree that Wise's brigade, detached from Johnson's division, fielded twenty-two hundred infantry in the Petersburg fortifications on the 15th, though the Federals, counting all the assorted units, made the figure higher. With Ransom's eighteen hundred returning and the loan of Gracie's brigade of about twelve hundred, Johnson's division (without Wise) would not run less than fifty-five hundred at the Bermuda Hundred lines. With Hoke's six thousand infantry, Beauregard would have at least thirteen and a half thousand infantry in his department, plus odd units, Dearing's cavalry, and a comparatively heavy force of artillery. To Lee, knowing no details, this force, behind powerful fortifications, seemed sufficient for containing the likes of "Beast" Butler.

It is at this stage that Lee becomes so involved in the myth that it is difficult to appraise his actions against the background of information he was known to possess. What was known after the fact, by everyone, was that late in the day of June 15th Smith's corps of Butler's army attacked south of the Appomattox River directly at Petersburg, and his assault struck the works before Hoke arrived after dusk. This brief fight was entirely between troops in Beauregard's department. In his epic he made it appear that this opening action at Petersburg climaxed the gathering of Grant's army on his front, about which he had been sending those "urgent reports" to Lee and which Lee, in his dullness, had ignored.

Beauregard had sent reports, but not about Grant's army and not to Lee. He had repeatedly wired Braxton Bragg that he must have reinforcements or he would be forced to abandon the Bermuda Hundred line in order to hold Petersburg. Bragg included these messages in a batch of telegrams which he sent, without comment, by a courier to Lee's camp at Riddell's Shop. From them, Lee learned only that the "enemy," unidentified, could force Beauregard's lines either at Petersburg or Bermuda Hundred without reinforcements. Without further details, Lee assumed that Hoke's division and Ransom's large brigade would constitute the reinforcements Beauregard requested.

In the messages seen by Lee, *the only reference* Beauregard made to Grant's army on June 15th placed it on the north side of the James River. In what seemed one of his routine cries, Beauregard stated that his position was "more critical than ever" because Grant was at the river crossing of Harrison's Landing. On the day before, A. P. Hill had picked up some prisoners from Warren's V Corps, around Westover, to the east of Berkeley Plantation, and the one certainty of Lee about Grant was that his army was not at Harrison's Landing.

From this the General could have reasoned, as it happened quite rightly, that Beauregard knew less than he about the Army of the Potomac. Obviously it never occurred to Lee that one of Grant's corps, Hancock's, could have spent the day marching sixteen miles in the Petersburg area, to within rifle range of the city's fortifications, without Beauregard being aware of it. And, despite Beauregard's stirring drama written some years later, not one message to anyone indicated his awareness of Hancock's presence on his front on the 15th.

Though this removes Lee from his role as dunce to Beauregard's protagonist, it does not explain his inaction during the day of June 15th. As his cavalry could gain no definite information and Beauregard sent none, he continued to await developments. Any precise information about the Army of the Potomac crossing the James River would have to come from the signal stations, mostly in Beauregard's department. Lee's usual subsidiary reports, from scouts and observant natives, sometimes spies, were all shut off. Considering that he did not even know of Beauregard's late afternoon engagement with Smith's corps at the Petersburg fortifications, he was given no reason to act with any urgency. All accounts of the day reveal a total absence of any emergency calls reaching Lee's headquarters. Colonel Walter Taylor passed the hours writing to his girl, and specifically stated "nothing of importance" was happening.

Yet it seems unlike the Lee of the campaign through Cold Harbor to do nothing on the third day of lack of contact with Grant's army in the midst of the enemy's aggressive offensive. Because General Lee appeared so often to act as if by divination, there might be a tendency to overlook his painstaking analysis of all information, weighed against the factors of terrain and objectives, before he made his deductions. Not once during the campaign, even with his hopes at the Wilderness, did the General commit his army without reasonable certainty of the enemy's direction of movement and intention. On June 15th, his only certainty was that the Army of the Potomac was in camp beyond the obscuring brush somewhere along the river.

During Lee's uncharacteristic inaction during the day of the 15th, it is probable that he reflected something of the apathy with which his soldiers had moved out two days before. With the army he shared an inevitable letdown after the prolonged tension from May 4th to June 3rd, and his own physical vigor had not returned in the breathless heat.

Then, he could not have been immune to the effects of Davis's departmental boundaries, dividing the minds of men with concepts of invisible barriers. When the barrier was a tangible such as the James River, the mental divisions would erect barriers in his thinking. As Lee's area of authority stopped at the James River, he was unquestionably conditioned by his habit of operating within the boundaries of his own department in protecting Richmond. It had been made abundantly clear to the commanding general of the Army of Northern Virginia that coordination between the departments was the responsibility of the commander in chief.

5

President Davis's actions are obscure during the crossing of Grant's army and Beauregard's duplication of Pickett's earlier lonesome defense of Petersburg. Neither he nor Mrs. Davis wrote about this phase at all. Kean, chief of the war bureau, and Jones, the war clerk diarist, mention only the President's chronic personality difficulties.

It is known that the President devoted some time to overriding Secretary of War Seddon on his appointments of hundreds of commissaries and quartermasters. Seddon was an amiable, cooperative gentleman of sound intelligence, high principles and happily possessed of a vastly wealthy wife. Already discontented with the anomalous position into which Bragg had maneuvered him, after the to-do over clerical appointments, the Secretary of War began to complain of the difficulties of getting along with the President.

Then Gorgas, the Pennsylvania genius of ordnance manufacture, was roundly scolded for advancing ordnance officers, which Davis claimed, according to Kean, to be "an invasion of his prerogative in designating persons to be preferred."

On June 13, Davis was reported to be quarreling with the chairman of the Senate military committee. On the same day, Senator Hunter and Senator Wigfall, meeting in Seddon's office, passed the time by making jokes about the commander in chief. Wigfall said the way to beat Grant was easy: "the President would put the old folks and children to praying at 6 o'clock A.M." Nowhere was there any mention of Davis's concerning himself with Grant's crossing of the James.

On June 15th he wrote Lee a letter which is missing from the records, though, judging by Lee's reply, the subject concerned Johnston's army, then retreating closer to Atlanta. Bishop Polk, the lieutenant general whom Lee and Davis had known at West Point, had been killed, and Lee's letter seemed to be an answer to the question of a successor. Tactfully avoiding any suggestions about a corps commander in the army of another general (who had also been with them at the Point), Lee did state that he could not recommend artillery chief Pendleton for such an assignment.

By all evidence, the attention of the commander in chief was not on the Richmond-Petersburg action. It may have been a period when the President was suffering one of his acute attacks of neuralgia or dyspepsia, or the excruciating pains that overindulgence in paper work brought to his one good eye. For whatever reason, in the usual atmosphere of politics and personalities, Davis left departmental co-ordination in charge of his Military Adviser, and Bragg simply shirked the responsibility. As in the previous Pickett crisis (and as he had reacted when in field command), the miscast neurotic became immobilized at the emergency.

Before noon of the 15th, Bragg had received the first of Beauregard's wires which stated the choice of actions confronting him by the approach of Smith's corps directly on Petersburg. "We must now elect between lines of Bermuda Hundred and Petersburg. We can not hold both. Please answer at once."

Obviously Bragg, if he wished to avoid the responsibility of making the decision, should have questioned Davis. Since he did not wish to acknowledge his incapacity, however, Bragg evaded Beauregard's direct question and wired him that Hoke was on the way.

Not to be put off, Old Bory wired back at 1:45 with his question more bluntly stated. "I did not ask your advice with regard to the movement of troops, but wished to know preference between Petersburg and lines across Bermuda Hundred neck, for my guidance, as I fear my present force may prove unequal to hold both." To this Bragg made no reply at all, and Beauregard's succeeding flurry of telegrams reduced him to total inanition.

By nightfall, Beauregard had experienced a hairline escape from his long-threatened disaster, and nothing had saved him except the Federals themselves. Baldy Smith's fight at Cold Harbor must have taken a lot out of his corps, for he advanced so cautiously against the wide stretch of fortifications at Petersburg, defended only by one brigade, that it was dusk before he effected a lodgment. Then he was too timid to move ahead in the falling light, though he could have walked into Petersburg with bands playing.

Hancock, who came up late in the afternoon, would have walked in, but a command breakdown from army headquarters held him in idleness while night fell. As Kautz operated on the flank with his usual ineffectuality, something like forty thousand Federal soldiers failed to take Petersburg against twenty-two hundred infantry and a couple of cavalry regiments.

By then, Beauregard might not know *who* was on his front (in one of his wires to Bragg he suggested the possible presence of Burnside) but he did know there was an awful lot of Yankees. He knew also that Petersburg was the objective, and, though Hoke's division was then on the field, that he would be overwhelmed in the morning without more troops. He did not inform Lee of this. Instead, he informed Bragg that he was going to abandon the line at Bermuda Hundred and move the troops there to Petersburg. Some time after nine o'clock that night he wired Bragg of his decision. "I shall order Johnson [division at Bermuda Hundred] to this point [Petersburg.] General Lee must look to the defenses of Drewry's Bluff and Bermuda Hundred, if practicable."

This was a decision of tremendous importance, as it exposed to Butler's troops the railroad and highway connecting Richmond and Petersburg. Once the enemy occupied these passageways, the two cities would be cut off from one another and Beauregard isolated at Petersburg. When Beauregard withdrew Johnson's divisions from the lines containing Butler during the night of the 15th-16th, with his offhand suggestion that Lee might remedy the damage, he demonstrated the extent of his unwillingness to cooperate with Lee. During that morning, when he wanted Lee to intercede with the war office for the return of troops, he sent a staff officer to the General's headquarters; that night, when he made a move which disrupted the whole defensive system of the Richmond-Petersburg line, he merely appended a line that the telegraph operator would send a copy of the wire to Lee. This was not done.

Because of the confusion caused by the broken connection between the cities, Bragg later opened a court of inquiry to charge Beauregard with dereliction of duty in abandoning the Bermuda Hundred lines. The fame-conscious Creole had meticulously kept a record of every message sent and received, and produced the exchange with the revelation of Bragg's refusal to act. When the anti-Beauregard administration was confronted with this evidence, that was the end of the persecution of Beauregard. As the administration looked after its own, no one inquired why Bragg, ignoring the General's urgent questions, had not at least advised Lee of Beauregard's nine o'clock announcement that he was abandoning the connecting defensive line.

Braxton Bragg, who created a vacuum at the interdepartmental clearinghouse and then shifted the blame to Beauregard, would logically seem to be the villain for Beauregard's romance of his "Defense of Petersburg." But this poor dyspeptic was too obvious as a scapegoat. Besides, Beauregard himself had done nothing wrong with Bragg. Though the reasons for his punctilious operations through the proper channels of Davis's system may have been suspect, his record with the war office was flawless.

With Lee it was different. From the beginning, Beauregard had evaded cooperating with Lee, of whom he was intensely jealous, and he had done a very bad thing in dropping in Lee's lap the problem of restoring abandoned lines, without even an exchange with the General. This was only a single, though the most clear-cut, illustration of Beauregard's consistent efforts to avoid sharing responsibilities with Lee. Having returned to Virginia to regain the glory, Beauregard was determined that the fight for Petersburg should be his alone.

Curiously, with all his fame, Beauregard had never won a battle as field commander of an army. He did many things well in his chosen profession, and his most fanciful strategies always contained some vital insight. In battle he was the opposite of Grant: he was never at the right place at the right time. Beauregard was most remembered for Shiloh, where he was victim of a myth that Albert Sidney Johnston's victory was lost when Old Bory succeeded to command. Petersburg was his chance to win once by himself.

In retrospect he conceived of the role of "Defender of Petersburg" as his distinction in military immortality, and he wrote his epic to fit this concept. In this it would not do at all to explain how Lee had been left in the dark, bypassed whenever possible and confused by contradictory messages. Very sensibly Beauregard did not attempt an explanation of his weird behavior with the commanding general of the other army. He did a shrewder, bolder thing: he rewrote the events to place the general whom he regarded as a rival completely in the wrong, and the skill of his authorship is attested by the endurance of the myth built upon his epic.

His fundamental technique was to make broad generalities as

statements of fact, buttress them with messages carefully selected
out of context, and omit those messages which revealed the actual
course of events. While Beauregard's success as a thematic dramatist
(it might be said he ghost-wrote his own biography) enshrined
him in legend, it has made the actual course of events difficult to
disentangle.

Lee, of course, never explained himself about anything. His staff
officers were as unaware as he of all the "urgent reports" supposedly coming to headquarters. Bragg naturally was reticent about the
whole affair. However, there is one element which Beauregard
overlooked and which has been largely neglected: the complete
exchange of messages came to light many years later.

Incredibly, in view of the usually accepted myth, General Lee
became first involved in any way with Beauregard's trouble south
of the river when he was awakened at two o'clock in the morning
of June 16th to learn that the defense lines between Richmond and
Petersburg had been abandoned.

6

When General Lee was awakened in his tent, at Riddell's Shop,
in the middle of the night, he began his most confusing day as an
army commander. Sitting up on his cot, he read a dispatch sent by
Beauregard at 11:15 P.M., which announced that he had abandoned
the Bermuda Hundred line to concentrate his forces at Petersburg.
He did not say why nor whose threat caused this drastic action.
Furnishing no details, making no inquiries about Lee's front or
Grant's army, he merely said, "Can not these lines be occupied by
your troops? The safety of our communications requires it."

To Lee, in the still darkness of the wooded countryside, there
must have come questions as to why he had heard nothing from
the War Department. Davis, Bragg, Seddon, somebody involved in
the operation of the departmental system must have known before
it happened that the safety of their communications depended upon
holding the lines at Bermuda Hundred. Why did Beauregard inform him after his troops were already withdrawn, when it was
too late for Lee's men to reoccupy the lines before daylight?
And why Lee at all? When two weeks before Lee had asked Beaure-

gard for troops for the Cold Harbor emergency, the commander of the department south of the James had referred him to the war office.

Forced since he assumed command of the army to operate within Davis's system, which controlled the movement even of a brigade, Lee was suddenly confronted with no system at all. The central control had ceased to exist, vanished. Faced with a sudden emergency affecting their whole defense, Lee's only course was to act on his own discretion and hurry some of his troops across the river to the abandoned lines.

The restful interlude for his soldiers came to an abrupt end. Troops were aroused, and the first brigade of Pickett's forty-five-hundred-man division was put on the black road at three in the morning. While headquarters tents were struck, the picketed horses brought up and saddled, Lee ordered Lieutenant General Anderson to follow Pickett and direct the action against Butler. Powell Hill was left in command of the troops stretched from Riddell's Shop to Malvern Hill. While it was still dark, General Lee and his staff started to ride toward the river crossing at Chaffin's Bluff.

Around nine-thirty in the morning of Thursday the 16th, Lee's party reached the high earthen walls at Drewry's Bluff, where the gunners held the U. S. Navy at bay. From its outer fortifications southward, about seven miles across a lightly timbered farm country separated the General from the newly built Fort Dantzler. This was the northern bastion of the abandoned Bermuda Hundred lines, anchored on a great bend in the James River.

Slowly the news reaching Lee outlined a chaotic situation. From Fort Dantzler along its whole length, the Confederate works were occupied by Butler's troops, who had swarmed across the flat country to the turnpike, one mile to the west, and on to the railroad at Chester Station, another two miles west of the turnpike. When Pickett's division made contact with Butler's troops in the area of Chester Station, the enemy occupied the turnpike and was beginning to tear up railroad tracks near Port Walthall Junction.

At one o'clock of the hot day a courier from Dick Anderson brought Lee the news that the enemy was firmly established between Pickett and the Bermuda Hundred lines, and could not be driven. More ominously, the enemy blocked the way between Richmond and Petersburg. Lee hastily dictated an order to hurry Field's division over to help Pickett in reopening communications between the two cities, and then to see about retaking the abandoned lines.

All this concerned only the emergency suddenly dumped on him at Bermuda Hundred. He was at least five hours by courier from his own army on the other side of the river, and no information came to him from his cavalry. By the still-operating telegraph to Petersburg, he could learn nothing definite at all from Beauregard, either about his situation at Petersburg or any information on Grant's army.

As soon as General Lee had reached Drewry's Bluff, he wired Beauregard, at 9:40, that Pickett was on the field and asked for information. "Please inform me of condition of affairs." Lee's first message from Beauregard had been sent at about the same time as his, and the two wires crossed. Beauregard's 9:45 wire read: "The enemy is pressing us in heavy force. Can you not send forward the re-enforcements asked for this morning and send to our assistance the division now occupying the trenches lately evacuated by Johnson's division, replacing it by another division?"

This was one of the most bewildering messages any general received in the war. Manifestly Beauregard had wired him earlier and asked for reinforcements against the unidentified "enemy" pressing him in heavy force. The possibility of more than Smith's corps attacking the Petersburg lines must have occurred to Lee; yet, if Grant's troops were supporting Smith, he would surely expect Beauregard to say so. In choosing between two fronts, the whereabouts of Grant's army was the one essential element required before Lee could act.

Beyond that, Beauregard blandly assumed that a division *had* reoccupied the lines he abandoned and showed his ignorance of Butler's position across the lines of communication. Then, making no inquiry about the conditions Lee faced, he asked for another division from the Army of Northern Virginia, so that the first could be sent on to the undefined situation at Petersburg. When Lee read these airy assumptions about a stable front at Bermuda Hundred, he had already ordered over the second division to clear the blocked passageway. To get another division to Petersburg, in answer to

Beauregard's sudden request for reinforcements, Lee would be forced to commit half his army to the south side of the river, when he knew nothing of what was actually happening at Petersburg.

In hurrying off a brief reply to Beauregard's message, Lee stated only the essentials and eliminated all the details of troop disposition. He wired: "Your dispatch of 9:45 received. It is the first that has come to hand. I do not know the position of Grant's Army and can not strip north bank of James. Have you not force sufficient?"

In Beauregard's epic, this key message in their exchange was omitted, along with Lee's first telegram sent from Drewry's Bluff which requested information on the "condition of affairs." These messages reveal that Lee had not been informed by Beauregard of the whereabouts of Grant's army or the conditions at Petersburg. These two carefully omitted telegrams pull the rug from under the myth of Beauregard's "urgent reports" that he was fighting Grant's whole army. Beauregard also omitted his reply, sent to Lee just before one o'clock, in which he said, "We may have sufficient force to hold Petersburg." There is certainly nothing "urgent" in this.

In Beauregard's rearrangement of the exchanges, he published a 7:45 A.M. telegram of his which he knew Lee had not received. In that telegram, containing his first request for reinforcements, he mentioned that a Federal prisoner belonged to Hancock's II Corps. Yet, in writing about this undelivered 7:45 telegram, in which he mentioned to Lee for the first time the presence of a soldier from Grant's army on his front, Beauregard wrote that he sent that wire "through a sense of duty," thus implying that by the morning of the 16th he despaired of achieving anything through Lee. Then, suppressing the wire from Lee which stated that the 9:45 telegram was the first he had received, Beauregard wrote that "No direct answer was received" to his 7:45 telegram.

Even this did not constitute the extent of Beauregard's distortion of the events in his effort to conceal his own confused behavior by constructing a case against Lee. In his flurry of disconnected telegrams sent to Lee at Drewry's Bluff during June 16th, Beauregard included a routine message which reported that signalmen had counted forty-seven enemy transports on the river through June 15th.

To this Lee replied during the afternoon, "The transports you mention have probably returned Butler's troops. Has Grant been seen crossing the James River?"

On this telegram, Beauregard built the summation which has been followed by his admirers: "This shows that Lee was still uncertain as to his adversary's movements, and, notwithstanding the information I had already furnished him, could not realize that the Federals had crossed the James and that three of their corps were actually assaulting the Petersburg line."

Here the shrewd Creole cleverly interwove a factual statement ("Lee was still uncertain") with a total untruth ("notwithstanding the information I had already furnished him") to arrive at a convincing conclusion about Lee's state of mind ("Lee could not realize").

There is no doubt that Lee was still uncertain, as he was constantly trying to obtain information from Beauregard. But his telegram, within the context of their correspondence, "shows" nothing else. Lee acknowledged Beauregard's information about the transports by stating, correctly, that they had returned Butler's troops. Since both he and Beauregard knew by then that Smith's XVIII Corps had returned to Butler, Lee dismissed this item about Butler and turned to the pressing point. "Has Grant been seen crossing the James River?"

The foundation of Beauregard's generalities would have to rest on his answer to this direct question, sent in midafternoon of June 16th. His answer, sent at seven in the evening, reads ". . . No information yet received of Grant's crossing James River. Hancock's and Smith's Corps are however in our front."

These words of his own were omitted from his romance of "The Defense of Petersburg." But this message, as received by Lee, reveals the falseness of Beauregard's statement about "the information I had already furnished him," and about "three of their corps" then "assaulting the Petersburg line." Two corps of the Army of the Potomac, Hancock's and Burnside's, in fact were combined in the assault with Smith's corps on the 16th, but Beauregard's wire shows that *he* did not know it then.

7

Beauregard's most significant omission (perhaps because it was the guiltiest point) was the fact that during these exchanges one third of Lee's army was fighting in his department to clean up the mess he had left at Bermuda Hundred. There was no question that Beauregard acted soundly, when Bragg remained silent, in evacuating those lines in order to concentrate his forces at Petersburg; but he could not have failed to recognize that his way of doing it, as he related to Lee, caused the needless emergency action. Because of this omission, to this day the impression remains that Lee's "whole army," with its image of a vast host, passed the days in futile desuetude in their camp north of the James River, while Beauregard fought off "Grant's whole army" at Petersburg.

On the contrary, to the survivors of the old First Corps, the fight with Butler's troops on June 16th for the turnpike represented a hard action. Field's division numbered only three thousand men to join Pickett's forty-five hundred in the battle to drive "Beast" Butler back to his cage.

Field came up during the afternoon and by nightfall the two divisions had, at least temporarily, reopened the way between Beauregard and Richmond. Pickett's men, marching out at three o'clock in the morning, fought on until eleven that night to reach the main Confederate line across Bermuda Hundred. However small the scale, by numbers engaged, this was a battle Lee had to win and it represented a joint action in Beauregard's department.

The engagement of Anderson's two divisions occupied Lee's mind when at half-past seven he wrote the commander in chief of what was happening. Despite the collapse of the center of the departmental system, the General continued the formality of reporting to the President, though he opened the letter by stating that he had first heard of the abandoned lines at "2 A.M." He mentioned almost in passing that he had "not learned from General Beauregard what force is opposed to him in Petersburg, or received any definite account of operations there, nor have I learned if any portion of Grant's Army is opposed to him."

It was after he had dispatched his letter to Jefferson Davis that

Lee received Beauregard's seven o'clock message stating that Hancock's corps, as well as Smith's, was on his front. Removed from the coloration and emphases of Beauregard's artful rearrangement, his telegrams as received by Lee were amiable, almost casual in tone, and through June 16th lacked any of the urgency which perpetuators of the myth have described (apparently without reading the messages). Beauregard's summation of the fighting for June 16th read: "There has been some fighting today without result. Have selected a new line of defences around the city, which will be occupied tomorrow, and hope to make it stronger than the first." Then, stating that "no satisfactory information yet received of Grant's crossing James River," he mentioned that Hancock was "in our front."

Here Lee was presented with an exercise in his deductive powers. Did the presence of Hancock's corps, fighting with Smith's corps of Butler's army, indicate that Grant had crossed his whole army over the James? As early as midday of the 14th, he had written Davis at length on his reasons for believing that Grant intended to cross the James. Yet a dangerous gap existed between expecting what Grant would do and knowing what Grant was doing, when Richmond was the stake of a wrong guess.

As none of Lee's critics have pointed out, there was nothing to prevent Grant from dividing his army. McClellan had sent part of his army south of the river from Harrison's Landing two years before. After all, Butler's army, with Smith, outnumbered Beauregard's forces, even with Hoke and Ransom, and it scarcely seemed necessary to use all of one hundred thousand additional troops to take a position from less than fifteen thousand men. The presence of Hancock's corps could mean no more than reinforcements for Butler's army, as Smith had reinforced Grant at Cold Harbor. Without more certainty than the presence of one corps from Grant's army at Petersburg, Lee could not leave Richmond unprotected.

In front of Lee's troops north of the James, the enemy had never grown silent. When Lee had drawn in his reconnoitering forces, the blue cavalry pushed forward in the concealing brush, caused alarms with limited forays, and always some apprehensive officer reported that enemy infantry was advancing. Though Lee's habitual apprehension over the capital may have contributed to the dampening of any sparks of divination, with the information he possessed, nothing short of divination would have justified his abandonment of Richmond in the presence of an enemy. If all regulars joined him on the south side of the river, a cavalry force could rush into the city.

On the night of the 16th, he had ordered Kershaw's division of the First Corps moved to the pontoon bridge at Chaffin's Bluff, ready to cross on the first definite information. With Kershaw detached, that left outside the fortifications only A. P. Hill's corps of fifteen thousand infantry, some artillery, and two slim cavalry brigades. The combined force numbered less than one Federal corps, and three Federal corps were unaccounted for, plus the cavalry division that operated actively through the day of the 16th.

After it was over, all Confederates knew that Burnside as well as Hancock had fought Beauregard on the 16th, and that Warren's V Corps crossed the river during the day and marched that night from Windmill Point almost to Beauregard's lines. Because of Beauregard's false generalities, it has been assumed that Lee could not be convinced of the presence of these three corps outside Petersburg. What Beauregard concealed was his primitive intelligence system which permitted all this enemy activity to pass unobserved in his sector. Lee, stranded at Drewry's Bluff, certainly never considered the possibility that three fourths of Grant's army could be in action, or movement, at Petersburg without Beauregard being aware of it.

Though the hot June days of the 15th and 16th do not represent inspired action by the worn, prematurely aging man, considering the information he possessed and his unwillingness to expose Richmond, it is difficult to perceive what else he could have done.

8

From his headquarters at Drewry's Bluff, isolated from half his army, General Lee began the day of the 17th with his by then habitual request of information. At six in the morning he wired Beauregard that "I am now cut off from all information," and asked, "Can you ascertain anything of Grant's movements?" To this Beauregard replied at nine o'clock: "Enemy has two corps in my front. Nothing yet positive known of Grant's movements." Then, with no mention of pressing dangers, he added, "Could I not be sufficiently reinforced to take the offensive [and] thus rid of the enemy here?"

As Beauregard on the night before had mentioned that Smith, of Butler's army, and Hancock comprised the two corps on his front, Lee assumed that the two corps in Beauregard's front on the 17th were the same as the night before. Since these two corps presented so little menace to the Petersburg fortifications that Beauregard suggested driving them away, there was nothing to indicate to Lee that Grant's full army had crossed the river.

It was the fifth day since Grant left Cold Harbor, and this represented a long time for Grant to be quiet. Lee had believed from the first that Petersburg was the objective; yet Beauregard reported "nothing yet positive known of Grant's movements." Until something positive was known, Lee could only wait at his transient headquarters at Drewry's Bluff. As for sending reinforcements for the purpose of taking the offensive, Lee replied, "Until I can get more definite information of Grant's movements, I do not think it prudent to draw more troops to this side of the river."

In writing of this exchange, Beauregard omitted his telegram (which Lee was answering) and used Lee's reply out of context to substantiate an outright lie. In fact, it was on the situation as of the morning of the 17th that Beauregard told the Big Lie which made the myth. He wrote, "I had failed to convince its [Army of Northern Virginia's] distinguished commander that I was fighting Grant's whole army. . . . There was no reason to hope for assistance of any kind. The Army of Northern Virginia was yet far distant."

At that time, one third of the Army of Northern Virginia was fighting on his front for the second day. In battling to retake all positions of the Bermuda Hundred line, Pickett's division assaulted with one final flare-up of its lost glory. The rebuilt brigades had then been together for several weeks. Shaken down by the Cold Harbor campaign, the unit took up where it left off at Gettysburg, and this time their charge carried all the way. The lines abandoned by Beauregard had been restored, and this won something of a desperate race.

The day before, Grant, on learning that Butler had broken out and was across the line of communications between the two cities, had sent two divisions of Wright's VI Corps to support Butler in holding the passageways. That morning, the 17th, part of Smith's corps was pulled out of line at Petersburg and sent back to Bermuda Hundred. Pickett, with the support of Field, re-established the strongly built lines before this heavy force could be fully deployed. This was fairly crucial action omitted from Beauregard's romance.

Probably Beauregard's most significant omission for June 17th was his telegram to Lee, asking if the commander of the Army of Northern Virginia knew the whereabouts of Warren's V Corps. It was fighting Beauregard.

With Hancock, Burnside and Warren operating on his front during the 17th, Beauregard was then facing three fourths of Grant's army. In the actual fighting, Beauregard was magnificent. Always a brave soldier, he directed the troops in the fortifications with a resourceful skill that never faltered.

Petersburg was on the south bank of the Appomattox River and, with this as a northern flank, powerful works in depth almost enclosed the city. Though the fortifications extended for ten miles, most of the Federal assaults were delivered on the three miles which faced to the east. Beauregard concentrated his fourteen thousand infantrymen in these sections under attack, with guns of all descriptions firing from high-walled emplacements. As nearly always the Confederate artillery was well served, though the old stationary guns were captured whenever a redoubt was overrun.

The odd collection of troops, many of them garrison regiments, had served together only since their gathering in Virginia in mid-May, and in maneuver little concert of action could have been demanded of the units. What was demanded was heroism, and no troops anywhere in the war stood their ground more steadfastly. Against successive waves which threatened to engulf them, the men refused to break.

The lines were not overrun by sheer weight of numbers because the attacks were disjointed. Cold Harbor, as climax to a month of slaughtering without winning a single decision, had for the time being crushed the offensive spirit in the Army of the Potomac. Never before had a major Federal force in Virginia delivered such poorly organized and feebly pressed assaults.

Even so, against any widening break or weakening resistance, the masses would have rolled on momentum alone. But the breeches made were quickly plugged and no unit, not even a company, was shaken in its determination. A single spirit seemed to pervade the lines. To Beauregard, this was as great an hour as he could have dreamed of. His courageous stand was unsurpassed in the war.

With his poor intelligence service supplying no information as to the enemy's identification, Beauregard probably gave little thought to whom he was fighting. His fragmentary and contradictory messages to Lee revealed his excitement. Under the circumstances, his unhelpfulness to Lee was understandable. At half-past three, after having sent Lee two wires in which he mentioned reinforcements for the purpose of taking the offensive, the enormity of the gathering enemy suddenly caused him to reverse his position. He wired Lee that he needed "reinforcements to resist such large odds as are against us. The enemy must be dislodged or the city will fall."

9

When it was all over, and he looked back on his performance, Beauregard wanted to be all hero. He wanted nothing on his carefully cherished record to show that in the battle action he grew agitated, and confused the General to whom he called on for help. So he took out of context a wire Lee sent from Drewry's Bluff to his son, Rooney, at Malvern Hill, immediately upon receipt of Beauregard's sudden threat of disaster. "Push after the enemy and ascertain what has become of Grant's Army."

Removed from its background, this message could certainly sound like the piteous appeal of a bewildered general, and Grant's admirers, going along with Beauregard's myth, have made the most of it. As the legend has it, there was Lee at headquarters at Riddell's Shop, surrounded by the supine Army of Northern Virginia in its full strength, crying helplessly, "What *has* become of Grant?"

When Lee sent his wire from Drewry's Bluff, his two cavalry brigades (no larger than 1862 regiments) were screening Hill's corps of fifteen thousand, all of the army remaining in the Riddell's Shop area. As the troopers carried too little weight to press effectively against the enemy cavalry, Lee had been husbanding their

strength. When Beauregard's three-thirty wire entered a new note
of desperation, but still gave no information, Lee's wire to his out-
sized son constituted an order to "push after the enemy" — that
is, to force a reconnaissance regardless of the cost.

At that time, the north bank of the James was at last cleared of
the enemy, but General Lee had no way of knowing this. The last
of the Federal infantry had not crossed until the night before, the
16th. Wilson's active cavalry division had withdrawn from A. P.
Hill's front after dark of the 16th and abandoned Wilcox's Landing
at midnight.

On the morning of the 17th Rooney Lee, encountering no enemy
on his front, had moved reconnoitering parties forward through the
brushy country to the east. When the parties reached Dr. Wilcox's
abandoned landing, the information was then immediately dispatched for General Lee. But the cavalry messenger had first to return fifteen miles to the river crossing at Chaffin's Bluff, from where
a courier started for Lee's headquarters at Drewry's Bluff. The
courier was on his way when Lee dispatched the three-thirty message to his son.

Before the courier reached General Lee, another telegram from
Beauregard was delivered to him at four-thirty. This was the first
wire from Beauregard which mentioned more than Smith's and
Hancock's corps on his front, and this was very general. A native
had told Dearing, the cavalry brigadier, that a large number of Federal troops had been crossing the James River, and "a Yankee soldier boy" had boasted to some civilians that thirty thousand troops
were marching from the river to join their fellows at Petersburg.
On these unreliable sources and the indefiniteness of the information, Lee began the shift of the rest of his army to the south side.
Kershaw's division was ordered to cross over from Chaffin's Bluff,
and Powell Hill was ordered to move his corps to Chaffin's Bluff,
ready to cross over.

Early that night, June 17th, General Lee received a telegram from
Beauregard which stated that prisoners taken belonged to the II and
IX Corps, and that captured Federals reported that the V and VI
Corps were coming up. This information was not accurate. War-
ren's V Corps, up at midnight on the 16th, had been fighting during
the day, while most of Wright's VI Corps had been diverted to

Bermuda Hundred in the battle for the abandoned lines. It was curious that the corps identification was made so slowly and inaccurately, as Federal troops wore the identifying badge of their corps, and every Confederate soldier probably recognized the Maltese cross that identified the V Corps.

After nearly one century of a persuasive myth, endlessly repeated in print, it is difficult to accept the undramatic fact that it was at the end of the fifth day after Grant withdrew from the Cold Harbor lines that Beauregard first informed Lee, and then inaccurately, of the presence of units of "Grant's whole army" on his front.

At ten o'clock on the night of the 17th, adhering to his latest line of impending disaster, Beauregard sent a wire stating that he would be forced to evacuate Petersburg without reinforcements. These last messages were "urgent reports," and Lee responded immediately. Kershaw, already on the south side, was ordered to hurry forward to Petersburg to report to Beauregard in the morning. Orders went to A. P. Hill, pausing at Chaffin's Bluff, to make a night crossing of the river and continue by the Petersburg Pike in a forced march. With the Bermuda Hundred line firmly secured again, Lee planned to move out Field's brigade-sized division and start these First Corps veterans on after Kershaw. In that division, the famous Texas Brigade, which John Gregg had led so dramatically at the Wilderness, numbered only 435 officers and men.

As an anticlimax, after Lee made these dispositions in response to something definite from Beauregard, Captain Chisholm of Beauregard's staff visited Lee's headquarters. He supplied the General with the first details Lee had received of the three-day action at Petersburg. By then Old Bory, with some certainty himself of the enemy force opposing him, sent two more staff officers to present his cause to Lee. One of them was Major Giles Cooke, probably selected because he had roomed with Colonel Walter Taylor at V.M.I. and, through his friend, could get to the General.

All this was unnecessary. Yet, though Beauregard had sent no one near Lee since Captain Paul received assurance of his requested reinforcements on the morning of the 15th, the last two staff officers entered the legend as applying the final pressure on the adamant Old Man.

All Lee's orders had been sent before the young men arrived. The ultimate result of Major Cooke's trip was that he asked Walter Taylor to assist him in getting transferred to Lee's staff. This his fellow Virginian did, and Major Cooke lived to become the last surviving member of Lee's staff.

After the excited staff officers had departed, savoring their moment with history, the General retired to his cot for some sleep before an early morning start for Petersburg. Though Beauregard had never asked General Lee to join him, where his army went, he was going too.

10

In this second emergency at Petersburg, the departmental system in the Richmond area at last vanished, as it were, by common consent. This did not shake the total structure of Davis's departments in what remained of the Confederacy, but Petersburg was lost to Beauregard as the First Military District of the Department of Southern Virginia and North Carolina. Now, with its homes in the range of Grant's heavier guns, the junction city became included in Lee's area of responsibility. This was the eventuality Beauregard had feared from his first apprehensions for the safety of his front and which, to the end, he tried to circumvent.

During the frantic calls of the 16th and 17th, all he asked of Lee was "reinforcements" — or, bluntly, Lee's own troops, to be sent to an unknown situation. Even in his drama of Petersburg, Beauregard unconsciously revealed that he never asked any cooperation on the total problem. All he ever asked was for the General to send him his army. The last thing he wanted around Petersburg was General Lee in person.

It is commonplace in the history of warfare for generals to seek the troops of their allies without the accompanying presence of the troops' commander. The French and British tried it with the Americans in World War I, and the British again in World War II. When Lee petitioned Beauregard for a combination in late May, to avoid any suggestion of this, he punctiliously requested Beauregard to lead his own troops as a wing in a joint action, and went so far as to ask Beauregard to name the place of his convenience. Had

Beauregard felt Davis was supporting him, judging from his own earlier suggestions, he would then have welcomed a combination. But Lee's coming into his department was something else. Recognizing his place in the commander in chief's hierarchy, Old Bory knew that when the gray Old Man came riding up on his gray horse, full General P. G. T. Beauregard became only second in command.

Before General Lee came the first of his famed soldiers. Kershaw's veterans of McLaws's old First Corps division arrived on the field at half-past seven in the morning of the 18th.

The men with Beauregard, making a withdrawal during the night, had fallen back nearly half a mile to a position where the engineers had traced a new line closer to the city. All night the soldiers had dug to throw up crude new works. These were no more than plain trenches, primitive protection from bullets from an enemy infantry advancing straight ahead. Had the Federals' "grand assault" moved on schedule, the three corps would have experienced little trouble in rolling over such obstacles before Kershaw's division arrived.

For the fourth day every combination of Grant's troops sputtered and faltered. The jaded Union soldiers, discouraged at finding those inevitable works in their path, had been momentarily cheered when they first entered the abandoned lines they had attacked for three days. But, on finding their unshakable enemy waiting for them half a mile farther on, the units never regained their momentum in any unison. By the time the blue groups re-formed, to begin their series of disjointed advances, Kershaw's brigades were deploying under their red battle flags. The exhausted men at the mounds of freshly turned earth did not need the regimental battle flags to recognize their own in the gaunt, hairy faces shaded by floppy hats. Johnson's division tried to raised a quavering cheer of greeting, but most of the men wept in relief.

As Bushrod Johnson's half-dazed soldiers staggered out, Kershaw's men, relatively fresh in comparison, fitted themselves behind the loose earth, fixed bayonets, and slid their shiny rifles across the top of the trench. Gun batteries from Porter Alexander's First Corps artillery rolled into line, with a creaking of swab buckets and a clanging of chains. As with the race which opened the campaign at Spotsylvania, Kershaw's brigades were ready when the enemy came on, and the battle for Petersburg was over when their rifles began to crackle.

At nine-thirty their right was strengthened by Field's division, scarcely more than three thousand survivors of the once great assault unit of John Hood, with the remnants of the old Texas brigade as fierce as when they charged up Gaines's Mill in another June two years before. Behind them Hill's three divisions were strung out for miles on the Petersburg Pike, the men choking with the dust and the sick falling out of line with the heat.

They were not needed. The spasmodic attacks continued into the afternoon, at spots striking strongly for one drive, but no coordination existed between the Federal units and there was no conviction in the assault. Meade stated flatly that "the moral condition of the army" could not support another offensive. The troops were finished by their own hammering campaign.

When General Lee rode onto the field at eleven-thirty, the issue was no longer in doubt. Beauregard greeted him most cordially. The Creole was proud of the line extemporized by his engineers, and escorted Lee outside the city to a position from which he could survey the lines of fresh mounds. Built on the chord of the arc of the innermost original fortifications, the quickly dug trenches followed the natural roll of the ground and were well drawn. These lines, under Lee's direction, would be developed into an intricate system which came to be called "The Trenches," and remained as a line of defense to the end of the war.

As soon as Beauregard obtained the former engineer's approval of the trenches, he turned to the subject of a joint action, or so he said. Lee never referred to the proposal. According to Beauregard, he proposed that when Lee's army came up, "our entire disposable force be thrown upon the left and rear of the Federal Army before it began to fortify its position." General Lee, "after some hesitation," rejected the plan on the grounds that his men needed rest.

If this was a true account, Lee probably hesitated in order to think of some tactful reason for rejecting such a harebrained scheme. Nothing could seem more absurd than for an exhausted force of twenty-two thousand men before casualties, with Bushrod Johnson's division too done in to occupy lines, to attempt to succeed at an assault over the same ground on which upwards of eighty thousand Federals were then failing. Yet, even to the end, Beauregard falsified the conditions in contrasting his inspired hour with Lee's dullness. "I urged that the Federal troops were at least as much exhausted as ours," he reported, with the clear implication that Lee's full army was gathered on the field at noon.

Hill's corps, covering more than twenty miles under a brutal sun, did not begin to come up until dusk and it was late at night when the end of the column reached Petersburg, heavily drained by stragglers who were simply unable to keep up. A survivor of the dusty march remembered the "water was so scarce that men fairly fought each other at every well we reached. . . . Regiments melted down to the dimension of companies and . . . a brigade would stretch for miles."

Though the exact hour when the Federals began to fortify their position was not given, according to their own reports lines were built long before the first of Hill's troops were given a lift on some railroad cars for the last few miles and reached the city before night. During the midday hours when the Federal army was supposedly exposed to a counterattack on their left, Hoke's division, closest to the river, was pinned down by Burnside's corps of the Federal right, with two divisions "established" (dug in) within one hundred yards of the main line of the Confederates.

Ignoring these factual details, Beauregard closed his epic by leaving the impression that his men, on the point of evacuating the city before the eight thousand of "Lee's army" arrived, were prevented from inflicting destruction upon the enemy only by the caution of the General who overruled him. "But I was then only second in command," he said, leaving posterity to draw its own conclusions.

Beauregard's effort to avoid his status contributed as much as any single factor to the confusion of the four days' defense, and his literary effort, designed to demonstrate the injustice of this status, has contributed to the enduring confusion of this last maneuver of the war in Virginia.

I I

Contrary to the existing views on the crossing of the James River, there was relatively little generalship involved for a comparative study between the three principals.

Grant's maneuver, a repetition of his earlier moves, was basically a vigorously executed troop movement in which his army expertly used all the technical and supporting services at their command. By chance, he moved into an area of a Confederate vacuum of command. In the departmental system, as no provision had been made for the half-mile of the James River, Grant's pontoon bridge entered an undepartmentalized area, unmarked on the charts. Bragg, the coordinator of the two departments divided by this boundary, simply quit and left the two generals to work out their conflicts as they might.

Beauregard's behavior with Lee was egocentric, unstable and devoid of judgment. Motivated by his unarticulated purpose of getting troops from Lee's army without involving Lee personally, he assumed no part in responsibility for the total problem, gave little to no definite information on his own, changed his attitudes and demands from hour to hour, went from proposals of counteroffensives to threats of evacuation, and never evaluated the military situation either to himself or to Lee. It is incomprehensible that he could not identify the units of troops attacking his entrenchments nor locate the whereabouts of any army that for three days was marching over a sixteen-mile road from the river to his lines.

When it is considered that Lee located Grant in the unfamiliar brushy country of the Totopotomoi before the quick crossing of the Pamunkey was completed, he would certainly doubt that Federal corps could be camped in another general's permanent front without that general knowing it. The most consistent line in Beauregard's variable messages was that the enemy was gathering, but troops of Butler's army were his only positive identification until the night of the 16th, when he identified one of Grant's corps, Hancock's. Yet even the next day, to the direct question of "do you *know* that Grant has crossed the river," the answer was "no." He had not established the whereabouts of Grant's army on his own front.

With this indefiniteness from the general on the field, who held no consistent viewpoint about his own situation, it would seem that Lee would be foolish to renounce his responsibility to defend Richmond and send off his army to a man who had been sounding alarms for the past month.

Though Lee could scarcely have acted any differently with Beauregard, he certainly did not act as he did when in command of the situation himself. The final point is that Lee was not in command. Beauregard and Bragg were products of the bureaucratic system and, when those parts of the system failed, Lee, with no authority beyond his own army, was caught between Beauregard's incoherence and Bragg's inanition.

While the operation was not among Lee's inspired actions, displaying nothing of that intuitive quality of genius, under the conditions imposed on him he calculated coldly, if deliberately, and never lost his poise or his patience. Because there was nothing else he could do — short of risking Richmond on a stroke of divination — Grant was able to complete his hurried maneuver during this hiatus in Confederate command.

Yet Grant was able to do nothing with the opportunity, and for a very simple reason. He had not anticipated the breakdown in the system which, in that instance, controlled Lee as the system had controlled the Confederate generals whom Grant met in the West. Grant expected Lee to shift over to meet him, as Lee had all the way from the Wilderness, and he staked the success of his move on its speed. The result of forced marches on tired troops in low spirits was to bring them on the field in no condition to exploit the unexpected Confederate lapse. The Federals pointed to one of their organizational breakdowns, another *if*, to explain the failure at Petersburg. Grant's hammering worked both ways and they all felt the strain.

If Grant had used imagination or boldness, two corps of infantry held north of the James, if no more than demonstrating, would have chained most if not all of Lee's twenty-eight thousand infantry to Richmond. Nor was there any logical reason for the combined attack of Hancock and Smith to be so hurried on the 15th that the two corps could not act in unison. There was a frantic element about the rush to get to Petersburg before Lee. Only the mechanics were well planned.

In abandoning the attempt to take Richmond directly, or to destroy its supply sources north of the James, Grant's purpose in the move to Petersburg was to isolate Richmond from the South in order to maneuver Lee's army into fighting on unfavorable conditions — or conditions not of Lee's choice. In this he was no more successful than from the Wilderness to Cold Harbor. As his efforts to isolate Richmond from its supply sources either north or south of the James were an outgrowth of his failure to capture the capital and/or to defeat Lee's army, Grant's campaign of maneuver in Virginia was a military failure. He had achieved none of his intentions, neither those with which he began nor those he improvised along the way.

In operating against the supply system of Richmond as a substitute for his original intention ("I will . . . operate directly against Lee's Army wherever it may be found") Grant's rush to get to Petersburg first with many times "the most" lost ten thousand more men, only to settle for an end he could have achieved without a single casualty — establishment of a siege. In this last movement of the campaign of maneuver, Grant's total losses more than surpassed the number of men of all arms with which Lee began the campaign.

Grant, whatever rationalization he later made and however events in other sectors appeared to support him, tacitly accepted his failure to achieve his self-selected assignment in Virginia. Though summer had three months to run, the hammerer abandoned "the line" on which he had resolved to "fight it out."

In this, the Federal commander in chief had no choice. Grant had eviscerated the army he inherited. The flower of the Army of the Potomac was gone, with unenthusiastic recruits filling the places of the veterans. No experienced soldier could have observed the army's dispirited floundering before the lightly manned Petersburg entrenchments and hoped for military victory in the field.

Swinton, the army's historian, wrote, "There was at this time great danger of the collapse of the war. Had not success come elsewhere to brighten the horizon, it would have been difficult to raise new forces to recruit the Army of the Potomac, which, shaken in its structure, its valor quenched in blood, and thousands of its ablest officers killed and wounded, was the Army of the Potomac no more."

This was Lee's achievement. Perhaps, all things considered, this last campaign was his greatest achievement. Certainly he never fought against such heavy odds nor under such crippling restrictions. At no time in the war were Lee's operations as seriously hurt by his lack of authority over his own area of the Confederacy.

Yet at the end of the campaign, despite all that he achieved under the conditions, it was not enough. The combination of Grant and the system proved too much for him. As with Grant, Lee had failed of his purpose. He failed to maintain a war of maneuver.

When he stood with Beauregard and looked at the new lines that were to become "The Trenches" in front of Petersburg, while the Creole uttered his vaporings about a counterassault, Lee must have looked at the lines the enemy was digging. For those works also were to be expanded into the Federal trenches, which faced, and loosely embraced, the Confederate lines around Petersburg until the end of the war. In one glimpse, General Lee viewed the end of maneuver and the beginning of the end.

I 2

Before Grant left the Cold Harbor lines, Lee had told Jubal Early, "We must destroy this army of Grant's before he gets to the James River. If he gets there, it will become a siege, and then it will be a mere question of time."

Lee was thinking in desperation when he talked of destroying Grant's army. He lacked the force for that, and such as remained was as drained of offensive potential as the Army of the Potomac. But he looked realities squarely in the face when he predicted the consequences of a siege.

In terms of generalship, Lee and Grant had done all they could, and the result was a stalemate. The decision of the war passed from their armies to other factors. The basic factor was starvation. The Federals had come full circle round to the plan advocated by the old Virginian, General Winfield Scott, commander in chief of the Union forces at the beginning. Though the details of applying starvation as a weapon were quite different from those Scott advanced in the innocent days of internecine war, the fact that one opponent could decide on starvation as a weapon placed the final test between the countries supporting the two armies.

In its effect on the final decision, the campaign achieved nothing for either side. If the situation was changed at all, "the mournful losses of life" in the Federal forces, to no immediate purpose, could increase the chances of a peace party at the polls in the Union. This potential effect, of course, depended on the ability of the Confederates on other fronts also to maintain stalemates into the November elections.

This was out of Lee's hands. Lee's problem was of a more personal nature. He must summon the inner strength to serve truly as a leader in a military impasse which he believed to be foredoomed.

The only escape from his situation was the abandonment of Richmond for a concentration farther to the south that would place his forces closer to sources of supply and remove Grant from the well-stocked naval bases on Virginia's rivers. Politically this may have been as disastrous as the fall of the city; anyway, the President would not hear of it. The once mobile Army of Northern Virginia must end its days withstanding a siege on a twenty-six-mile front, reaching from the swamps east of Richmond to the hot stretches south of Petersburg.

For Lee there would be no more riding along lines of his marching tatterdemalions, with the echoes of Stonewall Jackson's grim "Close up, men, close up," nor of Jeb Stuart's joyous "Follow me." He would be riding Traveler along lines of freshly turned earth, where his emaciated men sweated themselves faint in throwing up ever-lengthening works. The officers outside brigade headquarters tents were little known to him, some strangers. Of those who had campaigned with Lee, there were more ghosts than men at Petersburg.

Of the generals who had been prominent in his plans when he built the Army of Northern Virginia in another June, two years before, only A. P. Hill was left. Now his Third Corps, the makeshift little more than a year old, was the dependable force of the army. Hill had created an *esprit* in the three divisions, with their superb artillery, which made them the one entity then campaigning in the tradition of the army as its fame was won.

Hill achieved this morale by an intuitive understanding of the citizen-soldier combined with constant solicitude for his rights and comforts. The General visited his field hospitals to look after the sick and wounded, gave his personal attention to the operation of all the supporting services, and made himself available to any private soldier in his corps. He worked ceaselessly to develop his amateurs into capable officers, always talking to them privately. Though Hill was known to have torn an officer's insignia off his jacket when the man showed cowardice in front of troops, he never rebuked an officer for a mistake before others. These personal methods were exhausting and, with his undiagnosed illness, the vital energies of Powell Hill were ebbing. One of the men who loved him mentioned, without details, how much he suffered physically at Petersburg. Yet he rode as gracefully as ever, a familiar figure in his single-breasted shell-jacket and black slouch hat, accompanied only by one staff officer or a courier.

General Lee was fond of the warmly courteous soldier and respected the quality in him which his friends so often referred to as "chivalrous." They said of Hill, "In all his career he never advanced a claim or maintained a rivalry. The soul of honor and generosity, he was ever engaged in representing the merits of others." Yet Hill never had been a confidant of General Lee.

As a general, his dependable talent was as a tactician in the deployment and fighting of troops in an established situation. At Petersburg, the conditions at last were ideal for the projection of Hill's talents in corps command. As soon as his troops were rested, Lee ordered A. P. Hill to the flank of the line to the south of the heavy fortifications in front of the city, where the compact Third Corps could meet the enemy's movements. There would come the fighting which Lee never doubted that Hill would handle. But for discussions, where General Lee might wish to explore possibilities and to sound out attitudes, intense Hill was not the man.

General Lee faced the rest of the way alone. Where Powell Hill could at last find employment for his best talents, of all of Lee's gifts as a soldier, the only one he could use at its fullest potential was the quality of his leadership. This demanded a spiritual force that must be self-renewing without support from the outside.

The day after Lee's army reached Petersburg was a Sunday, and Lee attended morning services at the church. When leaving, the General rode through the streets toward his new headquarters outside the city. Erect on Traveler, his massive features set in the characteristic expression of calm resolution, Lee was the image of the legend. No child, seeing him for the first time, needed to look twice to know that he was beholding General Lee. None of the citizens in the besieged city, and none of the idle soldiers gathered on the quiet summer Sunday streets, could look at him and conceive of defeat.

This was the aura of the leader and, beyond his presence, the legend pervaded, sustaining the faith of the loyal by their faith in the invincibility of R. E. Lee. But always the miracles had been wrought by the alchemy of the combination of the soldiers and the leader, so that Lee and the Army of Northern Virginia became inseparably identified one with the other. This singleness was not so clearly recognized at the time as perceived by perspective; in the spring of '64 Jefferson Davis, as an example, had suggested that Lee leave Virginia and assume command of the Western Army.

As a man, Lee understood the oneness formed of his leadership and the soldiers, and he could convince no one that the soldiers' part of the combination was gone. He could not field a corps the size that A. P. Hill's "Light Division" had been two years before, and as the existing units fell away no replacements came. If his army moved as long as three days, he warned the war office, his animals would collapse. No one heeded him. It was as if Lee alone recognized and accepted the reality that the Army of Northern Virginia was a shell and a name.

Its last miracle, and perhaps its greatest, was the defeat of Grant's objectives, with the blunting of the offensive of the massive Federal forces. In performing that miracle, Lee knew that his army had also performed its last campaign of maneuver. For him the issue was reduced to "a mere question of time."

Epilogue

"The Very Best Soldier"

WHEN LEE ESTABLISHED a stalemate in Virginia with the siege of Petersburg, and the indirect siege of Richmond, the heartland of the older South presented the appearance of a continuing existence as the Confederacy. There was an obvious recession from its vast military front of the year before, when the nation had armies in the field from Pennsylvania to the lower Mississippi. But there were no serious indentations on its thousand miles of Atlantic coastline, nor penetrations in its productive areas from the ocean to west of the Alleghenies. West of the mountains, the army under Sherman presented the only serious threat from Tennessee to the Gulf of Mexico, including stretches in Alabama and Mississippi westward along the Gulf. Though isolated across the Mississippi River, a separate domain existed in Texas (ingeniously supplied by trading through Matamoras) and armies operated in the lost lands of Arkansas and Missouri.

In western Georgia, the railroad junction city of Atlanta occupied on its front the equivalent position of Richmond in the East. No armies had previously approached this center, where strong outlying works were built and where Governor Brown promised he could field the thousands of state militia whose votes had saved them from conscription, Military actions of various size radiating out from the Atlanta area gave an impression of military stability to the Confederate West. A brilliant victory by Forrest at Brice's Crossroads gave Old Bedford in his sphere the quality of invincibility which Lee sustained in his.

This appearance of stability was illusory. In the West there was no general with the prestige nor the diplomacy of Lee, who could gain compromises with the commander in chief and, in extreme emergency, break the barriers of the departmental system. As in Virginia even Lee had been able to circumvent the system only to the extent of fending off disaster and gaining a stalemate, in the West, where the commander in chief ruled supreme, nothing could save the Southern armed forces from the consequences of departmentalization.

This is not to imply that Jefferson Davis's control of the military establishment and its policy caused the collapse of the extemporized agrarian Confederacy before the might of an industrialized nation four times its size. Libraries are crowded with volumes explaining the reasons why the quickly formed confederation was unable to maintain itself against physical force long enough to be granted its independence. Yet, exhibiting an heroic quality of the spirit to endure physically weakening and mentally discouraging hardships, along with a remarkable ingenuity and inventiveness, its soldiers and citizenry maintained armies in protection of its vital areas in June, 1864. It was in relation to those armies and the remaining key positions that Davis's operation of his system doomed the Western Confederacy, regardless of what other forces may have been at work.

With the example of the Richmond-Petersburg front before his daily gaze, the obsessed President effected a faithful reproduction of the arrangement at Atlanta. Only minor details were changed, according to the different personalities. Atlanta's department was sealed off from departments to the east and to the southwest, and Joe Johnston, the commander of the main army, could not obtain troops from adjoining departments to concentrate against the enemy's main objective.

Within this standard procedure, the irrational element was Davis's sudden turn to offense for defense-minded Joe Johnston, outnumbered two to one. As Joe Johnston's reasonable protests were regarded merely as a subordinate's efforts to thwart the authority of his superior, the General's request for the one solution to his problem was dismissed as an excuse. But Johnston requested the one move feared by Sherman: Forrest turned loose on the Federal line of supplies.

It happened that the commander of the department to the southwest of Atlanta did not wish to relinquish Forrest. The great cavalry raider could serve better by guarding property in Alabama and Mississippi. Though it was natural for Davis to give departmental stability preference over a strategic objective, the case involving the Department of Alabama and Mississippi was special.

Civilian authorities and newspaper editors joined General Johnston's appeal for Forrest to operate on Sherman's communication, and Davis's back stiffened at the suggestion that those persons knew more than he did. Also the department commander, Major General Dabney Maury, a regulation-style West Pointer, was a gentleman both by birth and act of Congress, while Bedford Forrest, an unlettered ex-slave dealer, was a rough customer who made up his own rules of war as he went along.

It was not, as it has sometimes been made to appear, that Davis missed the native genius for warfare uniquely possessed by Forrest. Davis showed no appreciation of any of the "originals" in the Confederacy, and little interest in accomplishments which did not fit into the system under his control.

Stonewall Jackson was a discovery of Lee, who personally gave that unexpected genius his chance while the commander in chief was preoccupied with Joe Johnston in their 1862 misunderstanding. Outside Davis's area of concern, semi-autonomous domains were operated by Gorgas in ordnance, General Anderson in the cannon-producing Tredegar Iron Works, and young Dr. McCaw at Chimborazo Hospital, then the world's largest military hospital and the most advanced of any kind. (The President's bureaucratic medical director, Dr. Moore, reproached McCaw for negligence in his morning reports during the period when Chimborazo Hospital was achieving the lowest mortality rates in medical history until the sulfa drugs of World War II.)

Almost forgotten in the Navy Department, Secretary Mallory and Matthew Fontaine Maury, the oceanographer, were very imaginative in concepts and inventive in technology. The Confederate naval forces introduced the first ironclad warship, the first combat submarine, were extremely advanced in the use of underwater torpedoes and highly original in the production of the ram (notably the *Arkansas* and the *Albemarle*), designed to nullify the superior numbers and equipment of the United States naval forces.

This type of man, who recognized the need of new concepts and new methods adapted to the Confederacy's specific circumstances, appeared in numbers and in a diversity of fields surprising in an essentially agricultural people fighting for an anachronistic culture. As their achievements were not interrelated in a single policy, the special gifts of these men were as wasted in their areas as was Forrest's in the West. The misuse of Old Bedford was more dramatic because it was a focus of attention during a decisive campaign.

Jefferson Davis was acting according to form in restricting the Confederacy's greatest raiding force to fending off enemy cavalry dispatched specifically for the purpose of keeping Forrest from Sherman's lines of communication; and he merely repeated his pattern in Virginia when he refused to recognize a cause-and-effect strategy. The effect in Georgia was to permit Sherman to proceed to Atlanta untroubled by disruption to his supplies.

Since even Sherman, with his physical superiority, could not successfully attack dug-in troops at that stage of defensive warfare, Johnston executed an extremely skillful retreat and held the cautious enemy to a snail's pace. However, by the time he reached the environs of Atlanta without striking an offensive blow, he was ruined with the President.

It is true that Johnston was secretive and evasive with his superior. Though Johnston talked then and later vaguely of his "plans," he could only give ground, conserve his army, and hope for an opening in which he could deliver a counterstroke. The mutuality of the loathing between the two former West Point college mates made it impossible for Johnston to confide this to the President.

Someone should have told Davis that this was not the time to try to make up for all the lost opportunities of the past. A small army had been diverted from operations in the Lower South to help Sheridan drive Jubal Early out of the northern end of the Shenandoah Valley. This not only helped stabilize the military situation in the Lower South but reduced Sherman's supply of the replacements for losses which Grant had drawn upon. Of all times to hold on, this was it.

But Davis had seized upon the idea of an offensive as the one cure, and to get to the bottom of the matter with the recalcitrant Johnston, he sent Braxton Bragg to Atlanta. Bragg, of course, told the President what he wanted to hear, and General Joseph E. Johnston joined Harvey Hill in the growing legion of generals without commands.

Against Lee's advice, Davis then appointed combative John Hood, whose skill at maneuvering for personal advancement exceeded both his military abilities and good judgment. Hood was a fine fighter of troops and a better soldier than his disastrous career as army commander would indicate. However, having won the position of army commander on the understanding that Davis's offensive would be mounted, Hood was precommitted to attack a superior force.

It was not that Hood's offensive around Atlanta was poorly conceived. As even Grant's mighty hosts showed in Virginia, the times in the war were unfavorable for offense against an alert, determined enemy. Ten days after Hood's appointment on July 18th, the poor, doomed men of the Army of Tennessee had attacked themselves out of Sherman's path to Atlanta. The siege lasted little more than one month, and on September 2nd Sherman's triumphant army marched into the half-wrecked city.

The illusory stability in the Lower South was immediately exposed. With the fall of Atlanta the bottom dropped out of the Confederate West. What had seemed in early July to be a broad front of Confederate resistance was suddenly reduced to the single hold-out of Lee.

To the North, the good news of Atlanta's fall in early September obliterated the already dimming memory of Grant's catastrophic losses back in June. Within three weeks more, before the end of September, the army collected under Sheridan in the Valley finally overran Jubal Early's little force.

All the enemies accumulated by bitter Old Jube blamed him for the debacle. With a simple devotion not suggested by his harshness to others, Early accepted the calumny rather than excuse himself on the grounds of the disparity between his force and the enemy's. After carrying the war to the enemy for three months, at the end he had little more than ten thousand men of all arms against close to fifty thousand under Sheridan.

Such personal details, unknown to either side, had no relation to the effect of the loss of the Shenandoah Valley. Though the South tried to explain away the disaster by making Jubal Early the goat, none could escape the costly loss of the supply center nor the moral effect of this defeat in the region associated with Stonewall Jackson's great days. In the North, the sweeping aside of Early's remnants redounded to the glory of Sheridan, who was finally able to enjoy an uninterrupted spree in the destruction of personal property. By then, with the war suddenly, or so it seemed, contracted to a single siege, obviously no Democratic peace party had a chance in the November elections. The Lincoln Administration would be supported to the finish, and the end did not come mercifully.

2

With Sherman in Atlanta and the Confederate forces outside, Hood occupied the Federals until mid-November. Then a concentration of Federal forces formed an army to contain Hood's troops, while Sherman, after burning Atlanta, turned loose his soldiers on a march of pillage and destruction across Georgia to the port of Savannah. Hogs, chickens, milk cows were slaughtered, horses taken and barns burned. Family stores of bacon and corn meal were rooted out of hiding places and, if the women protested or the officer in charge of the raiding felt porky, the house was burned. By Christmas, when Savannah was occupied, Hood had wrecked the Army of Tennessee at Nashville, and the ragged, starving survivors were retreating into Mississippi.

In February, 1865, Sherman's army, with the men then hardened by vandalism into a mob, started northward through South Carolina with the self-declared purpose of vengeance on the breeding ground of secession. The soldiers were allowed full license to loot, and they raged like hoodlums through private homes, taking jewelry, silver, whatever struck their fancy. Home-burnings became more commonplace until the state capital at Columbia was reached, on February 17th, and this city was, according to Sherman, "totally burned." On the same day the ante-bellum, cosmopolitan planters' paradise of Charleston was entered, bringing to an end its four-year-siege from the harbor.

The month before, Fort Fisher, guarding the approach to Wilmington, North Carolina, had fallen to an amphibious attack. Whiting, who had failed in the field with Beauregard at Petersburg, gave his life in leading an inspired defense of the fort strengthened by his engineering skill. Braxton Bragg, with no functions left as Military Advisor to the President, was officially in command of the department, with headquarters at Wilmington. On February 22nd, five days after Charleston was occupied, Wilmington was entered, and the last port on the Atlantic was closed. The Confederacy was isolated from the world.

After that, the pace to the finish was accelerated. On land Sherman started northward again, entering North Carolina. Another army started eastward from the coast. Cavalry raiders struck in from the West, terrorizing isolated families and running off stock. Joe Johnston was plucked from exile and given command of a heterogeneous collection of troops, including remnants of Hood's army, assembled in North Carolina in Sherman's fiery path. This force "melted away," Johnston said, before his eyes. At every nightfall men simply walked off, the artillerists taking their personally owned mounts, to get home and look after their families.

Scattered fighting continued in stretches of the Lower South, and the small empire in Texas held on to its lonely existence. But the core of the Confederacy, as it existed in mid-June when Lee set his army to withstand the siege, had shrunk to the two hundred inland miles between Grant's and Sherman's armies.

By March, the Richmond-Petersburg fort had become an island, with its lines extended to more than thirty miles. Finally the lines were stretched too far for the declining army to man the works. The masses of the enemy poured over in waves and at last, eleven months after the campaign had begun, Lee was forced into the open.

He had nowhere to go and nothing to go with. When his survivors escaped from the overrun lines, Richmond was uncovered. Troops of Weitzel's command, established in a permanent line north of the James River, marched into the burning city, with the bands of a Negro division playing "The Year of Jubilee."

The evacuation of Richmond removed the last conceivable justification for Lee's army to remain in the field. Davis, however, fled the capital into some private world of his own, where he intended to carry on the resistance indefinitely.

The pride of the Army of Northern Virginia was forced to the humiliation of a flight, dignified by the name of a "retreat," through the bleak farm country to the west of Petersburg. The twenty-seven thousand of all arms — wagoneers, doctors, hangers-on — were overhauled at the courthouse town of Appomattox County. There was nothing at Appomattox to defend. It was simply a place-name in the cheerless countryside where the walking skeletons could go no farther.

3

Before the army of Northern Virginia was officially dissolved on the 9th of April, 1865, in the months of "the long agony" while the Confederacy was disintegrating around the Richmond-Petersburg stronghold, there were thousands of soldiers with Lee who never believed they could be defeated with Uncle Robert. At first there was the hope of the November elections, which gradually faded with the collapse of other fronts. Then, beyond all reason, the men hoped because General Lee was there as the image of invincibility.

When did he know, beyond all outside unreasonable hope, that their second war for independence was doomed? By his own words, he regarded a siege as numbering the days of his own army. But during the summer, while the Federal forces gained no decisions on other fronts and Jubal Early threatened Washington with his small army, Grant's grinding operations hacked away so slowly that obviously the enemy could achieve nothing definite against him before November. As an approaching finality is difficult for anyone to accept while it is still distant, and as Lee was by instinct a warrior, it is unlikely that he looked ultimate defeat squarely in the face when his army was first immobilized. Though he had said it would be a question of time, with the shape Grant's army was then in, it could seem possible that time might run out on the enemy before it did on the Confederacy.

Because nothing he said or wrote in his most personal letters, during the remainder of 1864, indicated any change in Lee's attitude, it would be impossible to select any given date when he recognized that all hope was gone for the Confederacy, when he accepted beyond reprieve the death of the cause for which he had sacrificed everything.

In terms of events, September 30th would be as close as any to the date when nothing remained to support the most desperate hope. By then General Lee had absorbed the news of the surrounding disasters — the fall of Atlanta at the other end of the line and the loss of the Shenandoah Valley at home. And on that day he observed the collapse of his own veteran troops in performing the simplest operation merely to maintain the siege.

When large-scale assault had passed from the Army of the Potomac in June, after the men were rested and the drooping morale rose, Grant began a monotonous pendulum movement of limited attacks south of Petersburg at the railroad to Wilmington and north of the James at the Richmond fortifications. This whittling away at Lee's men was a focus of attrition directly on the manpower of Lee's army in the deadliest wearing down of Lee's ability to maintain a force in the field. In one of these grim mathematical exchanges of replaceable Federal soldiers falling to bring down an irreplaceable Confederate, on September 29th a surprise attack took Fort Harrison, a pivotal link in the chain of fortifications east of Richmond.

These works were manned principally by artillerists on the stationary guns, mostly men unfit for strenuous campaigning, and life on the bluffs near the James River had been relatively easy for these garrison troops. The men tended little vegetable gardens and their camps, cooler and fresher than the trenches, sometimes served as refitting stations for worn-out units, low in numbers and suffering absentees from sickness. While reconditioning, the regulars were available to assist the garrisons in repelling attack.

At the time of the pre-dawn surprise attack on Fort Harrison, only the skeletal brigades of Johnson's Tennesseans and Gregg's Texans were north of the James, neither in the fort. The garrison troops in the earthen works, lulled by the quiet tenor of their days, were overwhelmed almost before they knew what was happening, and Johnson's and Gregg's veterans were hard put to it to prevent the Federal force from extending the breach and wrecking Lee's great system of fortifications.

Because of the critical location of the break, on the next day Lee rode personally back to the north side of the river, once more in front of the capital. With him he brought the other survivors of

Field's division, Hoke's division and some of Pickett's regiments. As carefully as he planned the masterpiece of Chancellorsville with Stonewall Jackson, the commanding general prepared an attack for retaking Fort Harrison with black-bearded young Hoke and burly, one-legged Charlie Field.

The assault opened on a flat-landed field of a size where General Lee could survey every detail of the waste of valiant life in uncoordinated, futile movements. Field attacked too soon and Hoke waited for the time of the order. Field's brigadiers acted without concert and their units were cut up separately. As his men fell back in disorder, Hoke's division advanced to receive alone the concentrated fire of the enemy. Then these brigades retired, considerably shaken.

At the first confused repulse, General Lee could not accept the finality of this breakdown in command in a rudimentary action of such limited scope. One of the soldiers who passed near to him wrote, "I had always thought General Lee was a cold and unemotional man, but he showed lots of feeling and excitement on that occasion." Then the soldier described the General "imploring the men to make one more effort to take the position for him."

The men were moved to make the effort, but only the spirit was willing and that briefly. The soldiers were too experienced to advance into concentrated fire, from an enemy behind works, under leaders whose lack of capacity made useless the sacrifice of life. Almost by common consent, the veterans of Lee's greatest campaigns broke backward and made their way to safety in unapologetic disorder.

The General did not try to rally them again. When he turned Traveler to the river bridge, leading to what was becoming the fort of Petersburg, that may have been the hour when the certainty of the Confederacy's inevitable defeat came over him. It could scarcely have come later.

4

On that last day of September, five months after the gathering of all his generals on Clark's Mountain, the Army of Northern Virginia revealed itself to be little more than an image in the memories of men. The generals of the last pageantry in the spring were dead or scattered on the pleasantly warm day of early autumn.

Broken Ewell remained in the token position of commanding the Department of Richmond. Longstreet, with a partially paralyzed arm from his wound, returned to the mundane assignment of commanding a permanent line outside Richmond north of the James River. The division of Charles Field, the man whom Longstreet had so bitterly opposed, were the only troops of the old First Corps north of the James. The other division in the command was that of Robert Hoke, the disappointment as a major general. Ewell, with the department, and Longstreet, with the line of works, were to last to the end, though poor Dick Ewell was to suffer the final indignity of being captured on the retreat to Appomattox, where he commanded some local defense troops from Richmond and a "battalion" of sailors.

Pickett's division had enjoyed its last moment of glory in driving Butler's troops out of the Bermuda Hundred lines. George Pickett became a shadowy figure in the last months, continuing in his baffling withdrawal from Lee's regard. In time the division, crowded with conscripts, would be pulled out of line and held as a reserve unit.

Dick Anderson, Longstreet's successor on the First Corps, fell steadily away from his one great hour at Spotsylvania. Defeatism settled on him earlier and more obviously than most, and gradually his "corps" was reduced to the hodgepodge division of Bushrod Johnson, formed at Petersburg in the May battles against Butler.

The Second Corps had mostly disintegrated in the Valley. Jubal Early, contemned and forgotten, was left there with a token force without any of the young division commanders who had flashed so brilliantly in the campaign against Grant. Robert Rodes and Dodson Ramseur were killed, young Ramseur with a letter in his pocket announcing the birth of a new son. John B. Gordon was brought back to Lee's forces around Petersburg.

Only the Third Corps sustained its entity all the way, despite the increasing absences of A. P. Hill. His lovely wife and two young daughters took a residence in Petersburg, and the physically failing general spent much time at home. Toward the end, when the possibility of evacuating Richmond was discussed, Hill said he would not want to survive the fall of the city, and it would almost look as if Little Powell made sure he did not. When the break came in the lines on Sunday morning, April 2nd, A. P. Hill hurried back from a sick leave to make a personal reconnaissance into the wooded no man's land beyond the heavy fortifications. He was accompanied only by his favorite courier, Sergeant Tucker. They encountered a couple of Federal stragglers and Hill rode toward them, calling to the men to surrender. They fired on him, and life was gone from the wasted body when Hill, toppled from the saddle, struck the damp earth.

Lee choked up when Tucker brought him the news, and his care-worn face reflected the stab of sorrow. Then, controlling himself, the General said, "He is at rest now, and we who are left are the ones to suffer."

In the cavalry, little was required of the reconnaissance for which Jeb Stuart had been famous, and Wade Hampton performed well enough those thankless chores of fighting the enemy off the rail-roads. Long before the end, the Weldon Railroad was severed beyond repair, and supplies came only by trickles to the island of defense. In 1865, Hampton took Calbraith Butler's cavalry back to South Carolina, to try to put heart into the hopeless delaying action against Sherman. The highly respected South Carolina grandee was not close to Lee personally, and no one ever took the place in his affections of "my poor Stuart," as Lee called him, nor of the "great and good Jackson."

The nearest intimate was John B. Gordon, the patriot soldier who had attracted Lee at the beginning of the campaign. Bringing high gifts of intelligence, devotion and tireless energy to his inspiring physical presence, the Georgian nonetheless reflected the change from the panoplied gathering in May when he, a brigadier at the beginning of the campaign, became the closest companion of the commanding general. Yet so relatively simple were the technical demands in defending fortified positions that Gordon could become the army's first non-professional corps commander. Like Hampton in the cavalry, he brought to his duties the stout heart which repre-sented the essential element of leadership needed in the trenches.

The ever-lengthening lines, the digging of which exhausted more and more men, were manned by the various units who had defended Petersburg, interspersed with the units whose pride was sustained by the place-names on their battle flags. Except for the marchings out and back forced on Hill's fading men, the once mobile army acted as a garrison force covering some thirty-odd miles of expanding front. Lee's army had finally been claimed by the system.

As the days ticked away the life of Lee's army, the commander in chief was at last undisturbed in his departments. No one importuned him for concentration of forces, no decisions need be made of where to shift troops. His defensive policy had ultimately achieved a totally static defense. Only time, not sudden actions, could change his charts.

Fittingly, one of Davis's last arrangements was to resolve Beauregard's second-in-command status by placing him in command of yet another department. This time Old Bory was given the official authority for the area in which driven, goaded John Hood took his Army of Tennessee. Beauregard's ambitions would not again delude him into trying to recapture glory in one of Davis's fantasy departments. He accepted the assignment outwardly with good grace, remained blandly detached from involvement with the details of the foredoomed disasters and, playing out his role of the French marshal, settled for the future with his reputation as it then existed.

Lee was at last in sole command of the Richmond area north and south of the James River, now that it was too late to do more than exercise the techniques of a professional soldier in defending a hopeless position until the surviving force was sufficiently weakened for the enemy to storm the walls. He had written to the commander in chief, "I think it is his [Grant's] purpose to compel the evacuation of our present position by cutting off supplies, and that he will not renew the attempt to drive us away by force. . . . It behooves us to do everything in our power to thwart his new plan of reducing us to starvation."

To the end, General Lee anticipated his immediate antagonist. On July 24th he wrote his son Custis his estimate of Grant: "His talent and strategy consists in accumulating overwhelming numbers." To meet this policy he could only continue to offer suggestions. Davis paid not the slightest heed to anything the General suggested, but Lee wrote letters as carefully composed as those in the earlier years.

He could not have hoped that any action would be taken this late in the day. Back in October of 1862 Lee wrote his wife a strangely ignored letter on the perils to the Confederacy caused by vanity of the spirit. Referring to the "hand of God" in their affairs, he wrote, "If our people would recognize it, and cease from their vain self-boasting and adulation, how strong would be my belief in final success." Obviously, he could expect no change of spirit in people with the tide running out in 1864.

In dutifully writing suggestions of measures that might be taken, he avoided the one subject which grew in his mind as the last military expedient. This was the abandonment of Richmond, a desperate measure surely enough, but one he preferred to prolonging the ordeal of starvation. Since he knew the President's answer beforehand, General Lee evidently found it pointless to try any more diplomatic maneuvers.

To his own army, his own front, he brought the best he had each day. Like a great artist, he could only bring everything there was in him. Nothing was withheld, unused or wasted, however futile he might have believed the end. For to recognize the hopelessness of a cause was not for Lee to act on the acceptance of defeat. Realistic evaluation was a proper function of the mind, not of the heart.

To Lee, as a deeply religious man, resignation to an event before it happened would be to anticipate the will of God. In Lee's concept of man's relation to life, this would have been inconceivable, a violation of the duty clearly revealed by each new sun.

A military community was dependent upon him for its existence, for the support of its morale and its honor. Small though the sum of the units in comparison with the enemy's might, more than fifty thousand men of all arms comprised the force from Richmond's fortifications to the lines southwest of Petersburg. Daily the spirits of some men failed, and they stole away from their former comrades. Some went directly into the enemy's lines for food, others home to obtain food and provide safety for their families. Daily too the bodies of men proved unequal to the strain, and those who did not die were invalided out of the army. Yet to the end, to all ends, the spirit and the flesh of others would endure as long as he led.

Lee knew that. As his own children, these men had been placed in his care and they gave him the same implicit trust. Yet as a parent who knows he cannot provide food for children whose eyes turn to him in hunger, Lee must have suffered from the inwardly held knowledge that he could not provide these trusting men with what they expected.

He did not want to tell them to surrender; he never wanted that. But, as in his unrevealed preference for abandoning Richmond and breaking out into the open, it would have been his preference to bring the slow agony to a quick end. On this, he wrote an extremely revealing passage.

In his saddlebags, General Lee kept loose sheets of paper, on which he wrote from time to time, without date, various maxims, proverbs and Psalms, selections from standard authors, and occasionally some reflection of his own. These were written in his own clear, strong hand, slanting to the right, with "f's" heavily shaded in the downward stroke. On one sheet of paper, he wrote this:

The warmest instincts of every man's soul declare the glory of the soldier's death. It is more appropriate to the Christian than to the Greek to sing:

"Glorious his fate, and envied is his lot,
Who for his country fights and for it dies."

To this the General added another line, as if on further reflection on the subject. "There is a true glory and a true honor: the glory of duty done, the honor of the integrity of principle."

This was all left to the man whose vaulting aspirations had carried him to the top of his profession and whom General Winfield Scott called "the very best soldier I ever saw in the field."

Bibliographical Essay
with Selected Bibliography

A N IMPRESSION seems to exist that Civil War history, in contrast to all others, consists of a body of immutable facts, and all left to do is to present this material in a different way — or, as some say, "rehash." The existing "facts" about the Civil War, which are demonstrable and indisputable, would provide an extremely limited statistical reference without deductions, development and interpretation, and no researcher yet has seen anything approaching all the material. Huge segments of material have never been worked and new material is constantly appearing: more than a hundred of Lee's personal letters and nearly that many from General W. H. F. Lee to his father have recently been discovered in a private collection, not at present available to researchers.

The Civil War was the first war in history on which a deliberate effort was made to collect and organize the records; yet the 128 bulky volumes of the *Official Records* provide no more than one-fifth of the officially collected data.

The National Archives contain thousands of jackets on company muster rolls, with separate sub-subjects such as the fuel requisitions and the hospital reports of individual companies in a regiment. Dr. Meriwether Stuart, of New York, is the only researcher I know of who is working on the National Archive jackets — in a combination of other sources — to develop the exact company rosters of a regiment at successive stages of the war. Pages from Dr. Stuart's work in progress reveal the fiction of such terms as "brigade" and "regiment" in Lee's army in the last year of the war. A similar study would have to be done for each regiment in each army for a student to know with any exactitude how many men actually were present for duty in each engagement.

As of now, every estimate of numbers is an approximation. The much-cited Livermore, as an authority on numbers, arrived at "estimates" on a complicated percentage computation system. Livermore used his system of estimates even for the Battle of Drewry's Bluff, in the 1864 campaign, when the precise casualty lists were published in the Richmond newspapers — copies of which were on file at the Boston Athanaeum. Approximations may be very close, but no historian in the field — until publication of Dr. Stuart's work — has ever been able to cite a single source which provided the exact number of men present in even a single regiment.

It is in the military aspects particularly, where most facts are assumed to exist, that the existing material is most confusing. Dense masses of frequently contradictory evidence are divided by gaps where little or no data exist, and no new research techniques were brought to this wilderness until after World War II, and these have been very little used since then. A large proportion of historically cited sources consist of no more than the opinions or impressions of individuals whose competence as witnesses would be questioned in any other field. Passed on across the decades, these "sources" assumed an historic infallibility, and currently even the subjective deductions which historians made upon this dubious evidence are cited as authoritative sources.

What the contemporary researcher is doing, now that the general story has been covered, is to work in aspects of the whole: in effect, he has become a "specialist." As an illustration, the outcome of the Battle of the Wilderness would be acceptable as a fact, but the realm of fact is left behind immediately the focus is narrowed to bring out the details. As described in the narrative, the distance which Hancock said he drove the Confederates ("about a mile and a half") and the distance which Wilcox said they fell back ("three hundred yards") are conflicting statements between two honest men. They were also the impressions of two excited men, moving through smoke over a bewildering terrain with which they were unfamiliar. As neither the Brock Road has changed its course nor the farm clearing yet been totally reclaimed by the brush, it is today possible to clock the distance on a mileage meter. This 1.2 miles between the points represents a demonstrable fact which is not cited in any source.

With this fact as a guide, the conflicting statements of Hancock and Wilcox can be resolved, though only approximately. Where no precise measure exists as a guide to resolve conflicting statements, the resolution must be made by weighing the factors of total background, the character of the witnesses, their viewpoints, and the probabilities. But suppose there were only one report — either Hancock's or Wilcox's? In using the report of either one, the researcher must be wrong.

The impossibility of arriving at definite conclusions, "facts," on even this one battle, is recognized by the conscientious historians of the National Battlefield Park Service at Fredericksburg. Concentrating on the four battles in the area over a period of years, they cannot determine for a certainty which are the Federal and which the Confederate lines in the stretch of the Wilderness between the Tapp farm and the Brock Road.

In reappraising the non-factual "sources," the most dramatic new research technique is the mine detector. By discovering the density of metal (bullets, shell fragments, bayonets, the flattened canteens and tin cups used in emergencies for throwing up earthworks) in a given area, the size of the action at a specific point can today be determined with far more precision than was hitherto possible.

Mr. N. F. Warinner, in working the fields around Richmond, believes that he discovered the inaccuracy of even one of the generally accepted, larger facts — the site of the Battle of Glendale (or Frayser's Farm) in the Seven Days Around Richmond. By the test of density of metal, this important engagement between Lee and McClellan certainly did not happen where historians have placed it for nearly a century. As of now, Mr. Warinner has not discovered to the satisfaction of modern research standards where the battle did take place.

In the Battle of Cold Harbor, coming to closer focus for details, the mine detector has both established where the May 31 breakthrough between Hoke and Kershaw did not happen and where it did. The late Dr. Douglas Southall Freeman, when working with inconclusive evidence, often traced the process of his deductions in his footnotes. Of the May 31 breach, he wrote that of the two ravines on the map which "conformed to the general description of the break," he selected the first ravine because the details furnished in Alexander and the *History of Kershaw's Brigade* "made it practically certain that the rupture was" there. This deduction represents the soundest possible evaluation of existing material. But the mine detector revealed that the action occurred in the second ravine a quarter of a mile away.

Though this illustration might seem a matter of no great concern, the re-creation of battles and armies has become a tedious accumulation of such small details, all adding to a body of material from which to make deductions that will, in turn, construct an approximation. With this emphasis on "research in depth" (as the current saying has it) — along with the widening body of background material and the interpretative nature of the reappraisals — the work of specialists, as well as the specialized interests of students, has exposed large gaps in the development of aspects of the whole.

On the Army of Northern Virginia, no work exists on the cavalry, though the valuable collection of Munford Papers is now at Duke; except for Dr. Bean's recent biography on Sandie Pendleton, the Second Corps chief-of-staff, no studies have been made on staff work in Lee's army — either of individuals or their functions; nothing has been done on the commissary and supply services which eventually wrecked the army; and Wise's lonely standard work on the artillery needs to be reworked to meet today's specialized criteria.

As no study has ever been made of the CSA department system, a major motive in this book was to fill the existing gap on the departmental structure within which Lee operated during the six weeks of the campaign from the Wilderness to Petersburg. In this, the purpose was to bring into a single pattern the relations of Lee and Davis, Beauregard and Davis, and Lee and Beauregard, and to treat both the south-of-Richmond operations and Lee's army as parts of one campaign — the single military problem which it was to the Confederacy, as it was a single coordinated objective of Grant's.

As my interest was primarily in the personalities of the leaders, rather than in military units, this specialized study, within the isolated aspect of a single campaign, opened into a research background even more confusing and contradictory than that of the events. The false generalities, the sheer nonsense, accepted on leaders throughout American history offer a curious paradox in a factual-minded people, and the written history of the Civil War is so clouded and cluttered by time-honored clichés that the indisputable facts on individuals often extend little beyond vital statistics.

The clash of interests and temperaments was as common in both armies as it is in business organizations today and all judgments of contemporaries on their fellows must be analyzed within the context of their relationship. Beyond that, all existing historical judgments must be analyzed according to the viewpoint by which the records of leaders were regarded.

As example, Sheridan, a favorite of Grant, became conspicuous in victory when the tide of his side came rolling in when the enemy was collapsing. With Sheridan viewed as a star of the winning team, he can assume the image of the irresistible conqueror on his campaign in the Valley. There is another view. When Sheridan finally broke Early, he commanded a force approaching fifty thousand superbly equipped and conditioned men of all arms against an underfed, physically weakened force of little more than ten thousand. In a losing cause, Early had outmaneuvered and outfought Sheridan for nearly two months before the weight of numbers and the strain of maintaining an unequal contest forced the inevitable result. With a shift in viewpoint, Early could become as heroic as the doomed defenders of Thermopylae.

This is a broad illustration, where the available facts are usually ignored because of the selections and arrangement determined by the viewpoint. Coming into closer focus, again where considerable available evidence is usually ignored, A. P. Hill has been made the scapegoat for the poor condition of his lines on the second day in the Wilderness, though the guilt lay over the whole army, from platoon leaders to the commanding general. The viewpoint of Southerners wished to avoid including Lee in the guilt.

The viewpoint of Southerners has also tended to de-emphasize the control which commander-in-chief Davis exercised over field general Lee, with the result that Northerners and Europeans have a false impression of Lee's authority. Though in perspective it seems monstrous that Davis exercised the authority of his rank over the South's greatest general and most revered citizen, correspondence between them establishes Lee's subordination as among the demonstrable facts.

To the contemporary mind, familiar with the Organization Man, Lee does not appear to be of smaller stature by his entrapment in a system; rather, he becomes more human by his foredoomed struggle to assert his individual ideas and more understandably tragic in his fall beneath the combined forces of the enemy and the system.

Though there is nothing new about bureaucracy, we are today more familiar with its operation and effects, as also today we are more aware of the plight of the individual in adjusting to systems. This conditioning of our minds influences our analyses, and we regard the individual from a viewpoint different from that of historians of another generation. We know more about the individual through the broadening fields of psychology, psychiatry and medicine, and through a tendency to study the individual as a variable who, like any other living animal, will react differently according to circumstance. Older generations were more inclined to regard the individual as a static quality. When his behavior on certain occasions seemed at variance with the accepted picture of him, it was the action that was a variation from the norm and not the man himself who was variable. Today, we are more interested in the springs of action within the man.

With this viewpoint, the researcher weighs all the evidence to try to understand the fundamental *why*, the cast of mind and nerves, the state of health, and the effect of specific circumstances on the total personality. The contradictions and gaps in existing material are even more puzzling here than in battles because of the known inadequacy of human beings to report objectively on their fellow men. Historians accept dialogue reported verbatim twenty years after the event, where in any courtroom on any day you can see witnesses confused about events that happened only weeks before and which concern them much more vitally than a past battle concerned some veteran remembering precisely the words used at a specific minute in another era.

Many years ago in Richmond there lived a prominent and learned old gentleman who had written, while the details were fresh in his mind, one of the classic memoirs of the war in Virginia. As the decades passed and a new generation (my own) appeared, this truly fine memoirist began to elaborate more in detail in conversational response to specific questions. When he had written his book, he told only where his outfit was and what it did; but, as our generation was eager to place the fabled leaders on the scenes, he accommodatingly described the last meeting of Lee and Jackson at Chancellorsville, what Pickett said at Gettysburg, and the spot where A. P. Hill fell at Petersburg. Finally, one Sunday, he took a group of us out to show us where Lee stood — and how he gave orders to couriers — during the Battle of Malvern Hill. Not only could the embarrassed old gentleman not find even the battlefield of Malvern Hill, but we had to show him the way back to Richmond.

One of my great-uncles, who had served in Pickett's division, was then in the Old Soldiers' Home at Richmond, with hundreds of other veterans better turned out in Confederate gray than they had been since the first months of the war. I told Uncle Robert of this encounter and he laughed. He said that if I would listen to the old men around him, all of them had held the most intimate private conversations with Pickett and Jackson and "General Lee himself." Then he said, "I fought for four years and not a single general has spoken to me yet. But, if I ever heard any of them talking to anybody in the language these fellows claim they heard, I'd've known we were goners."

As disenchanting as this was at the time, years later the dual experience (followed by experiences as a newspaper reporter) provided a healthy skepticism in reading accounts of what veterans reported they had heard and what leaders claimed they had said. It is not conceivable that a brigade front of Texans, rushing into battle, would all cry, "Lee to the rear!" Of all the "eyewitness" accounts of that scene in the Wilderness, the one that seemed most reasonable was that which reported several men shouting, "Go back, General Lee, go back!" Yet that was selected as merely the most reasonable. Of all the varying accounts, no one wrote down a single version at the time. This is on an event observed by sufficient persons to constitute a fact, however the details of the fact may differ.

Away from such a well-covered event, the researcher must play detective with the existing material when trying to reach conclusions about individual leaders. The material consists of words or actions attributed to an individual by others and of others' opinions of him; of his written reports before, during and after an engagement, his private correspondence written before and after the same engagement, *and* of words, actions and opinions he attributed to himself in retrospect. These factors must be considered against his total record as known and the larger generally known facts (as the outcome of an engagement), against the character of those writing about him and their relationships with him, and against the circumstances at the specific times when he is under scrutiny.

For the Army of the Potomac, a special study needs to be made of the political alignments which would explain many of the otherwise inexplicable uses and misuses of general officers. (Any of a dozen Federal generals, instead of Butler, would have taken Richmond in May, 1864, and Grant would probably never have been President.) The antagonism between McClellanites and anti-McClellanites continued for decades after the war to the obfuscation of many individual careers. To an outsider, it seems that Grant was unfair to the Old Guard in the army he took over — especially to Warren (though he was by no means blameless) and to Meade after the war.

In the Army of Northern Virginia, where Lee's authority in the field was absolute, the commanding general would appear to be the source of valuable opinion on subordinates, but it is extremely difficult to define Lee's final opinion of most general officers. On Jackson and Stuart, whom he loved and admired, his attitude is shown by the trust he gave them and his reaction to their loss. With most others, inferences must be made.

Of Dick Anderson, whom Lee termed a "capital" division commander when he promoted him to corps command, Lee's waning confidence can be traced by the increase of the most specifically detailed orders he sent the new corps commander. During the movements from the North Anna to Petersburg, when he sent A. P. Hill no specific orders at all, he almost hand-led Anderson by describing the exact line of march he must take, even to the name of the house-owner whose property marked a place of turn. From this, from Anderson's performances and his failing spirit, the inferences can be made, but the precise *why* in Anderson's case must remain a surmise.

In Dick Ewell's case, there is more certainty of Lee's recognition of his psychological impairment by one reference, in a letter to Seddon, of Ewell's shattered "nervous system."

Yet many general officers were eased out of Lee's army, by his circuitous methods of finding employment for them in other theaters, with little clue to the nature of their failing. The reasonable conclusion is that the men were simply incompetent, as none so transferred distinguished himself elsewhere. In 1864, when he no longer possessed a choice, Lee's statements revealed that he regarded a number in his army as incompetent, but, while they served with him, he never named them. As "incompetence" in Confederate officers has always been an unpopular and ticklish subject in the South, no one writing about Lee's army — veterans or historians — has ever pursued this special line, and the element of plain unfitness is the most elusive of all.

The next most elusive element is the factor which determined the limitations of certain men at a given level. Of course, by 1864, many brigadiers were out of their depth as general officers and countless colonels as field officers, but a number of pre-Gettysburg brigadiers — like Jim Lane, in Wilcox's division — performed consistently well and were never considered for promotion in any extremity. As most of these personalities were the subject of few references by their contemporaries, the exact nature of their limitation cannot even become a reasonable assumption. When Lee recommended Kershaw for promotion to division command, he said Kershaw was "quick, prompt and cool." The baffling element is that others, such as Lane, from what is known, also seemed quick, prompt and cool. But something else was lacking. That supposed body of facts, which is presumably being rehashed, is extremely deficient for those "hot for certainties" about the personality secrets of the less publicized general officers.

The significance of the current viewpoint is that the attempts at fresh appraisals are at least trying to develop total personalities and analyze their reactions in events, rather than to establish the events as set pieces and place within the action the unchanging men of history.

At one extreme are the friends, Grant and Longstreet. Grant was the same man as prewar failure, 1863 hero of Vicksburg, 1864 "butcher" and 1865 victor, and as postwar presidential calamity; Longstreet was the same man as security-minded garrison paymaster, as 1862 and 1864 dependable and as 1863 maladroit Cassius, and as postwar vilifier of Lee. They responded differently to different circumstances.

At the other extreme, Lee emerges as the whole person because his prewar, war and postwar career are totally free of contradictions: he acted like the same man under all circumstances. Yet nature's revolt at the iron self-discipline was reflected in the rapid deterioration of his previously superb physique. Because of this breakdown he fought differently in detail, as graphically illustrated at the North Anna, than he would have in full vigor. It is my opinion that his failing health, combined with the frustrations with Davis and his awareness that he was fighting his last campaign of maneuver, caused the desperation in his thinking when he clung to the purpose of assuming a counteroffensive after his depleted army revealed in every limited action that the physical weakness of the men and the loss of capable leaders had destroyed forever the potential of attack.

The best approach to Lee as a person was found in his letters and full wartime correspondence. These were made available to me through the project, *The War Papers of R. E. Lee*, a selection for one volume which Mr. Louis Manarin and I are editing under the sponsorship of the Virginia Civil War Commission. Only excerpts of a few Lee letters are scattered through Freeman, Jones, Fitzhugh Lee and (inaccurately) in the *Recollections of R. E. Lee, Jr.* Lee's dispatches to Davis are collected, his war messages and reports appear in various volumes of the *Official Records;* his letter-books are in the National Archives and three of the 1864-1865 letter-books are in the Virginia Historical Society. His reports on the 1864 campaign were lost when wagons were burned on the flight to Appomattox, and messages written during battle are almost nonexistent, because of his habit of giving verbal orders during action. Yet more than 6500 items of wartime correspondence have been found thus far and a trickle continues to flow in. Miss Janet Fauntleroy Taylor of Norfolk, the granddaughter of Colonel Walter Taylor, alone possessed thirteen unpublished items.

Lee's letters to his wife and daughters reveal, as his official correspondence never did during the May-June campaign, his apprehensions and expectations, as well as his opinions about the Southern Confederacy. (Beginning in October, 1864, his official correspondence becomes more outspoken in general criticism and his anticipations of the end.) As so little exists on his battle exchanges, his personal correspondence provided the clearest indication of his attitude toward the successive stages of the campaign. His words on what he wanted to achieve, and his grim knowledge of the physical inadequacies he must work with, formed the line I followed for his tactics, decisions and indecisions. For tracing the course of Lee's behavior during 1864, his total correspondence offered the basic source.

For any book on the Army of Northern Virginia, the work of the late Douglas Southall Freeman is the alphabet and the grammar. As Dr. Freeman researched from the most extensive collection of material then available, and was aware that his explorations opened up the whole field, he provided an incalculable service on sources to all students of Lee's army. For me there was his additional encouragement and guidance in working on aspects of the whole, beginning when I was twenty-one years old on my first job, as reporter on the Richmond *News Leader*. In those days the staff was small and Dr. Freeman's sphere as editor included that of managing editor, with the result that his tutelage was constant, immediate and paternal (though he was then only thirty-nine, and some years from publishing *R. E. Lee*). In research techniques, Dr. Freeman used the *Official Records* more broadly and deeply than anyone before him, but he had great respect for personal recollections which coincided with the generally accepted facts, and made far bolder use than is usually recognized of those witnesses for filling gaps in official data. Though his approach to General Lee was just this side of idolatry, he held far stronger opinions about some of Lee's subordinates than his books might indicate.

Once I asked him why he did not write what he knew about certain generals, and he said that, as editor of the state's largest afternoon newspaper, it would be unbecoming to stir up their children or grandchildren, with whom he was acquainted. He then suggested that it was up to the rising generations to speak the whole truth, as we saw it, and let the chips fall where they may. This I promised to do.

Yet, though my acquaintance with the descendants of Confederate generals is not wide, and I have no official capacity to consider, I encounter an insuperable restraint in making a statement as flat as I would in conversation — even about Jefferson Davis. The reasons for this restraint are indefinable.

Once when I made a derogatory comment about a Confederate prima donna, I was deluged with letters of denunciation by descendants and friends of descendants, some even appearing in the letter columns of the Richmond newspapers. This was the only occasion when I felt tempted to let go with all the facts (like a reporter quoting a politician verbatim), but professional training easily stifled the personal reaction, and anyway this general really wasn't worth another mention. So, a reluctance to tread on toes is not part of the restraint. There is something about the printed page (and perhaps the added years) that made it impossible to follow Dr. Freeman's advice as far as I had promised I would. In any event, the advice served to point me in a definite direction, and I wish to acknowledge this, along with his unfailing and generous support across nearly three decades. And I must confess to some sense of apology for what I have done, as he would see it, to General Lee.

A reviewer of my last book said, very good-naturedly, that I had admitted that Lee made mistakes at Gettysburg though the admission "came through gritted teeth." This is not true. My interest in Lee's mistakes is in why he made them. Though the reasoning processes may seem to constitute an apologia, my approach to his mistakes is the same as to those of Ewell or A. P. Hill. In fact, I feel personally more moved by Hill than by any general in Lee's army, including Lee, and actually it is of him that I write most defensively.

No member of my family ever served with Hill. By personal association, I should be a Longstreet man. Both my grandfathers served in the First Corps, one in Kemper's brigade of Pickett's division and one in a battery of the Richmond Howitzers in Cabell's artillery battalion; a great-uncle, Captain Blount, commanded a First Corps gun battery and a good one. But I do not believe that writers on the Confederacy are as motivated by personal attachments as is generally considered.

As objectively as is possible for a Virginian, I believe that Lee was the greatest soldier ever produced on the continent, but my admiration for him as a man grew as I studied him and learned the details of the frustrating restrictions against which he was forced to perform and which for so long he overcame. To the bitterest end, they never overcame him personally.

Yet the very heroic size of his fortitude removed him further from my immediate comprehension, and I was forced to write of him in the same way that his men saw him — awesome, complete, removed from common clay. In letters to his wife he grew quite fussy about her making correct counts of the homemade socks she sent, and the repairing of his worn-out drawers, but the fact that he liked fresh socks and neat underwear — and depended upon his wife to supply these mundane needs — brought him into no closer focus as a human being. If he walked into the room the next minute, I would not have the remotest notion of what conversation would interest him, though I would feel on safe ground to inquire after his daughters.

My impression of General Lee, or reaction to him, is formed not only by a composite of everything I have read on the war, and not only of what I have read of other wars and other heroes, but inevitably there is a coloration from the days of earliest memory, and even preconscious memory, that it would be idle to attempt to define. From this formative period, however, it is possible to know that he was never regarded as an historic figure, never remote like Washington. Always he seemed more personally identified with my environment than persons of history.

There was the manner in which the older members of my family (those who had fought with him) referred to "General Lee" or "Uncle Robert" that placed him within the horizons of the widening world of a child. It was as if he was a cousin or an uncle who lived in another part of the state whom I had not yet met, and I distinctly remember when I learned that I would never see him. This too cannot be cited as a source, but I can hear again the voices of those now dead in the rooms still here, and I *know* how the men felt about him, and that something of their feeling in me is ineradicable in trying to write about him.

To some extent those same impressions constitute my earliest "research" on the Army of Northern Virginia and the war period in Virginia. Fortunately there were realists in my family and their feeling for their fellow soldiers did not implant either hero worship nor a swords and roses romanticism. Perhaps because of their lack of sentimentality their attitude did implant the deepest admiration for those qualities Lee's men truly possessed and a profound compassion for what my grandmother would sometimes refer to as "the poor things." She was speaking not only of her brothers and uncles, her cousins and neighbors, but of all those who suffered for the Confederacy.

The Blount plantation was between Richmond and Petersburg, and in 1864 my father's mother was a girl of fifteen when Butler's soldiers over-ran the place where no men were, and later when parties of Union deserters came at night as marauders. I remember very vividly her descriptions — of the terror she and her sister and mother struggled to hide, and the outrage they swallowed — but I also remember that she often said, "The Confederates stole more from us than the Yankees did in that last year — the poor things."

I do not feel that these formative influences affected my viewpoint any more than my friends in the North were affected by theirs. It can be observed in the Northern papers that when a book is written about the Confederates, the reviewer invariably explains that this book shows "the Southern viewpoint" — i.e. not his. A reviewer never says of a book written of the Federal forces that it shows "the Northern viewpoint." Even when a book on the Northern side refers only in passing to "the Rebels," who serve chiefly as foils, no viewpoint is mentioned. This is perfectly natural and to be expected. However, it should not be implied that those writing about the winning side have been less formed by their particular influences than those writing about the loser, or that by definition they are more objective. Yet so deeply ingrained is the attitude which regards war writings as divided between the acceptable, or objective, viewpoint and the Southern, or subjective, viewpoint that books of mine have been attacked for not *conforming to the Northern viewpoint of the South.*

In this sense, there is no such thing as "viewpoint" to the writer. A writer working from research is, like a novelist, attracted to a body of material in which he feels at home. An historian who was attracted to Hannibal might, I suppose, as the Romans saw it, be writing from "the Carthaginian viewpoint." With enough perspective, he would be seen simply to be writing about Hannibal. He would not slight Scipio Africanus out of any viewpoint but simply because the troops of Hannibal were the center of his interest. Because Lee's army was the center of my interest (and I enjoyed a running start in general background), my research in history has been concentrated here as my stories and novels were placed in this background.

When the stage of systematic research with sources is reached, everybody today — whatever the side — apparently works with the *Official Records*. This should not imply a diligent, cross-referenced work through the total, poorly indexed series: a single campaign will be covered in about a dozen of the bulky volumes. The only people who could read straight through the 128 volumes are similar to those who can read straight through the *Encyclopedia Britannica*. Many of my space-filling dust-gatherers have never been opened, and never shall be by me.

Though the *Official Records* are indispensable (in the literal meaning of that abused word), recently they have come to be regarded reverently as something like an omnipotent IBM machine. One historian built a reputation on his publisher's insistent claims about his use of the *Official Records*, giving the impression that he was the Columbus of this infallible material. Humphreys in his book on the Army of the Potomac, published in 1883, and Henderson in his Jackson, published in 1898, both relied heavily on the *OR*, though some of the later published volumes were not available to them. As stated earlier, Dr. Freeman was the first historian to make extensive use of the full series, in *R. E. Lee*, published in 1934.

Though no work could be done without them, the messages, reports and correspondence in the collection were composed by all too fallible human beings. In working on *The War Papers of R. E. Lee*, we have discovered such commonplace errors as wrong dates. It could be very confusing to a student without depth of background to read a letter written by Lee from near Richmond on a day when he was actually at the North Anna, as this would show Lee possessing knowledge which he did not possess on the date of the letter as in the *OR*.

Aside from mechanical errors, which occur every day in the best organizations, the correspondence was written by men very aware of their self-glorification and self-justification. As an example, the casualties in Lee's army, as reported by individual Union officers, from the Wilderness to Cold Harbor, can be selected and added to reach a total which far exceeds the number of men Lee had to begin with. Both Federal and Confederate reports of unhappy affairs can be studied as classics in understatement, while Homeric epics on successful actions would leave the impression that the enemy would never be seen again. A case-hardened student of the *OR* does not even blink to find a "wrecked, demoralized" division standing steadily to its work a few hours later.

This implies no distrust of the *OR*. It only indicates the need to apply judgment and do considerable cross-referencing. As a matter of fact, a study of the *OR* is fascinating. Nothing is more illuminating on the character of a general than to compare his battle report, written in the quiet of camp months after the event, with the messages he sent during the tension, sometimes panic, of the unfolding action. (In this book, the story of Beauregard at Petersburg was built almost entirely on this method.)

In military books written from the Northern side, you will find few Southern sources listed in the bibliographies, and scarcely ever those regimental histories which supply the living details. So, in my bibliography, there are very few Northern sources listed. In my experience, and in talking with friends working the other side of the street, research of the enemy is limited largely to establishing the broader facts, those no longer open to interpretation. With the *OR* as the primary source, this factual material includes the approximate number of "present effectives," the system and quantity of supply and transportation; the relative quality of individual units and the caliber of their commanders; when and where which units moved, the conditions under which they came into battle, and the conditions under which they fought.

This is not quite as surface as it sounds. By reading the messages sent during action and the reports filed by individuals in the enemy's forces, it is impossible not to form some personal opinion of the enemy's soldiers and leaders. No matter how deeply a researcher's interests may be centered in the fortunes of Lee's army, he cannot read the details of combat without forming the opinion, say, that Hancock was a superb corps commander, that Sheridan was an overrated bully-boy and that Meade was a generous, fine gentleman in an unhappy situation. As in watching a sport, you always recognize players on the other team who would be very helpful to your side (and you wish at least they were on the bench), and some whom you watch without sense of apprehension.

Of course, beyond the details of the enemy's forces, it is necessary to know always the opposing general's intentions and plans of execution — his strategy and tactics. For Grant, basic sources were his messages in the *OR* and his *Memoirs*, and the superlative account of the campaign by Meade's chief of staff, General A. A. Humphreys. Humphreys's *The Virginia Campaign of '64 and '65* was also a steady source of reference, with the *OR*, for composition, movement and performance of the troops in the Army of the Potomac. Also extremely helpful were Meade's candid letters to his wife and Colonel Lyman's letters from Meade's headquarters.

Bruce Catton, in his trilogy on the Army of the Potomac, has performed a priceless service for Southerners which no Southerner has performed for the other side: he presented a composite study of individual units garnered from regimental histories.

At times in the past for specific subjects (as the entry of the Federal forces into Richmond) I have studied a number of narratives by soldiers in the Army of the Potomac, and I have read current books on Federal leaders and units. (An old-line gentleman of Proctor, Vermont, whom I was visiting during Roosevelt's first administration, apologetically explained the appearance of the New York Sunday *Times* at his door by saying that he liked to know what the other side was up to.) This general reading, and the specific research in the past, left an impression of men and units, the tone of an army, though none was consulted for this book and none is listed.

For the Army of Northern Virginia, along with the *OR* and Freeman, the 53 volumes of the *Southern Historical Society Papers* are invaluable. These personal accounts were written by veterans, from generals to privates, soon after the war, when memories were fresh, and the first editor was the Reverend J. William Jones, formerly chaplain of the Army of Northern Virginia and of Washington (and Lee) College, when General Lee was president. Though the *SHSP* lack the official imprimatur of the *OR*, and the inaccuracies and personal biases are manifest, they contain the best and the most source material on Lee's army. As example, Colonel Venable's account of the 1864 campaign, as seen from Lee's headquarters, is nowhere else to be found; nearly all the personal narratives of staff officers and most of the scant material on Powell Hill are scattered through the volumes (which badly need an index).

Though personal narratives of Confederates — in the *SHSP*, similar collections and in published books — are abundant and voluble, the subjective Southerners usually wrote more on their own feelings about the whole thing than informative chronicles of their outfits. The similarity of the details of their misfortunes, their opinion of officers, the enemy and the conditions, provide in bulk a general agreement on the attitude of the Confederate soldier at successive stages, which makes a composite of these recollections an extremely valuable gauge to the state of the army in the 1864 campaign.

The really good unit histories are few. Clark's five volumes of North Carolina Regiments is a standard, though somewhat repetitious and with rather dispiriting prose. It is rich in detail on the troops with Hill and contains fine accounts of the Battle of the Wilderness.

By all odds the single best unit history is Caldwell's history of the Gregg-MacGowan (S.C.) brigade, with Wilcox's division, Third Corps, during the 1864 campaign. Dickert's *History of Kershaw's Brigade* is also excellent, very informative about the personnel of officers and useful on the 1864 campaign.

Casler's *Four Years in the Stonewall Brigade* is perhaps the best ac-

count of the life of a private soldier and, though it lacks the balance of
Caldwell and Dickert, and their information on officers, it gives an unforgettable impression of the brigade. Worsham's *One of Jackson's Foot
Cavalry*, a history of Richmond prewar Company F in the Second Corps,
is interesting and informative for its trace of the change of a *corps
d'élite* into a unit of "Lee's Miserables." McCarthy's *Detailed Minutiae
of Soldier Life in the Army of Northern Virginia*, though written by a
captain in a company of the Richmond Howitzer Battalion, is generally
and rightly regarded as indispensable for living up to its title.

Histories of the literate artillerists abound, and the one I found the
most useful was Stiles. *The Long Arm of Lee*, by Jennings Cropper Wise
(not a participant), is the standard on the army's artillery; it is unequaled
for its account of the officer personnel, though by current standards it is
lacking in the details of battery action.

With all my admiration for the beguiling writing and unforgettable
pictures in *Jeb Stuart*, by the late John Thomason, the best source for
Stuart, as for Wade Hampton, is Cooke's *Wearing of the Gray*. Blackford and McClellan, Stuart's young staff officer, contain good accounts
of the cavalry during Stuart's lifetime.

Of general stories by literate observers, Alexander is rightly regarded
as the best, though Sorrel is very good and was quite useful in this book,
as was Taylor's *Four Years with General Lee*.

Though Henderson's *Stonewall Jackson* stopped at Chancellorsville,
and his study of the Wilderness Campaign is a brief chapter in his published works, his unsurpassed analyses of the Confederate military operations and his emphases on the Confederate leadership make his books, to
me, a prime and stimulating source of study for any period in the Virginia theater.

Battles and Leaders has lost some of its aura of authority, as too many
contributors (of both sides) used their narratives to air their own grievances or — like Beauregard in his epic in Volume 4 — to build a case in
distortion of the records. Yet it is still an excellent source for details, especially of terrain, and its maps are among the very best.

For help on the difficult terrain of the Wilderness, I am greatly indebted to Mr. Ralph Happel, of the National Battlefield Park Service, at
Fredericksburg, and I wish to acknowledge my gratitude for the loan of
his manuscript, and his patient, unfailing and extensive cooperativeness.

I am indebted to Mr. McDonald Wellford, of Richmond, whose family owned the Catherine Furnace, for placing at my disposal his accumulation of records of wartime life and activities in the Wilderness country.
I also wish to thank Mr. Wellford, Dr. Beverly Randolph Wellford, and
Mr. Joseph Heistand, rector of St. Paul's Church, for their knowledge-

able companionship in working the battlefields. Without them, the way would have been longer and much lonelier.

I am indebted to Mr. N. P. Warinner, of Highland Springs, Virginia, for guidance on Confederate ordnance, for his findings with the mine detector, and for consultation on the fighting around Richmond — especially Cold Harbor — and to Mr. R. E. Stivers, of Silver Spring, Maryland, for valuable gleanings from his projected biography of Pickett.

I wish to thank Dr. Meriwether Stuart, of Bronxville, New York, for pages from his work in progress on regimental records compiled from the National Archives jackets on company rosters, and for much enlightenment on the techniques of his research and the findings. I am grateful to Mr. John Warren Cooke, of Mathews, Virginia, for the loan of the diary of his father, Major Giles Cooke. Major Cooke was the officer from Beauregard's staff who, after taking Beauregard's last "urgent" appeal to General Lee, effected a transfer to Lee's staff and lived to become his last surviving staff officer. I am indebted to Dr. W. G. Bean, of Washington and Lee University, for the use of letters by a young staff officer of Jubal Early, in the 1864 campaign.

For help on books and research, I am very grateful for the friendly cooperation of Miss Mary Clark Roane and Mr. Hubel Robins, of the Collectors Old Book Shop, Richmond. And again, as always, I wish to thank the staffs of the Virginia Historical Society, the Confederate Museum, and the Virginia State Library.

Also again, I wish to thank my friends in the Richmond medical profession — Dr. Wellford, Dr. Harry Warthen, Dr. Dupont Guerry, III, Dr. David Markham, Dr. E. L. Kendig, Jr., and Dr. St. George Tucker — for guidance on the physical condition of leaders, particularly the mysterious ailments of A. P. Hill.

I am grateful to the Medical College of Virginia Hospital for the opportunity of looking at their Civil War records. Nothing revealed more in detail, and more in pathos, the equipment of a Confederate soldier than their lists of the belongings left by soldiers who died in the hospital.

Finally, I wish to thank the Governor of Virginia, the Hon. J. Lindsay Almond, Jr., and the Virginia Civil War Commission, for giving me the opportunity to work on *The War Papers of R. E. Lee,* with its access to Lee's total correspondence, and Mr. Louis Manarin, for his splendid work in processing the correspondence and making the items readily accessible.

As to maps, I worked from Steele, the *OR* Atlas, and *Battles and Leaders.* Most of all, to rank with the *OR,* Lee's correspondence, *SHSP,* Freeman and personal narratives, are the fields themselves. After the reading and the map studies, come the fields; from the fields, there is a return to reading and maps; and then, the process begins all over again with the fields. The *feeling* of the scope of a battle comes finally only with a familiarity with a field such as one has with his own room.

There the student knows more than any general on the field knew, because at that moment in time he alone in all the world is standing there with the knowledge of where everything was happening on every part of the field at the same time. At least, that is the researcher's sensation. In that moment of omniscience, he forgets the conflicting evidence from which he made his deductions, the gaps which he filled with reasonable assumptions, and the panorama unfolds not as if it were partly his own re-creation, but as if he were watching the action happen in a rollback of time.

Of books consulted, as an understanding of the army and its leaders is necessary for an understanding of a specific campaign, I have included some books on the army, on Lee and his generals, which may treat of the 1864 campaign only in passing, and a few not directly at all. But I have omitted all books on the war which are not concerned strictly with this army and its leaders, and as at least pertaining to the 1864 campaign. As example, no biographies or memoirs of generals not with the army in 1864 have been included (except Henderson's *Jackson* as mentioned, which was more a study of war) and no accounts restricted to other campaigns, however vividly they may portray segments of Lee's army.

For general studies of the CSA — particularly its civil leaders, the operations of the War Department and of President Davis in relation to the military, and the wartime life of Richmond — I used my own *Experiment in Rebellion* (Garden City, 1946) and *The Land They Fought For* (Garden City, 1955), both of which contain complete bibliographies on the broader phases of the war and of the non-military aspects. My *Death of a Nation* (New York, 1958) is a study of the army's general-officer personnel during the Gettysburg campaign in its reorganization, following Jackson's death, which continued with only individual changes into the 1864 campaign. These books are not otherwise listed.

I would like to say that no critical evaluations are implied by my selections and omissions in the following bibliography: many good books which had no direct application to this campaign were highly enjoyed and contributed to a general knowledge.

Agassiz, George R., ed. *Meade's Headquarters, 1863-65: Letters of Col. Theodore Lyman from the Wilderness to Appomattox.* Boston, 1922.
Alexander, E. F. *Military Memoirs of a Confederate.* New York, 1907.
Annals of the War, Written by Leading Participants North and South.

Philadelphia, 1879. (Contains General Wilcox's account of the Wilderness.)

Battles and Leaders of the Civil War. 4 vols. New York, 1887-1888.

Beale, R. L. T. *History of 9th Virginia Cavalry.* Richmond, 1899.

Bean, W. G. *Stonewall's Man: Sandie Pendleton.* Chapel Hill, 1959.

Black, Robert C., III. *Railroads of the Confederacy.* Chapel Hill, 1952.

Blackford, Susan Leigh, compiler. *Letters from Lee's Army.* New York, 1947.

Blackford, William Willis. *War Years With Jeb Stuart.* New York, 1945.

Bradford, Gamaliel. *Confederate Portraits.* Boston, 1917.

———. *Lee, the American.* Boston, 1912.

Brooks, U. R. *Butler and His Cavalry* . . . Columbia, S.C., 1909.

Bushong, Millard Kessler. *Old Jube: A Biography of General Jubal A. Early.* Boyce, Va., 1955.

Caldwell, J. F. F. *The History of a Brigade of South Carolinians.* (New edition) Marietta, Ga., 1951.

Casler, John O. *Four Years in the Stonewall Brigade.* (New edition) Marietta, Ga., 1951.

Catton, Bruce. *A Stillness at Appomattox.* Garden City, 1953.

Chamberlaine, William W. *Memoirs of the Civil War.* Washington, 1912. (This observant officer served in Hill's corps.)

Chamberlayne, C. G., ed. *Ham Chamberlayne — Virginian.* Richmond, 1933. (Among the very best letters of the war, by a battery commander in Hill's corps in the 1864 campaign.)

Clark, Walter, ed. *Histories of the Several Regiments . . . from North Carolina* . . . 5 vols. Raleigh and Goldsboro, N.C., 1901.

Cockrell, Monroe F., ed. *Gunner With Stonewall: Reminiscences of William Thomas Poague.* Jackson, Tenn., 1957. (Poague commanded the Third Corps gun battalion at the Tapp farm.)

Cooke, John Esten. *Robert E. Lee.* New York, 1875.

———. *Wearing of the Gray.* New York, 1867.

Dame, William Meade. *From the Rapidan to Richmond.* Baltimore, 1920.

Daniel, Frederick S. *Richmond Howitzers During the War.* Richmond, 1891.

Dickert, Augustus D. *History of Kershaw's Brigade.* Newberry, S.C., 1899.

Dictionary of American Biography. Dumas Malone, editor. New York, 1928- (Sketches of general officers, though far from complete.)

Douglas, Henry Kyd. *I Rode With Stonewall.* Chapel Hill, 1940. (Following the death of Jackson, Major Douglas transferred to the staff of General Edward Johnson, with whose division he served in 1864.)

Dunaway, Wayland F. *Reminiscences of a Rebel.* New York, 1913.

Early, Jubal A. *A Memoir of the Last Year of the War for Independence in the Confederate States of America.* Lynchburg, Va., 1867.

Eckenrode, H. J. and Conrad, Bryan. *James Longstreet, Lee's War Horse.* Chapel Hill, 1936.

Eggleston, George Cary. *A Rebel's Recollections.* New York, 1875.

Evans, Clement A., ed. *Confederate Military History.* 13 vols. Atlanta, 1899. (Biographical sketches of general officers; complements *DAB.*)

Fletcher, W. A. *Rebel Private, Front and Rear.* (New edition) Austin, Texas, 1954.

Freeman, Douglas Southall. *R. E. Lee.* 4 vols. New York, 1934.

————. *Lee's Lieutenants.* 3 vols. New York, 1942-1944.

————. *Lee's Dispatches to Jefferson Davis.* New York, 1915. (This is correspondence not included in the *OR.*)

Gordon, John B. *Reminiscences of the Civil War.* New York, 1903.

Grant, U. S. *Personal Memoirs.* New York, 1885.

Hamlin, Percy Gatling. *Old Baldhead: General R. S. Ewell.* Strasburg, Va., 1940.

Harrison, Walter. *Pickett's Men.* New York, 1870.

Hassler, William Woods. *A. P. Hill: Lee's Forgotten General.* Richmond, 1957.

Henderson, George F. R. *Stonewall Jackson and the American Civil War.* (American one-volume edition) New York, 1936.

————. *The Civil War, A Soldier's View: A Collection of Civil War Writings,* edited by Jay Luvaas. Chicago, 1958. (Contains his study of the campaign from the Wilderness to Cold Harbor.)

Howard, McHenry. *Recollections of a Soldier and Staff-Officer.* Baltimore, 1914.

Humphreys, Brigadier General A. A. *The Virginia Campaign of '64 and '65.* New York, 1883.

Hunton, Eppa. *Autobiography.* (Privately printed) Richmond, 1933. (General Hunton, a survivor of Gettysburg, commanded a brigade with Pickett in 1864.)

Jones, Rev. J. William. *Personal Reminiscences of General Robert E. Lee.* New York, 1875.

Livermore, Thomas L. *Numbers and Losses in the Civil War.* (New edition) Bloomington, Ind., 1956.

Loehr, Charles T. *History of the 1st Virginia Regiment.* Richmond, 1884.

Long, A. L. *Memoirs of Robert E. Lee.* Richmond, 1886. (This is General Long, one-time staff officer, who commanded Second Corps artillery in 1864.)

Longstreet, James. *From Manassas to Appomattox.* Philadelphia, 1896.

McCarthy, Carlton A. *A Detailed Minutiae of Soldier Life in the Army of Northern Virginia.* Richmond, 1882.

Macon, T. J. *Reminiscences of the 1st Company of Richmond Howitzers.* Richmond, N.D.

Malone, Bartlett Y. *Diary of* . . . W. W. Pierson, Jr., ed. Chapel Hill, 1919.

Marshall, Charles. *An Aide-de-Camp of Lee* . . . Major General Sir Frederick Maurice, ed. Boston, 1927.

Maurice, Major General Sir Frederick. *Robert E. Lee, the Soldier.* Boston, 1925.

McClellan, H. B. *Life and Campaign of Major-General J. E. B. Stuart.* Richmond, 1885.

McKim, Randolph H. *A Soldier's Recollections.* New York, 1910.

———. *The Soul of Lee.* New York, 1918.

Meade, George Gordon. *Life and Letters of George Gordon Meade.* 2 vols. New York, 1913.

Mixson, Frank M. *Narratives of a Private.* Columbia, S.C., 1910.

Moffett, Mary C., ed. *Letters of General James Conner, C.S.A.* (Privately printed) Columbia, S.C., 1933. (Conner was judge-advocate of Ewell's corps in the 1864 campaign.)

Moore, Edward A. *The Story of a Cannoneer Under Stonewall Jackson.* New York, 1907. (With the Second Corps in 1864.)

Morgan, W. H. *Personal Reminiscences of the War.* Lynchburg, Va., 1911.

Oates, William C. *The War between the Union and the Confederacy.* New York and Washington, 1907. (This literate narrative by a regimental commander in Law's brigade contains an account of the Law-Longstreet feud.)

Official Records of the War of the Rebellion. 128 vols. Washington, D.C. 1902.

Owen, William M. *In Camp and Battle with the Washington Artillery of New Orleans.* Boston, 1885.

Photographic History of the Civil War. 10 vols. New York, 1911.

Pickett, George E. *Soldier of the South* . . . *War Letters to His Wife.* Boston, 1928. ("Edited" is a charitable euphemism for the imaginative doctoring performed by the general's widow, La Salle Corbell Pickett.)

Roman, Alfred. *The Military Operations of Gen. Beauregard.* 2 vols. New York, 1884. (Roman was little more than amanuensis for Beauregard's autobiography.)

Royall, William L. *Some Reminiscences.* New York and Washington,

1909. (Contains the account by Colonel Palmer, Hill's chief-of-staff, of the controversial night in the Wilderness.)

Scott, W. W., ed. *Two Confederate Items*. (Pamphlet) Richmond, 1927. (Contains day-by-day diary of Captain Wingfield, 58th Virginia, Ewell's corps, during 1864 campaign, and Judge Moncure's *Reminiscences of the Civil War;* as a trooper in the 9th Virginia Cavalry, Moncure rode with General Lee as guide on the night ride from Spotsylvania to the North Anna, through the young soldier's home neighborhood.)

Seitz, Don. *Braxton Bragg . . .* Columbia, S.C., 1924.

Sorrel, G. Moxley. *Recollections of a Confederate Staff Officer*. (New edition) Jackson, Tenn., 1958.

Southern Historical Society Papers. 53 vols. Richmond, 1876-1959.

Steele, Matthew Forney. *American Campaigns*. 2 vols. Washington, 1909.

Stiles, Robert. *Four Years Under Marse Robert*. Washington, 1903.

Tankersley, Allen P. *John B. Gordon*. Atlanta, 1955.

Taylor, Walter H. *Four Years With General Lee*. New York, 1877.

Thomas, Henry W. *History of the Doles-Cooke Brigade*. Atlanta, 1903.

Thomason, John W. *Jeb Stuart*. New York, 1933.

Venable, C. S. *The Campaign from the Wilderness to Petersburg*. (Vol. 14, *SHSP*, pp. 522-542.)

Walker, James A. *Address on the Unveiling of the Statue of Gen. A. P. Hill, Richmond, Va.* (Vol. 20, *SHSP*, pp 370-386.)

Warner, Ezra J. *Generals in Gray*. Baton Rouge, 1959. (Biographical sketches of general officers.)

Welch, Spencer Glasgow, Dr. *A Confederate Surgeon's Letters to His Wife*. (New edition) Marietta, Ga., 1954. (Dr. Welch was with Hill's corps in the 1864 campaign.)

Wiley, Bell Irvin. *The Life of Johnny Reb*. Indianapolis, 1943.

Williams, T. Harry. *Beauregard: Napoleon in Gray*. Baton Rouge, 1954.

Wise, Jennings Cropper. *The Long Arm of Lee: The History of the Artillery of the Army of Northern Virginia*. (New edition) New York, 1959.

Wood, William Nathaniel. *Reminiscences of Big I*. (New edition) Jackson, Tenn., 1956. (Lieutenant Wood served in the 19th Virginia, Pickett's division.)

Worsham, John F. *One of Jackson's Foot Cavalry*. New York, 1912. (The 21st Virginia was in Edward Johnson's division in 1864 and involved in the breakthrough at Spotsylvania.)

Index

Index

ALABAMA BATTALION, 5th, 124-125, 132
Alabama brigade, 211
Albemarle, 39
Alexander, Brig. Gen. Porter, 116, 141-143, 199-200, 211, 213, 264, 349
Ammunition issue (Confederate), 77-78
Anderson, Brig. Gen. George T. ("Tige"), 139, 151, 155, 161, 162
Anderson, Lieut. Gen. Richard H., background and qualities, 114-115, 183, 287, 289, 371; Wilderness, 128, 133, 160, 161, 169; moved up to Longstreet's command, 175, 182, 287; Spotsylvania, 182, 183-184, 188-192, 209, 211, 286-287; Bethesda Church, 280; promoted to Lieut. Gen., 289; Cold Harbor, 292; Petersburg, 336
Anderson's Corps. *See* First Corps
Anderson's Station, 256, 257
Appomattox County, 368
Archer, Brig. Gen. James Jay, 111
Armistead, Gen. Walker, 230
Army of Northern Virginia, plans for *1864* campaign, 3-4; makeup, morale and officers, 3-33 *passim*, 71-72, 76-82, 218, 303; "Lee's army," 5, 8, 358; sense of family in, 26; problem of detached brigades, 39-40, 169; uniform, equipment and morale of individual soldiers, 62-65; replacements, 66; decline in morale, 66-67; aggregate, 71-72, 253, 312, 320, 356; underestimated by Grant, 132; outfought Grant's army, 171; lacked strength to win, 172; Lee's recognition of accomplishments and failures, 175; defensive stand, 176, 179; elements of chance, 183; cavalry,

186, 310; weaknesses, 186, 198; return of detached brigades, 245; personnel changes, 194-195, 270, 293; bureaucratic control hurts organization, 302; importance of Virginia Central to, 314; Grant's conclusions, 316; on Beauregard's front, 343; last campaign of maneuver, 358; humiliation of retreat, 367-368; last days, 368, 370-372; *See also* First Corps, Second Corps, Third Corps
Army of the Potomac, in camp prior to *1864* campaign, 3-4; politically dominated, 5; possibilities for strategy, 31-32; real command by Grant, 49; makeup and morale, aggregate and losses, 53-54, 70-71, 171-172, 214, 218, 256, 266, 315; crossing of Rapidan, 61; Wilderness, 69-70, 73, 83, 99, 131-133, 155, 171-172; retains initiative, 172-173; subsurface conflict, 184-185; Spotsylvania, 212-214, 218, 224-225; "on to Richmond" campaign, 228, 230-231; withdraws from Spotsylvania, 249, 250-251; "battle" of North Anna, 265-266; "sidling movement," 267-269; Bethesda Church, 279; Cold Harbor, 292, 315; disappearance and probing for, 317-327, 344; Petersburg, 349; last days of campaign, 354-355
Army of Tennessee, 13, 171, 365, 366
Artillery (Army of Northern Virginia), aggregate, 71-72; Second Corps, 90; Third Corps, 115-116; First Corps, 141-143
Atlanta (Ga.), importance, 58; military action, 361-362; fall, 364-365
Atlee (Va.), 269, 270

BARLOW, BRIG. GEN. FRANCIS (U.S.), 120, 123
Barringer, Brig. Gen. Rufus, 303
Barton, Brig. Gen. Seth, 275
Battle, Brig. Gen. Cullen, 90, 92, 96, 97
"Battle of the Patients and the Penitents," 304
Baum, Courier, 166
Beauregard, Gen. Pierre Toutant Gustave, 74, 75, 141; commander Department of Southern Virginia and North Carolina, 40-41, 231-232; "sick" for Petersburg situation, 234-235, 237, 239; background and characteristics, 239-241, 344; appointed full general, 241; Davis's antipathy, 242, 246; question of joint action with Lee, 242-243, 244, 350; preparations for attack on Butler, 243-244, 255; unwillingness to co-operate with Lee, 245-246, 255, 266, 292, 327, 333, 334, 348-349; Lee's meetings with, 277-278, 250-253; sends reinforcements to Lee, 282; messages to Lee, 303, 335, 337, 338, 339, 341, 342, 343, 344, 345, 346, 347; and the Lee myth, 319-320, 327-334, 338, 342, 343, 345, 350; requests for reinforcements, 327-329, 337, 338, 339, 345, 347, 348; withdraws troops from Bermuda Hundred, 332, 335; felt injustice of his status, 351, 373
Belle Plain (Va.), 250
Benning, Brig. Gen. Henry Lewis ("Rock"), 139, 154-155, 175
Berkeley Plantation, 323-324
Bermuda Hundred, Butler's base, 74, 232, 233; Beauregard abandons lines at, 329, 332, 333-337
Bethesda Church, 284
Birney, Major Gen. David Bell (U.S.), 118
Blackford, Lieut. Col. W. W., 28
Borcke, Baron Heroes von, 28
Bragg, Gen. Braxton, 171, 367; similarity to Longstreet, 10; ineptitude at Chickamauga, 15; Military Adviser to War Department, 40, 47; characteristics and failures, 47, 237, 332, 333; and Beauregard, 234-235,

326-327, 332; ignored Pickett's messages, 235; approved reinforcements to Lee, 282; commander in chief for departmental co-ordination, 302
Breathed, Major James, 142, 190
Breckinridge, Brig. Gen. John, in Shenandoah Valley, 74, 304, 311; decides to join Lee, 226; Hanover Junction, 252; North Anna, 265; Cold Harbor, 293-294, 297; wounded, 304
Brice's Crossroads, 361
Brigade (Confederate), basic battle unit, 77-78
Brigadier Generals (Confederate), 78
Bristoe Station, 108
Brock Road, Federal army on, 72, 181, 184-185, 188; Meade to defend passage, 93-95; Longstreet's path opened to, 162-164; Longstreet's scheme, 165-166; confusion, 168, 169, 173; held by Meade, 169, 170. See also Wilderness
Brockenbrough, Col. John M., 111
Brown, Major Campbell, 84, 85, 199
Brown, Col. J. Thompson, 99
Brown, Widow (Mrs. Richard S. Ewell), 18-20, 84, 87
Bryan, Brig. Gen. Goode, 141, 155, 191, 192
Burnside, Gen. Ambrose E. (U.S.), IX Corps of, 70, 71, 157, 158, 159, 168, 169, 171, 172, 175, 213, 264, 277, 342, 344, 351
Butler, General Benjamin (U.S.), secondary army threatens Richmond from the south, 74, 172-173, 175, 226, 232-233; incompetence, 235-236, 238; driven back by Beauregard, 243-244; at Petersburg, 336, 343-344
Butler, Brig. Gen. Calbraith, 186-187, 272, 305, 307-308, 309, 372
Byrd, Col. Williams, 52

CARTERS, Lee's maternal ancestors, 59, 60
Casler, Private John O., 203
Catharpin Road, 61, 104-105, 109, 134, 155
Catherine Furnace, 53
Cavalry (Army of Northern Vir-

ginia), function as "eyes of the infantry," 27-29; condition and equipment, 29-30; waning strength, 69, 71, 176, 305

Chaffin's Bluff, 324, 326

Chamberlayne, Hampden, 5

Chambersburg (Pa.), 28

Chambliss, Brig. Gen. John, 186

Chancellorsville, 11, 13, 70, 161, 171, 176

Charleston (S.C.), importance, 58; Sherman devastates, 366

Charlottesville, 306

Chesnut, Mrs. Mary Boykin, 15

Chester Station, 336

Chew, Lieut. Col. Robert Preston, 142

Chewning Hill farm, 158-159

Chickahominy River, 294, 299; Grant crosses, 317, 320-321

Chickamauga, 15, 138

Chisholm, Capt. A. R., 347

City Point (Va.), 74

Clark's Mountain, 61; meeting of Lee and his generals, 3, 12, 17, 24, 31-33, 370

Clingman, Brig. Gen. T. L., 283, 285, 290, 294

Cold Harbor, battle of, 284-290, 294, 296, 297-298; Sheridan's cavalry, 284; deterioration in Lee's command, 289; Grant's army, 292; Lee's army, 292, 294; casualties, 297-299; trenches, 321

Colquitt, Brig. Gen. Alfred H., 238, 243

Columbia (S.C.), burned by Sherman, 366

Company (Confederate), group spirit, 77

Confederacy, strained resources, 4, 58; military departments, 36-38; delusions as to future status, 56-57; breakup of, 367-369; certainty of defeat, 370; uniforms, equipment and morale of individual soldiers, 62-65

Confederate naval forces, 363

Conner, Judge Advocate James, 19

Conscripts, confederate, 66

Cooke, Major Giles, 347, 348

Cooke, Major John Esten, 29, 86

Cooke, Brig. Gen. John R., 111-112

Cooke, Philip St. George (U.S.), 112

Cooper, General Samuel, 235, 241

Corps (Confederate), a complete army in itself, 79-80

Corse, Brig. Gen. Montgomery, 231, 275

Crawford, Brevet Major-Gen. Samuel (U.S.), 95, 98, 105, 108

Crook, Brig. Gen. George, 304

Crouch, Nichols, 86

Crutchfield, Stapleton, 90

Cullen, Dr. J. S. Dorsey, 166

Custer, Gen. George Armstrong (U.S.), 274, 307-308

Custis, George Washington Parke, 60

Cutler's division (U.S.), 156, 258

Cutshaw's battalion, 200, 203, 224

Dahlgren, Col. Ulric (U.S.), 69

Daniels, Brig. Gen. Junius, 90, 96, 97, 209

Davis, President Jefferson, 70; and Longstreet, 16; Lee's handling of, 24; military differences with Lee, 36-42, 227-228; nature and policies, 42-48; unaware of new offensive phase, 55; Lee's attempts to get back detached troops, 73-76; inability to grasp intangibles, 76, 81, 330; system of departments and dispersal of troops, 228-229, 231, 232; and Beauregard, 235, 241-242, 246; Lee's request for reinforcements, 292; administrative quarrels, 331, 332; personal control of military establishment, 362; and Johnston, 363, 364-365

Davis, Brig. Gen. Joseph, 111, 112, 161

Dearing, Brig. Gen. James, 243, 304

Democratic Party (U.S.), 57, 58

Department of Alabama and Mississippi, 363

Department of Cape Fear, 229

Department of Henrico, 235

Department of North Carolina, 229-231

Department of Northern Virginia, 37-38

Department of Richmond, 232, 235, 371

Department of the South Atlantic, 241

Department of Southern Virginia and North Carolina, 40, 231, 239, 348

Departmental system, effects of, 228-229; breakdown of, 348, 352, 353; Lee circumvents, 362

Division (Confederate), largest unit directly commanded by one man, 78-79

Dobie, Capt. Alfred E., 166

Doles, Brig. Gen. George, 90, 96, 97, 302

Douglas, Major Henry Kyd, 67, 205

Drewry's Bluff, 38-39, 74, 232, 233, 238, 324, 326, 327; Lee's headquarters, 333, 336, 342

EARLY, MAJOR GEN. JUBAL, 176, 253; influence on Ewell, 20, 170; harshness and ability, 88-89, 182, 193; Wilderness, 97, 169-170, 171; temporarily replaces Hill, 175, 193, 217; replaces Ewell, 269; Bethesda Church, 278-280; Cold Harbor, 292, 294; command in Shenandoah Valley, 312-313; effect on military pattern in Virginia, 314; overrun by Sheridan, 365; last days of campaign, 371

Echols, Brig. Gen. John, 297

Eggleston, George Cary, 277

Ely Ford, 32, 61, 94

Elzey, Arnold, 312

Emancipation Proclamation, 57

Enfield rifles, Confederate issue, 64

Enon Church, 273

Evans, Col. Clement, 206, 253

Evans, Gen. N. G. ("Shanks"), 80-81

Ewell, Lieut. Gen. Richard Stoddert ("Old Baldhead"), nature, record and personal life, 9, 17-20, 86-88; marriage, 18; advance to Wilderness via Old Turnpike, 35, 55, 61, 70; detached brigade of, 39, 41; requests orders, 84-85, 91; Lee's limiting orders, 85-86, 91-92; Wilderness, 91, 93, 97, 98, 99-100, 108, 132-134; ignores discretionary orders, 100-101; immobilized by Lee's discretionary orders, 132-134, 159, 169-171; Early's influence on, 170; unfit for high command, 175; Spotsylvania, 198, 200-201, 203; ill health, 265; commander of Richmond defenses, 269; replaced by Early, 269-270; capture of, 371

Ewell, Mrs. Richard S., 18-20, 84, 87

Ewell's corps. See Second Corps

FARLEY, CAPT. WILL, 28

Field, Major Gen. Charles, refuses verbal order from Lee, 135; his division, 137, 139, 371; background, 139-140; Wilderness, 141, 151, 153, 156, 157, 160, 161, 167-168, 170, 174; wounded, 175; Cold Harbor, 289; Bermuda Hundred, 344

Field's division, Spotsylvania, 192; Cold Harbor, 294; Petersburg-Richmond front, 337, 340, 347, 350; Fort Harrison, 370; last days, 371

Finegan, Brig. Gen. Joseph, 297

First Corps (Army of Northern Virginia), 13; Wilderness, 61, 134-135, 137-143, 148, 151-156, 161-169; aggregate, 71; under Anderson, 182; Spotsylvania, 182-184, 188, 189, 191, 213, 224; Hanover Junction, 254, 255; North Anna, 263; Cold Harbor, 285, 286-287, 290, 294, 296; last days, 371

First Manassas, battle of, 77, 80, 241

Florida battalions, reinforcements to Lee, 292; Cold Harbor, 297

Forrest, Gen. Nathan Bedford, 361, 362-363

Fort Dantzler, 336

Fort Fisher, 366

Fort Harrison, 369, 370

Fort Monroe, 38, 195, 230

Frank, Brevet Brig. Gen. Paul (U.S.), 162-163

Fredericksburg, 32, 93, 94, 164, 167, 171

Fredericksburg & Potomac Railroad, 263

GAILLARD, COL. FRANKLIN, 175

Gaines's Mill, 153, 291-292, 300

Georgia brigades, 88-89; Wofford and Bryan, 191-192; Evans, 206, 207, 253

Germanna Ford, 32, 53, 61, 91, 94, 133

Getty, Brig. Gen. George Washington (U.S.), 109, 118

Gettysburg, 111, 112, 115, 134, 141, 160, 170; Longstreet's conduct, 10-11, 14-15; Ewell's unfitness, 18, 85; end of hope for decisive Confederate victory, 65

Gibbon, Major Gen. John (U.S.), 119, 155, 156, 157, 164

Gordon, Brig. Gen. James, 186, 221, 259, 271

Gordon, Major Gen. John B., under Early, 88-89; Wilderness, 97, 98, 120, 121, 169-171, 174; elevated to division command, 194, 253; Spotsylvania, 205-208, 211; Bethesda Church, 280; last days of campaign, 371; Lee's closest companion, 372

Gordonsville, Longstreet at, 35, 52, 137

Gorgas, Brig. Gen. Josiah, 331, 363

Gracie, Brig. Gen. Archibald, 328

Graham, Col. R. F., 236

Grant, Gen. Ulysses S. (U.S.), 5, 12, 13, 14; Lee's unfamiliarity with, 31, 32; his authority, nature and background, 35-36, 49-52; three-pronged objective on Richmond, 37-38; with Army of the Potomac, 44; offensive policy in relation to Lee, 48; concept of total war, 49-50, 267-268; underestimated Lee, 54, 83; confidence and hammering tactics, 93, 173, 198, 213-214, 299, 315; Wilderness, 118, 124, 131-133, 168, 171-172; recognized Lee's accomplishments, 175; retains initiative, 175-176; Spotsylvania, 192, 214; fundamental difference from Lee, 227; "sidling movement," 249-250, 267; refuses battle at North Anna, 267; admits Cold Harbor a mistake, 299; diversionary attacks, 303; purpose in Shenandoah Valley, 304; objective to cut Confederate supply lines, 314-315; attempts to force Lee out of entrenchments, 315; "stole a march on Lee," 319; whereabouts a mystery after Cold Harbor, 337-347; campaign of maneuver in Virginia a military failure, 353-354

Gregg, Brig. Gen. John, Texas brigade, 139, 347; Wilderness, 152, 153

Gregg's division (U.S.), 70, 273, 308

Griffin, Brig. Gen. Simon G. (U.S.), 93, 94, 95, 96, 97

Guiney's Station, 73, 251

Hagwood, Brig. Gen. Johnson, 236, 238, 283

Hammond, Col. John (U.S.), 105

Hampton, Major Gen. Wade, brigades under, 186; withdrawal from Spotsylvania, 252; as division commander, 272, 273

Hampton's cavalry, and Sheridan's cavalry, 273-274, 305-308; Trevilian's Station, 320; last days of campaign, 372

Hancock, Gen. Winfield Scott (U.S.), II Corps, 69-70, 94, 109, 118-120, 123, 124, 126, 143-145, 148, 155-157, 160, 163, 164, 168, 169, 201, 205, 207, 251, 261, 263, 264, 265, 297, 318, 326, 332, 341, 342, 344

Hanover County, 254

Hanover Junction, 90, 232, 252-254

Hanovertown, 268-269

Harris, Brig. Gen. Nathaniel, 115, 210-211

Harrison's Landing, 323

Haskell's battalion, 190

Haw's Shop, 273

Hays, Brig. Gen. Harry, 88, 194, 204

Henagan, Col. John W., 152, 175, 190, 288

Heth, Major Gen. Harry, 69, 70, 294; Wilderness, 110-112, 117-124, 126-129, 144-145, 151; Spotsylvania, 209; Jericho Mills, 257, 259

Hill, Lieut. Gen. Ambrose Powell, 34, 35, 55, 181, 336; background and characteristics, 9, 11, 12, 20-24, 57, 110-111; Longstreet's feud with, 11, 114, 139; advance to Wilderness, 61, 62, 68-70, 83-84, 94; Lee with, 69; aggregate of his corps, 71, 79; Wilderness, 99-100, 104, 106, 107, 123-130, 135-136, 143, 145, 148, 149, 151, 152, 158-160, 164; illness, 104, 108, 126, 129, 175, 193, 265; almost captured, 116-117, 158-159; Jericho Mills, 257-258; Lee rebukes, 258, 260; talents in corps command, 356-357

Hill, Major Gen. D. H., 37, 113, 237, 239, 243-244, 253, 312

Hill's Corps. *See* Third Corps

Hoke, Major Gen. Robert, detached in North Carolina, 39-40, 41, 75, 89, 169; command of district, 231, 232; commands division in Beauregard's army, 246; sent to reinforce Lee, 281, 292; background, 283; failure to co-operate with Anderson, 287; Cold Harbor, 292, 294

Hoke's division, sent as reinforcements for Lee, 281-282, 292; Cold Harbor, 284-286, 294; detached and ordered to Drewry's Bluff, 324, 326-328; Petersburg, 351; Fort Harrison, 370; last days of campaign, 371

Hoke's old brigade, 194, 238, 253, 263, 280, 281

Hood, Major Gen. John B., 23, 77, 135, 138, 139, 350, 365, 366

Hood's Texans, 139

Hooker, Gen. Joseph (U.S.), 133, 168, 171, 172, 175

Hotchkiss, Jed, 19

Humphreys, Gen. A. A. (U.S.), 71, 264, 273, 277

Humphreys, Brig. Gen. Benjamin, 141, 151, 190

Hunt, Major Gen. Henry (U.S.), 90

Hunter, Gen. David (U.S.), 303-305, 311, 313

Hunter, Senator R. M. T. (Confederate), 331

Hunton, Eppa, 275

Hygeia Hotel, 230

Imboden, Brig. Gen. John, 226

Jackson, Gen. Thomas J. ("Stonewall"), 5, 87-91 *passim*, 161, 163, 168, 171; genius of, 8-9; meteoric rise and career, 13-14, 363; and Ewell, 17-18; the Stonewall brigade of, 77, 204-205; *1862* Valley campaign, 313

James River, boundary of Lee's operations, 37-38; arrival of Butler's army, 74; enemy gunboat control, 314; Grant crosses, 317, 318; course, 324

Jefferson, Thomas, 306

Jenkins, Brig. Gen. Micah, 138-139, 165-166, 175, 302

Jericho Mills, battle of, 257-258

Johnson, Major Gen. Bushrod, 236; division head in Beauregard's army, 246; Bermuda Hundred, 328, 333; Petersburg, 349-350

Johnson, Major Gen. Edward ("Allegheny"), 23, 42, 67, 92; eccentricities, 89-90; Wilderness, 95, 97, 98; Spotsylvania, 194, 196, 200-204, 214, 217-218; Lee exonerates, 202-203

Johnston, Gen. Albert Sidney, 241, 334

Johnston, Gen. Joseph E., 142, 241, 242; rebuilds Army of Tennessee, 47-48; Atlanta, 58, 362-363, 367; relations with Davis, 363-365

Johnston, Brig. Gen. Robert D., 90, 195, 205, 207, 280

Jones, Rev. J. William, 22

Jones, Brig. Gen. John M., 90, 91, 92, 95, 96, 99, 203

Jouett, Jack, 306

Kautz's cavalry (U.S.), 237, 304, 318

Keitt, Brig. Gen. Laurence Massillon, 288-289

Kemper, Brig. Gen. James Lawson, 221, 275

Kershaw, Brig. Gen. Joseph, background, 140-141; Wilderness, 141, 151, 152, 154, 155, 156, 157, 160, 161, 165, 166; Spotsylvania, 189, 190, 191, 192; Cold Harbor, 285, 286, 287, 289, 290, 294; Chaffin Bluff, 342; Richmond-Petersburg front, 346, 347, 349, 350

Kershaw's old brigade, 175

Kilpatrick, Brig. Gen. Judson ("Kill Cavalry") (U.S.), raid on Richmond, 69

Kirkland, Brig. Gen. W. W., 105-106, 107, 111, 120, 121, 122

Knoxville, siege of, 11, 12, 15

Lane, Brig. Gen. James, 113, 121-124, 132, 144, 208, 258, 302

Latimer, Major Joseph W., 143

Law, Brig. Gen. Evander, 11, 12, 15, 16, 138, 139, 154, 157, 165, 302

Lee, Agnes, 68

Lee, Ann Carter, 59

Lee, Major Gen. Fitzhugh, 27, 30, 221, 308; Spotsylvania, 186-191; as division commander, 272-273; Cold Harbor, 285, 294

Lee, Gen. Robert E., Clark's Mountain meeting, 3, 5, 31-33; declining health, 4; loss of initiative from growing weakness of his army, 4, 45, 172-176, 179, 280; confidence in "Uncle Robert" and his indestructibility, 4-5, 65-66, 368; personification of a cause, 5-6; the legend, 6-7, 28-30, 32-33; method of operating, 8-9; and Longstreet, 14-17; and Ewell, 20; and Hill, 24; and his staff, 24-31; and Jeb Stuart, 30; anticipation of Grant's strategy, 32, 34, 35-36, 51-54, 61-62; headquarters in tent to prevent reprisals, 34-35; military differences with Jefferson Davis, 36-42, 48; problem of detached brigades, 39, 75-76, 81-82, 169; relative freedom with his own army, 43-46; unfamiliarity with Grant's nature, 48, 50; gamble to seize initiative, 54-55; aware of new Federal offensive phase and the South's problem, 55-56; distaste for slavery, 57; hopes for stalemate, 58-60; family background, 59-60; unaware of morale changes in his army, 67-68; rides to Wilderness with Hill, 69, 83-84, 104; poor intelligence on Army of Potomac, 70, 72; correspondence with Davis as to area of command, 73-75; importance of *esprit* or morale, 76-77, 81; Wilderness lack of confidence shown by orders to Ewell, 85-86, 100; and to Hill, 107; worry over gap between Ewell and Hill, 107-108, 116, 117, 120, 159; assumes control of Third Corps, 108; slowed down by lack of trust, 109-110; almost captured at Widow Tapp's farm, 116-117; statuesque image, 126-127, 130; allowed men to sleep in disorder, 128, 129, 130-131; quickened by combat, 132-133; offensive plans for second day in Wilderness, 133-136;

wept at sight of First Corps in April, 138; "Lee to the rear," 148, 153, 206-207; bitterness with MacGowan, 150-151; puts trust in Longstreet, 160; devotes time to straightening lines, 168-169; checks on Ewell's inactivity, 170; outfought Grant in Wilderness, 171-172; concern over fate of Richmond, 173; acceptance of incompletion of Wilderness assault, 174; losses of men and generals, 174-175; must wait on Grant's next move, 176, 179; moves to Spotsylvania, 192; beginning of collapse in command organization, 193; acts as field commander, 193-194; evades Davis's table of organization, 194; as an engineer, 195, 230; vagueness in command, 199-201; exonerates Johnson in "mule shoe" action, 202-203; "Mule Shoe" action, 206-214; narrowly escapes death, 210; gives army rest after Spotsylvania, 217, 224-225; news of Stuart's death, 218, 223; crippling restrictions by Davis, 227-228; advises Davis of Grant's co-ordinated drive on two fronts, 230; one of Confederacy's full generals, 241; conflict with Beauregard, 245-246; has moral support of Davis, 246; retreat to cover Richmond, 251-253; arrives at Hanover Junction, 253; seeks combination with Beauregard, 254-255, 266, 270, 348-349; illness, 256, 258, 260, 265, 266, 274, 293; sharp rebuke to Hill, 258; Jericho Mills, 258-259; felt lack of Stuart, 259; a military opportunist, 260-261; tactical coup at North Anna, 264; changes in his army, 269-270; organizes cavalry to fight Sheridan, 272-273; meetings with Beauregard, 277-278, 350-352, 353; asks Davis for more troops, 278; endorses Early's offensive at Bethesda, 278-280; wires Beauregard for reinforcements, 281-282, 292; decides against further offensive, 281; Cold Harbor battle, 284-290, 292, 301; new field headquarters at Gaines's Mill, 291-292; struggle

Lee, Gen. Robert E. (*continued*)
against bureaucratic control, 302;
moves to counter Grant's, 303-304;
sends cavalry to Shenandoah Valley, 305, 312-313; the myth, 319-320,
327-330; concentration of army at
Riddell's Shop, 324; Beauregard's
evasiveness to Grant's whereabouts,
337, 338, 339, 342, 343, 346, 352-353;
mystery as to Grant's whereabouts,
337-347; wire to son Rooney at Malvern Hill, 345-346; trenches, 350;
failure of his last campaign, 355; appearance on Traveler, 358; and the
departmental system, 362; image of
invincibility, 368; attempt to retake
Fort Harrison, 369-370; area of command in last days of campaign, 373;
on Grant, 373; on perils to the Confederacy caused by vanity, 374; a
deeply religious man, 374-375
Lee, Mrs. Robert E., 6, 291
Lee, Major Gen. W. H. F. (Rooney),
27, 28, 60, 303, 323; promotion to
Major General, 186; Spotsylvania,
199; Cold Harbor, 294; reported
whereabouts of Grant, 322; at Mal-
vern Hill, 345-346
Letcher, John, 311
Lewis, Col. William G., 253
Lexington (Va.), 311
Lieutenant-General (Confederate), du-
ties and qualities, 80
Lincoln, President Abraham, 50, 57,
58, 76
Little River, 263
Lomax's brigade, 186, 192, 221
Long, Brig. Gen. Armistead, 90, 116,
199-200, 224-225
Long Bridge, 317, 322
Longstreet, Lieut. Gen. James ("Old
Pete"), background, characteristics
and feuds, 9-17, 114, 138-140, 141; at
Gordonsville, 52, 55; advance to
Wilderness, 61, 94; Lee awaits ar-
rival, 128-130, 132, 133, 136; slow to
arrive, 134, 137; Wilderness, 143,
148, 151, 153, 155-156, 160-161, 163-
164; fanciful scheme, 164-166, 168-
169; wounded, 166-167, 175, 182, 193,
218; last days of campaign, 371

Longstreet's Corps. *See* First Corps
Louisa Court House, 306
Louisiana brigades, 88, 194, 204
Louisianians, 77, 89
Lyman, Col. Theodore (U.S.), 54
Lynchburg, 311, 313

MacGowan, Brig. Gen. Samuel, 113,
121, 122, 123, 150-151, 158, 175, 212,
258
MacGowan's brigade, 212, 257, 321
McAllister, Col. Robert (U.S.), 163
McCandless, Col. William (U.S.), 98
McCaw, Dr. James B., 363
McClellan, Gen. George (U.S.), 12,
23, 49, 71, 230
McClellan, Major Henry, 132, 135, 137,
223
McGuire, Dr. Hunter, 19
McIntosh, David, 116
McLaws, Major Gen. Lafayette, feud
with Longstreet, 11-12, 16, 140, 141
Madison, President James, 34
Mahone, Major Gen. William
("Billy"), Wilderness, 115, 161, 162,
167; promotion, 193; Spotsylvania,
209-211; Jericho Mills, 257, 259; Cold
Harbor, 294, 296, 297
Major-generals (Confederate), duties
and qualities, 79
Mallory, Secretary Stephen, 363
Marshall, Major Charles, 25
Martin, James ("One Wing"), 238,
283
Mattaponi River, 252
Maury, Major Gen. Dabney, 363
Maury, Matthew Fontaine, 363
May, Benjamin, 163
Meade, Gen. George Gordon (U.S.),
nominal command of Army of Poto-
mac, 49, 51, 93, 184; his estimate of
his army, 71; Wilderness, 94-95, 118,
156, 169, 171; Spotsylvania, 214; clash
with Sheridan, 219; Cold Harbor,
290; on Lee, 299
Mechanicsville, 278, 291
Merritt, Brig. Gen. Wesley (U.S.),
185, 187, 188
Milroy, Major Gen. Robert Huston
(U.S.), and his "weary boys," 304
Minié ball, 64, 73

Mississippians, 210
Mixson, Frank, 174
Morale, importance to Lee, 76-82
Morgan, John, 226
Mott, Brevet Brig. Gen. Samuel (U.S.), 118
"Mule Shoe" action, Spotsylvania, 197, 200-208, 211-213

NANCE, COL. JAMES D., 175
Navy, Confederate, 363
Navy, U.S., 317
New Bern (N.C.), 39, 75
New Cold Harbor, 291
New Market, 226
New Verdiersville, 72, 105
North Anna, 252, 261-266, 267
North Carolina, significance for Richmond campaign, 229-230
North Carolina brigades, 89, 186, 207, 259, 271, 280-281, 303

OLD CHURCH ROAD, 278, 284, 291
Old Cold Harbor, 291
Old Turnpike, Wilderness, 35, 85, 91, 93-94, 95-98, 169-170, 174
"On to Richmond" campaign, 228, 230-231
Orange (Va.), 52, 93
Orange & Alexandria Railroad, 32, 34
Orange County, 34
Orange Court House, 32, 34, 35, 52
Orange Plank Road. See Plank Road
Orr rifles, 257
Ox Ford, 256, 257, 261, 263

PAGE, MAJOR R. C. M., 201
Palmer, Col. William, 122, 128, 129, 130, 143, 144, 154, 159, 181, 182
Pamunkey River, 252, 268, 271
Parker's Store, Wilderness, 70, 94, 105-106, 118, 141
Patrick Henry, 317
Paul, Col. Samuel B., 326
Pegram, Brig. Gen. John, 89, 99
Pegram, Willie, 89, 116, 142, 205, 213
Pelham, John, 28, 142
Pemberton, Lieut. Gen. John Clifford, 270

Pender, Major Gen. Dorsey, 22, 110, 113
Pendleton, Lt. Col. Alexander (Sandie), 18-19, 67, 91
Pendleton, Brig. Gen. W. N. (Reverend), Lee's chief of artillery, 18, 25, 149, 181, 199
Perrin, Brig. Gen. Abner, 115, 211
Perry, Brig. Gen. Edward A., 115, 297
Petersburg, 74, 231, 303-304, 314, 316, 318, 335, 337, 344, 345; battle of, 349-351
Pettigrew, Johnston, 105, 111
Peyton, Major Charles S., 26
Pickett, Major Gen. George E., 169, 230; detached brigades of, 39, 41, 138; at Petersburg, 74; makeup of his division, 78-79, 232-233; marriage, 230, 231; Commander of Department of North Carolina, 231, 232-233; at Gettysburg, 231, 233-234; ordered to report to Lee, 232; characteristics, 233; trapped at Petersburg, 234-235; receives support against Butler, 236, 238-239; nervous collapse, 239; Cold Harbor, 289; loss of Lee's confidence, 371
Pickett's division, after Gettysburg, 231; Hanover Junction, 253; North Anna, 263; return to First Corps, 275; Cold Harbor, 294; Richmond-Petersburg action against Butler's troops, 336, 340; Bermuda Hundred, 343; last days of campaign, 371
Plank Road, Wilderness, 61, 69, 70, 72, 84, 93-94, 104-136 passim, 141, 143-145, 149-156, 159, 160-163, 165, 168, 170, 173-174
Plymouth (N.C.), 39
Poague, Col. William, 107, 116, 125, 142, 149-150, 153, 154, 213
Pole Green Presbyterian Church, 274
Polk, Lieut. Gen. Bishop, 331
Pope, Major Gen. John (U.S.), 176
Port Royal, 250
Port Walthall Junction, 236, 336
Posey, Brig. Gen. Carnot, 115
Potomac River, enemy gunboat control, 314
Price, Channing, 28

RAMS, Confederate use of, 39
Ramseur, Major Gen. Dodson, 90, 96, 133, 208-211, 218, 279-280
Randolph, George W., 87
Ransom, Brig. Gen. Mat, 238
Ransom, Major Gen. Robert, 232, 236, 238, 243, 246, 270, 275, 304, 312
Rapidan River, 3, 31, 32, 41, 53, 61, 133, 165
Rappahannock River, 32, 314
Rations, Southern, 63-64, 69, 77, 275-276; Northern, 70
Regiment (Confederate), group spirit, 77
Republican Party (U.S.), 57
Revolution, difference from Civil War, 56-57
Richmond, Grant's objective, 35, 38, 51, 173; Lee's responsibility for, 37, 54, 55; defenses of, 38-39, 195, 221; the heart of the Confederacy, 51, 58; Federal raiding parties on, 69; Butler's threat south of the James, 74, 75, 173, 233; fieldworks around, 195, 221; Sheridan's raid, 220, 222; Seven Days Battle, 291; Grant's decision to isolate, 314, 315; burning and evacuation, 367-368
Richmond, Fredericksburg & Potomac Railroad, 73, 263
Richmond Howitzers, 86, 276
Richmond-Petersburg railroad, 233
Riddell's Shop, 322, 324, 336
Rifle (Ewell's horse), 87, 88, 97
Rifles, change in range of, 197-198
Roanoke Island, 230
Robertson, Brig. Gen. Jerome (Doctor), 139
Robinson, Brig. Gen. James S. (U.S.), 189, 190, 191
Rockbridge artillery, 25
Rodes, Major Gen. Robert, 92; background and nature, 90; Wilderness, 96-97; Spotsylvania, 195, 196, 208-212; Bethesda Church, 279
Rosser, Brig. Gen. Tom, 30, 104-105, 190, 191, 257, 259, 272, 294, 308

SAVANNAH (GA.), fieldworks around, 195

Scales, Brig. Gen. Alfred, 113, 121, 123, 124, 208, 258
Scott, Gen. Winfield (U.S.), 356; high opinion of Lee, 59; Lee's letter of resignation to, 131; quote on Lee, 375
Second Corps (Army of Northern Virginia), under Ewell, 19-20; advance to Wilderness, 35, 61, 70; influence of Widow Brown over, 84; Wilderness, 85, 91, 93-101, 169-170; makeup, 88-91; division commanders, 193-197; Spotsylvania, 197, 217-218, 224-225; at Hanover County, 251, 253, 254, 255; North Anna, 263-265; Cold Harbor, 296; Shenandoah Valley, under Early, 312
Second Manassas, Battle of, 11, 17, 22, 134, 176
Seddon, James, 37, 331
Sedgwick, Major Gen. John (U.S.), VI Corps of, 70, 95, 109, 209, 218, 251. See also Wright
Seven Days, battle of, 9, 11, 291
Seven Pines, battle of, 11, 112
Shady Grove Church, 189, 284
Sharpsburg, battle of, 22
Sharpshooters (Confederate), 64
Shenandoah Valley, part of Lee's command, 38, 73-74; Lee's breadbasket, 52, 314; Breckinridge in, 73-74; Grant's objectives, 226, 303-305; Sheridan's operations, 310-311; importance of keeping communications open, 314; enemy vanished from, 318-319; loss of, 365-366
Sheppard, William L., 86
Sheridan, Gen. Philip (U.S.), 109; nature, 30; Wilderness, 155, 164; ruthless tactics of total war, 180, 219, 220, 311; resentment of Meade, 184-185, 219; advance to Spotsylvania, 185, 187, 188; hatred of Southerners, 219; raid on Richmond, 220-222; rejoins Grant's army, 268, 271, 273-274; action against Gordon's North Carolinians, 271; refers to "demoralization" of Lee's men, 272, 276, 277; Cold Harbor, 284, 286; raids in Shenandoah Valley, 303-306; Trevilian's station, 308, 309; rebuilding cavalry,

309, 310; command in Shenandoah Valley, 310-311, 313; conquered Jubal Early's force, 365

Sherman, Gen. William Tecumseh (U.S.), 47; takes Atlanta, 364-366; pillage of Georgia, 367

Shirley plantation, 59, 60, 323

Smith, Major Gen. William F. ("Baldy") (U.S.), XVIII Corps, 255, 281, 290, 297, 318, 324, 326, 328, 332, 341, 342, 344

Smith, Brig. Gen. William ("Extra Billy"), 89

Smith, Maj. Gen. Martin, Lee's chief of engineers, 26, 160, 161, 197, 215

Sorrel, Col. Moxley, 151, 162-163, 165-169, 182

South Carolina brigades, Kershaw, 190, 212, 287-288; Calbraith Butler, 305, 308; MacGowan, 321

South Carolina Regiment (20th), 292

South Carolinians, in Butler's new brigades in Hampton's cavalry division, 272-274

Spencer repeating carbine, Federal issue, 30, 73

Spindler farm, 189

Spotswood, Governor Alexander (Colonel), 52

Spotsylvania, battle of, advance to, 181-184, 188-189; Anderson's divisions at, 183-184, 188, 189, 191; Warren's V Corps at, 184, 188-189, 190, 191; Sheridan's corps at, 187, 188; Stuart's cavalry corps at, 187, 188, 189, 191; armies meet at, 189-192; Lee acts as field commander, 193-194; field fortifications, 195-197; battle resumed, 198; Mule Shoe debacle, 200-208, 211-213; losses, 214, 218

Spotsylvania Court House, 181-182, 189

Springfield rifles, Confederate issue, 64

Stafford, Brig. Gen. Leroy, 89, 99

Stafford's Louisiana Brigade, 89, 194

Starvation as a weapon, 355-357

Staunton, 303

Steuart, Brig. Gen. George H. ("Maryland"), 90, 204

Stiles, Major Robert, 86, 87, 166, 321

Stone, Col. John Marshall, 112, 161-162

Stonewall Brigade, 203, 204, 217

Stratford Hall, Lee's birthplace, 60

Stuart, Major Gen. James Ewell Brown (Jeb), personality, background and staff, 27-31, 185-186, 188; intelligence details as to Grant's moves, 69; aggregate of his cavalry, 71; Verdiersville escape, 72-73; advance toward Wilderness, 84, 85; action in Wilderness, 104-105, 107, 124, 132, 155, 171; almost captured with Lee and Hill, 116-117; cavalry losses, 176; Spotsylvania, 185-188, 191-192, 286, 287; death, 218, 221, 223; encounter with Sheridan's cavalry, 220-221; Lee's prophetic statement, 223

Suffolk, siege of, 11, 13

Sweeny, Joseph, 28

Swinton, William, Campaigns of the Army of the Potomac, 354-355

Tapp farm. See Widow Tapp's farm

Taylor, Col. Walter, Lee's chief of staff, 25, 26, 67, 117, 330, 347

Telegraph Road, 221, 251, 269

Terry, Col. William R., 275

Texas brigade, 77, 347; "Lee to the rear," 148, 152-154

Third Corps (Army of Northern Virginia), under A. P. Hill, 21; advance to Wilderness, 61, 70, 72, 73; action in Wilderness, 104-136, 151-153, 158; under temporary command of Jubal Early, 193; at Spotsylvania, 213, 218, 224; retreat southward, 251, 253, 254, 256, 257; North Anna, 263-264; Cold Harbor, 285, 294, 296; skirmishes and reconnaissance, 322-324; Petersburg, 342, 345-347, 350-351; last days of campaign, 371

Thomas, Brig. Gen. Edward, 113, 121, 122, 208, 258

Todd's Tavern, 94, 109, 181

Torbert's division (U.S.), 274, 307, 308-309

Totopotomoi Creek, 274, 276, 277

Traveler, Lee's horse, 4-5, 68, 83, 136, 153, 205, 210, 256

Trenches, Lee improvises, 300, 350, 355

Trent Reach, 318

Trevilian's Station, 306, 308, 309
Tucker, Sergeant, 106

VENABLE, COL. CHARLES S., Lee's aide-
de-camp, 25, 62, 124, 129, 130, 153,
199, 201, 206, 209, 210, 257, 258, 265,
299
Venable Street (Richmond), 291
Virginia, influence on Lee, 7
Virginia brigades, 186, 206, 207
Virginia Central Railroad, 34, 52, 263,
270, 271, 274, 305, 306, 309, 314
Virginia Military Institute, 226
Virginia Regiment (21st), 204
Virginians brigade, 89

WADSWORTH, BRIG. GEN. JAMES SAM-
UEL, (U.S.), 95, 97-98, 108, 125, 126,
132, 143, 145, 156-158
Wagons for general officers only, Con-
federate, 68; Federal, 70
Walker, Brig. Gen. Henry Harrison
("Mud"), 111
Walker, Brig. Gen. James A., 90, 204,
209
Walker, Col. Lindsay, 115-116
Warren, Major Gen. Gouverneur
(U.S.), V Corps, 70, 93, 94, 95, 133,
184, 188-189, 192, 209, 211, 257, 258,
261, 263, 264, 278, 279-280, 342, 344,
346
Washington, George, 59, 60
Washington, Martha, 60
Washington (D.C.), Early's threat to,
313
Washington Artillery Battalion (New
Orleans), south of James River, 71-
72, 232
Waterways, enemy gunboat control,
314
Webb, Major Gen. Alexander S.
(U.S.), 157, 158
Weitzel, Major Gen. Godfrey (U.S.),
367
Weldon (N.C.), 232
Weldon Railroad, 230, 372
Westover, 323

White House, Grant's headquarters,
279, 290
Whiting, Major Gen. W. H. C., 229,
231, 232, 243, 244, 246, 366-367
Whitworth sharpshooter rifles, Confederate issue, 64-65
Wickham's brigade, 186, 191, 221
Widow Tapp's farm (Wilderness),
Hill's deployment, 106-107; headquarters at, 107, 125; Lee, Hill and
Stuart narrowly escape capture, 116-
117; Federal attack (2nd day), 143-
144; Poague's artillery success, 149-
150, 153; fluctuations of battle, 153,
157, 173
Wigfall, Senator Louis T., 331
Wilcox, Major Gen. Cadmus, 50, 69;
Wilderness 112-114, 117, 118, 120-
123, 126-130, 136, 143-145, 151; Spotsylvania, 208, 211, 212; Jericho Mills,
256, 257, 258-259; Cold Harbor, 294
Wilcox's Landing, 317, 322, 323, 346
Wilderness, 32, 34; description of terrain, 52-54; Lee anticipates Grant's
passage, 54-55; Grant's entry into,
61, 69, 83; Lee's advance to, 84; Old
Turnpike action (first day), 93-101;
effect on troops, 95-96; exploited by
Lee, 98, 132, 134; Plank Road action
(first day), 104-136; Lee's worry
over gap between Ewell's and Hill's
Corps, 107-108, 116-117; First Corps'
advance to Plank Road and relief of
Hill, 137-143; action along Plank
and Brock Roads (second day), 143,
145, 148-155, 158-163, 167, 169; Longstreet's fanciful scheme to roll Grant
back, 163-166, 168-169; Meade retains passageway, 169; Grant outfought by Lee, 171-172; Grant's decision to depart, 173, 176; disaster
area after battle, 173-174; Lee's assault inconclusive, 174; a campaign
in itself, 176
Wilderness Tavern, 70, 94, 100
Williamsburg Stage Road, 322
Willis, Col. Edward, 280
Wilmington (N.C.), 231, 366; importance of port, 37, 58; taken by Federal army, 367

Wilson's cavalry (U.S.), 70, 190, 191, 322, 346
Windmill Point, 318
Wise's brigade, 238, 328
Wofford, Brig. Gen. William, 140, 160-162, 165, 167, 191, 192, 290
Wright, Brig. Gen. Ambrose R. ("Rans") (U.S.), Wilderness, 95, 97, 98, 115; given command of Sedg-wick's VI Corps, 251; with VI Corps, 251, 263-264, 289, 290, 297, 344, 346

YORK RIVER, 314
Young, Judge Advocate General H. E. (Major), 26
Young, Brig. Gen. Pierce, 186, 187, 259, 272, 305

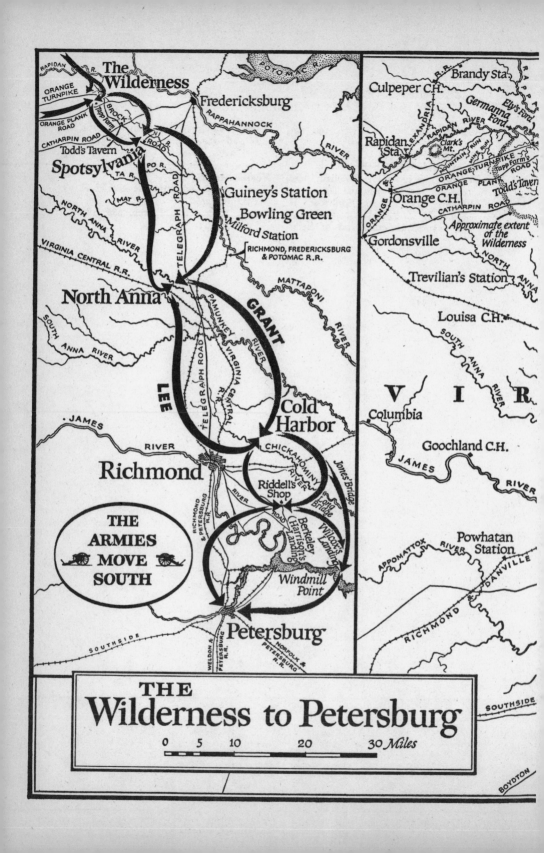

THE
Wilderness to Petersburg

0   5   10   20   30 *Miles*

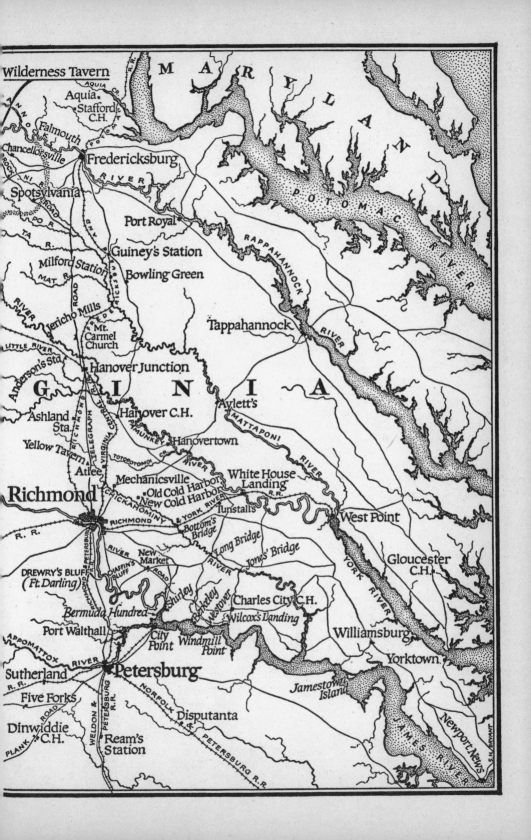